THE GOSPEL, FREEDOM, and THE SACRAMENTS

THE GOSPEL, FREEDOM, and THE SACRAMENTS

Did the Reformers Go Far Enough?

BARRY C. NEWMAN
Foreword by John W. Woodhouse

RESOURCE *Publications* · Eugene, Oregon

THE GOSPEL, FREEDOM, AND THE SACRAMENTS
Did the Reformers Go Far Enough?

Copyright © 2015 Barry C. Newman. All rights reserved. Except for brief quotations in critical publications or reviews, no part of this book may be reproduced in any manner without prior written permission from the publisher. Write: Permissions, Wipf and Stock Publishers, 199 W. 8th Ave., Suite 3, Eugene, OR 97401.

Resource Publications
An Imprint of Wipf and Stock Publishers
199 W. 8th Ave., Suite 3
Eugene, OR 97401

www.wipfandstock.com

PAPERBACK ISBN 13: 978-1-4982-3744-4
HARDCOVER ISBN 13: 978-1-4982-3746-8

Manufactured in the U.S.A.   03/29/2016

Scripture quotations marked (NIV) are taken from the Holy Bible, New International Version®, NIV®. Copyright © 1973, 1978, 1984, 2011 by Biblica, Inc.™ Used by permission of Zondervan. All rights reserved worldwide. www.zondervan.com The "NIV" and "New International Version" are trademarks registered in the United States Patent and Trademark Office by Biblica, Inc.™

Greek Bible text from: Novum Testamentum Graece, 27th revised edition, Edited by Barbara Aland and others, © 1981 Deutsche Bibelgesellschaft, Stuttgart.

Greek Bible text from: Novum Testamentum Graece, 8th revised edition, © 1898 and 1993 Deutsche Bibelgesellschaft, Stuttgart 2001.

The Interlinear Hebrew-Greek-English Bible, Four Volume Edition, Copyright © 1976 by Jay P. Green, Sr., general editor and translator, Wilmington: Associated Publishers.

All English textual material of Scripture has been taken from the New International Version of the Holy Bible except in those instances where the text clearly indicates by its context that an independent translation or paraphrase is being offered. Where appropriate that text is referred to by the symbols—NIV.

All Greek textual material of the New Testament has been taken from the Nestle–Aland Greek English New Testament. Where appropriate that text is referred to by the symbols—NAG.

All Hebrew textual material of the Old Testament has been taken from The Interlinear Hebrew-Greek-English Bible Where appropriate that text is referred to by the symbols—IHG.

Contents

Foreword by John W. Woodhouse • vii
Preface • ix
Acknowledgements • xi
Introduction • xiii
Abbreviations • xvii

Part 1: Law and Freedom
DAY 1: The Conscientious Believer • 3
DAY 2: The Role of Law in the Life of a Believer • 10
DAY 3: The Galatian Problem • 17
DAY 4: Slavery, Freedom and Life in the Spirit • 23

Part 2: Baptism
DAY 5: Baptismal Practices and Beliefs Today • 33
DAY 6: Baptismal Practices in the Gospels and the Acts of the Apostles • 42
DAY 7: Baptismal Words as used Outside of the New Testament • 55
DAY 8: "Βαπτισμα" in the New Testament • 69
DAY 9: "Βαπτιζω" in the New Testament • 79
DAY 10: Matthew 28:18–20 • 93
DAY 11: More on Matthew 28:18–20 • 100
DAY 12: The Conclusion to Matthew 28: 18–20 • 111
DAY 13: Objections Considered • 117
DAY 14: More Objections Considered • 129
DAY 15: Decision Day • 139

Part 3: The Lord's Supper
DAY 16: What they Call it, what they Believe and what they Do • 147
DAY 17: The Last Passover Meal • 153
DAY 18: "This Do in Remembrance of Me" • 161
DAY 19: "You are Doing This in Remembrance of Me" • 172
DAY 20: The Last Passover Meal in John and the Lord's Supper in Hebrews • 183
DAY 21: Bread and the Breaking of Bread • 191

Day 22: The Lord's Supper in the Acts of the Apostles • 203
Day 23: Agape Meals • 217
Day 24: Corinthian Meals—The Cup of Blessing which we Bless • 227
Day 25: Corinthian Meals—The Table of the Lord • 241
Day 26: Corinthian Meals—The Cup of the Lord • 252
Day 27: Corinthian Meals—the Markets and being a Guest at a Meal • 266
Day 28: Corinthian Meals—Corinthian Behavior • 271
Day 29: Corinthian Meals—the Lord's Supper • 282
Day 30: Corinthian meals—the Last Passover Meal • 291
Day 31: Corinthian Meals—the Last Passover Meal—Consequences for the Corinthians • 301
Day 32: The Lord's Supper—Final Considerations • 309

Part 4: The Gospel and the Sacraments
Day 33: The Gospel in the New Testament • 321
Day 34: Implications for the Proclamation of the Gospel • 338

Bibliography • 347

Foreword

This is an important book.

Its subject matter guarantees that it will be controversial, but its arguments are of great importance for all of us who believe that Christian thought and practice—even ideas and customs that have a long and honored history—must be shaped by the teaching of Scripture.

Christian faith believes the word that God himself speaks to us in the Scriptures. By this word he teaches, corrects, rebukes, comforts, and encourages us.

In this book Barry Newman takes us on an intriguing journey as two believers explore what they should believe and practice in the matter of what have traditionally been called the "sacraments" of Baptism and the Lord's Supper.

Christian thinking about the sacraments has a remarkable history. In the sixteenth century Reformation, with its emphatic affirmation of the gospel of God's grace, the human response of faith in the person and work of the Lord Jesus Christ, and the authority, clarity and sufficiency of Scripture, the sacraments were a critical battleground. Misunderstandings of the sacraments had obscured the gospel of grace, confused the simplicity of faith, and compromised the priority of the word of God. A thorough re-thinking of the sacraments was essential.

Nonetheless, even among the leading Reformers, there were sharp differences in understanding the sacraments. Specifically the names of Luther, Calvin and Zwingli represent three significantly different understandings of the Lord's Supper.

Evangelical Christians today who are persuaded that the Reformers were essentially right in their core convictions still often have difficulties with the sacraments. Too often in church life we find it difficult to preserve a Reformed understanding of the sacraments. From time to time we are criticized for "neglecting" the sacraments. Some respond to this criticism by giving the sacraments a more prominent place in church life. Many remain confused.

Is it possible that there has been a fundamental misunderstanding about "sacraments" from very early times?

Misunderstandings and misrepresentations of the Christian gospel and of the Christian life did emerge from the beginning. The disciples of Jesus misunderstood him repeatedly in various ways, as the New Testament Gospels testify. Likewise, as the

Foreword

apostles proclaimed the gospel and people came to faith in Christ, it is astonishing how quickly departures from the truth arose. The years and centuries after the period of the New Testament likewise involved disputes and controversies. Misunderstandings were not always easily recognized or simple to refute. The teaching of Scripture is our sure guide.

This book asks fundamental questions, challenging basic assumptions behind most Christian thinking about the sacraments. The conclusions reached may seem radical. That, I believe, is what happens when we allow our thinking and practices to be shaped by the word of God.

John W. Woodhouse
Former Principal of Moore Theological College, Sydney

Preface

Why write a book entitled "The Gospel, Freedom and the Sacraments"? Because in the light of the gospel and the freedom it brings, there is a question that needs to be considered concerning the sacraments. Is participation in them mandatory? This book raises and discusses that question with respect to the sacraments of Baptism and the Lord's Supper. The conclusion reached is contrary to the beliefs of almost all for whom this question is important.

Acknowledgements

I owe a great debt to my loving wife, Laurie, for her patience during the completion of this work and to my dear daughters, Linda, Kathryn, Beth, Victoria, and Alexandra, together with my wife, for their support and for critiquing the manuscript. A special word of thanks is due to my friend and colleague of many years, Colin Gauld who, in his usual painstaking manner, reviewed the work in considerable detail and made a number of significant suggestions. I have always valued his advice. Thank you also to my fellow travellers and friends, John Woodhouse, Peter Bolt, George May, Robert Doyle, and Bruce Hall for their encouragement and insights. In particular, I am very grateful to John, for stimulating my thinking not once but many times, to Peter for his help in translating a number of Greek texts external to the New Testament, to George for a single but fundamentally important question he once asked me, and to both Bruce and Robert for treating me with a respect I do not think I deserve. I also wish to convey my thanks to Professor Edwin Judge for his ready ear and for his helpful advice on a number of technical problems. My thanks are also due to Bishop Donald Robinson for his honesty, encouragement and his readiness to reflect. None of these people, however, bear any responsibility whatsoever for any aspect of this work. My thanks also to the people of Lord Howe Island who by their cheerful hospitality, unwittingly, gave me the freedom to start work on this book, during one of the Island's balmy winters, while I endeavoured to fulfil my responsibilities there as a clergyman who wasn't a clergyman. Finally, what a great debt, an unpayable debt, I owe to my heavenly Father who in my late teenage years indelibly inscribed upon me the absolute necessity of searching for the truth and following it no matter what the consequences.

Introduction

What some people regard as a sacrament, others consider only as an ordinance. In this book, while references to "sacraments" tend to dominate over references to "ordinances," both are always in mind. Furthermore, some people believe that there are only two sacraments or ordinances while others assert there are more than two or fewer—one or none. This book considers only two sacraments or two ordinances if you prefer to see them as such. They are baptism and what is commonly called "The Lord's Supper," "Holy Communion" or "the Eucharist." However, much of the discussion has relevance for any so-called sacrament or ordinance.

The style that dominates this book is characterized by conversations between two people. Although, as far as we know, Socrates wrote nothing of note himself, his pupil Plato, a man of the fourth and fifth centuries BCE, wrote many works in which Socrates is depicted as engaging in dialogue with a person he is endeavoring to instruct—though Socrates himself would not necessarily call it instruction. Often he asks questions and waits for the other to respond but not always. Sometimes he makes statements meant to provoke the other to change his thinking. What Plato created became known as "Socratic Dialogue."[1] This work is largely one of dialogue and after a fashion it is similar to Socratic dialogue in style.

By way of another illustration, Joseph Agassi, an extraordinary man of the twentieth and twenty-first centuries, of whom the description "philosopher and historian of science" does not do justice, published a work in 1968[2] that was based on a series of dialogues. It details conversations held between himself and his eleven year-old son and is structured as though these conversations were held over 21 days. His Table of Contents lists Week I, Week II and Week III as major headings with each week divided into the days Monday to Sunday. For each day there is a heading depicting the subject matter covered on that day. The present work mirrors this type of structure to some extent. It is divided into four "Parts" with each Part made up of a number of Days. At the end of almost every Day there are "Explanatory Notes." Two of the Parts are also

---

1. An introduction to Socratic Dialogue could be gained by reading *Plato The Republic*, a translation of Plato's *Republic*, by Lee.

2. Agassi, *The Continuing Revolution: A History of Physics from the Greeks to Einstein*.

Introduction

accompanied by "Author's Comments." These latter provide additional information about those involved in the dialogue that would otherwise not be available.

There are only a few footnotes and they all occur in this Introduction. However the "Explanatory Notes" take the place of those footnotes that would normally appear throughout the rest of this book, because in dialogue there are no footnotes. However, these Explanatory Notes also often contain much material that is related to the dialogue for the Day providing information that would not normally be likened to a footnote. Rightly or wrongly, in these Explanatory Notes, I've endeavored to provide information for both the novice and the expert. To assist the reader, each explanatory note, including what constitutes a footnote, occurs approximately in the same order in which the subject matter to which it refers occurs in the main body of the text. When following the dialogue, every now and again, the reader might consider it a pity that certain items of information seem to be omitted. I could not possibly anticipate every wish but the reader might be surprised to discover here and there that the material sought for is in fact provided in the "Explanatory Notes." Indeed, it might be of some benefit to briefly peruse the "Explanatory Notes" for the Day, immediately upon "listening to the conversation" that occurred on that Day, in order to gain an impression of what might be found in those notes. The reader should be warned however, that because of the style of this work, he or she is essentially following a dialogue, not reading an academic paper—the "Explanatory Notes" lack a certain rigor being somewhat informal and conversational in nature.

A further example of a writer who might well have used the "dialogue strategy" here and there, is the Apostle Paul. Unfortunately, our translations tend to mask this possibility. In particular it has been claimed that 1 Corinthians 8:1–11:1 conforms to what is known as "ancient deliberative rhetoric," Paul firstly stating what he considers to be a Corinthian position to which he himself then responds.[3] Those chapters assume some significance in the third Part of this book, though the main member of the pair engaged in the dialogue claims that his arguments are not dependent upon the acceptance of that thesis.

It is now proper for me to refer to the participants in the dialogue, GB and TS. They are entirely fictitious in character. Of course GB's pastor, referred to here and there, is also fictitious as is everybody mentioned in connection with either TS or GB. Even the "Author's Comments" and to some extent the "Explanatory Notes" have this fictitious element written into them, though the sources referred to and the acknowledgements made in the "Explanatory Notes" are real.

In this work of fiction GB has only recently come to faith, while TS has been a believer for some time. GB is in his late twenties, TS is in his middle fifties. You will learn more about GB when you read the opening chapter.

What TS has to say throughout the dialogue varies enormously from being simple and folksy to quite complex and highly focused. Matters are sometimes simply

---

3. Fotopoulos, *Food Offered to Idols in Roman Corinth*, 195–207.

Introduction

put because TS needs to take into account the limited understanding that GB has of the way Christians think and behave. On the other hand, GB is extremely zealous and conscientious in his reading of Scripture and sometimes GB displays such an understanding of Scripture and of ideas raised by TS that TS is astonished. But ultimately this considerable ability of GB together with his strong motivational drive enables TS to raise for consideration, matters which often require considerable concentration and reflection.

The relationship between TS and GB develops over time. To begin with, there is a type of formality that characterizes their conversations. Thankfully, however, after a few days this changes. They start to feel more at ease with each other because they begin to understand and appreciate each other better. TS sometimes embarks on a tangent or argues his case, probably unnecessarily, at considerable length but GB good humoredly never ceases to appreciate what TS is trying to do. Occasionally their memories of what they had discussed on some previous day fails and they travel a little over the same ground again. Very occasionally one corrects the other but without causing offence.

In his dialogue with GB, TS often becomes quite technical. In particular he is not averse to discussing the use of Hebrew and Greek words and phrases, while never claiming to be a language expert. While at the time of the conversation, it is quite clear to GB how TS pronounces this word or that, a reader unfamiliar with any such pronunciation and only being offered the Hebrew or Greek symbols will find it difficult to know any phonetics involved. Consequently, when a Hebrew or Greek word or phrase is first introduced in the text, it is accompanied by a simple phonetic equivalent, which should hopefully give the reader unfamiliar with Hebrew or Greek, some clue as to how the word or phrase might sound. The only sophistication introduced into the phonetic "equivalents" is to place a macron over a vowel where the vowel is perceived to be long. In the case of a Greek word or phrase, the Greek itself is used throughout the text. In the case of a Hebrew word or phrase, the phonetic equivalent is used throughout. Understandably it is also the case that as they speak, either TS or GB, from time to time, wish to emphasize a word or phrase. The text indicates this by placing the word or words in italics. There are a few instances where TS, and one instance where GB, produces a paraphrase of a portion of Scripture which conveys an understanding of the text contrary to that commonly held. Where the paraphrase is considered to be of significance, the words of the paraphrase appear in italics.

In determining the frequencies and locations of certain Hebrew words in the Old Testament I consulted Mandelkern's Veteris Testamenti Concordantiae Hebraicae atque Chaldaicae[4] and for the frequencies and locations of certain Greek words in the New Testament I consulted, Moulton and Geden's A Concordance to the New

---

4. Mandelkern, *Veteris Testamenti Concordantiae Hebraicae atque Chaldaicae.*

Introduction

Testament.[5] To access the Greek text of the Septuagint I consulted Brenton's *The Septuagint with Apocrypha: Greek and English*.[6]

It is possible to read any of the Parts out of order and for them still to make reasonable sense. However it should be noted that the discussion of some objections that are raised in Part 3 is limited because such discussion has already occurred in Part 2, the objections being in principle the same. It would even be possible to read some of the Days in isolation from other Days and for the substance of that Day to be well understood, though adopting this strategy could lead to some confusion. Skimming the material for a Day here and there might be a reasonable procedure, particularly where the reader regards the material of that Day to be relatively trivial. For instance, Day 5 entitled "Baptismal Practices and Beliefs Today" and Day 16, which deals with much the same but in connection with the Lord's Supper, might be of little interest to some. Additionally, some of the Days make for rather heavy reading and the reader may choose to skip a Day here and there, perhaps to return to it later. For example, Day 7 goes into considerable detail on how a number of Greek words, including those related to baptism, were used in the world outside of the New Testament, much of Day 11 is devoted to the use of three prepositions, Day 21 has a great deal to say about "bread" and the "breaking of bread" as referred to in and outside of the Old and New Testaments, and Day 26 pays considerable attention to libations and toasting in the Greco-Roman world. Yet for TS, though he sometimes does go "on and on," the general thrust of the material he introduces on those and other Days is, rightly or wrongly, regarded by him as important for the case he is trying to make. Regardless of whatever way, you, the reader, decide to read this book, it is important to realize that in this work of fiction the overall argument develops in the order presented. Consequently, I think that reading most of it by following the sequence given is the method likely to prove to be the most beneficial.

Finally, though it is certain that TS is sometimes in error, has not considered some issues in sufficient detail, and is unaware of some relevant matters of fact, I hope that these things alone do not mean that what he says will be lightly dismissed by you the reader. I think a number of his arguments are worthy of further investigation, rather than being cast aside as too unnerving to be true. After a while, you might find yourself to be a fellow traveler having more sympathy with what he said than you initially thought possible.

I hope you enjoy the dialogue that follows.

---

5. Moulton and Geden, *A Concordance to the Greek Testament*.
6. Brenton, *The Septuagint with Apocrypha: Greek and English*.

Abbreviations

Chr	Chronicles
Col	Colossians
Cor	Corinthians
Dan	Daniel
Deut	Deuteronomy
Eph	Ephesians
Exod	Exodus
Ezek	Ezekiel
Gal	Galatians
Gen	Genesis
Heb	Hebrews
Hos	Hosea
IHG	The Interlinear Hebrew–Greek–English Bible
Isa	Isaiah
Jer	Jeremiah
Judg	Judges
Kgs	Kings
Lev	Leviticus
LXX	The Greek Septuagint
Macc	Maccabees
Mal	Malachi
Matt	Matthew
Mic	Micah
NAG	Nestle–Aland Greek English New Testament

Abbreviations

NIV	New International Version of the Holy Bible
Num	Numbers
Phlm	Philemon
Pet	Peter
Prov	Proverbs
Ps	Psalm
Rev	Revelation
Rom	Romans
Sam	Samuel
Tim	Timothy
Thess	Thessalonians
Zech	Zechariah
Zeph	Zephaniah

PART 1

Law and Freedom

Day 1

The Conscientious Believer

TS goes to the door of his home and meets GB for the first time. After they introduce themselves TS invites GB to come inside and proceeds to his lounge room where they sit in two old but very comfortable chairs. It is a day of getting to know each other although it is mainly GB telling TS about his extraordinary recent past.

GB: Thanks for agreeing to have a chat with me.

TS: It's a pleasure. You mentioned in your email that we hadn't met before and that's true. From what you said, however, a mutual friend—I know her well—suggested you contact me.

GB: I don't know her all that much. I met her at my church, only a few months ago. But I was talking to her about my problem and she thought you might be able to help.

TS: I'll help if I can. What do you want to talk to me about?

GB: It's fairly complicated and it's got a lot to do with my past. I suspect we'd need to meet a few times, if you'd be happy with that. The other thing is, because what I want to ask you about is, I think, fairly unusual, and Christians might be a little concerned that I am raising these matters in the first place, could we keep our conversations confidential—at least for now?

TS: I don't have any problems with discussions being confidential unless they're of a criminal nature.

GB: No, no! There's nothing criminal about what I'd like to discuss with you. It's theological!

TS: No worries then. And as far as meeting with you a few times, that's not a problem either. But you're a bit of a mystery. What's it all about?

GB: Well I won't beat around the bush. The truth is, I've spent a number of years as the leader of a cult—well, what you'd call a cult. There were a large number of us. I know I'm young but they made me their leader almost from the beginning. They could've picked other people instead of me. It might have been my forthright manner or that I seemed to be so sure of myself. I don't know. Anyway, as time went on, we all thought we were very important. We were the enlightened ones! And we were very conscientious. We tried promoting our beliefs to others and were quite prepared to cope with those who mocked us. After a year or so of being their leader I began to think of myself as the most conscientious and most able of them all. Then everything began to change. Slowly but steadily, what I will now call, "a profound sense of reality," began to undermine my confidence. What I had been playing at seemed to be incredibly unreal. By the end of the next year I became thoroughly disillusioned with everything we stood for.

TS: What happened?

GB: Sorry. I really don't understand what happened. It was as though I was having a type of brain transplant—a transplant for the better. In the end it seemed to me that it was as though we had all been drugged. It now became obvious to me that we'd all been suffering under some terrible delusion. I felt completely lost and utterly stupid. Yet everyone looked to me as their leader. I'd been blind and realized that I'd been responsible for misleading many others. I was however, far too embarrassed to explain to anyone the profound change in my thinking. Throughout that long period of my reassessing what I was doing and what I believed, I kept my deep-seated doubts to myself. So, one day, I simply walked out on them–without any explanation! They were devastated and in shock. But I had to. . . . I know I'm talking a lot–I'm a bit nervous. Sorry. It's still so fresh in my mind.

TS: You've got nothing to be sorry about. You've obviously been through a terrible experience. What was the cult all about?

GB: I'll get to that. Anyway I had to leave everything. I had to get away from it all. I couldn't continue to live a life of what I now saw as utter stupidity. My self-confidence evaporated and I felt so bad about myself that I really couldn't see any point to life—at least not to my life. As a last resort—I'm sorry to put it this way—I decided to test the possibility that *Jesus* might be somebody, unlike me, of some significance! I did know a fair bit about him. I won't go into how that came to be. Or at least I thought I knew a fair bit about him. Perhaps there was some truth to what some people claimed for him. That was my thinking. Maybe he had been, or even now, was, somebody far more important than even me!! Hmm! Maybe some of those things he said were really worth something. Maybe he could give some direction to my life. Maybe he was someone or had something worth dying for. I would go for that! You see I was a zealot at heart. I'm still a zealot. I know myself well enough to say that!

TS: So you tried to find out about Jesus or more about him than you previously knew. And what conclusion did you come to? Have you come to any conclusion yet?

GB: I focused on the Gospels of the New Testament, but also some of Paul's letters. I studied them from an historical point of view. I read works opposed to Christianity. I simply wanted to get to the truth about this man. I was desperate. Gradually I became convinced, quite convinced, that Jesus rose again from the dead, much the way the Gospel writers claim. That was a little over a year ago. Since then I've been reading the Bible as a whole, over and over, and I realize that I have much to learn. Though I've started going to church, I haven't talked to many Christians about what I've been reading and learning but perhaps I should've.

TS: So you think it would be helpful if we chatted about the Scriptures, perhaps book by book, and what they say?

GB: Oh no! That would be too much. Another time perhaps! Anyway, I think I've worked a lot out but I do have a couple of particular problems that I want to raise—fairly serious problems. They relate to my previous life in the cult.

TS: Okay but before you tell me about those, I'll be very direct. Do you think you're a genuine Christian?

GB: I'm pretty sure I am! Yes, of course I am! By the way, I don't mind using the word "Christian," though I know the word only occurs in the New Testament two or three times. However, sometimes I prefer to refer to myself as a believer in the Lord Jesus Christ or just as a believer when I'm in Christian circles.

TS: "Believer" or "Christian" is okay with me. But I think I see your point. Perhaps I should be more judicial in my use of the word "Christian." . . . Have you read that book in the New Testament entitled 1 Thessalonians?

GB: Yes, a number of times. I found it one of the easiest of New Testament books to understand.

TS: Paul wrote at the beginning of that letter how the Thessalonians had turned from idols to serve the living and true God and to wait for his Son from heaven, Jesus, who rescues us from the coming wrath. Do you think that applies to you?

GB: Yes it does, absolutely, although I've learnt that my idols are different to their idols, if you know what I mean. And I'm waiting for his Son to bring the universe, as we know it, to a close, and to come again, recognizable by all as God's Son, the one whom he has made Lord. I do believe this Son, Jesus, has rescued me from the anger of God, which otherwise I would have suffered under at his great judgement day. I do understand that he's in charge.

TS: How long have you been a Christian, a believer!?

GB: I guess just about a year.

Part 1: Law and Freedom

TS: You seemed to have discovered an awful lot in a year! You've discovered the gospel, the good news—the great news. And you express yourself so clearly.

GB: Thanks, but I feel I've started rather late and am still confused about a number of things.

TS: Believe me, you're still quite young! And the truth is, by the kindness of God, you've discovered what many others fail to perceive all their lives. You've been born a second time. You are a child of God. Your sins have been forgiven, you've been justified through faith in Christ Jesus, you have peace with God and you've received the gift of his Holy Spirit. I know that I'm using very Christian language but what God has done for you is extraordinarily significant. I find it difficult to express it otherwise, without cheapening what I'm trying to say. Certainly, what God has done for you should never be treated lightly.

GB: I know, I know. I couldn't agree more. It's wonderful really. Once I was indeed blind but now I really do see! However let me cut to the chase. You asked me what the cult was all about. In the world of that cult to which I belonged, that cult which I led, there were many rules and regulations. *That's* what the cult was all about! This must sound *ridiculous* but there were all these ceremonies that we rigorously took part in. I led them! We were, well, particularly myself, concerned to get everything right. I was meticulous in my conformity to the rules and in my participation in the rituals. I think my zealousness led to my disillusionment. I could never get it all right all the time. It was impossible. I began to see more and more my inability to make the rituals perfect in every way. I realize that for people—people probably like you—this is very difficult to understand. At the time, however, I had no idea how consuming the rituals were. I realize this sounds *utterly* ridiculous but it wasn't ridiculous to me or to any of us. I told you that we were, well I realized that I was, stupid, blind and in a way, drugged, though we weren't on drugs!

TS: I'm glad. And yes, I don't understand what it must've been like. I've never had anything like that sort of experience, though I think I can appreciate just a little of what you're saying. It's too easy for others to say you were, as it were, drugged. Most of the world is in a type of drugged state. Most people are blind to the ultimate realities concerning God and his Son. But you've been delivered. And you've tasted the freedom of the gospel. As a believer in the Lord Jesus who has done everything for you, you simply need to live by that same Spirit whom God has freely given to you. I am sure you know that now. His fruit is love, joy, peace, patience, kindness, goodness, faithfulness, gentleness and self-control. And he will cultivate in you this fruit more and more as he himself changes you by his Spirit and makes you more and more like the Lord Jesus whom he glorifies.

GB: I know now the reality of what you've just said and I am very grateful to God for his kindness, such great kindness. But now, let me tell you why I have come to you for advice. I am concerned about two Christian ceremonies—I hope you don't mind my calling them that—baptism and the Lord's Supper. You see, I've never been baptized, not even as an infant, and I've never partaken of the Lord's Supper, or what some call "Holy Communion." And these days, as you might understand, I'm somewhat worried about ceremonies or rituals. I've been trapped before! I know however, that Christians are pretty strong about participating in these rituals. And if I were to be baptized and if I were to take part in the Lord's Supper, I'd want to understand what I'm doing, what these ceremonies are really all about, and why I really needed to take them on. This is where I need your help—someone's help. Could *you* help me? This is what I really want to talk to you about. I want to know the truth. To be honest I can't see what they have to do with Christianity, at least if they're compulsory. Have I come to the wrong person? Do you think it's wrong of me to be concerned about such things? If you'd rather not chat with me about these worries of mine then please feel free to say so and I can leave you in peace.

TS: There's absolutely no problem. I'd be delighted to talk with you about these matters. Actually, I'm quite moved by your story and your worries. As far as your attitude is concerned, I think that you'd leave some Christians, ones who've been around for quite a while, in the shade. . . . I'd like to give you an immediate response but it would be too slick and you deserve far more than a simple piece of advice from me. To some extent, you're going to have to work on the issues involved yourself but I'm very willing to help you as much as I can. I think I now know why my friend suggested that we have a chat. The truth is, that over the last couple of years I've been working on these very issues myself and it would help me, as well as, I hope, help you, if we talked about these things over a number of days, perhaps many, many days, if you were agreeable. But in the mean time I want you to know, for what it's worth, that I think that one day you'll worry no longer. And I don't think that you need to see the matter as an urgent one. Believe me! You've placed your confidence in the Lord Jesus, the one who has secured your very being in himself. . . . That's the really important issue!

GB: I can see that you're trying to be helpful and I'd like to believe what you're saying. Anyway, I do believe in him.

TS: For sure! Look, the more relaxed we can be and perhaps the more time we can take over our discussions, the more profitable that time will be. For one, I hope that you and I can get to know each other better. And it would be a pleasure and a privilege for me to sit down and talk with you, but at leisure. However, I think you should realize that the matters you've raised are complex. That will become obvious if we're seriously going to consider how most Christians understand baptism and the Lord's Supper. So, why don't we agree to meet as many times as we think necessary? I think today has been good. I've learnt a lot about you and I think I know where you're coming from. But I suspect I now need to sit down and work out how we might proceed.

So, what about meeting again tomorrow or on whatever day is convenient? My place, if that's okay with you. What do you think?

GB: That sounds good to me. And tomorrow would be fine and yes your place here, if that's not a problem for you. I'm on vacation at the moment and have a lot of time on my hands. . . . Look, I really do appreciate your being prepared to meet with me. However, in all honesty, as far as getting together on a *number* of occasions, yes I think that might be necessary, but in the course of time you might change your mind about wanting to chat with me. I suppose it's also possible that and I might even change my mind about wanting to chat with you! I'm simply being honest.

TS: And I appreciate your honesty. Let's take things a day at a time then and see how we go. See you tomorrow.

EXPLANATORY NOTES: DAY 1

During this first day TS referred to a number of Christian sentiments based on Scripture. There were two occasions when his Biblical references were more explicit. The first entailed a quote from 1 Thess 1:9–10 (NIV). The second concerned the fruit of the Spirit that Paul wrote of in Gal 5:22–23 (NIV).

The Greek word translated "Christian" occurs three times in the New Testament—Acts 11:26, 26:28; 1 Pet 4:16 (NAG).

Day 2

The Role of Law in the Life of a Believer

Today TS chats with GB about some of the things that Jesus said concerning the Jewish law. He thinks they need to seriously address some of the very pointed statements that Jesus made about the Law, before doing anything else.

TS: So, you've never been baptized and never partaken of the Lord's Supper.

GB: That's right.

TS: What are you really concerned about? Are you worried that God might be displeased with you if you aren't baptized and if you don't take part in the Lord's Supper?

GB: Well, I am a little. More than a little!

TS: Perhaps someone has said to you that Jesus instituted these two ceremonies and commanded that those who wish to be his followers should obey him in these matters along with all of his other commands.

GB: You've hit the nail on the head. And I don't wish to disobey him at all. It's just that I want to understand the truth of things. One problem I have is that different people have different views on how you should be baptized and what happens in the Lord's Supper and what these ceremonies really mean. From what I've read and been told, both ceremonies seem very important. My other problem is that I've come from a world of ceremonies, a world of rituals, as I've explained. I must confess that I find it a little strange that Christianity also has rituals.

TS: You're right to be concerned about disobeying God under any circumstances. You should certainly pray to him about your difficulties. Your heavenly Father knows you have a heart to obey him and that you want to understand what you should be doing and why.

GB: I do pray to him about my worries and my ignorance. And I've been hoping that you could help me. Maybe God will answer my prayers through you or if not through you, through someone else.

TS: Please feel free to talk to other people. I don't have any special hold on the truth. I get things wrong just like everybody else.

GB: Don't worry. I've learnt to be cautious but for the moment I've come to you. . . . You indicated yesterday that you thought that what we would need to look at is complex in some way or another. Where do you think we should begin? I am somewhat anxious to get things sorted out as soon as I can.

TS: Again, I want to say that I really don't think you should be too anxious. We can and probably need to take our time. Last night I thought long and hard about how we might proceed. If you're happy to chat with me over quite a few days, I think you'll find that what we discuss is certainly novel in some aspects but also exciting. It's always exciting to learn new and important things. It will take us some time to get to where you want to go but that's because we need to negotiate our way carefully through a number of matters in order to arrive at our destination safely. But, if at any stage you say to me "That's enough thanks," then we'll call it quits.

GB: From the little you've said to me so far, I hope we don't quit.

TS: I, likewise! It's refreshing to chat with someone who has only recently come to faith in the Lord Jesus and who is so eager to, as you put it, "get things sorted out." . . . I think it would help if we started by taking a look at the way Jesus looked at the Law, the Jewish Law. I know that doing that might seem a little strange but I think it will lay a type of foundation for us. You're familiar with what is commonly called "The Sermon on the Mount" in Matthew's Gospel?

GB: Yes I've read Matthew chapters five, six and seven a number of times.

TS: I'm not going to say that everything that Jesus said on that occasion is easy to understand and I know that experts differ here and there over a few details and even over some substantial matters. But for starters, consider the following—Jesus having said that he had not come to abolish the Law or the Prophets but to fulfil them, then said that until heaven and earth disappeared not the smallest letter or pen mark would by any means disappear from the Law until everything was accomplished. Furthermore he warned that anyone who broke one of the least of the commandments and taught others to do so would be called least in the kingdom of heaven but promised that whoever practiced and taught the commandments would be called great in the kingdom of heaven. These are very serious statements aren't they?

GB: Absolutely! But I don't know any believers who take the Jewish law as seriously as Jesus seemed to. For instance, the ones I know don't observe the Sabbath although I've heard of some Christians who do. And I know that some of the prophets condemned the nation of Israel for the way it did not *respect* the Sabbath. Keeping the Sabbath seemed to have been very important. And I know there were other Sabbaths over and above the seventh day of the week Sabbath. And there were special feast days—the Feast of Tabernacles and of course the Passover Festival—and special Sabbaths associated with those feasts. And what of the agricultural laws that we can't fulfil if we don't live in an agricultural setting? And we certainly don't carry out any of the laws that relate to the sacrifices nor do we observe the dietary laws. Again I've heard that some Christians do have dietary prohibitions but none that I know worry about what they eat, unless it's for reasons of health. What is Jesus saying here? Or has the modern Christian got it wrong?

TS: You obviously know a fair amount for a new believer! And you're right to make the points you've just made and to ask those questions. I think it's important to realize that Jesus having said these things, then went on to speak, in considerable detail, about issues that had no obvious connection with Sabbaths or sacrifices or dietary laws! For example, he spoke of anger, lust, loving one's enemies, hypocrisy, loving wealth, worrying about material matters, seeking first the kingdom of God, being judgmental and seeking good gifts from God.

GB: I know. It's all a little puzzling.

TS: Let me continue. Interestingly, in spite of the obvious lack of reference to Sabbath keeping and the like, none the less, the bulk of his teaching on that occasion seems to be enclosed within references he makes to the Law and the Prophets. Towards the beginning, as we've already indicated, he claims he has not come to abolish the Law and the Prophets but to fulfil them. Towards the end of this so-called "Sermon on the Mount," he says that doing to others what you would have them do to you *is* the Law and the Prophets. I know he doesn't say this right at the very end but it's only followed by his pointing out alternatives from which people must choose—entering through a narrow gate or a wide one, recognizing a good tree from a bad one by its fruit, and building a house on rock or on sand.

GB: And I remember that with that last choice he said something about hearing his words and acting on them. The focus is really all about his teaching isn't it? But why then does he refer to the Law and the Prophets and claim such importance for the Law?

TS: I think, it's because for Jesus the Law and the Prophets require a fulfilment, and he sees himself as bringing about that fulfilment. There is a focus on the importance of the Law because the Law specifically embodied the will of God for his people. We know that Jesus was the perfect obedient Son and perhaps in that sense he fulfilled the Law. Is he however, also fulfilling the Law—that is, giving a full expression of what is inherent in the Law—in the actual teaching he gives on this occasion?

GB: This would be to understand "fulfilment of the Law" in two senses.

TS: Yes and there may be more than two senses! I wish I were more confident of what Jesus is really getting at when he marries both his statement on the importance of the Law and his statement on his fulfilling the Law and the Prophets. My consolation is that even the experts differ. However, I can say with some confidence that most of what he says on this occasion is concerned not about things such as dietary laws and feast days *et cetera* but about how we should treat one another, how we should see ourselves, how we should see God and what should be our prime goal in life. In fact what he says seems to go deeper than the Law as it's normally understood. He seems to get at the heart of things, indicating what the Law ultimately points to.

GB: That would make sense of his teaching being the fulfilment of the Law. It's quite clear to me that in his day there were groups of people who by their rigorous rule keeping thought they were living a life that was the ultimate in how to please God. They seemed to believe that they were indeed fulfilling the requirements of the Law. Yet I think that Jesus wanted to point out otherwise.

TS: I am still amazed at how much you know! I am sure you have in mind those described as the Pharisees and the scribes. What must have astonished them and others who looked up to them, was Jesus saying that unless people's righteousness exceeded that of the Pharisees and the scribes they would in no way enter the kingdom of heaven. Fulfilment of the Law required much more than the rule keeping of the Pharisees and the scribes. And, as I think Jesus made clear, none of us have been able to fulfil what *is* required. The righteousness he spoke of is way beyond any standards we create for ourselves. Thanks be to God for his great gift, the Lord Jesus Christ, who became sin for us, he who knew no sin, so that in him we might become the righteousness of God.

GB: I understand that and wholeheartedly agree. I am ever so grateful to God for his viewing me as being *in* his Son, *in* the Lord Jesus. And I now think that I'm a little clearer on what Jesus was saying in his "Sermon on the Mount." But how does this relate to my concerns?

TS: Well, in all that Jesus said, and no matter how we understand Jesus fulfilling the law there is no mention of ceremonial requirements. In fact, once, when a scribe questioned Jesus about the greatest commandment in the Law, Jesus replied that it was—"You shall love the Lord your God with all your heart, with all your soul and with all your mind." And that there was a second like it, "You shall love your neighbor as yourself." On this occasion he concluded these words with "All the Law and the Prophets hang on these two commandments." Ceremonies and other matters such as dietary laws and Sabbath keeping seem to take a back seat when you consider these two commandments. And of course, interestingly, these commandments are found in the Law!

Part 1: Law and Freedom

GB: But might loving God with all your heart, soul and mind not entail obeying those other commands—ones that relate to dietary laws, special days and special feasts and even the sacrificial requirements? I'm just asking. I don't really think the answer is "Yes."

TS: I don't know if this helps, but have you read how Mark in his Gospel, after recording what Jesus said about, what enters the stomach does not make anyone unclean, added, "By declaring this, Jesus indicated that all foods are clean." I know this statement only refers to dietary laws, but Jesus, in fulfilling the Law, seems in fact to overthrow some aspects of the Law. Indeed, I think the fulfilment of the law is accomplished in various ways—by his life, through his teachings and in his death. In his life he perfectly obeyed the Law. In his teachings he brought to the fore what is entailed in the Law. In his death he accomplished for us what no animal sacrifice of the Law could ever achieve—a clean slate!

GB: I know that believers don't have to worry about the sacrificial system because Christ is our sacrifice and has brought all of that to an end. But I do worry about special days. Of course for me, what I am concerned about mainly is "baptism" and "the Lord's Supper."

TS: I know, I know. We'll get there but it's important to have a broad perspective before considering those things head on.

GB: By mentioning how Jesus saw himself and the Jewish Law are you trying to suggest that maybe there's no law that says we have to be baptized or that we need to participate in the Lord's Supper?

TS: I don't want to say anything like that or even similar to that, at least not at this stage. I think we have a long way to go before we would ever want to consider saying something like that, even as a possibility. I think we need to continue laying a foundation before we start to look at your questions more directly. However, I suspect we've dealt with enough for today. Can we talk again tomorrow or would another day suit you?

GB: No, tomorrow would be fine.

TS: Well, tomorrow, I think it would be helpful to look at a letter that the Apostle Paul wrote to some Christians in a Roman province called Galatia. It would have been written not too long after they had become believers—maybe only a few years at the most. Paul seems to have had perspectives on the Jewish Law similar to those that Jesus had. He would say he learnt from Jesus. In another letter of his, one he wrote to Christians in Rome, he said something very close to what Jesus said as recorded by Matthew—"Love is the fulfilment of the Law." But I'm off the track. In the letter to the Galatians he said some serious things about the gospel and its ramifications for both Jew and Gentile Christians but with the Gentile believers mostly in mind. In that letter he raised issues relating to circumcision, food laws and special days. Is there any possibility that you could read through that letter overnight? It would help if you could, but there's no problem if you can't.

GB: I've read it before but can read it again, tonight. Many thanks for today. I'll see you tomorrow.

PART 1: LAW AND FREEDOM

EXPLANATORY NOTES: DAY 2

TS made a number of references to sections of what is commonly called the Sermon on the Mount. There are two accounts of this "sermon," one in Matt 5:1–7:29 (NIV) and the other in Luke 6:27–7:49 (NIV).

One prophet that speaks at length about the profaning of the Sabbaths by God's people is Ezekiel. See Ezek 20:13–24 in particular.

There are several references in the Old Testament to the various festivals that Israel was commanded to keep. Lev 23:1–44 refers to a number of these.

TS mentioned Christ being the great gift from God. He was alluding to 2 Cor 9:15 (NIV) and associated it with an earlier statement by Paul in 2 Cor 5:2 (NIV)—a reference to the one who knew no sin.

The text that TS referred to when speaking of Jesus responding to a question by a scribe is Matt 22:35–40 (NIV).

Mark 8:18–19 (NIV) is the text that TS had in mind when he mentioned what Jesus said about food and the comment by Mark that Jesus, by saying what he did, declared all foods clean.

TS quoted from Rom 13:10 (NIV) when referring to Paul writing that "Love is the fulfillment of the Law."

Day 3

The Galatian Problem

Given the concerns that GB has about ceremonies or rituals, TS thinks it appropriate if they reflect on what Paul wrote in his letter to the Galatians. TS and GB wander around parts of the text fairly freely, even spending some time on some of the events in the life of the apostle Peter. Not being in any hurry, well, TS is not in a hurry, they only look at the first three chapters.

GB: Hi there. I've read Galatians again and I believe I've got the gist of it. At least I think I understand it better than I did the first time. Let me see if I've got this much right. Obviously Paul wasn't very happy with them was he? At one stage he called them foolish and rhetorically asked who'd bewitched them! Circumcision seemed to be the main problem. Certain Jews, who while seemingly recognizing Jesus as the Messiah, at the same time, were insisting that Gentiles who had become believers should be circumcised just as they had been. I take it that from Paul's point of view these Gentile believers, having put their faith in Christ Jesus, were justified by their faith in Christ and not by any rite such as circumcision, though it had been an extremely important rite for every Jewish male.

TS: Spot on. And in referring to those who *seemingly* believed that Jesus was the Messiah you've pointed to the difficulty that I suspect most of us have, in understanding exactly what their faith, I mean the faith of those who were trying to disturb the others, amounted to. Were they genuine believers or not? It's difficult to tell. They were certainly Jewish. But Paul doesn't speak very well of them. . . . Now, the Galatian letter is an exceptional letter from many points of view. It's the only letter that we have of Paul's, well, that we're confident that Paul wrote, that doesn't in its early stages have a word of encouragement, praise or thanksgiving. Paul was very concerned about what had been happening to the believers, that is the ones to whom the letter is addressed.

He says he was astonished that they seemed to be so quickly—yes, they hadn't been believers for very long—so quickly deserting God—the one who had called them by the grace of Christ. By "the grace of Christ" he meant something like the kindness of God shown to them through his Son. It is by Christ alone that we can be forgiven and made right with God.

GB: Sure.

TS: Well, Paul was very concerned that they were turning to a different gospel, which he exclaimed was really no gospel at all. His view was that the grace of Christ was being denied and the genuine gospel undermined. Interestingly, the word "gospel" and the verb, often translated "preach the gospel," when taken together, occur relatively more often in the Galatian letter than in any other document of the New Testament. It's only in the Acts of the Apostles that the noun and the verb, lumped together, occur more frequently.

GB: But I'm not *exactly* sure what the letter has to do with baptism and the Lord's Supper, though I could hazard a guess.

TS: I think the Galatian letter does say something about the sacraments, as they're termed by many people, but only indirectly. I don't think there's any direct reference to them in the letter. At least that's my point of view. But to continue. Circumcision, which was part of God's contractual arrangement with Abraham and therefore before the Law came into existence, wasn't the only issue that Paul raised. Just as fundamentally, he was concerned with the Law itself. He was very concerned that these Galatian believers, I guess they were mainly Gentiles, were observing "days and months and seasons and years" as though they felt they *had* to be observed. I take it that since the infiltrators, as Paul referred to them, were Jewish, those days, months, seasons and years were *Jewish* special days and months *et cetera*. It seems to me that what Paul had in mind was such as Sabbath observance and keeping the Passover and the other Jewish festivals, like the Feast of weeks, the Feast of Trumpets, the Day of Atonement and the Feast of Tabernacles. Those festivals are mentioned in Numbers, chapters twenty eight and twenty nine in the Old Testament with details of the various sacrifices to be performed when they occurred.

GB: I can understand some people thinking that Paul thought there was something wrong with the Law but it seems to me that that's not true. Do you mind if I give an account of what I think he says about the Law?

TS: Of course not!

GB: He points out that if anyone hopes to be justified before God by keeping the Law he is entirely mislead. Instead, he argues from the Old Testament, that all who rely on observing the Law are under a curse. They are under a curse because everyone who does not do everything written in the book of the Law, all the time, is cursed, and no one obeys the Law all the time and in every respect—I'm starting to think about my own experience in the cult! His view is that the law came into existence to make transgressions, sins, obvious. Living under the Law only made it clear that you were a breaker of the Law. It acted like a custodian showing people up for what they were really like until Christ finally came. The only way anyone could ever be justified was by faith and when Christ came that would be more obvious. Have I got that right?

TS: Absolutely!

GB: And I could follow his argument about the promises God made to Abraham. One was concerning his faith in God and how God as a consequence counted that faith as righteousness. Another was that through Abraham all the nations—that is, the Gentiles—would be blessed. Yet, as Paul made clear, these promises were made before the law was ever given and like an unalterable will, that a person might make in anticipation of his death, the law, when it came, could not alter what God had promised, what he had contracted to do beforehand. It wasn't that the Law was in opposition to the promises of God, it was that the Law and the promises simply served different purposes. Have I got that right?

TS: I think so. Paul was trying to make it clear that this focus on circumcision and the observance of special occasions was like living in the past. However, a new era had begun with the coming of Christ but an era that God had always planned for. And it wasn't only circumcision and special days and occasions that had become a problem. There may have been a number of other matters, but one additional area of concern for Paul was that of the Jewish dietary food laws.

GB: I was wondering when you were going to mention those.

TS: Well what you ate and what you didn't eat was very important for a Jew. Did you notice how Paul referred to certain people having a reputation as leaders and then, almost out of the blue, produced the name of Peter, charging him with hypocrisy and even leading Barnabas astray? I wouldn't like my name being mentioned in such a manner and having it for all to see in a letter being circulated among a lot of people! I take it that it wasn't being circumcised, or deciding to make certain occasions special or deciding to eat only certain types of food, that in themselves were the issue. It was whether or not keeping the regulations were seen, among other things, as essential for gaining God's approval. In fact, as you've just said, trying to live under the Law simply indicated that you were a failure—you broke the Law, you were a sinner. Your failure meant you gained God's disapproval. Sure, as Paul pointed out, Jews looked upon the Gentiles as sinners but Jews were sinners also. And now that Christ had come, to focus on things like circumcision as mandatory, for Jews or for anybody, in order to avoid God's displeasure was a terrible mistake. In truth, Paul was unconcerned about whether a man was circumcised or not. His view was that neither being circumcised nor being uncircumcised meant anything. What really counted was being a new creation.

GB: I really can't understand how Peter got it wrong. From what Paul said he had been having meals with Gentiles but when certain Jews came along, he absented himself from the Gentiles. Maybe he didn't think what the Gentiles were doing or not doing was wrong, it was just that he worried about what these Jews thought of his behavior. I remember reading in the book of Acts how earlier Peter had been taught by God through a vision that it was okay to go into a Gentile's house and even share a meal with him. Do you mind if I go through what I recall happened on that occasion?

TS: Of course not.

GB: Peter was hungry but fell into a trance. In a vision he saw a sheet coming down from above with lots of animals and birds on it, animals and birds that from his perspective were unclean. And he heard God speak, commanding him to get up, kill the creatures, and eat them. The vision focused on the food laws didn't it? And I guess the "killing" had to do with preparing the animals and birds for food. This happened three times. Peter had never eaten such unclean creatures before yet in the end these visions and what God said in them convinced him to enter the house of the Gentile. He even seems to have let some Gentiles into his own house beforehand. Later he saw the Holy Spirit being given to this Gentile and others who were with him. If I remember correctly, his name was Cornelius. And in the end Peter stayed with him and the others for a few days. The man was a centurion and I suppose that meant he was probably well off and could afford to have a large house. Anyway, I take it that Peter "staying with him" meant that Peter would have had meals with him. Later, perhaps not too much later, Peter stood up to certain Jews in Jerusalem who took issue with what he'd done. But in this letter, Paul says Peter was afraid of the group claiming that people needed to be circumcised, a group of people that had come from a person called James.

TS: That James was almost certainly the James who was the leader of the church in Jerusalem. However, I'm really not sure of the exact part he played in this whole business. And as far as Peter is concerned, I suppose he was just like what any of us might be. Sometimes we feel the pressure of other people so much that we act insincerely and contrary to what we really know to be true. However, it was a very serious matter. What Peter did would make it appear to others that God had not extended his mercy to the Gentiles or that if he did, it would depend upon their being obedient to at least certain features of the Law. You might recall in the book of Acts how on another occasion, back in Jerusalem, Peter recounted to a meeting of important church folk, as we might call them, what God had taught him before and during the time that he was with Cornelius. Yes, Cornelius was his name. At that meeting Peter made it clear that God did not require Gentiles to be circumcised. We can't be sure of the chronology but perhaps this meeting occurred after the occasion mentioned in Galatians.

GB: I suppose it's difficult for us to understand the pressure Peter was under. Paul on the other hand seems as solid as a rock on the issue of circumcision. He is firmly committed to the view that God does not now make it a requirement for anybody. To go back to the Law, having been delivered from its curse, is simply to portray oneself as, again, a breaker of the Law. Actually, I must admit that I found what Paul wrote at this particular point a little difficult to understand but that's my guess as to what he was saying. Is it okay if I continue by indicating what I think is abundantly clear in this part of Paul's letter?

TS: Go ahead.

GB: For Paul, to rely on the works of the Law was not only to be found guilty under the Law, but it was to treat the death of Christ as though it was of no use and that faith in him was futile. To rely on the works of the Law would be to deny God's kindness towards us, his grace, and we ourselves would be, and would be seen to be, trying to contribute to our own salvation. I was really impressed with what he wrote towards the end of chapter 2. I wrote it down for myself. "The life I live in the body I live by faith in the Son of God who loved me and gave himself for me. I do not set aside the grace of God, for if righteousness could be gained through the law, Christ died for nothing."

TS: They're very impressive words aren't they? Paul understood ever so clearly how to live. The special days, dietary laws and circumcision were being viewed as essential in order to gain God's approval. But Paul knew that approval only came by Jesus Christ, God's Son and faith in him alone. You must have noticed how concerned Paul was, in the letter, to indicate how he didn't receive the gospel from someone else and that it wasn't made up and that "It came through a revelation of Jesus Christ." It seems to me that he was saying that Jesus himself had revealed the gospel to him, directly, though I am not quite sure what that would have amounted to. It's clear however that he was absolutely confident that he knew what the gospel was. Indeed, it had changed his whole life. An extremely well educated and zealous Jew had become a staunch defender of the gospel of Jesus Christ, the same Jesus Christ whom he had once persecuted. He was no mean Jew and he came to be no mean believer in Jesus Christ the Lord, an apostle to the Gentile world, as well as the Jewish one. . . . That's enough for now. I feel I am getting a little carried away. Shall we continue discussing Galatians tomorrow?

GB: You're not going over the top at all, and yes, tomorrow would be fine. A great letter!

PART 1: LAW AND FREEDOM

EXPLANATORY NOTES: DAY 3

God's covenant with Abram/Abraham regarding circumcision can be found in some detail in Gen 17:1–14 (NIV)

In their references to Peter and his experience with Cornelius, TS and GB discussed what Paul wrote in Gal 2:11–14 (NIV) and what Luke wrote in Acts 10:1–8, 11:1–18, 15:7–11 (NIV).

GB quoted from Gal 2:20b–21 (NIV).

Day 4

Slavery, Freedom and Life in the Spirit

Being determined to finish working through Galatians, TS deals with the last three chapters of the letter more systematically than he had when considering the first three. Towards the end of the day GB wants to discuss the phrase "being baptized into Christ." TS is reluctant to do so and instead asks a question about what some of GB's church friends might say about Paul not mentioning exceptions to his general principle.

TS: Yesterday we only looked at the first half of Galatians. Today we're going to work on the second half.

GB: I decided to read through Galatians again last night, just to check on a few things and it was clear what we'd done and what we hadn't.

TS: Do you think we'd made some *mistakes* yesterday?

GB: No, no. It was really just to go over what Paul said and to prepare myself for today.

TS: You're very conscientious. You put some of us to shame. . . . I'm sure you are now quite aware that about half way through the letter Paul begins to focus on the issue of freedom.

GB: Yes. Wonderful freedom! I know what it's like to be free.

TS: Would that a few more of us appreciated our freedom in the gospel. . . . Anyway, back to Galatians. It's as though Paul is asking the rhetorical question, "If freedom is available and if with that freedom there is a life really worth living, who would want to remain a slave?" Appealing to features of his Roman world, he argues that a child, even a child who has a future inheritance awaiting him, as a child, is like a slave. He is subject to guardians and trustees until his father determines otherwise. Similarly, he contends that we are bound in slavery by the basic principles of the world. Given what follows I suspect he might have had in mind Jews only at this point but I'm not sure.

Whether Jews only or Jews and Gentiles, I think by the phrase "the basic principles of the world" he means something like, the systems by which we live. In the case of Jews it meant living under the Law and it is now, in what follows, clearly the Jew upon which he focuses. Continuing his argument he indicates that their circumstances had changed however, when in the fullness of time, when God's timing had reached its climactic point, the Son of God came. He came to redeem from slavery those who were under the Law, so that they might receive the full rights that belong to sons. He then makes a point of saying that Jesus was born under the law himself. I think his position is that somehow or other, Jesus being born under the Law enables him to act for others who are also under the Law.

GB: I noticed that you used the word "we"—"*we* are bound in slavery"—and "the systems by which *we* live." It's easy isn't it and not inappropriate, to see ourselves in the text?

TS: Quite so. But I was simply trying to follow Paul. Paul himself was using the first person plural. What I mean by that is that in the Greek the reference is to "we." First person singular is the situation when the reference is to "I." But I should comment on Paul's use of "we." It's not always clear whom Paul is including when he uses the first person "we" or "our" or to whom he's referring when using the second person "you" or "your." Paul has the difficulty of writing to a mixture of people—Jews, Jewish proselytes, Gentiles who were not Jews but who were rather familiar with Jewish teaching, perhaps because in the past they had attached themselves to a Jewish synagogue, and also presumably some Gentiles who had only recently become familiar with Jewish ideas. It may be that in this part of his letter, he's referring to himself and fellow Jews and Jewish proselytes when using the first person and that he's addressing the others when using the second person. The reality, however, might not be as simple as that. Having made the statement that in Christ there is neither Jew nor Greek, he may have felt he had the freedom here and there to be flexible in his use of the first or second person plural. By "second person" I mean either "you" referring to one person—that would be second person singular—or "you" referring to more than one person—that would be second person plural. Third person singular is a reference to "he," "she" or "it" and third person plural is a reference to "they."

GB: I understand what you're saying and don't worry about explaining "first person plural" and so on. I understand that as well. I know English is not my area of expertise but I have studied some languages. What Paul said—it's one of his wonderful statements, isn't it? A wonderful statement of the truth that I've learnt—that in Christ there is neither Jew nor Greek, neither slave nor free, and neither male nor female.

TS: True. A great statement! I should have mentioned it earlier. But let me continue. Having written about "we" being bound by the basic principles of the world, but then focusing on those who were under the Law, he then writes of "you"—those who beforehand did not know God. I think it's clear that here he has those who were Gentiles in mind. They're the ones he describes as having been slaves to what were no gods at all. He then asks how come they were now returning to those same weak and wretched basic principles. These words are very telling. He's asking how they could go back to such a terrible way of life. How could they be so stupid! Remember how he has just referred to these basic principles, but possibly with Jews only in mind. In the end, for Paul, Jews and Gentiles have a similar problem. Paul characterizes both Jews and Gentiles as having been in slavery to what he considers to be the basic stuff of the sinful world, but probably in different senses. For the Jew, his slavery was evidenced by his failure to keep the Law though the Law was still the center of his life. For the Gentile, his slavery was evidenced by his worthless idolatry, but to have the gods on side was considered essential for life to be lived at all successfully. The point is, Paul saw that all people are bound in slavery in this world, one way or another.

GB: Although I wasn't sure about some of what Paul said, I thought that aspect of it was fairly clear.

TS: You would have noticed then, that continuing with his reference to slavery he uses the story of two women—Sarah and Hagar, to make his point that slavery means being a child of the slave woman, Hagar, the personification of *earthly* Jerusalem while freedom means being a child of the free woman, Sarah, the personification of *heavenly* Jerusalem.

GB: I did. However, I must confess that I'm not all that familiar with the Old Testament. Yet it seems obvious that he assumes that his readers, both Jews and Gentiles, would have been familiar with the story of Hagar and Sarah.

TS: That's interesting isn't it? And it surprises me. It appears that the Gentiles by whatever means had become quite familiar with what was basically the Jewish Scriptures. Maybe it was because, having become believers, those Scriptures were by and large their only Scriptures.

GB: What became apparent to me, as I read through Galatians again, was how much Paul wanted his readers to appreciate that they were subject to a negative response from God if they were going to subject themselves to legal requirements. Appealing to that statement in the Old Testament, I've now got the text in front of me—"Get rid of the slave woman and her son."—Paul is being very pointed isn't he? On the other hand, it's like a rallying call to them all, when he writes, "Therefore, brothers we are not children of the slave woman but of the free woman. It is for freedom that Christ has set us free."

TS: But still he indicates his considerable concern when he exhorts them to stand firm in that gospel of freedom and not to submit themselves, again, to a yoke of slavery. He warns them about being cut off from Christ and falling away from grace. And he seems to indicate that if one gives in to this legalism, just a little, it will affect them through and through. He makes use of a saying, "A little yeast works through all the dough." and then he returns to the subject of circumcision again. It's obviously a matter of great concern. They are being strongly urged by these "infiltrators" to submit to circumcision. They must strenuously resist. Of all the problems, circumcision seems to be the main one.

GB: And doesn't he speak harshly and perhaps, it seems to me, sarcastically, about those who are attempting to lead them astray—"I wish they would mutilate themselves!"

TS: They're certainly harsh words.... Paul then seems to anticipate what for some might be considered a genuine objection to his position. It's as though he hears someone saying, "Won't the idea of living in this world of freedom from the Law lead people into sin?" In response, if response it is, he writes that their freedom must never be used to indulge in sin. Rather they are to serve one another in love. Like Jesus, as we mentioned earlier, Paul refers to all of the Law being summed up in that one commandment of loving one's neighbor as oneself. Remember, he said that sort of thing in Romans as well. By the way, have you noticed that it's at about this point in the letter that he begins to make several references to the Spirit?

GB: Yes. However I think his first reference to the Spirit is in about the middle of the letter where he refers to the Galatians having begun their new life with the Spirit and how God has given the Spirit to them not because they have obeyed the law but because they have believed what they have been told. Then he refers to how God has sent the Spirit of his Son into their hearts, because they are sons, and then how the Spirit calls out "Father."

TS: You have a good memory.

GB: I also have the text in front of me!

TS: But you knew exactly where to look.... And now having appealed to that law about loving one's neighbor, he makes reference to walking by the Spirit. Next he refers to the idea of the sinful nature and the Spirit being contrary to one another, being in conflict with one another. He then follows this up with the idea of being led by the Spirit and then makes a wonderful statement about the fruit of the Spirit. Obviously he sees that the answer to that question, "Won't living in a world of freedom from the Law result in our living sinful lives?" is, "No. We live by the Spirit whom God has freely given to those he calls his children and the Spirit will lead us in the way of righteousness." It isn't freedom to do what one likes. And it isn't just freedom from the curse of the Law. It's enablement to "walk in step" with the Spirit because God has given his children a special life lived by his Spirit. His last words on the Spirit refer to sowing to the Spirit. This results in the reaping of eternal life. Sowing to the flesh results in decay. I think the idea behind "sowing to," is "living where your interest lies." It can only be with respect to the things of the Spirit or, alternatively, to the things of the flesh.

GB: It's so clear that for Paul a life lived under the Law is not a righteous life. It's a failed life. Life lived by the Spirit is the life that promises the most in terms of righteousness. I know that we can never in this life reach the standard that God requires and that the righteousness that we need is granted to us because of who Christ is and what he's done. But to have the very Spirit of God at work in us is the way to go!

TS: Sometimes just listening to you I find it difficult to believe that you've only been a believer for about a year.

GB: In reality I realize that I know so little.

TS: Well, just a few more comments on Paul's letter. It's sobering that although towards the end of the letter Paul focuses on how the Galatians should treat one another with love and care, he again raises the subject of circumcision. It's obviously a considerable problem, as we mentioned before. He compares how he glories in the cross of the Lord Jesus Christ, their Lord Jesus Christ, whereas those trying to persuade them to be circumcised, want to glory, as he puts it, in their flesh. He claims that in trying to force circumcision on them, these others are seeking to avoid difficulties in their own lives. They are avoiding being persecuted by fellow Jews. Peer pressure can be considerable and exceedingly significant in affecting the way we behave. It's at about this point that he makes that statement, "Neither being circumcised nor not being circumcised counts for anything. What does count is being a new creation." Indeed, a new creation brought about by the Spirit!

GB: It's fairly obvious isn't it? Paul sees undergoing circumcision, observing special days and having dietary regulations as unnecessary for one's salvation and those who regard them as obligatory are in opposition to the grace of God and the work of the Spirit. Does Paul express similar views in any of his other letters?

TS: In one way or another, yes. For example in his letter to the believers at Colossae, though there he was dealing with different matters than those facing the Galatians, he writes "Let no one pass judgement on you in questions of food and drink or with regard to a festival or a new moon or a Sabbath." It was an entirely different situation but one can see similar theological perspectives coming to the fore.

GB: Thanks. Now that you've mentioned it, I do recall something of those words in that letter. . . . Look, I hope you don't mind what I'm about to say. But I need to raise the issue. I know that baptism is not the concern of the Galatian letter but I noticed the reference by Paul in that letter to being baptized into Christ. You haven't made any reference to that part of the letter. In fact I thought you said that Galatians didn't have anything to say about either of the sacraments.

TS: Well, I think I said that it did say something about the sacraments, though *indirectly*. I'm sorry, but could we leave that verse aside for the moment, at least until we start looking at the matter of baptism as a whole? Actually could we leave discussing that verse for quite a while?

GB: Sure. Whatever you think is best.

TS: I think you would find it most helpful if we *didn't* deal with that text until sometime down the track. . . . Before we finish for the day, we could now ask two interesting questions about the Galatian letter. "What did Paul not say and what exceptions to his general position did he not specify and why?" and "What would you or your believing friends at your church wish Paul had said, to make things clearer and again, why?"

GB: I think you have asked more than two questions! I suppose you have in mind that he didn't raise as exceptions, being baptized, keeping the first day of the week as a Sabbath or participating in the Lord's Supper? I suppose you also think that my friends at my church might say something like, "It would've been helpful if Paul had made it clear that his concerns did not include, the sacraments of baptism or the Lord's Supper."

TS: Well, something like that.

GB: I don't think my friends would make that sort of statement at all! If I were to ask them whether or not they saw any implications arising from the Galatian letter for those ceremonies, they would probably say, "No," because those practices were so much part of the ordinary life of those early Christians. I think they would say that if they *were* to be thought of as exceptions, it was well understood by Paul and the recipients of the letter that they were just that—exceptions.

TS: I guess you're right about what your friends might think. I was being somewhat naïve. However, as a counter argument I'd say that it seems fairly clear that Paul is arguing from principles. That although mention is made of specific matters—dietary food laws, the observance of special days, and circumcision, it is submitting to the "stuff" of the world, either the Jewish or Gentile world that's the problem. I think it's significant that having referred to the problem by using the Greek words, "τα στοιχεια του κοσμου" *(ta stoicheia tou kosmou)*, which we could translate "the basic principles of the world" and then the simple word "στοιχεια," "the basic principles," a few verses later, he then chooses, towards the end of his letter, to use the word "στοιχωμεν" *(stoichōmen)* which we could translate "let us walk in accordance with the principles." A moment ago I spoke of the word as "walk in step." He chooses to use this word, a verb, when referring to how to live life by the Spirit. Believers need to abandon the principles by which they used to live their lives and live life by the basic principles of the Spirit. In arguing from principles he appeals to principles! He argues that at a fundamental level both Jew and Gentile get it wrong. There is a fundamental problem because a fundamental principle is involved. It isn't a question of whether or not a custom or ceremony is helpful. It's a matter of whether or not such are regarded as obligatory.

GB: I understand your argument but I can't imagine that you'd convince many others that certain ceremonies aren't obligatory. Indeed people might claim that the phrase "being baptized into Christ," obviously relating to Christ and also being part of a very positive statement, is indicative of at least the practice of baptism being both acceptable and necessary! I'm sorry to bring that verse up again.

TS: And again, I think you're probably right. What I mean is, I can imagine people arguing that way. As I said, why don't we leave a discussion of that text until later on—maybe much later on? Perhaps I should not have mentioned those "two interesting questions," at least not at this point in our discussions. I think now however, we've spent enough time on the Galatian letter, unless of course you want to say something more about it.

GB: No. I think we've basically covered the main elements of the letter, at least as far as I can see.

TS: All I'd ask however, would be for you to keep in mind what Paul wrote in that letter as we progress in our discussions. And you might also note how what he wrote is not inconsistent with what Jesus spoke about in his Sermon on the Mount.

GB: Now that you mention it, even though Jesus in that address couched what he said within the framework of the fulfilment of the Law—you said something like that—which I realize is not the same as simply talking about the Law, there *is* a consistency between what Jesus taught there and what Paul wrote in Galatians. I find it remarkable!

TS: Well, perhaps not so remarkable. Our Lord Jesus Christ whom God had sent into the world was the same Jesus who appeared to Paul whom God, the Father of our Lord Jesus, had appointed to be an apostle to the Gentile world and the people of Israel. You might expect there to be a consistency.

GB: I remember reading about how Jesus appeared to Paul and how God explained to Paul what he had in store for him. In God's plans Paul was obviously really special.

TS: How very true. . . . At this point we both might benefit from a few days break, but could we get together say, next Monday, to begin to have a look at the whole question of "baptism"?

GB: Monday would be fine. I'm looking forward to finally tackling one of my concerns, head on.

TS: See you in three days' time then but I feel I should warn you that we're going to take our approach to baptism rather slowly, beginning perhaps by thinking about how baptism is practiced today.

GB: Okay. Slowly it is!

Part 1: Law and Freedom

EXPLANATORY NOTES: DAY 4

The phrase, "the basic principles of the world," the other phrase similar to that one, "the weak and wretched basic principles," and the verb that could be translated, "walk in step," referred to by TS, can be found in Gal 4:3, 9, 5:25 (NIV) respectively, and the associated Greek word or phrases have been taken from NAG.

In citing Paul's reference to Hagar, TS was referring to Gal 4:30, 31 (NIV). GB makes a further comment quoting from Gal 4:30b, 31 (NIV).

Paul's reference to "A little yeast . . . ," quoted by TS can be found in Gal 5:9 (NIV).

There was a reference by GB to Paul's sarcastic comment about mutilation. The comment is located in Gal 5:12 (NIV).

The statement, "Neither being circumcised nor being uncircumcised counts for anything," quoted by TS, can be found in Gal 6:15 (NIV).

In referring to another letter in which TS claimed that Paul expressed some views similar to some of those expressed in his letter to the Galatians, TS quoted from Col 2:16 (NIV). In fact a reference to Col 2:8–23 (NIV), as a whole, might have been more helpful.

The phrase, "being baptized into Christ," that GB raised with TS, is located in Gal 3:27 (NIV).

In mentioning Jesus appearing to Paul and Paul being appointed to be an apostle to the Gentile world and the people of Israel, TS was referring to material recorded in Acts 9:1–19 (NIV), although the word, "apostle" does not appear in those verses. Furthermore, the passage speaks of "the Lord" choosing him, rather than "God."

PART 2

Baptism

Day 5

Baptismal Practices and Beliefs Today

Although it is evident to TS that GB wants to focus on his own predicament very early in their discussions, TS tries to alleviate his concerns and proceeds to mention some of the beliefs about baptism that people hold today and some of the baptismal practices in which they engage. It is obvious that TS wants GB to see how much these beliefs and practices vary from Christian group to Christian group.

GB: Hi. You mentioned on Friday that we are now going to think about how baptism is practiced today. I know that practices vary somewhat and that people can hold different beliefs about its purpose.

TS: One of our difficulties is that even within the one denomination, what people think baptism is all about can vary depending upon whom you talk to and whether they rely on a confessional or doctrinal statement. However a brief trip to the Internet can give you a general idea. Even then I'm sure that some people would disagree with some aspect of the description of what their particular group really believes and practices. In fact if people were to overhear our discussion they might be concerned about the accuracy of what I'm likely to say. I hope it won't be too misleading.

GB: Well, in the end it's a matter *I* have to decide on, although learning about other people's ideas, even if I don't have a completely accurate picture, will still be interesting and maybe helpful. Are there any Christians who don't practice baptism at all?

TS: I know the Quakers don't and the Salvation Army doesn't either. Neither of them considers that it's necessary. Regarding the Quakers, not all of them see themselves as specifically Christian and those who do seem to emphasize the "inner life" and being "baptized in the Spirit" rather than external rituals such as baptism. In the case of the Salvation Army I understand that originally the position adopted was for pragmatic reasons. They didn't see themselves as a separate denomination and didn't want to be seen to be taking sides with any one group as opposed to another. So it was thought that the best thing to do was not to have the rite or custom performed at all. Today, the Salvation Army, as a distinct denomination is quite happy if any of its members wish to be baptized by this group or that. It's simply that they don't offer the possibility of baptism to their members themselves.

GB: I can understand that others who think being baptized is essential are not all that happy with either of their positions.

TS: True and most denominations seem to believe that it's essential. However, those who think so, differ very much amongst themselves as to what being baptized means, what effect it has or should have, why it should be practiced, how people should be baptized, who should baptize and who should or should not be baptized. One can understand why historically the founders of the Salvation Army decided not to have it as part of their corporate life!

GB: I know that one of the main differences between the various denominations or Christian groups is with respect to whether the baptism of infants is regarded as appropriate or whether only adults or at least those old enough to make responsible decisions for themselves, should be baptized.

TS: You're quite right. It's one of the really important differences between the various groups. Those who hold that only so called adults should be baptized include the Baptists, Pentecostals, the Churches of Christ and the Seventh Day Adventists. The position they adopt is that a person, before being baptized needs to, on her or his own volition, repent and then put their trust in the Lord Jesus Christ, though they may express things a little differently to this. Other people, such as the Roman Catholics, Lutherans, members of the Church of England and the related Episcopalians or Anglicans, those of Greek or Coptic Orthodoxy, Congregationalists, Presbyterians, and the United Methodists, a largely American denomination founded in 1968, while happy to baptize adults, more commonly practice the baptism of infants.

GB: But those who believe in the practice of baptism don't all do the same thing when they do baptize, do they? I know that some baptize by completely immersing the person in water and others just pour water over the head or part of the head of the person.

TS: Yes, that's right. There's also the practice of sprinkling, where droplets of water are gently flung, as it were, upon the person. Often, in the case of baptism by immersion, the person is fully immersed, although sometimes it can be that the person, while standing in a pool of water, being half immersed, has water poured over his or her head. Interestingly, the Church of England suggests that an infant can be "dipped," that is, immersed, unless it's thought that the young child would not be able to cope. And the practice, in at least some of the orthodox traditions, seems to be that of immersion both for infants and adults.

GB: I guess that what the person who carries out the baptism says when they are baptizing varies from denomination to denomination or group to group as well.

TS: Yes, there is some variation but not all that much. It's become very common to refer to baptizing in the name of the Father and of the Son and of the Holy Spirit, although some simply refer to baptizing in the name of Jesus. This latter practice used to be much more common. Oh, and by the way, some people are immersed three times. I take it that this is done either to correspond to the three-fold name or to mirror the three days Jesus was in the tomb. Immersing people three times was also a practice carried out in ancient times.

GB: Who are allowed to baptize?

TS: That varies, but what's new? Generally however, it has to be someone in authority. Historically at one stage in the western church it had to be a bishop. Often now that means a priest or presbyter in the particular church, although some churches are happy to have a layperson baptize, especially if that person is also a preacher.

GB: What do people think happens when a person is baptized?

TS: That's a crucial question and perhaps more important than any we've raised so far. The reason why some insist that a person should only be baptized when of "mature age," as it's often put, is because their view is that the ceremony or "rite" must at least symbolize the fact that the person him or herself has on their own volition come to faith in Christ. That's why such baptisms are sometimes called "believer's baptism." It's the person being baptized who, as one of mature age, is the believer. In being baptized, the believer, in some sense or another, is understood to have been crucified with Christ and to have been raised with him. Furthermore it's generally agreed that such a baptism should be quite public, the believer making it clear to others, the transformation he or she has experienced, even if some years before, in Christ.

GB: I guess that those who baptize infants might also have the same view, that is that the infant, in being baptized has been crucified and raised with Christ and that it's important for the baptism to have been performed publicly.

TS: With regards to the idea of being crucified and raised with Christ, I suppose so, although I'm not sure. With respect to the baptism being performed publicly, I think it's generally recognized, that whether or not the person being baptized is of mature age, the extent to which a baptism is made public might be quite limited.

GB: I think I have an idea of what being crucified and raised with Christ means but I wouldn't have automatically associated that theology with baptism. None the less, I realize how the ritual of baptism, especially when it involves immersion, can be understood as symbolic of dying and coming back to life. Are there other ideas about what's involved when a person is baptized?

TS: Well, some consider that being baptized indicates that the person is entering into the church tradition or denomination within which the baptism took place. Consequently for some there is no oddity about a person being baptized more than once. There could have been a believer's baptism or even the baptism of an infant at one time, and then some time later a separate, most likely adult baptism for the same person as an indication that the person was now becoming a member of a different denomination or tradition. Another idea relates to the connection between baptism and the forgiveness of sins. Baptists and Seventh Day Adventists, for example, generally regard "baptism" as a sign and not as the means by which a person is brought into a relationship with God, that is, a person is not saved by baptism. However, some from the Churches of Christ, for example, seem to have the view that upon a person being baptized his or her sins are, at that point, forgiven, the person now being in a new relationship with God.

GB: Would that also be the situation with those who believe that infants can be validly baptized?

TS: Do you mean in connection with what happens when a child is baptized, with respect to their standing with God?

GB: Sorry, Yes.

TS: Well, again, things are not that simple, but generally speaking that, or something like that, seems to be the case. Roman Catholics, Lutherans, Episcopalians, Presbyterians, Congregationalists, United Methodists and those of an Orthodox faith are of the view that something of considerable spiritual significance occurs at the moment of baptism. What it is that is believed to occur, however, differs. The belief of some is that a person is saved by faith, that such faith is the gift of God and that that faith is bestowed upon the infant being baptized, by God's grace. For others, the idea seems to be that a work of God has begun in baptism but that it needs to develop as the child develops. This might require some sort of assistance given perhaps by Godparents as well as perhaps by the parents who may make certain promises on behalf of the child. As the child matures, and perhaps after some formal instruction, the person, perhaps a pre-adolescent or adolescent, might be required to undergo another ceremony called "Confirmation." In that ceremony, he or she would be confirming for himself or herself what others did on their behalf at their baptism. It also appears to be the case that generally the baptism of the infant is seen as his or her entrance into "the church," or coming to belong to "the church" though what is understood by the term "the church" would differ from group to group. For some, unless a person, as an infant or adult, has been baptized, there can be no forgiveness of sins, no matter how that forgiveness is brought about. Baptism is seen to be that important.

GB: I know that some refer to "baptism" as an "ordinance" and others refer to it as a "sacrament." What is going on here?

Baptismal Practices and Beliefs Today

TS: Interesting that you should have picked that up. The term "sacrament" has its roots in the Latin word, "*sacramentum*" meaning an oath. I think that the taking of an oath, particularly in a secret society, was often accompanied by the making of a sign. So the term "sacrament" took on the notion of a "sign" being made. Some refer to a sacrament as "a visible sign" of something that's not really observable by simply looking at what happens on the outside. It is deeply spiritual. Some also refer to the sacrament of baptism, as well as other sacraments, as a mystery. I think they are regarded as "mysteries" because there is a belief that some aspect of being baptized or partaking of the Lord's Supper, to take those two as examples, is mysterious. The idea is that something has happened that can't be observed with our physical senses—it is spiritual—and it can't be fully comprehended. Indeed sometimes the word "sacrament" is applied to just the bread and the wine of what some people call the Eucharist, bread and wine changed into the body and blood of Christ.

GB: I see. . . . But with respect to baptism, whatever else some people believe about it, I can readily see how it can be understood as a sign, as symbolic of something.

TS: Yes. However, I think that most who apply the term "sacrament" to baptism consider baptism as more than just a Christian ceremony that points to something else—a sign. I am pretty sure that almost all those who see "baptism" as a sacrament, see it as a rite or ceremony instituted by God and also one in which some especially significant 'grace' is bestowed upon the person being baptized, as I've already pointed out. Interestingly, Roman Catholics and generally those who belong to one of the Orthodox traditions believe there are seven sacraments.

GB: Seven? What are they?

TS: In addition to those that are sometimes referred to as dominical sacraments—sacraments considered to be directly instituted by Jesus—baptism and the Eucharist or the Lord's Supper—many believe that there are five other sacraments. They go by different names but it's not uncommon to refer to them as the sacraments of ordination, anointing the sick, penance or reconciliation, confirmation and marriage. Lutherans are not dogmatic about the number of sacraments but basically settle on just two. However Episcopalians and many others who approve of the baptism of infants, some of whom might believe that there are seven sacraments, consider that the dominical sacraments of baptism and the Eucharist are of fundamental significance.

GB: Sorry, I didn't mean to get off the track. I was just curious.

TS: I was the one who mentioned the seven! Back to baptism. Where baptism is regarded as a sacrament, the general position, perhaps understandably, is that one cannot be baptized a second time and that indeed a baptized person should not try to be baptized again. If God has begun a work of grace in a person, child or adult, through the baptism of that person, how can the need for a second baptism arise? Also, understandably, many of those who see baptism as absolutely essential for gaining one's salvation, consider it better to have a person baptized as an infant rather than later, given that anything might happen in the interim.

GB: But what of those who see baptism as only an ordinance? What do they mean by that?

TS: Whether baptism is referred to as a sacrament or not, probably every tradition that considers the rite as very important conceives of it as an ordinance. That is, they see it as something that has been ordered by God or Christ. Those who view it *only* as an ordinance also see it as a sign though generally they might prefer to use the terms "symbolic" and "symbolizes" in statements they make about it. It is regarded as symbolic of very significant matters. However, if considered only as an ordinance and not also as a sacrament it is not understood to convey directly in itself any special grace from God. Yet, it's not as though a person might not regard the experience as a blessing, if as an adult he or she is being baptized or that others, witnessing the baptism, might not be blessed whatever the age of the person being baptized. It's just that they don't tend to see the ceremony in itself as bestowing that blessing. So some believers think there are two ordinances, rather than two sacraments. One is baptism and the other is the Lord's Supper. However, Seventh Day Adventists, and I don't think they're alone, believe that there are three such ordinances, they wouldn't call them sacraments, foot washing being the other ordinance.

GB: I didn't realize how many different understandings of the rite or ceremony of baptism there were. How could a new Christian trying to size things up objectively and without pressure from others, make up his or her mind? What am I supposed to decide from all that you've said?

TS: I've said this before and I say it again. Please don't worry about this matter at this stage. You don't need to worry. And if when chatting to somebody about what I've been saying today he or she tells you that I didn't get it right with respect to their particular denomination or the church that they attend or that I omitted saying something very important about what they believe and practice, please give them my apologies. I've simply been trying to give you a picture of the variety of positions adopted by some. In fact, in some cases, practices and beliefs adopted by a group seem to change over time, even if ever so slowly.

GB: How can anyone be claiming, even by implication, that their practice with their understanding of what it means, is the real baptism?

TS: Well might you ask! However, in thinking about the whole complex situation, we could see the various practices and beliefs as Roman Catholic baptism and Presbyterian baptism and Baptist baptism *et cetera*, and treat them as different customs. That way of proceeding might be helpful. In fact I sometimes think we would be far better off referring to them as different customs however else we describe them.

GB: But surely some of these "customs" have got to be wrong while some might be, I stress, "might be," right!

TS: Of course, though we shouldn't be too hasty to judge. I'm not saying that *you* are. It's just that history seems to teach us that we all get some things wrong! What I think might be helpful at his stage would be to try and indicate some criteria by which to judge certain practices.

GB: I hope there aren't too many! Criteria I mean.

TS: Well, I want to propose four but I might think of more later on. I think one needs to answer the following questions—Is the practice and the beliefs that go with it helpful? Is either the practice or the associated beliefs misleading? Is any claim that there is historical precedence for that practice or associated beliefs a correct claim? Is the practice mandatory and for what reason?

GB: I think you actually asked five questions!

TS: Well, maybe! . . . I probably need to think more about how to phrase them! . . . What should we do now? I think we can call it quits for today. I suppose when we next meet we could have a look at the practice of "baptism" in the New Testament, although to begin with, let's restrict that to the Gospels and the Acts of the Apostles. I think examining what they say about baptism and its practice will be more helpful than some of the things we've talked about today.

GB: None the less, what we, or mainly you, talked about today was interesting. You made clear to me the great range of ideas that people have about baptism and how it should be practiced.

TS: That's what I was trying to do. But regarding our next meeting, I'm wondering if we couldn't have another break for a day or so?

GB: Would a few days be possible? Meeting up again, say, next Thursday? That would give me time to read through the Gospels and the Acts of the Apostles again with my focus being on what is said there, about baptism.

TS: No problem. And not a bad idea to read through those documents beforehand. It can only help. And as we proceed it might also be helpful if you could keep in the back of your mind what we dealt with earlier—law and freedom and especially that letter that Paul wrote to the Galatians. Just as a backdrop. So, see you on Thursday.

Part 2: Baptism

EXPLANATORY NOTES: DAY 5

The following Internet addresses give some account of the beliefs and practices concerning baptism held by various denominations or groups. However most of them relate to an Internet site associated with a particular church or churches within the denomination or group. The reader may wish to consult many more sites particularly where his or her interest is in beliefs that people have about the existence, nature and number of sacraments.

Anglicanism (Australia)—http://www.anglican.org.au/content/home/about/students_page/How_do_Australian_Anglicans_worship.aspx.

Church of England—http://www.churchofengland.org/weddings-baptisms-funerals/baptism/christening-faqs.aspx.

Episcopalian Church—http://www.episcopalchurch.org/page/holy-baptism.

With respect to Australian Anglicanism, the Church of England and the Episcopalian Church, articles XXV, XXVI and XXVII of their Book of Common Prayer relate to the matter of baptism. Article XXV makes it clear that baptism is considered a sacrament ordained by Christ.

One particular point of interest might be the reference to the Church of England practice of baptizing by dipping. One can find a reference to this, for example, in the rubrics accompanying the "Publick Baptism of Infants" in the 1662 Book of Common Prayer.

Baptists—http://www.baptisthistory.org/pamphlets/baptism.htm.

Churches of Christ (Australia)—http://cofcaustralia.org/wp-content/uploads/2011/12/baptism_booklet_print.pdf.

Congregationalism (Bristol CT, USA)—http://www.firstchurchbristolct.org/images/bapwedfun/BaptismBooklet.pdf.

Coptic Orthodoxy—http://www.copticchurch.net/topics/thecopticchurch/sacraments/1_baptism.htm.

Greek Orthodoxy (Australia)—http://www.greekorthodox.org.au/general/faq/faqbaptism.

Lutherans (Church of Canada)—http://www.whatyoubelieve.ca/believe.php?id+4.

Pentecostalism—http://people.opposingviews.com/pentecostal-baptism-ceremony-2927.html.

Presbyterianism—http://www.presbyterianmission.org/ministries/today/baptism/.

Quakers—http://www.fgcquaker.org/explore/faqs-about-quakers.

Roman Catholicism—http://www.vatican.va/archive/ccc_css/archive/catechism/p2s2c1a1.htm.

Salvation Army—http://www.salvationarmy.org.au/en/Who-We-Are/vision-and-mission/Positional-Statements/Positional-Statements/THE-SACRAMENTS/.

Seventh Day Adventism—http://www.sdanet.org/atissue/books/27/27-14.htm.

United Methodism—http://www.umc.org/site/apps/nlnet/content2.aspx?c=lwL4Kn N1LtH&b=4951419&ct=6480489.

TS mentioned that baptizing in the name of Jesus only, used to be much more common than baptizing in the name of the Father and of the Son and of the Holy Spirit. His main evidence for this is that in the Acts of the Apostles, the name in which people were baptized was either, "Jesus Christ" or "the Lord Jesus"—see Acts 2:38, 8:16, 10:48, 19:5 (NIV). *The Didache*, dated late first to sometime in the third century CE, contains one of the early references to baptizing in the name of the Father and of the Son and of the Holy Spirit (section 7). See also Stevenson, *A New Eusebius*, 126 (section VII).

A reference to the practice of being "baptized" three times during the ceremony of baptism can be found in *The Apostolic Tradition*. 21. 12–18, ostensibly composed by Hippolytus, perhaps around 200 CE. See also, Stevenson, *A New Eusebius*, 155–56.

Day 6

Baptismal Practices in the Gospels and the Acts of the Apostles

TS believes that the next thing that he and GB should discuss should be the ministry of John the Baptist and then how the early disciples and others became involved with the practice of baptism. It is a little odd but TS begins to refer to John by an unusual title that GB had never come across before. TS also raises a few questions about who was baptized and who was not both when John was baptizing and when Jesus was engaged in his earthly ministry.

TS: Hi there. Are you ready for today?

GB: Yes of course.

TS: I think we need to begin our look at baptismal practices in the New Testament by focusing on "John the Baptist," although I prefer to call him "John the Immerser."

GB: Why? You don't really think that some people believe he was a Baptist!

TS: I hope they don't! But if someone did, it wouldn't surprise me. My reason for referring to him as "John the Immerser" is because I think he was given that name as a type of nickname—not a hurtful one but a very descriptive one. He was doing something that as far as we know no one else had done and certainly not anything like on his scale. Josephus in his work, *Jewish Antiquities* refers to him by the same name. Of course Josephus was probably using the name by which he had become popularly known, the same name that appears in the Gospels. You see, it looks as though John had acquired a reputation for immersing people in water. He did quite a lot of it. It appears that many, many people had been "immersed" in water by John.

GB: But didn't other people do that *sort* of thing?

TS: Not really, at least, as I said, not as far as we know. It's true of course that in Jesus' day washing ceremonies of one sort or another were fairly common at least amongst Jewish people. Washing ceremonies or rituals of various kinds have probably often been practiced here and there, practices adopted by different groups from different cultures at different times. Around about the time of Jesus, in his world, there was a group called the Essenes who had fairly strict rules that stipulated the need to undergo a variety of washing procedures on different occasions and for different reasons. Then there were also the Pharisees. They likewise were meticulous in their concerns about the need to wash not only themselves but also things like plates upon which food for eating was to be placed. But both with respect to the Essenes and the Pharisees, it seems that when the body or parts of the body were washed you washed yourself. In the case of John's procedure, *he* was the one who placed you under the water. You didn't immerse yourself. It was also a one-off situation.

GB: What about when Gentiles became Jewish proselytes? I've heard about how they underwent a type of baptism. Did John copy what was done there?

TS: We don't know for sure, but it seems that the practice of these Gentiles being immersed in water came a little later than John's ministry, maybe towards the end of the first century. However, whenever the practice was adopted, it was such that in this case also, the person immersed himself or herself. What is also interesting is that outside of the New Testament, in the Greek literature, at least up until the beginning of the second century, the verb that's used to describe what the Jews did in their washing ceremonies and in the proselytizing of Gentiles is not the word used of John in the New Testament. The word used there is "βαπτιζω" (*baptizō*) but the word most commonly used for the Jewish washings was "λουω" (*louō*). "Βαπτιζω" conveys the sense of "immersing"—I want to talk a lot about that word later on—whereas "λουω," carries the plain sense of "washing." There is another Greek word, "βαπτω" (*baptō*), that can be associated with the idea of washing and found in the Jewish literature but it has primarily the sense of "dipping." I think I'd like to talk a little more about Greek verbs that have the sense of "washing" or similar, a little later, if I don't forget.

GB: Why then did John start doing what seems to have been unique or almost so?

TS: A good question. According to the fourth Gospel, John said he was sent by God to "baptize." I will sometimes say "immerse" because I think that better describes what he did—as I said I want to spend some time looking at the verb involved, later on, down the track. I think we should understand that what he said about God sending him to baptize indicated among other things, that what he was doing was quite unusual. He needed to justify publicly what he was doing, this unusual thing, immersing others, by explaining that God had sent him to do it. I'm pretty sure that he saw himself as a prophet who had been given a special mission by God to carry out this practice. That he immersed others probably contributed to many people's belief that he *was* a prophet. In his immersing people rather than people immersing themselves, the emphasis was on God who had sent him rather than on the people. He also explained that he was "baptizing" so that "the lamb of God might be revealed to Israel." He was preparing others in Israel for the one who at the beginning of John's ministry had not yet made a public appearance. That one, "the lamb of God," was the one who in the end had to be the main focus. He was the one, John said, who would baptize with the Holy Spirit and fire, whereas he was only baptizing with water.

GB: Was what he was doing something like a sign? Was it something like what Ezekiel had to do and what Hosea had to do? They had to do certain things that would point to a spiritual reality. I've read their books.

TS: You've read quite a lot and understood them as well! I'm not trying to be patronizing. I'm just coping with my astonishment! Yes, I think that's quite possible. In fact Ezekiel spoke of God sprinkling clean water and people becoming clean. Perhaps John saw himself as somehow or another connected with what Ezekiel had said. The New Testament reports that John preached a "baptism of repentance" for the forgiveness of sins and the idea of forgiveness can carry with it the notion of being cleansed. Indeed Paul, once when recounting his personal experience, mentioned Ananias, the one who had been instructed by God to explain certain things to him, saying to him that he needed to be baptized and to wash away his sins. John may have seen himself as fulfilling the promise of God recorded in Ezekiel. However "immersion," as I'd like to point out again later, in the Greek world, often carried with it the notion of death by drowning. What John may have been indicating was that in a person's repentance that was accompanied by their being immersed they were to see themselves as dying to an old way of life. Upon coming out of the water they could be seen to be rising to a new way of life.

GB: If that's the case, then the repentance that John was calling upon people to make was quite radical and life changing. When I think about it, of course that's the case.

TS: Absolutely. He was preaching that the rule of God, his kingdom, was about to burst in upon the world and although people should have always repented of their sinful ways this necessity was now ever so much more apparent.

GB: I recall how he clearly indicated how this repentance should show itself in various ways and the examples he gave were indeed radical! Of course this demand for repentance couldn't possibly be what was required of Jesus when he was baptized by John.

TS: Of course not. But doesn't the baptism of Jesus indicate his willingness, right at the beginning, to "stand in our place"? He was the Lamb of God to be slain for sinners and seemed to know it from the very start of his ministry. No wonder God spoke to him and said, "You are my beloved son; with you I am well pleased."

GB: How grateful I am to Jesus for standing in *my* place. . . . Now some of those who later became disciples of Jesus had already been baptized by John hadn't they—Simon Peter and his brother John?

TS: Certainly Peter and very probably John. Had Philip and Nathaniel—Nathaniel who probably had another name, Bartholomew—had they also been baptized by John? We tend to assume so. Were some of the disciples baptized twice—once by John and then by Jesus—with the focus at their second baptism being on him? That seems hard to believe. Had other disciples such as Matthew been baptized as well, if not by John, perhaps by Jesus? We really don't know. There is no evidence that other disciples had ever been baptized by anyone. An assumption that they must have been could be correct but I'm not sure.

GB: What are you trying to say?

TS: There was a very rich tax collector called Zacchaeus who wasn't one of the original twelve but he became a follower under very unusual circumstances. He came upon Jesus one day, well actually Jesus came up to him, and Jesus told him that he wanted to stay at his house for the day. Zacchaeus responded whole-heartedly and soon declared forthrightly that he would give half of his possessions to the poor and if he had defrauded anyone he would pay them back four times the amount whatever it was. Zacchaeus had completely changed his attitude towards money. He had been a tax collector for the Romans, and a chief tax collector at that, with plenty of opportunity for a type of "white collar" crime. And now he enthusiastically centers his attention upon Jesus. He has completely changed direction. In response, Jesus says that today salvation has come to his house. My question is, did Zacchaeus now need to be baptized at some later stage? He had repented and turned towards Jesus and Jesus had accepted him without his taking part in any ceremony. And if *he* were not baptized, would all the disciples have needed to have been baptized?

GB: You may have something there. I remember the story. I think as a backdrop there were those who murmured their displeasure at Jesus because he so closely associated himself with one they thought so poorly of.

TS: That's right. Jesus concluded his words about salvation having come to Zacchaeus's house by stating that Zacchaeus was also a son of Abraham. He followed this up with a statement about himself saying that he, the son of man, came to seek and to save the lost.

GB: Do you think that John the Baptist, John the "Immerser," do you think he had been baptized, baptized by someone?

TS: Another interesting question! . . . I find it difficult to imagine so. Perhaps of some relevance is what he said when Jesus came to be baptized by him. According to one of the Gospels, on that occasion John tried to deter him from undergoing baptism, suggesting that Jesus should be baptizing him, not the other way around. I think this might indicate that, no, John hadn't been baptized, though he didn't see himself being baptized as inappropriate.

Part 2: Baptism

GB: You've raised the possibility of Jesus baptizing. I thought I read somewhere that Jesus did not baptize, only his disciples.

TS: You're right. That's what the fourth Gospel says although that situation may have only applied over a particular period of time. My own view is that probably Jesus never baptized anyone, but who knows? An interesting question is to what extent the disciples baptized as part of any responsibility that Jesus gave them during his earthly ministry. When Jesus sent the twelve out, two by two, visiting village after village to heal the sick and to drive out evil spirits, he told them to preach the kingdom of God but there is no mention of their having to baptize. Mark however, makes it clear that they preached that people should repent. That would have been part of their message about the kingdom of God.

GB: As you say, interesting. . . . Did John baptize in his own name and when the disciples of Jesus baptized did they do so in the name of Jesus?

TS: There is no evidence that John baptized in anybody's name, that is, that he uttered someone's name over the person being baptized at the time of their baptism. What we do know is that the apostles, after the resurrection of Jesus, baptized either "in the name of Jesus Christ" or "in the name of the Lord Jesus." Each of those expressions is mentioned twice in the Acts of the Apostles. However, what the disciples actually did or what they said, when they baptized during the earthly ministry of Jesus, we really don't know. None the less, because the baptisms that they conducted all had to do with Jesus, they were all in effect in his name, even if a statement to that effect was not made at the time. I guess the same would apply to John and his baptisms. With respect to the baptisms recorded in the Acts of the Apostles, where people were baptized "in the name of," it's just possible that this was simply what the baptisms were all about, without those precise words being used on the occasion. My own view is that the words themselves or words just like them were in fact used. Regardless, I think that down the track we should ponder on what that phrase, "in the name of," in the context of baptism, would have meant.

GB: I seem to have read last night or the night before that there were some Ephesians who acknowledged that they had been baptized into John's baptism but who didn't seem to be all that familiar with Jesus. However, when Paul pointed out to them that John had told people to believe in the one who was going to come after him, who in effect was Jesus, they were then willingly baptized in his name. That means they were baptized twice!

TS: True. I suppose if the answer to that question I asked a moment ago were "Yes," that is the question about whether any of the original disciples of Jesus' had been baptized twice—once by John and then again by Jesus—then the Ephesian situation would have been similar to what happened then. But as I said earlier I find it hard to believe that any of the twelve *had been* baptized twice. Anyway, for these Ephesians,

Baptismal Practices in the Gospels and the Acts of the Apostles

and I guess it would have been the same if any of the twelve had been baptized twice, the baptisms were essentially quite different baptisms. One related to the teaching of John and the other to the person of Jesus whom they didn't seem to know too much about until Paul explained things to them. And for the Ephesians it is quite possible that the time difference between the two baptisms was considerable. And upon being baptized in the name of the Lord Jesus and upon Paul laying his hands on them, the Holy Spirit came upon them in a very remarkable and public way. So as strange as the two baptisms might appear to us, that they took place wouldn't have been strange to God! However, I do want us to have a closer look at this episode and how it's recorded, sometime down the track.

GB: The obvious giving of the Holy Spirit in association with being baptized, at least in the Acts of the Apostles, seems to be a feature of those early days.

TS: Well the giving of the Holy Spirit on these occasions really stood out—clearly witnessed by others, on at least four different occasions—the Day of Pentecost, about 50 days after Jesus left this earth, then later when Peter and John visited certain Samaritan believers, then later still when Peter conveyed the message, "the word," to the Roman centurion Cornelius and those with him, and finally when those Ephesians had things explained to them by Paul. Are you familiar with all of these occasions?

GB: Yes. I remember. I just finished reading the Acts of the Apostles last night—of course I've read it before—though I did so in a hurry.

TS: Perhaps the book of Acts records these remarkable outpourings, clearly observed by others, to make the reader aware of God's mercy being freely available to such distinctly different groups of people. Of course the early Apostles and others, apart from any who might later read Luke's account— Luke wrote the book of Acts—would have themselves been equally aware of God's outstretched and generous hand.

GB: It seems like those being baptized were probably all adults, well certainly not children.

TS: You're probably right, although some people like to point out that when a Philippian jailor was baptized the account mentions not only his being baptized but also all from his household. This probably implied that all those "under his roof," as it were, went along with his decision, perhaps somewhat automatically, although maybe not. Whether or not those who were baptized included young children and even slaves is unknown. There was also a businesswoman, Lydia who, when she was baptized, had her household baptized along with her as well.

GB: But I wonder what the early believers did when they had children, after they had become believers? If households tended to operate as one or even if they didn't, a child of a believer was presumably very likely to become a believer, even without making a conscious decision. Did that child have to be baptized later? Or is that how infant baptisms came into being?

TS: We don't know what the really early believers did with the children born to them, born, as it were into Christian households. Personally, I would have thought that if the parents were genuine believers, and it seems from the book of Acts, that upon becoming a believer, no matter who you were, you were then baptized, parents still didn't need to think that their children should also be baptized. The family had become a family of believers. Of course when a child matured, he or she might then decide to abandon the faith of their parents but that would be a new situation. If only one parent had been a believer that might have complicated the matter. But anyway, to try to answer your question, in the course of time, perhaps following on from what might well have been an early practice—the baptizing of the young children of believers—perhaps an understandable practice, whatever we might think of its suitability—a serious problem began to manifest itself. When Christianity became an established part of the culture of a society, children, infants, were baptized in order for them to become automatically members of "the church," "the church" that was now being equated with the religious Christian arm of that society. It wasn't that these children were necessarily children of serious believers. They were children born to people, genuine believers or not, who were automatically, from the time of their own birth, part of the Christian fabric of their society.

GB: Do you think that the idea that something such as special grace being conveyed to a person upon their being baptized arose because children, who couldn't answer for themselves, being merely infants, would need God to do something special for them?

TS: I'm not really sure. Some would say that special grace has always been conveyed to any person being baptized. Baptism is sometimes spoken of as one of the means of grace. I've no doubt that for persons of mature years baptism that's undertaken with sincerity and for the right reasons is an event in their lives that is a source of blessing not only for themselves but also for others. In that sense, their baptism is certainly a means of God's grace. I am concerned however, about the notion that infants because they're infants and cannot enter into any conscious relationship with God must at their baptism be recipients of some special grace. I don't know where in Scripture that idea comes from. . . . Anyway, your suggestion could be correct. I think that the belief about special grace being conveyed might well have arisen in connection with what otherwise might have been considered to have been an oddity—the baptizing of children who, because of their infancy, could not repent or believe. The idea that special grace was being bestowed upon the child might have provided justification for the practice of infant baptism over and above the view that parents or guardians, by having their children baptized, were committing their children to the same position held by themselves.

GB: Okay. A tricky one for some people! . . . Repentance! It's clear that John associated repentance with baptism. And on the Day of Pentecost, Peter commanded his listeners

Baptismal Practices in the Gospels and the Acts of the Apostles

to repent. But was the need for repentance in association with baptism stressed on all occasions?

TS: In the Acts of the Apostles, just as the giving of the Spirit accompanying a baptism is not always mentioned, so too repentance is only mentioned in association with baptism from time to time. I think we should assume that both the giving of the Spirit and the demand for repentance were always involved. On the day of Pentecost, the words of Peter were, "Repent and be baptized . . . in the name of Jesus Christ for the forgiveness of sins; and you shall receive the gift of the Holy Spirit." I think it's safe to assume that repentance was always a factor—people always needed to repent in one way or another—turning from sinful self-centered living to a mode of life characterized by care for others and a genuine desire to please God, turning from idols to serve the one true and living God, or turning from opposition to Jesus to acceptance of him as the Messiah and Lord. And whether the receiving of the Holy Spirit was made obvious by some manifest external sign or not, I think we likewise should assume that the Holy Spirit was always given when people genuinely repented and turned to Christ.

GB: When you think about it, what John the Immerser, as you describe him, was doing, what the early disciples of Jesus were doing and what the Apostles were doing, wasn't only unique—they were "immersing" people, using your word, and the immersions were one-offs—but in time, their baptisms were probably also becoming fairly common, in the good sense of the word. And consequently many people got to know about them or at least got to hear of them.

TS: That latter point is something not generally appreciated. All four Gospels record how great crowds became familiar with the practice. I know is sounds like an exaggeration but Mark states that "the whole Judean countryside and all the people of Jerusalem" went out to John the Immerser. And at one time it appears that the disciples of Jesus were baptizing even more disciples than John! I suspect that by the day of Pentecost what John and the disciples of Jesus were doing was very well known. What Peter claimed people should do on the Day of Pentecost would've been, in some sense, no surprise. However, the practice may not have been that well known or known at all in the Gentile world, though Jews living in the Gentile world may have heard about it.

GB: That makes sense of the Ethiopian eunuch automatically asking to be baptized upon having that servant passage—as I think it's called—in Isaiah, explained to him by Philip. I read how he had been returning from Jerusalem where he had been worshipping God. He was obviously a well-read person of some Jewish persuasion given that he had a copy of a Jewish scroll. Surely he would have also been very familiar with what the followers of Jesus had been doing in and around Jerusalem. So when he understood something of the significance of Jesus, upon seeing some water, he understandably asked what could prevent *him* from being baptized. It was a very natural question for this new believer to ask! I see that now. But did the Ethiopian miss out on something by his baptism being not all that public?

Part 2: Baptism

TS: I know people often speak of the public nature of baptism and one can see that going public in such an obvious way can be of considerable benefit for both the person being baptized, and the believer or believers who witness the baptism. It could also be of great benefit for any non-believer who observes what is happening and what is said. However, I don't think that the Scriptures indicate that it has to be all that public. It's primarily something for the believer to do. Its symbolism can be witnessed and understood by others but I think its symbolism is primarily for the new believer before God. I'm sure that the Ethiopian would have had one or more officials looking on, but it seems to me that what drove him to ask to be baptized, then and there, was something he wished to do, solely with himself and Jesus in mind. By the way do you remember how the text refers to both of them going down into the water and coming up out of the water? I think that indicates that something like "going right under" was the case.

GB: I agree. I've suddenly realized that the baptisms seem to have occurred in water that was there naturally.

TS: Well, we can't be certain that all the baptisms were like that. It's true that there was a Jewish view that natural running water was the best type of water for the most significant of ceremonial washings. However I think that John the Immerser baptized in the Jordan and in other "country" settings because the "countryside" was the place of his ministry—not somewhere in the big city of Jerusalem where the religious hierarchy held sway, nor even in some place in the towns. To begin with, his ministry took place in Judea in the wilderness area of the Jordan, probably an area just north of where it enters the Dead Sea. Later it's mentioned that he baptized at Aenon, which seems to have been a place or area further north, near the Jordan, but in Galilee. At the river Jordan itself, water would've been freely available for people to be fully immersed.

GB: I must have missed that reference to Aenon.

TS: When it is mentioned, note is made of there being "much water there." The fact that so many people were baptized on the Day of Pentecost, probably necessitated that some were baptized in some of the formally constructed pools in Jerusalem such as the Bethesda Pool and perhaps even in some of the stone "upright baths" that archaeologists have discovered in various places in ancient Jerusalem and elsewhere. Certainly there is no hint in the New Testament that a certain type of water or a certain type of container for the water was important. It was repentance that was fundamental, and with that repentance, belief in the message and the person of that message.

GB: We've covered a lot of ground today. This has been a heavy session. However, I must confess I'm becoming more interested in just thinking, recalling and learning about the issues than in trying to sort out my concerns!

TS: Learning is fun but of course also helpful! Tomorrow, why don't we have a look at the way the Greek words relating to "baptism" are used in the Greek-speaking world up to and around the time of Jesus, even up to the beginning of the second century after Christ? And then perhaps the day after that or whenever is suitable, we can see how these same words are used yet again but throughout the New Testament. Would tomorrow and the day after be okay?

GB: No problem. Looking forward to both days!

Part 2: Baptism

EXPLANATORY NOTES: DAY 6

The description by Josephus of John as the Immerser can be located in Josephus, *Josephus IX,* Book XVIII, 117, line 1, 80–81.

The Greek text of the New Testament that relates to John being described as John the Immerser and that lies behind the word "baptize" relies upon NAG.

A description of washing practices by the Pharisees and by the Essenes can be found in Ferguson, *Baptism*, 63–65, 68–71 respectively.

There are two references in the New Testament that relate to washing practices by the Pharisees. They can be found in Mark 7:4; Luke 11:38 (NIV).

Jewish proselyte practices are discussed in Ferguson, *Baptism*, 76–82.

The uses of "βαπτω," "λουω" and "βαπτιζω" are discussed in Ferguson, *Baptism*, 38–47, 65–67, 47–59, respectively.

The reasons given by John as to why he was baptizing can be found in John 1:31–33 (NIV).

"Enacted" signs in Ezekiel and Hosea can be located in Ezek 4:1–5, 12:1–11, 24:15–23; Hos 1:2–9 (NIV).

The reference by Ezekiel to "sprinkling with water" can be located in Ezek 36:25 (NIV).

References to John preaching a baptism of repentance are found in Mark 1:4; Luke 3:3; Acts 19:4 (NIV).

The account of Paul recalling what Ananias said to him about being baptized can be found in Acts 22:16 (NIV).

The "Jesus, the Lamb of God" quote comes from John 1:29 (NIV).

Matt 3:11; Luke 3:16 (NIV) refer to the one coming after John baptizing with the Holy Spirit and fire whereas Mark 1:8; John 1:33 (NIV) simply refer to his baptizing with the Holy Spirit.

See John 1:35–40 (NIV) for the calling by Jesus of two disciples of John the Immerser, one being Peter and the other possibly being John, the brother of Andrew.

The episode involving Jesus and the tax collector Zacchaeus can be found in Luke 19:1–10 (NIV).

The account of John the Immerser trying to deter Jesus from being baptized and his suggestion that he should be baptized by Jesus rather than the other way around, can be found In Matt 3:13–14 (NIV).

The reference to the disciples of Jesus baptizing rather than Jesus himself can be found in John 4:1–2 (NIV).

Baptismal Practices in the Gospels and the Acts of the Apostles

The account of Jesus sending out the twelve, two by two, can be found in Matt 10:1–16; Mark 6:7–13; Luke 9:1–6 (NIV). Luke 9:2 (NIV) records Jesus telling them to preach the kingdom of God and Mark 6:12 (NIV) records that they preached that people should repent. Luke 9:6 (NIV) records that they preached the gospel. All three gospels refer to the tasks of healing and driving out evil spirits.

References to people being baptized in the name of Jesus Christ and in the name of the Lord Jesus can be found in Acts 2:38, 10:48 (NIV), and Acts 8:16, 19:5 (NIV) respectively.

The episode of Paul dealing with the Ephesians who originally only knew of John's baptism is recorded in Acts 19:1–7 (NIV).

TS did not believe that any of the original disciples of Jesus had ever been baptized twice—once as a disciple of John and a second time as a disciple of Jesus. At the same time he conceded that the Ephesians mentioned in the Acts passage were baptized twice, although in the discussion of Day 9 he recognizes that there is an argument that this second immersion was not a literal water baptism. However, given that he thought it more likely that the Ephesians had been baptized twice, he could have mentioned one significant difference between the two situations. Any member of the twelve, who had originally been baptized by John, had almost certainly heard John refer to Jesus, the one who was to come, the one more important than John. To some extent, John himself made the connection between being a disciple of John and being a disciple of Jesus. In the Ephesian situation, that connection had to be made by a third person, someone who had had no overt connection with either John or Jesus, or at least Jesus in the flesh. That the Ephesians were baptized twice is more understandable than if any of the disciples of Jesus had been baptized twice, given the weaker connection between the two baptisms in the case of the Ephesians.

The four occasions when specific mention is made in the Acts of the Apostles of the giving of the Holy Spirit to those people being baptized or about to be baptized can be found in Acts 2:38, 8:17, 10:45, 19:6 (NIV).

The Philippian jailor and his household, and Lydia and her household are mentioned in Acts 16:31–34 (NIV) and Acts16:15 (NIV) respectively.

The comment about whole crowds coming out to witness John's baptisms can be found in Mark 1:5 (NIV).

That the disciples of Jesus were baptizing more people than John is mentioned in John 4:1 (NIV).

Phillip's encounter with the Ethiopian Eunuch is recorded in Acts 8:26–39 (NIV).

The different types of water used in Jewish washings are discussed in Ferguson, *Baptism*, 63–64.

John's ministry around the Jordan is referred to in Matt 3:6; Mark 1:4; Luke 3:3; John 1:28 (NIV).

John's ministry near Aenon is referred to in John 3:23 (NIV).

"Upright baths" are discussed in Ferguson, *Baptism*, 64.

Day 7

Baptismal Words as used Outside of the New Testament

Today's discussion mainly revolves around how the Greek verb "βαπτιζω" was used externally to the New Testament. TS hopes that GB will begin to appreciate how a Greek speaker would understand what the word normally meant or did not mean, depending upon the context. Other verbs are also mentioned along with some nouns related to that verb.

GB: Hi. Yesterday you mentioned that today we were going to look at the way Greek words relating to baptism were used outside of the New Testament.

TS: Well, in particular, we will need to consider the Greek verb "βαπτιζω," which I've already mentioned, and the Greek noun "βαπτισμα" (*baptisma*). These are the main words used in connection with baptism in the New Testament. There are other related words in the New Testament but I'll refer to them later.

GB: Couldn't we deal with those words now and then focus on the main words, at leisure, as it were?

TS: Okay, sure. If you like! There's the one I've already referred to, without giving the Greek word itself, that given the information available to us, is found only once outside of the New Testament, at least up until the end of the first century CE—"βαπτιστης" (*baptistēs*). It's the word I translate as, "Immerser." Used by Josephus, as I said, I think it was a type of nickname, a good description for John who was baptizing in the river Jordan. In the New Testament it occurs twelve times and always refers to John. You might classify it as a technical word in character. That is, it has a highly specific usage. Then there's the verb "βαπτω." It can be found extensively outside of the New Testament but it only occurs a few times within the New Testament. Either outside or inside of the New Testament it seems to have the notion of "dipping" or similar. I mentioned that word earlier as well. It can also have the technical sense of "dying." Then there's the noun "βαπτισμος" (*baptismos*). It's not found outside of the New Testament at least up until the end of the first century CE and it occurs only three times within the New Testament. In these instances the reference seems to be to ceremonial washings.

GB: Yesterday you said that we would leave New Testament usages until tomorrow. Are we going to look at *these* words and how they are used in the New Testament in more detail, tomorrow?

TS: Maybe. If either of us thinks that would be helpful. I don't mind. Perhaps any reference again to these words will just come naturally.

GB: Okay. About the verb "βαπτιζω," was it a specialized word in the Greek-speaking world?

TS: No, not really! Using a search engine, under the name, *Thesaurus Linguae Graecae*, we can locate about one hundred instances of the verb outside of the New Testament, examining from about the sixth century BCE up until about the end of the first century or the beginning of the second century CE. Nine of these have "βαπτιζω" in a derived form, there being one or more instances of "ἀβαπτιζω" (*abaptizō*), "ἐμβαπτιζω" (*embaptizō*), "ἐπιβαπτιζω" (*epibaptizō*), "καταβαπτιζω" (*katabaptizō*) and "διαβαπτιζω" (*diabaptizō*). I think we can consider them simply as instances of "βαπτιζω." They just happen to have a prefix attached. Some instances of "βαπτιζω," in whatever form, are in a negative statement—something is not the case. However most are used in a positive sense. Of the one hundred or so occurrences, about forty belong to the period up until the end of the second century BCE and about sixty are found in the period beginning the first century BCE to the end of the first century CE or slightly beyond.

GB: What's the point of considering two periods? Wouldn't the last period be the one we're interested in, corresponding, as it does, roughly, to the times of the New Testament?

TS: The usage of any word can change over time and perhaps, on first thoughts we should only look at the usage in that period. However, appealing to how the word was used in an earlier period could add to our sample if the usage for each period were somewhat similar—the bigger the sample, the more useful the information.

GB: My suspicion is that you're going to tell me that the usage of the verb in those two periods is reasonably similar?

TS: Well, yes. Perhaps without any exception, the verb in both periods carries with it the notion of "being immersed," "being engulfed" or similar. The contexts in most cases make that clear. Furthermore one can analyze its usage for both periods in terms of four reasonably distinct categories. The percentage occurrence for each of the categories is much the same, recognizing that in some instances, only small numbers are involved.

GB: I am not sure I follow.

TS: Sorry. Let me explain further. The verb is sometimes used to refer to a literal physical "immersion" in a fluid medium. Some examples are, ships being submerged, that is they sink, men being submerged, that is they drown, soldiers wading through a sea along a narrow beach with water up to their waists. The submerging of ships resulting in their being lost and the submerging of people resulting in their death are probably the two most common usages of "βαπτιζω." However, it's sometimes also used in ways that I will refer to as abstract, rather than literal, in character. I think we can discern three different types of abstract usage. Firstly, it can be found in a metaphorical sense or in the form of a simile but where there is an allusion to a fluid medium. As examples for this usage there is a reference to an oracle speaking of the city of Athens, that it might be immersed but that it would be impossible like a bladder to sink, and another to a person who, likening himself to a cork on the surface of the sea, is not immersed. Secondly, there is an abstract usage that involves a person or persons being or not being "immersed" or more simply put, being or not being "in" an alcoholic stupor. A fluid medium of sorts is still in the background. Thirdly, the verb is sometimes used to refer to situations where there is no direct or indirect reference to a fluid medium. One example is that of a person being overwhelmed in verbal engagements. Another is that of people not being overwhelmed by taxes.

GB: However, these four categories, one literal and three abstract, are ones that you've created.

TS: Yes, but I think they are reasonably distinct, as I've said. Though I must admit an ancient Greek might be quite amused at my classifying usages as either literal or one of three abstract usages. He or she might simply see "βαπτιζω" as a word that fulfills various functions. Anyway, using these categories as a test of consistency across the two periods, the percentages, in order of, literal physical immersion in a fluid or fluid type medium, metaphorical or similar usage with an allusion to a fluid medium, reference to alcoholic stupor and an abstract usage where there is no direct reference to a fluid medium are 77, 5, 8 and 10 for those instances found before the first century BCE and 64, 14, 8 and 14 for those instances found in the period first century BCE to the end of the first century CE or slightly beyond.

GB: I think I follow. Using the different categories that you've created, the usage for the two periods appears to be reasonably similar. But is the usage for the two periods similar in any other ways?

TS: Yes. Generally the word is used in what might be described as a fairly intense situation such as a person drowning or a ship sinking but it's not limited to those situations. The "being immersed," "being engulfed" or "being overwhelmed" is often of a fairly substantial nature, involving, for instance, either a weighty matter such as a person being in debt, or something having to be endured over a period of time or a situation reaching some terrible finality, such as death. However in a few instances the usage seems to be of a less intense character, for example, where the reference is to bathing or dipping, where perhaps an alternative Greek verb could've been used. Possible alternatives would include the word "βαπτω" and that other word that I referred to yesterday, "λουω." However it's difficult to argue that such alternatives would indeed have served just as well. By not seeing it as an intense situation we might be misunderstanding what is intending to be conveyed.

GB: Sorry for interrupting, but what has such an analysis to do with similarity of usages for the two periods?

TS: Yes, I almost got side tracked there. The point is this, for each period, 90 percent of the instances seem to be of the more intensive type and 10 percent of the less intensive type. Of course, in some cases, it isn't all that easy to make a judgment as to which category an example belongs.

GB: And are there any other similarities?

TS: Again, yes. One can examine the parts of speech used for the two periods. The verb can be classified as being a participle or an infinitive, or whether it's in the indicative, imperative, subjunctive or optative moods and again the percentages for each of the periods in terms of these six categories are surprisingly similar. The percentages for usage as a participle or infinitive, or involving the moods, indicative, imperative, subjunctive or optative for the period sixth century BCE to first century BCE are 43, 25, 18, 3, 3 and 10 respectively and for the period first century BCE to first century CE the percentages are 44, 19, 24, 2, 7 and 5, also respectively. You need to keep in mind that with some small numbers and six categories, the total percentage won't always add up to 100 and differences involving small numbers aren't all that significant.

GB: I think I understand. I don't know what an "optative mood" is. And I'm a bit rusty on the other moods. "Indicative" is when you have a straight out statement or a question. I think "imperative" is when it's a demand or a request, and "subjunctive" has something to do with uncertainty, but I guess my understanding of the moods doesn't matter.

TS: Yes, don't worry about the moods. Besides, how you define the moods can depend on the language they're being applied to.

GB: Is that it? I mean with respect to comparing the two periods.

TS: Well, there's one last similarity I could refer to though I don't think it's worth all that much. It involves the grammatical voices of the verb. I'm sure you're familiar with active and passive voice but in Greek there is also a voice described as middle voice. Don't worry about what that voice is all about though often it seems to operate just like active voice. Now, as a further complication, there can be a form that a verb takes that is distinctly middle voice and there can be a form that can be either middle or passive voice. In this latter case the context often helps you decide whether the middle or passive voice is involved. But all this means that a verb like "βαπτιζω" can have a form that belongs to one of four different categories—active, middle, passive or, middle or passive.

GB: So how do the two periods compare using these four categories?

TS: For the period sixth century BCE to first century BCE, the percentages for the instances when the verb has the form for the active mood, the middle mood, the passive mood and the middle or passive mood are—38, 5, 0 and 58 respectively. The corresponding percentages for the period first century BCE to first century CE are—42, 0, 8 and 49. The usage of "βαπτιζω" for the two periods, when the voices are considered, is much the same.

GB: You've gone into a lot of detail to indicate that the usage of "βαπτιζω" for the two periods is similar!

TS: Well, as I said, we could have simply looked at usages in the period, first century BCE to first century CE but a sample of ninety nine—that's the actual total we end up with—is somewhat more helpful than a sample of fifty nine, which is the number we would have if we limited the sample to that period. We should have more confidence about the way a word is used looking at a sample of ninety nine than if we examined only a sample of fifty nine.

GB: I get it. One of the things that has already struck me is the extent to which "βαπτιζω" was used in an abstract sense. Considering both periods as one, it was about 30 percent of the time wasn't it?

TS: Yes. Combining the two periods, the percentages for, literal usage, abstract usage with an allusion to a fluid medium, abstract usage with reference to an alcoholic stupor and abstract usage with no reference to a fluid medium, are 70, 10, 8 and 12, respectively. One hundred minus seventy, or ten, eight and twelve added together, makes thirty—30 percent. You are spot on.

GB: Was the verb ever used for a ceremonial washing or a water rite of some sort?

TS: I know I've been using the word "rite" but it is not clear that "rite" was a Greek concept in those ancient days. However, I think because it's in popular usage today I'll continue to use it, whether I'm referring to Greek literature of whatever source, or modern day practices.

GB: Fair enough. I'll try to keep in mind what you've said. But to return to my question, was the verb ever used for a ceremonial washing of some sort?

TS: In all of the ninety nine available occurrences, I think there is only one that clearly refers to a rite. In the *Septuagint*, a Greek version of the Old Testament and some other literature, and sometimes referred to by the Roman symbols for the number seventy, *LXX*, there is a reference to a person immersing himself because of his having been in contact with a dead body. However, there are two or three other instances that possibly relate to a ceremonial cleansing if not an established rite. One, also in the *Septuagint*, refers to a woman, Judith, who immerses herself in some flowing water, privately at night. This may have been for reasons to do with ritual cleanliness though one can't be certain. Another, also in the *Septuagint*, refers to a Syrian called Naaman immersing himself in the Jordan seven times. You may have come across him in your reading of the Old Testament. There is just one other possible instance that might be considered a ceremonial washing. The reference, found in one of the writings of Plutarch, a Greek historian who became a Roman citizen, concerns the scenario of a man being instructed to "immerse" himself in the ocean to get rid of a curse. But it was a one off situation, just like that relating to the Syrian Naaman. That's it!

GB: You mean outside of the New Testament it's basically just an ordinary word without any obvious religious connotations?

TS: Yes.

GB: Three of those four instances that you've just mentioned come from what you've referred to as the *Septuagint* or *LXX*. Do you think there is any significance in that?

TS: I don't know. It could be that Jews, using the Greek language, began to see "βαπτιζω" as a word that could rightly be associated with ritual cleanliness. I'm not sure. I know that with reference to that person called Naaman, in the complete account of what he had to do, the verb "λουω" is used at least three times but "βαπτιζω" only once.

GB: Hmm. You use "immerse" or "overwhelm" as your main words when referring to the verb. Would either one or the other be suitable in English translations in almost all cases?

TS: Well, in many instances, yes, but not all. It often has the sense of "being immersed" when used literally such as a fishing spear that upon falling into the water is only partly immersed because of the way it's made, or a dart thrown into water flowing along a channel being barely immersed because of the water's rapid flow. "Being overwhelmed" is often the sense when the use is metaphorical or of some other abstract nature. A couple of examples—some robber chieftains overwhelmed the city of Jerusalem while it was under siege; in the *Septuagint* the prophet Isaiah speaks of his being overwhelmed with iniquity. However, there are often better words one could use. In the case of the robber lords I've just mentioned, maybe "swamped," used metaphorically, as a ship might be swamped, conveys a more accurate sense than "overwhelm." In some instances words such as "engulf," "envelop," "submerge," "plunge" or "sink" are probably more suitable. There's no general rule. And certainly

Baptismal Words as used Outside of the New Testament

there is no single English word that would be suitable in a translation of the Greek word in all instances.

GB: I suppose that when there is some indication of a physical medium into which the immersion takes place, that that medium is always water or at least part water.

TS: Well, almost always. There is one reference to a hand being immersed in blood and another to a sword being immersed in a neck. I know that both blood and a neck contain "water" but one normally wouldn't think of them as primarily water.

GB: Thanks for all of that. For me, one of the most fascinating things is that "βαπτιζω" wasn't a religious word. But now, what about the noun "βαπτισμα," that's the other noun, that we haven't discussed so far, isn't it?

TS: Yes. You don't forget much do you! . . . Prior to the end of the first century CE we can only find two usages of "βαπτισμα" outside of the New Testament. One of these can be found in Josephus's *Jewish Antiquities* and it's a reference to the baptisms of John. The other can be found in Plutarch's *On Superstition* where, in a remark on various so-called superstitions, one of which had to do with smearing yourself with mud, he includes in his list, "immersions." Look, something that I ought to mention is that the verb in the form of a participle often took the place of the noun. That's probably why the noun itself is relatively rare. In fact, almost one half of the ninety nine instances of the verb we have been looking at are in the form of a participle, not that the participle is always being used as a noun. Regardless of what I've just said however, we ought to realize that as limited as its occurrence is, the noun "βαπτισμα" is obviously a counterpart of the verb "βαπτιζω."

GB: I can see how "βαπτιζω" and "βαπτισμα" and even "βαπτισμος," which you also mentioned earlier, are related. They each have a "z" or an "s" sound as part of their pronunciation, whereas "βαπτω" has no such sounds. Is there any significance in that?

TS: Well, I believe that the Greek letter "*zeta*," which we pronounce a little like the English letter "z," that we find in the verb, indicates that there is some intensity to its meaning. The Greek letter "*sigma*" which sounds like an "s" and is found in our nouns, is derived from the "*zeta*" and conveys a similar intensity. That is, the action, in the case of the verb, that underlies its usage has some "strength" to it. For example, sprinkling would be regarded as a mild activity whereas "drowning" or "being overwhelmed with worry" would be regarded as an intensive situation. As you might remember from what I said earlier, about 90 percent of the actual usages of "βαπτιζω" can be judged to be intensive in character. In only about 10 percent of cases, might another verb have been appropriate. But as I also said, whether or not some of these instances were of an intensive nature or not is difficult to tell.

GB: What are some of these other verbs that sometimes might prove to be adequate replacements?

TS: I've already mentioned "βαπτω," which seems to relate to dipping or dyeing. I've also referred to "λουω." It's used when reference is being made to the washing or bathing of a person or the washing of an animal. Then there's "νιπτω" (*niptō*). It's often associated with washing *parts* of the body. "Πλυνω" (*plunō*) is used when the washing or the cleaning of clothes is involved. Of course, it's always possible to find some overlap in usage. Less likely candidates would be "ῥαινω" (*rainō*) which refers to sprinkling and "χεω" (*cheō*) that relates to pouring. All of these words can also be found with the prefix "ἀπο" (*apo*). The prefix adds to the word the notion of thoroughness, a type of "intensity." There are other words that I could mention but I reckon that's enough. And the only verb of relevance for us is "βαπτιζω," with its accompanying noun "βαπτισμα." It may be of interest to realize that the form "ἀποβαπτιζω" (*apobaptizō*) is not found. "Βαπτιζω" doesn't require a prefix to convey the notion of "intensity." That's already written into the word.

GB: How do you know these things?

TS: Easy, I just look up something like a Liddell and Scott's *Greek-English Lexicon*. You wouldn't have heard of these lexicons but they're easy to find in a decent theological library. Look, I think we should call it a day for now. I know we've discussed the water baptismal ceremony as referred to in the Gospels and the Acts of the Apostles but we now need to look more specifically at how "βαπτιζω" and "βαπτισμα" are used throughout the New Testament. We will again refer to some of those instances that we've already covered but we will also look at some texts that we've never yet mentioned. We could do that tomorrow, if that's still okay with you.

GB: No problem. But before we go, I think I know where you're heading, at least at this stage. Are you going to suggest that generally whenever we come across "βαπτιζω" or "βαπτισμα" in the New Testament, we should be thinking that something like "immersion," "engulfment," "envelopment," "being overwhelmed" or similar is involved?

TS: Yes, unless there are fairly good reasons to the contrary. The underlying sense in most instances seems to be that of "being surrounded" but just as there is no one suitable word to translate all known occurrences of the verb as found in the Greek literature outside of the New Testament, so one would expect, at least to begin with, the same situation when dealing with the verb as found in the Greek literature of the New Testament.

GB: But in the New Testament the verb is usually translated "baptize." Am I correct?

TS: Unfortunately, yes. I think we are misled by many of our English translations. But now, let me make one last comment for today. As with the usage of "βαπτιζω" outside of the New Testament, there might be an argument that here and there in the New Testament, less "intense" words compared to "βαπτιζω," or words other than "βαπτισμα" could've been used as alternatives. However, I don't think that for us much hangs on whether this is true or not.

Baptismal Words as used Outside of the New Testament

GB: Sure. I understand. . . . And I'm pretty confident you're going to suggest that we should look for usages that are somewhat abstract in character as well as literal ones?

TS: Again, yes. But enough for now! See you tomorrow. Cheers.

Part 2: Baptism

EXPLANATORY NOTES: DAY 7

I made extensive usage in the years 2012 and 2013 of *Thesaurus Linguae Graecae*, a special Research Project at the University of California.

Josephus uses the word "βαπτιστης" in his *Jewish Antiquities*. See *Josephus IX*, Book XVIII, 117, line 1, 80–81.

"Βαπτιστης" in The New Testament is found in Matt 3:1, 11:11–12, 14:2, 8, 16:14, 17:13; Mark 6:25, 8:28; Luke 7:20, 33, 9:19 (NAG).

"Βαπτω" in the New Testament is found in Luke 16:24; John 13:26 (twice); Rev 19:13 (NAG).

"Βαπτισμος" in the New Testament is found in Mark 7:4; Heb 6:2, 9:10 (NAG). However, it should be noted that there is a variant reading for Col 2:12, where the word is either "βαπτισματι" (baptismati) or "βαπτισμω" (baptismō). NAG prefers "βαπτισμω," the word being related to "βαπτισμος."

With respect to the usage of "βαπτιζω" outside of the New Testament, there is a degree of artificiality in deciding what belongs to the period sixth century BCE to the end of the second century BCE ("Prior to 1 BCE") and what belongs to the period at the beginning of the first century BCE to the end of the first century CE ("1 BCE to 1 CE"). The authors included by TS in his investigation are given below. The names used are as given in the *Thesaurus Linguae Graecae* and where the number of times the author or source represented in the sample is greater than one, the actual number is given in parentheses.

Prior to 1 BCE—*Septem Sapientes, Aesopus et Aescopica* (five), *Pindarus, Alcibiades, Zeno Eleaticus, Zeno Citieus, Euenus, Hippocrates et Corpus Hippocraticum* (three), *Plato—Ethydemus—Symposium* (two), *Aristophon, Aristoteles, Eubulus, Demosthenes Atheniensis, Duris, Hecataeus Abderita, Menander Atheniensis, Philochorus, Epistulae Privatae* (Απολλωνιος Πτολεμαιωι), *Nicander Colophonius, Polybius Megalopolitanus* (six), *Anonymus Photii, Septuaginta* (four), *Agatharchides Cnidius* and *Posidonius Rhodius* (two).

1 BCE to 1 CE—*Diodorus Siculus* (three), *Heraclitus Scriptor Quaestionum Homericarum, Philo Judaeus* (six) *Strabo* (six), *Dioscorides Pedanius, Heron Alexandrinus* (five), *Vitae Aesopi, Apollonius Sophista, Epictetus, Flavius Josephus* (fifteen), *Plutarchus* (eighteen) and *Soranus*.

It is clear that most of the occurrences found "1 BCE to 1 CE" come from just two sources—Josephus and Plutarch. Their usage was analyzed individually and against all other authors or sources of the period, for the categories—literal usage involving a fluid or fluid-type medium, abstract usage where a fluid medium is in the background, abstract usage involving alcoholic stupor, and abstract usage with no allusion to a fluid medium. The analysis revealed that their contributions were not significantly abnormal. Percentages for Josephus, Plutarch, and all other authors or sources, respectively, for the period were, 73, 50, and 69 for the first category, 13, 28, and 4 for the second category, 7, 17, and 4 for the third category and 7, 6, and 23 for the fourth category. In all but the first category the actual numbers were six or less in any category of usage or any author or source category, meaning that the percentage differences observed were of little significance. These results together with results for the abstract categories combined, appear in Table 1 below, where "LF" represents a literal usage involving a fluid or fluid-type medium, "AF," an abstract usage where a fluid medium is in the background, "AAS," an abstract usage involving alcoholic stupor, and "A," an abstract usage with no allusion to a fluid medium. The numbers outside of the parentheses are the absolute numbers of instances for each category.

Category/Author	LF (%)	AF (%)	AAS (%)	A (%)	Total (%)	AF, AAS, A combined (%)
Flavius Josephus	11 (73)	2 (13)	1 (7)	1 (7)	15 (100)	4 (37)
Plutarchus	9 (50)	5 (28)	3 (17)	1 (6)	18 (100)	9 (50)
All other authors	18 (69)	1 (4)	1 (4)	6 (23)	26 (100)	8 (31)
All authors	38 (64)	8 (14)	5 (8)	8 (14)	59 (100)	21 (36)

Table 1
Types of usage of "βαπτίζω" by *Flavius Josephus*, *Plutarchus*, all other authors and all authors for the period 1 BCE to 1 CE

I am indebted to Edwin Judge of Macquarie University, Sydney, for alerting to me the probability that "rite" was not a Greek concept, the word "rite" coming from the Latin "*ritus*" and there not appearing to be an equivalent to "*ritus*" in the Greek language.

I am indebted to Peter Bolt of Moore Theological College, Sydney, for informing me that the presence of "ζ" in a verb such as "βαπτίζω" gives to the verb some intensity in meaning.

A number of examples of the use of "βαπτίζω" outside of the New Testament are given below, together with the authors involved. The list includes the usages referred to by TS.

Polybius in *Polybius, The Histories, Book I–II,* Book I, chapter 51, section 6, 156–57 mentions many vessels being sunk in an engagement at sea.

Strabo in *The Geography of Strabo III,* Book VI, chapter 2, section 9, 90–91 refers to a person floating on a particular lake not being immersed.

Diodorus Siculus, in *Diodorus Siculus: Library of History, VIII,* Book XVI, chapter 80, section 3, 60–61 refers to a river in flood submerging a number of soldiers, drowning them.

Strabo in *The Geography of Strabo,* VI, Book XIV, chapter 3, section 9, 320–21 mentions soldiers marching through a sea near a narrow beach immersed in water up to their waists.

Plutarch in *Plutarch Lives, I,* Theseus, 24, 5, 54–55 refers to an oracle speaking of Athens that it might be immersed but like a bladder it would not be possible for her to sink.

Pindar in *Pindar, Olympians Odes,* Pythian 2, 80, 238–39 compares himself to a cork floating on the surface of the sea that is not immersed.

Plato in *Plato III,* Symposium, 176, section B, line 5, 94–95 refers to people who had been overwhelmed by an excessive amount of wine.

Josephus in *Josephus VI,* Book X, 169, lines 1–2, 252–53 writes of a man immersed by drunkenness into a stupor and then being murdered.

Plato in *Plato II,* Euthydemus, 277, section D, line 1, 398–99 refers to a young man overwhelmed by the verbal strategies of certain professionals.

Diodorus Siculus in *Diodorus Siculus. Library of History, I,* Book I, chapter 73, 6, line 6, 252–53 refers to people under certain circumstances not being overwhelmed by taxes.

LXX, The Wisdom of Sirach 31:25 refers to a person "immersing" himself from a dead body.

LXX, Judith 12:7 refers to a woman, immersing herself in a fountain or spring.

LXX, 4 Kings 5:14 speaks of Naaman immersing himself seven times in the river Jordan.

Plutarch in *Plutarch's Moralia II,* On Superstition, 166, A, line 6, 460–61 refers to a superstitious man consulting with others because of his frightening dreams and being advised by a woman to immerse himself in the sea.

Polybius in *Polybius VI,* Book 34, chapter 3, section 7, 332–33 refers to a fishing spear that upon falling into the water is only partly immersed because of how it is constructed.

Strabo in *The Geography of Strabo,* V, Book XII, chapter. 2, section 4, lines 6–8, 352–55 writes of a dart, being thrown into water flowing rapidly through a channel that is barely immersed in the water due to its rapid flow.

Josephus in *Josephus III,* Book IV, 137, line 2, 40–41 writes of robber barons who overwhelmed the city of Jerusalem while it was under siege.

LXX, Isaiah 21:4 refers to the prophet Isaiah saying that iniquity overwhelms him.

Baptismal Words as used Outside of the New Testament

Plutarch in *Plutarch's Moralia IV*, Greek and Roman Parallel Stories, 306, section C, line 4, 262–63 mentions the Roman general, Postumius Albinus, who immersed his hand in his own blood in order to write upon a shield.

Josephus in *Josephus II*, Book II, 476, line 4, 508–09 relates an account of a man who committed suicide by plunging a sword into his own neck.

For convenience, the analysis of "βαπτίζω" outside of the New Testament for two different time periods is here presented in tabula form, where "LF" represents a literal usage involving a fluid or fluid-type medium, "AF," an abstract usage where a fluid medium is in the background, "AAS," an abstract usage involving alcoholic stupor, and "A," an abstract usage with no allusion to a fluid medium. The numbers outside of the parentheses are the absolute numbers of instances for each category. See Table 2.

Category/ Time Period	LF (%)	AF (%)	AAS (%)	A (%)	Total (%)
Prior to 1 BCE	31 (77)	2 (5)	3 (8)	4 (10)	40 (40)
1 BCE to 1 CE	38 (64)	8 (14)	5 (8)	8 (14)	59 (60)
Totals	69 (70)	10 (10)	8 (8)	12 (12)	99 (100)

Table 2
Types of usage of "βαπτίζω" for the time periods "Prior to 1 BCE" and "1 BCE to 1 CE"

For convenience the analysis by TS of "βαπτίζω" in terms of different parts of speech for the two periods is here presented in tabular form. Again, the numbers outside of the parentheses are the absolute numbers for each category. See Table 3.

Part of Speech/ Time Period	Participle (%)	Infinitive (%)	Indicative-Mood (%)	Imperative-Mood (%)	Subjunctive Mood (%)	Optative Mood (%)	Total (%)
Prior to 1 BCE	17 (43)	10 (25)	7 (18)	1 (3)	1 (3)	4 (10)	40 (100)
1 BCE to 1 CE	26 (44)	11 (19)	14 (24)	1 (2)	4 (7)	3 (5)	59 (100)

Table 3
Incidence of six different parts of speech for "βαπτίζω" for the time periods "Prior to 1 BCE" and "1 BCE to 1 CE"

For convenience the analysis by TS of the usage of "βαπτίζω" in terms of four different voice forms for the periods "Prior to 1 BCE" and "1 BCE to 1 CE" is also given in tabular form. See Table 4. The absolute numbers for each category are given outside of the parentheses.

Part 2: Baptism

Voice Form/ Time Period	Active (%)	Middle (%)	Passive (%)	Middle or Passive (%)
Prior to 1 BCE	15 (38)	2 (5)	–	23 (58)
1 BCE to 1 CE	25 (42)	–	5 (8)	29 (49)

Table 4
Incidence of four different voice forms for "βαπτιζω" for the time periods "Prior to 1 BCE" and "1 BCE to 1 CE"

In Conant, *The Meaning and Use of Baptizein*, the usage of "βαπτιζειν" (*baptizein*)—the infinitive of "βαπτιζω"—in ancient texts and well beyond the first century CE is discussed. Without the assistance of any computer program he mentions sixty seven of the ninety nine instances referred to in this work.

The two references to "βαπτισμα" outside of the New Testament for the period first century BCE to first century CE are found in *Plutarch's Moralia II*, On Superstition, 166, A, lines 9–10, 460–61 and in *Josephus's Jewish Antiquities IX*, Book XVIII, 117, line 4, 80–83.

TS made mention of Liddel and Scott's *Greek-English Lexicon*. The version used by this author was Liddell and Scott, *An Intermediate Greek-English Lexicon*.

Moulton and Milligan, *The Vocabulary of the Greek New Testament* is another resource that could be used for the same purpose as that referred to by TS in using Liddel and Scott's *Greek-English Lexicon*.

Day 8

"Βαπτισμα" in the New Testament

Today TS chooses to discuss how the Greek noun "βαπτισμα" is used in the New Testament. While making some reference to each occurrences he chooses to focus his attention on a few metaphorical usages and another six, which for the purpose of discussion, he labels as "problematic." The day finishes with a lengthy consideration of a text to be found in 1 Peter.

GB: Hi. So today we're going to look at how "βαπτιζω" and "βαπτισμα" are used in the New Testament.

TS: Well we could, but I think it would turn into a very long day. I'm going to suggest that in this session we concentrate on the noun "βαπτισμα" and leave the verb until the next time we meet.

GB: No problem.

TS: But I should point out that in the New Testament the verb occurs many more times than the noun, and consequently our session today might be much shorter than when we meet to discuss the verb.

GB: Okay. That will mean I'll have an early mark today but a late one next time!

TS: Probably! But who knows how this day will really develop? . . . I've got to admit that teasing the noun and the verb apart is not a simple matter. There are a number of texts where both the noun and the verb appear in close association with each other. In those cases, while discussing the noun we will be inevitably making some comments about the verb. But I'll try not to say too much about the verb in those instances.

GB: I can see how things might get complicated.

TS: I'll try to make it as simple as possible. For starters, the noun "βαπτισμα" can be found twenty times in the New Testament. Of these twenty instances, eleven clearly refer directly to the literal water baptisms carried out by John, three usages are clearly metaphorical and six are worth considering as possibly metaphorical or in some other way abstract rather than literal in usage. I shall refer to these six usages as "problematic."

GB: What about discussing the metaphorical ones first.

TS: Sure. You can find them in Mark 10:38 and 39 and Luke 12:50. Each of them refers to the suffering, that is, the death of Jesus and the two Gospel accounts refer to the same occasion. Just to cite Luke, Jesus says "I have a baptism with which to be baptized and how constrained I am until it is accomplished." You can see how the verb "βαπτιζω" is involved. I think it's very clear that Jesus is referring to the suffering associated with his death.

GB: And they are the only three texts that are clearly metaphorical?

TS: Well, they are the only three about which there is no dispute.

GB: And as you've said, they really just come from the one occasion.

TS: Yes. But the same situation is also true with some of those eleven instances that relate to the water baptisms that John carried out. There are three texts—one in Matthew chapter 21, another in Mark chapter 11 and the third in Luke chapter 20—each seemingly referring to the one occasion where Jesus is asked by what authority he does certain things. Jesus responds by challenging his opponents to state their beliefs about John's authority. There are two other texts—one in the first chapter of Mark and the other in the third chapter of Luke—where the Gospel writers record an identical matter—John came preaching a baptism of repentance. That leaves six other texts that are independent of one another that also refer to John's water baptisms.

GB: Fair enough. . . . From what you said a moment ago you are going to argue that some or all of those other six instances you have regarded as "problematic" might be metaphorical in usage.

TS: Well, at least metaphorical to some extent. We should consider them, one by one. To begin with let's have a look at Acts 18:25. The text refers to a man called Apollos who had been instructed, as it says, "in the way of the Lord," and who taught about Jesus accurately, though he only knew the "baptism" of John. The phrase "the baptism of John" could be a reference, at least in part, to the teaching that went along with the baptism of John. If that's the case, then the noun "βαπτισμα" in that text, is not being used in a simple literal sense but nor is it acting as a simple metaphor. Its immediate reference would be to the literal water baptism conducted by John but its ultimate reference would be to the teaching associated with that baptism. The text would then be understood to refer to Apollos and, mainly, his knowledge about that teaching. Similarly, the phrase "a baptism of repentance" which I've just referred to, found in

Mark and Luke but also in the chapters 13 and 19 of Acts, it seems to me, point to both the act itself and the teaching associated with that act.

GB: I see what you mean. In Acts 18:25, the noun "βαπτισμα," while being grounded in the literal water baptism would actually be a cognitive trigger for focusing on the teaching.

TS: Well, that's what I'm proposing as a possibility.

GB: How could Apollos teach about Jesus if he only knew about the teaching of John that was associated with his water baptism?

TS: I'm not quite sure but we do know, we've mentioned this earlier, that when John was baptizing he spoke about the person who would come after him and who would baptize with the Holy Spirit and fire. Of course that person was Jesus. So, I guess, to that extent and in that way, Apollos could've been speaking about him, by referring as John did, to the one to come, while also speaking about the teaching of John concerning the need for repentance.

GB: Yes. That makes sense.

TS: For our next case let's go to a few verses in the early part of Acts chapter 19. Here we're told about how Paul came across a group of people in Ephesus who seemed to know something about the faith, particularly some aspects of John the Immerser's ministry, but seemingly little about Jesus. You referred to them a couple of days ago, on Thursday, and I made some comments about the situation.

GB: Yes. I remember.

TS: Well, in three verses in that chapter the verb "βαπτιζω" occurs three times and the noun "βαπτισμα," twice. Let's put aside the way the verb is used until later. And I've already mentioned one of the instances where the noun is used—it occurs in the phrase "a baptism of repentance" in verse 4. Verse 3 is the other place where the noun is found. Literally, the verse could be translated, "He (Paul) said to them, "Into what then were you baptized?" They said, "Into John's baptism." I think the situation here is similar to what I've suggested for Acts 19:3 and 18:25. In my view it's possible that here again, the noun, while having a primary association with a literal water baptism, is to be understood as having a more substantial reference to the teaching associated with that baptism, the baptism of John.

GB: You could be right. However, I wouldn't think that that's the traditional way those verses are viewed.

TS: I'm sure that's true. However, I make the suggestion because I think the possibility is worth considering. Let me continue by next referring to a few verses early in chapter 6 of Paul's letter to the Romans. Most translations would read something like this—"How can we who died to sin, still live in it? Or, are you ignorant that all of us who were baptized into Christ Jesus were baptized into his death? We were buried therefore by baptism into death so that as Christ was raised up from the dead . . . so also we should walk in newness of life."

GB: So here we have two instances of the verb and one instance of the noun.

TS: Yes. And now, I'm going to find it very difficult not to discuss the verb while discussing the noun. I hope you don't mind.

GB: No, not at all. I think I can see the problem.

TS: Okay. Given that in the Greek-speaking world, it's not uncommon to find the verb in association with people drowning, "death" could be the concept that's largely in mind here, not a literal water baptism. Yet, I am not claiming that such a baptism could not form part of the background to the text. None the less, a more "neutral" translation, one that doesn't tend to pre-empt our understanding of the text, could be as follows—"Are you ignorant that all of us who have been immersed into Christ Jesus were immersed into his death? We were buried therefore with him by immersion into death so that as Christ was raised from the dead . . . we too might walk in newness of life." The association of "newness of life" with the resurrection of Jesus bespeaks of an intimate involvement of the believer with Christ in his resurrection. Why would the same sort of thing not hold with respect to his death? Is he not saying something like, "You have died to sin because you are enveloped in Christ Jesus and he died." The concept of "being in Christ" is not an uncommon one for Paul. . . . I am using "enveloped in Christ Jesus" as another way of referring to "immersed into Christ Jesus."

GB: If I understand you correctly, you're suggesting that rather than primarily making a reference to a water ceremony, Paul is referring to these believers as being somehow or other caught up in the death of Jesus as well as being, somehow or other caught up in his resurrection—they are thoroughly in him both with respect to his death and with respect to his resurrection. You're suggesting that here there is a fundamental spiritual reality in mind rather than a baptismal water rite. Am I correct?

TS: Yes. And using words such as "immersed" and "immersion," a quite legitimate usage, enables us to see that more clearly. If the spiritual reality is to the fore and not a water ceremony, then both the noun and the verb are being used metaphorically.

GB: Makes sense to me! Other instances where you think the noun is being used metaphorically? I think we have three to go.

TS: Yes, and there are three to go. The fourth and fifth verses of Ephesians, chapter 4, speak of "one body," "one spirit," "one hope," "one Lord," "one faith" and "one baptism." I would have thought that in this instance, something like "the one spiritual reality of being immersed in Christ" is what the last item refers to—not some water rite. None of the other matters refer to that particular spiritual reality. Why couldn't Paul have that in mind?

"Βαπτισμα" in the New Testament

GB: And given that all the other "ones"—"one body," "one spirit," and "one hope"—are spiritual realities, one might expect that the last "one," "one baptism" would be of a spiritual nature also. I know that we can invest a spiritual reality in the baptismal water ceremony itself but surely a water baptism would really be in the background, if it were there at all. I think I'm beginning to argue like you!

TS: I guess so! . . . To our next text. In Colossians 2:12 we find a reference to "You were buried with him (Christ) in baptism, in which you were also raised with him, through faith in the working of God who raised him from the dead." This is very much like what Paul wrote in Romans, chapter 6—"we were . . . buried with him by baptism into death." I should point out however, that the prepositions governing "baptism" in Colossians chapter 2 and Romans chapter 6 are in fact different. The phrase in Romans is "by baptism," or "through baptism," the preposition involved being, "δια" (*dia*). The phrase in Colossians is "in baptism," the preposition being "ἐν" (*en*). The translations reflect this difference. However, I do not think that the difference is all that significant. The constructions in which the noun is *imbedded* are different—Romans refers to "baptism into death" and in Colossians the clause ends with "baptism"—and so, one might argue, the noun requires different prepositions in these phrases anyway.

GB: And I take it that you are suggesting that as in Romans chapter 6, the usage of the noun in Colossians is also metaphorical?

TS: Yes. However, here in Colossians, because the construction is different, I think a word different to "immersion" may be more suitable. I'm not entirely happy with what's in my mind at the moment, but it's all I can think of right now. We could translate the text as follows—"You were buried with Christ in envelopment, in which you were also raised with him." Hmm. That's very awkward isn't it? Perhaps an expanded paraphrase makes better sense—"You were buried with him by being enveloped in him, in which envelopment you were also raised with him."

GB: It still sounds a bit awkward but I understand what you're saying.

TS: I'll put my mind to it and see if I can come up with something better later on. I can understand people claiming that water baptism itself unites the believer with both the death and resurrection of Christ. However, my position is that Paul could be speaking simply of being enveloped in Christ with respect to both, his burial, that is, his death, and his resurrection, without making any direct reference to water baptism whatsoever. Paul might, as with other texts we've already discussed, have the literal water ceremony in the back of his mind, but again the spiritual realities, I'd argue, would surely be to the fore of his thinking.

GB: Given that you referred to "unites," could "You were buried with Christ in baptism" be understood to mean, "You were united with Christ in his burial, that is, his death"? If so, our understanding would be that they were united with him in his resurrection also. "United" might be a better word than "enveloped."

TS: Your suggestion has appeal, but the verb "βαπτιζω" to which the noun "βαπτισμα" is obviously related, never seems to convey the sense of "union" either in the Greek-speaking world outside of the New Testament or anywhere in the New Testament itself. I think the sense being conveyed in our text is one of being "completely in him" or perhaps better "enwrapped by him," "being engulfed in him," "immersed in him" or "being enveloped by him." You have however made me think a little more about the text. In a burial, either with the body being placed in a tomb or being interred in a grave, there really is a type of "envelopment." The text actually refers to "buried" rather than "made dead" and I think the imagery of "envelopment" better fits "buried" rather than the notion of "being dead."

GB: I follow you.

TS: But additionally, I notice that Paul, unlike what he wrote in his letter to the Romans, in his letter to the believers at Colossae, links "βαπτισμα" with "being raised." Paul connects both the ideas of "death" and "being raised" in Romans but doesn't extend the imagery of "immersion" to being raised from the dead. Strictly speaking, "immersion" relates only to something like "drowning" not "being resuscitated." My guess is that if, in his thinking, the sense of "envelopment" or similar, rather than "immersion" was mainly to the fore, then Paul might have considered that "βαπτισμα" was not an inappropriate word to connect both "buried" and "being raised." But again, the concept is not that of "union." The idea involved is more than that. It's envelopment. As I come to think of it now, "envelopment" is not an inappropriate word for this verse, as awkward as the translation I gave seems!

GB: . . . You've got one "problematic" usage of the noun to go!

TS: Yes. I hope it's not been too wearying.

GB: No, not at all.

TS: It occurs in the first Epistle of Peter, chapter 3, verse 21. In verse 20 of that chapter reference is made to eight persons in Noah's ark being saved, as the writer, Peter, puts it, "through water." By "through water" Peter might have meant that floating on the flood waters was their means of escape but more likely or perhaps as well, the "through" might refer to their having gotten safely through the water which was all around them—to begin with—water continually rising in height and rain continuously pouring down from above. And in the end they came through this terrifying set of circumstances safely. Whatever we think was precisely being said here, in the next verse Peter says, "Baptism, similar to this, now saves you. Not as a removal of dirt from the body but as an appeal to God for a clear conscience through the resurrection of Jesus."

GB: I remember reading this verse, some time back, and was a little disturbed then because, as you know, I've not been baptized. But are you about to suggest that the reference is not to a literal water baptism?

"Βαπτισμα" in the New Testament

TS: Exactly. But before we look at the text in some detail, I think we need to remind ourselves of that occasion in the Gospels where the noun *is* clearly used metaphorically.

GB: Sure.

TS: Remember, it relates to the suffering of Jesus. Though Jesus would have spoken in Aramaic, Mark and Luke both record in Greek that he saw his oncoming death as a baptism, using our Greek word for "baptism"—clearly a baptism to be endured. I am also tempted to start referring to how the verb is also clearly used in a metaphorical way in the same passages—again with reference to suffering. But that's actually unnecessary, except to say that in Mark, the verb is used metaphorically in the same way that it is used of Jesus to refer to the sufferings that the disciples would one day have to endure.

GB: Okay. Where are you going with this?

TS: Well, the epistle of 1 Peter, where our problematic text occurs, has a great deal to say about suffering—the suffering of believers and the suffering of Christ. In the first chapter Peter writes of his readers having to suffer grief in various trials and follows this by speaking of the prophets predicting the sufferings of Christ. In chapter 2 he writes that if for doing good they suffer they have God's approval. To this, they were called, he writes, because Christ had suffered for them. In verse 16 of chapter 3 he writes that his readers need to keep a clear conscience, it being better to suffer for doing good than for doing evil. At the beginning of chapter 4 he speaks of Christ suffering in his flesh and says that his readers should have the same attitude since the one who suffers in his body is done with sin. Let's not go into exactly what he meant by this. Towards the end of chapter 4 he warns them not to be surprised at the fiery trial they were suffering and that they should rejoice that they were participating in the sufferings of Christ. And it doesn't end there. But you get the picture?

GB: Absolutely. Their suffering and the suffering of Christ are obviously important features of the letter.

TS: So now let's have a look at that verse we're primarily interested in—1 Peter 3:21 and the verse just prior to it. Peter uses powerful images that run into one another. There are eight people in the ark and they are delivered from their terrible ordeal through water. He then writes that this is a "figure" or an "echo," "ἀντίτυπον" (antitupon), of what saves them—a baptism. He then quickly adds that this is not a reference to the removal of dirt from the body but rather the pledge of a good conscience toward God.

GB: And you think that Paul in his reference to "baptism" has in mind "suffering"? I'm not sure how it fits with their being saved!

TS: Let me say again what he wrote but I'll put it as an expanded paraphrase—"*The eight in the ark had a frightening time during the flood but in the end they were safely delivered from that watery environment by their floating on water. Water of course is* *involved in the water ceremony of baptism, but metaphorically it can also refer to suffering. What happened to those eight on the ark is symbolic of your situation. You need to endure your baptism, your considerable suffering—suffering you endure for doing good. This endurance of your suffering can be seen as your salvation, your spiritual health. Of course, by referring to "baptism" I am not referring to a thorough immersion in water for getting rid of dirt from the body. And, anyway, having endured, you come out of your suffering with a good conscience, before God."*

GB: That makes some sense. I am not sure it would convince everybody, but it's possible that what you're saying is basically what Peter was saying. I can see how a baptismal water ceremony may have been in the background but that ultimately "baptism" or "immersion" was actually a metaphorical reference to suffering.

TS: Well, I think so but I admit that it's complicated. Peter has a number of images in his mind that he freely links together. I should also point out that Peter makes it clear that fundamentally their safety did not depend upon their endurance in suffering but on Jesus Christ. He follows up what he said about the flood and their "baptism" by saying that it—their suffering—saves them by or through, "δια," the resurrection of Jesus Christ. His reference to the resurrection only and not to the death of Jesus may have been triggered by his having followed up his appeal to "baptism" with his mention of the good conscience—a sign of the new life in Christ.

GB: Peter certainly piles ideas on top of one another!

TS: Yes he does! . . . I think we could now call it quits for the day. We've covered all the occurrences of the noun. Could we meet again, to look at the verb, say on Monday or would some other day suit you better?

GB: Monday would be fine.

"Βαπτισμα" in the New Testament

EXPLANATORY NOTES: DAY 8

The twenty instances of "βαπτισμα" in the New Testament are found in—Matt 3:7, 21:25; Mark 1:4, 10:38–39, 11:30; Luke 3:3, 7:29, 12:50, 20:4; Acts 1:22, 10:37, 13:24, 18:25, 19:3–4; Rom 6:4; Eph 4:5; Col 2:12; 1 Pet 3:21 (NAG).

The eleven instances of "βαπτισμα" in the New Testament associated with John's literal water baptism can be located in Matt 3:7, 21:25; Mark 1:4, 11:30; Luke 3:3, 7:29, 20:4; Acts 1:22, 10:37, 13:24, 19:4 (NAG).

The three instances of "βαπτισμα" in the New Testament that are clearly metaphorical are located in Mark 10:38, 39, Luke 12:50 (NAG).

The six instances where "βαπτισμα" in the New Testament is arguably used metaphorically, according to TS, can be found in Acts 18:25, 19:3; Rom 6:4; Eph 4:5; Col 2:12; 1 Pet 3:21 (NAG). As mentioned in Explanatory Notes: Day 7, there is a variant for "βαπτισματι" in Col 2:12, the variant being "βαπτισμω." Obviously TS has chosen the former possibility rather than the latter.

The phrase, "the baptism of repentance"—"βαπτισμα μετανοιας" (*baptisma metanoias*)—is mentioned in Mark 1:4; Luke 3:3; Acts 19:4 (NAG).

Knox, Robinson, and M'Neile are three writers who consider that some of the usages of the noun "βαπτισμα" in the New Testament, Matt 28:19 aside, generally considered to be literal, might be or are indeed metaphorical or abstract in some sense, in character. See the following.

In the chapter "New Testament Baptism" in Knox, *Broughton Knox*, 263–309, it is evident that Knox believes that in Acts 18:25, the noun stands for the body of doctrine taught by John, that in Rom 6:4 it is highly likely that it refers to Christ's death, that in Eph 4:5 it refers to all being united as one in the death of Christ and that in Col 2:12 the relevant phrase should be translated, "buried with him in his baptism"—"baptism" referring to the death of Christ.

Robinson, writing in "Towards a definition of baptism" believes that the noun in Rom 6:4 has the sense of either "Christ's baptism of death" or "the believer's involvement in Christ's death." He also thinks that the noun in Eph 4:5 might refer to "baptism in the Spirit" and that in Col 2:12 the noun either refers to Christ's baptism, that is his death, or to being baptized with the baptism with which Christ was baptized, that is, again, his death.

Robinson and Knox consider that "baptism" as it is used in 1 Pet 3:21 refers to the suffering the Christian suffers because of his faith. Robinson adds that this suffering is a sharing in the suffering that Christ endured. For an extended discussion by Knox on 1 Pet 3:13–22 see the chapter—"Addition to manuscript on Baptism," 311–15.

Part 2: Baptism

As part of the baptismal controversies of the mid-nineteenth century in England, M'Neile, in, *Baptism doth save*, 12–14, submits that both Rom 6:3 and 4 and the noun in Col 2:12 relate to spiritual baptism involving conversion, which he equates with regeneration and renewal. I am grateful to Peter Bolt for bringing this tract to my attention.

Examples of Paul's use of the notion of "being in Christ" or similar can be found in Rom 8:1 ("ἐν Χριστῷ" Ἰησου [*en Christō Yēsou*]—those who are in Christ Jesus), 6: 23 ("ἐν Χριστῷ Ἰησου τῳ κυριῳ ἡμων") [*en Christō Yesou tō kuriō hēmōn*]—the free gift of God is eternal life in Christ Jesus our Lord); 1 Cor 15:22 ("ἐν τῳ Χριστῷ" [*en tō Christō*] in Christ all shall be made alive); 2 Cor 1:21 ("εἰς Χριστον" [*eis Christon*]—God who establishes us with you in Christ), 5:17 ("ἐν Χριστῷ" [*en Christō*]—if anyone is in Christ), 12:2 ("ἐν Χριστῷ|"—I know a man in Christ); Gal 3:28 ("ἐν Χριστῷ Ἰησου"—you are all one in Christ Jesus); Eph 2:10 ("ἐν Χριστῷ Ἰησου"—created in Christ Jesus), 13 ("ἐν Χριστῷ Ἰησου"—in Christ Jesus you have been brought near); Col 1:28 ("ἐν Χριστῷ"—every man mature in Christ), Phlm 23 ("ἐν Χριστῷ Ἰησου"—my fellow prisoner in Christ Jesus). The Greek texts can be found in NAG.

The following may be of some interest. Either inside or outside of the New Testament "εἰς" would seem to be a suitable preposition when following the verb "βαπτιζω," the verb and preposition together conveying something like the sense of "immersed into." However, see a discussion on prepositions used in association with "βαπτιζω" on Day 11 where TS states that in the New Testament the preposition "ἐν" is found following the verb "βαπτιζω" fifteen times and the preposition "εἰς" is found following the verb "βαπτιζω" only eleven times. In the Pauline epistles "εἰς Χριστον" appears about eight times while "εἰς Χριστον Ἰησουν" appears twice. Not all instances have the sense of "being in." One of the instances of "εἰς Χριστον" can be found in Gal 3:27 and one of the instances of "εἰς Χριστον Ἰησουν" can be found in Rom 6:3. In each of these cases, the phrase follows the verb "βαπτιζω." By comparison however, in the Pauline epistles "ἐν" is the main preposition used when the object is Christ or Christ Jesus. In those epistles there are forty six instances of "ἐν Χριστῷ Ἰησου," twenty five instances of "ἐν Χριστῷ, five instances of "ἐν τῳ Χριστῷ," four instances of "ἐν Χριστῷ Ἰησου τῳ κυριῳ ἡμων," two instances of "ἐν ... κυριῳ Ἰησου Χριστῷ and one instance of "ἐν κυριῳ Ἰησου Χριστῷ," although not all instances have the sense of "being in." The verb "βαπτιζω" is not associated with the preposition "ἐν" in any of these instances. The Greek texts can be found in NAG.

The notion of "being in him," that is, being in Christ is of course not limited to the word for Christ but can also be found in other expressions such as "in the Lord."

Day 9

"Βαπτιζω" in the New Testament

Having discussed a couple of days ago how the noun "βαπτισμα" is used in the New Testament, TS hopes that today they will spend most of their time doing the same thing but with the verb "βαπτιζω." Again one of the main points for discussion is what he considers "metaphorical" and "problematic" usages. For GB, the highlight is how TS understands the 1 Corinthians text that speaks of "being baptized on behalf of the dead."

GB: So today we're going to be looking at the verb "βαπτιζω" and presumably that text in Matthew chapter 28 to do with the great commission.

TS: Sorry if I've mislead you. The way I'm thinking, I suspect we won't be looking at that text for a day or two yet. I feel we need to cover a few more things before that would be appropriate. And indeed, I want to get something out of the way before starting on "βαπτιζω." There are two verbs that I've mentioned before, "λουω" and "βαπτω" and I should refer to their use in the New Testament.

GB: Sure.

TS: Well, in the New Testament "βαπτω" occurs four times, meaning, either "dip" or "dye" in those instances, and "λουω," occurs six times, on each occasion, having the sense of "wash." "Απολουω" (*apolouō*) also occurs in the New Testament and can be found twice, meaning something like, "wash thoroughly." None of these words really have any relevance for us, given our interests, but I thought I should make some reference to them again, before proceeding with "βαπτιζω." By the way, each of these four verbs are in the form of the first person singular of the present tense, indicative mood—"I am doing such and such." This is a common way of referring to Greek verbs, whatever grammatical form they have in a particular text. I've been referring to verbs in that way from the beginning.

Part 2: Baptism

GB: Thanks. I understand.

TS: Anyway, the verb "βαπτιζω" in one grammatical form or another occurs seventy six times in the New Testament. And I'd like to begin with two instances of "βαπτιζω" that while somewhat relevant are of no real importance. Just to get them out of the way really.

GB: They are?

TS: In Mark 7:4 and in Luke 11:38 "βαπτιζω" is used to describe a certain washing procedure that was carried out by Jews in the time of Jesus. Verses 2, 3, and 4 of Mark read something like this—"And they (the Pharisees) observed that his disciples (the disciples of Jesus) ate bread (perhaps the meaning is, "had a meal") with defiled hands, that is, unwashed hands. For the Pharisees and all the Jews do not eat unless they wash their hands intensely, observing the tradition of the elders. And when they come from the market place they do not eat unless they bathe themselves. And there are many other things that they have 'taken on board' to hold to—the washing of cups and pitchers and bronze containers." The Greek word for "unwashed" comes from the adjective, "ἀνιπτος" (*aniptos*) and you can see how that word is related to the verb, "νιπτω" that I mentioned a few days ago. I said then, that that verb is often used when washing parts of the body is what is in mind and it's the verb that is translated "wash" in "unless they wash their hands." The word for "washing" in "the washing of cups *et cetera*," is the noun, "βαπτισμος" that I referred to on Saturday. Washing those utensils would surely involve their being immersed. Finally, to our verb. I have translated the word, "βαπτισωνται" (baptisōntai), occurring in verse 4 and coming from our verb, "βαπτιζω," "they bathe themselves" whereas others might translate it as, "they wash themselves." My point here is that I don't think that what they did when they came from the market place was a simple washing, say, of the hands or feet, otherwise, I think, the word, "νιπτω" would have been used. I suspect that when they came from the market place they immersed themselves—that is, they bathed themselves, to some extent or another.

GB: I see what you're saying. And the Luke 11 text?

TS: Here the reference is to a Pharisee who is surprised that Jesus did not wash before coming to a dinner. Obviously he, the Pharisee, would've washed beforehand. Or, should I have said, "Here the reference is to a Pharisee who is surprised that Jesus did not *bathe* before coming to dinner" and that, "Obviously he, the Pharisee would've *bathed* beforehand"? Though I could be wrong, I suspect that the same sort of situation as that recorded in Mark is being referred to here, whether coming from a market place was involved or not, particularly if a type of formal dinner was involved, which I suspect was the case—the Pharisee had invited Jesus to dine with him. And interestingly, Jesus responds with a reference to the general habit of the Pharisees cleaning the *outside* of their eating and drinking utensils but then in an extremely pointed manner says that, by comparison, *inside* they are full of extortion and wickedness. By the way, I would expect that they cleaned the inside of their eating and drinking utensils as well, but Jesus chose to say what he said in order to make a point.

GB: Thanks for all that but, yes you're right, these two occurrences of our verb, whether your view of how they should be understood is correct or not, are not all that relevant given my interests.

TS: Well then, back to the other usages of "βαπτιζω" in the New Testament—seventy four of them! Oh, and by the way there are no examples in the New Testament of "βαπτιζω" occurring in a derived form, that is, with a prefix, as was the case outside of the New Testament.

GB: Sorry for interrupting, but I suppose that most of these seventy four instances are associated with a literal water baptismal ceremony.

TS: Well certainly more than half. From my point of view the verb is used with reference to John's water baptism, in one context or another, twenty nine times. All but three of these instances are to be found in the Gospels, the three exceptions being located in Acts. There are another twenty four instances where "βαπτιζω" is fairly clearly used to refer to literal water baptisms, the baptisms having been performed mainly by the apostles but also by others, one example being a person called Ananias. He's the one who baptized Paul.

GB: Does that mean that the remainder of the ones we're looking at, excluding the usage in Matthew chapter 28 and the two texts that refer to Jewish washing ceremonies, a total of twenty, if my maths is correct, are possibly abstract in character? Or are there some that refer to being immersed in water but a rite or ceremony is not involved?

TS: Your maths is good! Of that twenty, I don't think there are any instances where a non-baptismal water immersion is involved. And regarding the possibility of abstract usage, it's fairly obvious that at least twelve of them are metaphorical.

GB: The metaphorical ones occur where?

TS: There are references to being baptized in the Holy Spirit in Matthew 3:11, Mark 1:8, Luke 3:16, John 1:33 and Acts 1:5 and 11:16. And there are references to being baptized in the sense of suffering, either the suffering of Jesus or the suffering that the disciples are to endure, in Mark 10:38—twice, Mark 10:39—twice, and Luke 12:50. Some of the texts relating to the Holy Spirit refer to the same occasion. Likewise with some of those texts that relate to suffering. This is also true with some of the texts where a literal "immersing" in water is involved.

GB: You mentioned baptism as a reference to suffering when you were discussing the noun.

TS: Yes.

GB: You said there were twelve usages of "βαπτίζω" that were clearly metaphorical. You have only mentioned 11.

TS: You're good! But I hadn't forgotten. The other clear metaphorical usage can be found in the first epistle of Corinthians, chapter 10, verse 2. There the reference is to the Israelites being baptized into Moses in the cloud and in the sea. The "sea" that he has in mind is probably the "Sea of Reeds" that the Israelites, under the leadership of Moses, had to cross in their escape from Egypt. The "cloud" that he mentions would have been that cloud by which God revealed his presence and by which he lead his people, again under the leadership of Moses, to the promised land.

GB: I remember reading about that in the book of Exodus.

TS: Well, while it's clear that a watery environment is in Paul's mind, the baptizing, the immersing, is into Moses, a person. My guess is that Paul, with a watery situation at the back of his thoughts feels free to use a word often associated with water, but with his focus actually on Moses, the one that led the Israelites. The Israelites were *under* Moses—his authority and leadership. I think the usage is fairly obviously metaphorical.

GB: An odd text, at least to my way of thinking!

TS: Well, for both of us, but presumably not for Paul.

GB: A little bit off the track, but it seems to me that the very large number of times that the verb and the noun referred to a literal water baptism must have seemed a little odd to a Greek-speaking outsider.

TS: I think you're right and I suspect I know why you think that.

GB: Well, a few days ago you pointed out that at least in the case of the verb, in almost all known instances of its use outside of the New Testament up until the end of the first century, it appears to be simply an ordinary non-religious word. There are only a few instances where it is associated with what we would call a religious activity. Yet in the New Testament, the majority of instances of both verb and noun *are* associated with a *very* religious ceremony—a literal water baptism.

TS: Exactly. Yes, in the New Testament both verb and noun, more often than not, seem to take on a technical aspect—they are indeed used to refer to a religious ceremony. I guess that explains why, for example, in the Latin Vulgate, an early Latin translation of the Bible, the verb is always translated using a Latin word that doesn't seem to have been in common usage—"*baptizo,*" "I baptize." It's simply a transliteration of the Greek word "βαπτίζω." There were a few ordinary Latin words, such as "*mergo,*" "*immergo,*" "*demergo*" and "*summergo,*" one or more of which could've been used, perhaps "*summergo*" being the most suitable. However, presumably the translators thought it necessary to use a word that was really just the original Greek word transformed into a Latin word.

"Βαπτιζω" in the New Testament

GB: Of course, now that I think about it, the English translations appear to have done the same thing. "Baptize" and "baptism" seem to be simply transformations of the Greek words involved.

TS: You're right. Indeed the Spanish, French and Italian languages, languages, having Latin as one of their roots, also have words that are much like transliterations of "βαπτιζω." And I think it's worth pointing out that this can be unhelpful, particularly if a metaphorical usage is involved. In fact by such an approach I think it's difficult for us, in some instances, to recognize such a usage. Because, in the New Testament, the verb and noun are transliterated in all instances, even in the clearly metaphorical cases, we tend to think that something like a technical usage, concerning a ceremony, is involved in almost all instances. The only exceptions are when the context is such that we cannot escape the fact that a non-literal usage is involved. We even imagine that what we recognize as a clearly metaphorical usage is odd, odd because it is metaphorical. Yet in ordinary Greek usage, on the basis of the evidence available, a metaphorical or otherwise abstract usage is not at all that uncommon. It is the case 30 percent of the time, as you so readily observed, if you remember!

GB: Well, moving on—speaking like this, I feel as though at this point *I* am in charge of the discussion—what about the other eight from the twenty. The eight usages that you have not said are clearly metaphorical?

TS: Again! You certainly keep the numbers in your head. I think I need to refer to their usage at this stage as "problematic" in the same way that I referred to some of the usages of "βαπτισμα" as "problematic." We've already come across three of them when we were looking at that noun. They occur in Acts 19:3 and Romans 6:3—twice. The other five are located in the 1 Corinthians 1:13, 12:13 and 15:29—twice, and Galatians 3:27.

GB: You'll need to remind me what you said about the texts in Acts and Romans.

TS: I didn't say all that much. But it went along the following lines. At the beginning of Acts 19 there is that reference to Paul finding some disciples in Ephesus who didn't seem to know anything about the Holy Spirit let alone having received him. We've already referred to that situation twice before. In verse 3 it's recorded that Paul asks them "Into what then were you baptized?" To which they reply "into John's baptism." I suggested the other day that with respect to the noun of that verse and now I suggest that with respect to the verb of that verse that a reference is being made to the *teaching* of John the Immerser, while not denying that there is a connection with the literal water baptism that he administered. In each of verses 4 and 5 the verb "βαπτιζω" occurs again. In verse 4 it is still in association with John and what he did but I think that what Paul says there, "John baptized with the baptism of repentance" is more focused on the water ceremony while still reflecting the teaching of John. In verse 5, the writer records that after Paul had told them that John had told people to believe in the one coming after him, that is Jesus, these disciples were now baptized in the name of Jesus. I think that *here* the reference is to a literal water baptism. I assumed that that was the case when I discussed it with you last Saturday and Thursday. But I could be wrong about that understanding of verse 5. It could be argued that the text means that in Paul instructing them about Jesus these disciples were now immersed into the *teaching* of Jesus.

GB: I guess so. And Romans?

TS: Yes, well there the argument was that the references to baptism and being baptized—the verb occurs in verse 3 of chapter 6 twice—relate to the idea of death. "Those who have been baptized into Christ Jesus have been baptized into his death." I can understand some arguing that the first use of the verb is with respect to a literal water baptism while the second might well be metaphorical in character. I suggest that Paul in saying something like, "being immersed in Christ Jesus" implies at least "being immersed in his death" without there being any pointed reference to a literal water baptism in either use of the word.

GB: I've got it. Can we now move on to the texts in 1 Corinthians?

TS: Sure. Are you in a hurry?

GB: No. Sorry. I'm happy with what you've said about Romans 6 and now I'm ready for 1 Corinthians!

TS: Okay. Firstly let's look at 1 Corinthians 1:13. Verses 10 to 17 of that chapter have a lot to do with the baptismal water ceremony. In fact the verb "βαπτίζω" occurs six times in verses 13 to 17. I think five of the six instances fairly clearly relate to that water ceremony. However, "βαπτίζω" in verse 13 might be the exception. In leading up to that verse, Paul tells the Corinthian believers that he's been informed that there are various factional groups amongst them—that some of them refer to themselves as belonging to Paul, others to Apollos, others to Cephas—which is another name for Peter—and others to Christ. By mentioning himself first, I think Paul wants his readers to immediately caste aside any idea that he himself should be the focus of a group. By mentioning Christ last, I suspect that he wants his readers to see that Christ is the only one upon whom their focus should ultimately rest. Having just mentioned Christ, Paul then rhetorically asks the questions, "Is Christ divided? Was Paul crucified for you?" Undoubtedly, Paul is making it clear to them firstly that these divisions should not exist—for there are no divisions within Christ—and secondly that there is only one to whom they owe their allegiance, only one whom they should follow, that is, the one who was crucified for them and it certainly wasn't Paul!

GB: Paul is a model for pointing others to Christ and away from himself!

TS: Too true. Would that we all took notice of the way he spoke and acted! But to continue. He follows up his rhetorical question about himself being crucified for them, to which the answer is a resounding "No," with a further rhetorical question—"Were you baptized into the name of Paul?" Of course the answer is again "No." But here is our problem! Is he simply asking that when they were baptized in a water ceremony, was the name of Paul uttered over them or, alternatively, that when they became believers was it essentially in terms of who Paul was and what he had done and said? Were they enveloped in him and his teaching, teaching which centered on the Christ? Given that the matter of to whom they owe their allegiance is in mind, it could be that it's the latter possibility. However, I am torn somewhat between the alternatives and probably lean towards the former one. So, although I still consider the text a problematic one, I am inclined to think that the reference is to a literal water baptism. He certainly goes on from this point stating that he baptized hardly any of them, naming just a few that he did baptize. And it's obvious that here he's referring to literal water baptisms.

GB: It's difficult for me to think that he wasn't referring to a literal water baptism in all instances but what of the next text that we should look at?

TS: The next one we should consider is found in 1 Corinthians 12, verse 13. A little like verse 5 in Ephesians chapter 4 in which the noun occurs, in 1 Corinthians 12:13 Paul says "By one Spirit we were all baptized into one body—Jews or Greeks, slaves or free." I really think he's referring to being all one in Christ, all being caught up in him. He wants to refer to them as being members of the one body but that that body is Christ. One becomes a member of that body, as he puts it, by "being made to drink of one Spirit." . . . Notice the powerful imagery of "*drinking* of the one Spirit." I think his use of "baptized" is also a use of imagery. They are all one, all having been enveloped in Christ. We have already mentioned the metaphorical usages of "βαπτιζω" in the New Testament that speak of being baptized in the Holy Spirit. Surely drinking of the one Spirit in this verse is a reference to *receiving* the Holy Spirit.

GB: I suppose that some might argue that whether Jew or Greek, slave or free, they had all been baptized in the same type of a literal water baptism, one that referred to Jesus. However, I agree that the reference to the Spirit makes a spiritual type of baptism rather than a literal water one more likely.

TS: Next I'd like to discuss Galatians 3:27. It's the text you raised with me when we discussing the Galatian letter over a week ago now. I'd prefer to leave the two occurrences of the verb in 1 Corinthians 15:29 to the last.

GB: No problem. Yes, I remember that text in Galatians. I wondered if it wasn't a reference to what some would say was the sacrament of baptism.

TS: Well, I'll try to explain now why I don't think it is a reference to a literal water ceremony. In the verse leading up to verse 27 of Galatians chapter 3, Paul writes, "You are all sons of God through faith in Christ Jesus." Then in verse 27 he says, "For as many of you as were baptized into Christ, have put on Christ." And follows this with, "There is neither Jew nor Greek, neither slave nor free, neither male nor female, for all are one in Christ Jesus." I think Paul is saying something like, "*Because you have been enveloped in Christ, meaning that like clothing, you have put on Christ, the one who is God's Son, you are all sons of God through faith in that Son, Christ Jesus. And consequently, being enveloped in him, being clothed with him, being in him, the distinctions of Jew and Greek, or slave and free or male and female do not apply.*" Notice the imagery of putting on clothing. That there is also imagery in the use of "βαπτιζω" should not surprise us.

GB: I agree. I think your way of understanding the text makes sense and I now suspect that it's not a reference to the sacrament at all. It seems to me that to argue that a literal water baptism is the prime reference is to claim enormous significance for a ceremony. This would be particularly odd given the Galatian letter as a whole—a letter in which, as you made clear, Paul is concerned to downgrade the significance of the ritual of circumcision and regulations such as observing special days and dietary laws.

TS: And I'm sure you also remember that in our discussions of that letter you said that some people would simply say that the rite or ceremony of baptism would've been an exception and such an obvious exception that there would be no need to mention it *as* an exception.

GB: And you said that Paul seemed to be arguing from a position of principle rather than just dealing with isolated individual items.

TS: Well, I think I said something like that.... But now for our last text—1 Corinthians 15:29, a text that contains the verb "βαπτιζω" twice. This Corinthians passage is particularly interesting since it seems to refer to the very unusual practice of people being baptized on behalf of the dead.

GB: I remember coming across that verse and thought it rather odd. Surely Paul didn't believe that that was an appropriate practice. Yet, the text seems to suggest that if someone were baptized in place of someone who had died but who had not been baptized, then that dead person somehow or other would receive some sort of benefit. Weird! Was he just referring to what some people mistakenly believed and practiced? I know that his main concern was to argue for the reality of the resurrection from the dead but this seems a strange way to do that.

TS: Well, members of the Church of the Latter Day Saints don't believe that what Paul wrote was weird. They're committed to that belief and conscientiously carry out the practice of being baptized on behalf of the dead, on an ongoing basis.

GB: Is there any evidence outside of the text in 1 Corinthians for that sort of practice being carried out by early believers?

TS: No I don't think so. But the text exists and it's been a difficult one to come to grips with for centuries.

GB: I don't suppose we're going to be any better off!

TS: I wonder! What if we consider "βαπτιζω" in that text to have a metaphorical character? Would that throw any light on what Paul was referring to?

GB: What would be a metaphorical understanding?

TS: Let's take it slowly. Traditionally the text reads something like, "Otherwise what do people mean by being baptized on behalf of the dead? If the dead are not raised at all, why are people baptized on their behalf?" The verb "βαπτιζω," as we've mentioned, occurs twice. Before we look at things from a metaphorical point of view, it might be helpful to ponder on a couple of translation problems. The preposition "ὑπερ" (*huper*) can mean "on behalf of" but equally, a good rendering would be "for the sake of." Secondly, the adverb "ὅλως" (*holōs*) normally means "wholly" or "completely," not obviously something like, "at all." To translate it as "at all" is a little odd, but such a translation does fit in with the text as normally understood. Furthermore, it might help us to keep in mind that for Paul "the dead" can mean those who are physically dead or those who are in principle dead, or spiritually dead.

GB: Could you give me some examples of Paul writing like that?

TS: Well, in 2 Corinthians, chapter 5 Paul writes, "If one died for all then all died." More to the point and particularly relevant is his statement in the present chapter of 1 Corinthians, a few verses earlier than our verse, that "In Adam all die." He follows this with "So, also, in Christ shall all be made alive." Here, only seven verses before the one under discussion, Paul, in effect, writes of "death" as a type of "death in principle" or "spiritual death."

GB: I get the point.

TS: Regarding a metaphorical understanding of "βαπτιζω," one possibility is that the verb relates to suffering. We've already come across that in the Gospels where Jesus refers to his own suffering and that to be endured by his disciples but also in 1 Peter where again the suffering of his followers, as I've argued, is in view. "Being immersed" in this sense is "being overwhelmed." There is also a first century CE work outside of the New Testament where "βαπτιζω" is used metaphorically in direct association with "sorrow," with the translation "overwhelmed by sorrow" being a suitable one.

GB: I suspect you already have an idea on how to understand the text!

TS: I'm not all that subtle in my approach am I?

GB: No. Not really. Anyway, what would be your translation?

TS: Recognizing that in the original Greek, there would be no clear signs of where a sentence ends or begins, it could go something like this—"For what is the point of people being overwhelmed in suffering for the sake of the dead if those who are completely dead are not raised? Why are people overwhelmed in suffering for their sake?" Read this way, the text interconnects with the following verses—"Why am I in peril every hour?" "I die every day" and "What do I gain if humanly speaking, I fought with beasts at Ephesus?"

GB: What you're suggesting is that Paul is saying something like—"*What is the point of suffering so much, for the sake of those who are as good as dead, if in the end they simply really do die and there is no resurrection. Why would anyone put up with so much anguish if in the end there was no point to what one was doing?*"

TS: Exactly! Couldn't have put it better myself!

GB: Understood that way, the text has nothing to do with a literal water baptism! And the suffering is the suffering that Jesus spoke of—the baptism that his followers would experience—isn't it? It all makes sense now and the text fits in naturally not only with his main argument about the resurrection from the dead but also with the verses that follow about his own suffering and that of others like him!

TS: Notice then the power of considering that "βαπτιζω" is sometimes used in a metaphorical sense.

GB: And not just the verb but also the noun "βαπτισμα" as we discussed on Saturday!

TS: Anyway, enough for today. It's been quite a bit longer than yesterday. Tomorrow, if that's okay with you, we'll look at the verse that I think is of most interest to you—Matthew 28:19.

GB: About time! Tomorrow it is. I'm wondering where you're heading, though I have a sneaking suspicion.

"Βαπτιζω" in the New Testament

EXPLANATORY NOTES: DAY 9

In the New Testament the verb "βαπτω" is found in Luke 16:24 John 13:26 (twice); Rev 19:13 (NAG).

The verb "λουω" is found in the New Testament in John 13:10; Acts 9:37, 16:33; Heb 10:22; 2 Pet 2:22; Rev 1:5 (NAG).

The verb "ἀπολουω" is found in the New Testament in Acts 22:16; 1 Cor 6:11 (NAG).

The seventy six instances of the verb "βαπτιζω" in the New Testament are located in Matt 3:6, 11 (twice), 13, 14, 16, 28:19; Mark 1:4, 5, 8 (twice), 9, 6:14, 24, 7:4, 10:38 (twice), 39 (twice); Luke 3:7, 12, 16 (twice), 21 (twice), 7:29, 30, 11:38; 12:50; John 1:25, 26, 28, 31, 33 (twice), 3:22, 23 (twice), 26, 4:1, 2, 10:40; Acts 1:5 (twice), 2:38, 41, 8:12, 13, 16, 36, 38, 9:18, 10:47, 48, 11:16 (twice), 16:15, 33, 18:8, 19:3, 4, 5, 22:16; Rom 6:3 (twice); 1 Cor 1:13, 14, 15, 16 (twice), 17, 10:2, 12:13; 15:29 (twice); Gal 3:27 (NAG). The occurrence in Mark 16:16 being part of the longer reading to Mark, is omitted.

The following table may be of some interest especially when compared with Table 3 to be found in the Explanatory Notes: Day 7. The numbers outside of the parentheses are the absolute numbers of instances for each part of speech.

Part of Speech	Participle (%)	Infinitive (%)	Indicative Mood (%)	Imperative Mood (%)	Subjunctive Mood (%)	Optative Mood (%)	Total (%)
New Testament Occurrences	16 (21)	12 (16)	45 (59)	2 (3)	1 (1)	–	76 (100)

Table 5
Incidence of six different parts of speech for "βαπτιζω" for occurrences in the New Testament (NAG)

Likewise, the following table might be of some interest especially when compared with Table 4 to be found in the Explanatory Notes: Day 7. The numbers outside of the parentheses are the absolute numbers of instances for each voice form.

Voice Form	Active (%)	Middle (%)	Passive (%)	Middle or Passive (%)
New Testament Occurrences	30 (39)	–	33 (43)	13 (17)

Table 6
Incidence of four different voice forms for "βαπτιζω" for occurrences in the New Testament (NAG)

"The Great Commission" text is found in Matt 28:19 (NIV).

The two texts where "βαπτιζω" is used to refer to Jewish washing ceremonies are Mark 7:4; Luke 11:38 (NAG).

Part 2: Baptism

The twenty nine instances of "βαπτιζω" associated with John's literal water baptism are found in Matt 3:6, 11, 13, 14, 16; Mark 1:4, 5, 8, 9, 6:14, 24; Luke 3:7, 12, 16, 21 (twice), 7:29, 30; John 1:25, 26, 28, 31, 33, 3:23 (twice), 10:40; Acts 1:5, 11:16, 19:4 (NAG). Acts 19:3 is omitted from the list it being problematic as to whether that instance referred to a literal water baptism or not. See later in the discussion that followed.

The twenty four instances of "βαπτιζω" associated with a literal water baptism being carried out by someone other than John the Immerser are located in John 3:22, 26, 4:1, 2; Acts 2:38, 41, 8:12, 13, 16, 36, 38, 9:18, 10:47, 48, 16:15, 33, 18:8, 19:5, 22:16; 1 Cor 1:14, 15, 16 (twice), 17 (NAG).

The twelve clearly metaphorical usages of "βαπτιζω" can be found in Matt 3:11; Mark 1:8, 10:38 (twice), 39 (twice); Luke 3:16, 12:50; John 1:33; Acts 1:5, 11:16; 1 Cor 10:2 (NAG). The texts where reference is made to the Holy Spirit are—Matt 3:11; Mark 1:8; Luke 3:16; John 1:33; Acts 1:5, 11:16. The texts where reference is being made to the suffering of Jesus or his disciples are—Mark 10:38 (twice), 10:39 (twice); Luke 12:50. The remaining text is 1 Cor 10:2 where Paul refers to the "fathers" being baptized into Moses. This verse is further discussed in the Explanatory Notes for Day 11.

The eight usages of "βαπτιζω" categorized by TS as "problematic" can be found in Acts 19:3; Rom 6:3 (twice); 1 Cor 1:13, 12:13, 15:29 (twice); Gal 3:27 (NAG).

TS was almost correct when he said, "in the Latin Vulgate . . . the verb ('βαπτιζω') is always translated by a Latin word—'*baptizo*.'" Of the seventy six occurrences of "βαπτιζω" in the New Testament, seventy four are translated by the word "*baptizo*" in the Latin Vulgate, with the other two instances, to be found in Mark 6:14, 24, being translated by the Latin word "*baptista*." "*Baptista*" is the Latin word used to translate the Greek word "βαπτιστης." The eleven occurrences of "βαπτιστης" in the New Testament are all translated by that same Latin word in the Latin Vulgate. Of the twenty occurrences of "βαπτισμα" in the New Testament, all are translated by the Latin "*baptismus*" in the Latin Vulgate with all of the three occurrences of "βαπτισμος" in the New Testament being translated in the Latin Vulgate by the word, "*baptismatus*." Clearly a type of transliteration is in use for the verb and all three nouns when translating from the Greek to the Latin of the Latin Vulgate.

TS mentioned that the Spanish, French and Italian languages have words that are in effect transliterations of the Greek word "βαπτιζω." Meaning "I baptize," the words are—"*bautizan*" (Spanish), "*baptize*" (French) and "*battezzato*" (Italian).

As mentioned in the Explanatory Notes: Day 8, M'Neile in *Baptism doth save*, 15–16, believes that Rom 6:3–4 refers to conversion which he considered equivalent to regeneration.

The chapter "New Testament Baptism" in Knox, *Broughton Knox*, 263–309, makes it clear that Knox believes that in Acts 19:5 the verb in association with "the name of the Lord Jesus" was probably metaphorical in character representing the acceptance of

Jesus as Lord and obedience to his teachings, that in 1 Cor 1:13, being baptized in the name of Paul is a reference to being a disciple of Paul as a leader of the Corinthians, that "baptized" in 1 Cor 12:13 is being used metaphorically to stress "the unity of the Christian group that the giving of the same Spirit of God to each creates" and that in Gal 3:27 being "baptized into Christ" is equivalent to the Christian sharing in Christ's death and burial.

Robinson, in "Towards a definition of baptism," believes that the verb in Rom 6:3 has the sense of "baptized with the baptism with which Christ is baptized," that is Christ's death, that being "baptized by one spirit into one body" in 1 Cor 12:13 is a possible reference to being baptized with the Spirit and that with Gal 3:27 in mind "putting faith in the proclamation of Christ crucified and finding justification thereby and being sealed in the Spirit in the manner described in Gal. 3:2–5" is probably "epitomized by Paul as an experience of being 'baptized into Christ' without any necessary implication of water-baptism."

Dunn in "The Birth of a Metaphor–(Part I)" and "The Birth of a Metaphor–(Part II)" argues that the references to "baptize in Holy Spirit" in Mark 1:8; John 1:33 and "baptize in Holy Spirit and fire" in Matt 3:11; Luke 3:16 are metaphorical and that Paul's references to "baptized" in Rom 6:3; 1 Cor 12:13; Gal 3:27 are also metaphorical. See also his "Baptism," 451, where he writes, "the imagery of 'baptized in Spirit' is both coined as a metaphor from the rite of baptism and set in some distinction from, even antithesis to, the rite of baptism."

Examples of Paul's use of the notion of "being in Christ" can be found in Rom 8:2; 1 Cor 15:22; 2 Cor 5:17, 12:2; Gal 3:28; Eph 2:10, 13; Col 1:28; Phlm 20. The preposition "ἐν" is used in all instances (NAG).

White in "Baptized on Account of the Dead" suggests that the "dead" when first referred to is to be understood metaphorically as a reference to the apostles, but literally when occurring the second time. He also suggests that "ὅλος" is to be understood to mean "truly," that it modifies the literally dead and that "ὑπερ" is to be understood causally. His translation of 1 Cor 15:29 becomes, "Otherwise what will those do who are being baptized on account of the dead (that is the dead figuratively speaking; that is, the apostles)? For if truly dead persons are not raised at all, why at all are people being baptized on account of them (that is, the apostles)?"

Murphy-O'Connor in "Baptized for the Dead" believes that both the verb "βαπτιζω" and the noun for "dead," when used first, are to be understood metaphorically. His suggested translation for the first part of 1 Cor 15:29 is "What will they do who are being destroyed [i.e. the apostles] on account of (the resurrection of) the dead?" By "the dead" here he understands those "who for the spirituals [i.e. πνευματικοι in Corinth] were not worth bothering about."

Part 2: Baptism

For one statement of the view of baptizing on behalf of the dead held by the Church of the Latter Day Saints (the Mormons) see http://www.mormon.org/faq/baptism-for-the-dead.

Paul's statement, "If one died for all then all have died" can be found in 2 Cor 5:14 (NIV) and his statement, "In Adam all die. So also, in Christ shall all be made alive." can be found in 1 Cor 15:22 (NIV).

I am indebted to Peter Bolt for highlighting for me the idea that Paul sometimes sees the dead as those who are "in principle" dead.

The reference to the idea of "being overwhelmed by sorrow" occurring in literature external to the New Testament, mentioned by TS, can be found in Vitae Aesopi, *Vita Pl vel Accursiana* where the word "βαπτιζομενος" is used.

Day 10

Matthew 28:18–20

The day finally arrives when they turn their attention to Matthew 28:19 but also to the verses on each side. However, they begin the day by briefly thinking about another text—one understood by some to refer to baptism but in which the words "baptize" and "baptism" do not appear. They then proceed to consider the setting of Matthew 28:19 but only briefly examine that verse before deciding to continue the discussion the following day.

TS: Hi there. Are you ready for Matthew 28:19?

GB: I'm as ready as I'll ever be. However, as anxious as I am for us to consider that verse, I wonder if we couldn't do something else first.

TS: Sure. What's on your mind?

GB: We've been looking at how the Greek words "βαπτιζω" and "βαπτισμα" are used in the New Testament. However, are there passages in Scripture that don't contain such words but still seem to relate to "baptism"? If so, before examining Matthew 28:19, could we have a very brief look at those passages?

TS: Well, there are some passages that don't contain those words and that some people think do relate to "baptism" but I don't think it will be all that helpful to spend much time on them. . . . Perhaps we could look at just one. There's a verse in Hebrews that goes something like this—"Let us draw near with a sincere heart in full assurance of faith, with our hearts sprinkled clean from an evil conscience and our bodies washed with pure water." It's verse 22 of chapter 10.

GB: I can see how some might think that something in that verse relates to a water ceremony.

TS: A small point, but there is no Greek word for "clean" in the text though it is legitimate to see it as understood. A thing to note is that the writer is using highly metaphorical language throughout this part of his letter. In verse 19 he refers to "the sanctuary." In verse 20 he refers to "the curtain" and in verse 21 to "the house of God." All three metaphors relate to the ancient tabernacle. Given the nature of these verses, it should be no surprise to discover that verse 22 contains other metaphorical elements. To begin with, he refers to "hearts sprinkled." You might remember the Greek word for sprinkle is "ῥαίνω." It's never used of the water rite anywhere else in the New Testament and indeed doesn't carry with it the notion of immersion at all. Surely the idea at this point is that the "evil" of the evil conscience that we have is washed away. By what means is that "evil" washed away? Verse 19 says, "We have confidence to enter the sanctuary by the 'blood of Christ.'" The death of Christ deals with our evil. The verse makes no mention of "baptism."

GB: But what do we make of the last part of verse 22?

TS: You mean, "Our bodies washed with pure water"?

GB: Yes.

TS: The use of the word "pure" is interesting. Nowhere else in the New Testament is there a reference to the water being used in a baptismal ceremony being "pure." Surely again, we have a metaphor. The text simply says, "Our bodies washed with pure water." Taken literally, it refers to the fact that in order to have a thoroughly good bath to remove all dirt, one would need to have "pure water." But the writer is not fundamentally interested in bodily cleanliness. And taken literally it's not talking about a water ceremony. It might be argued that understood metaphorically it could refer to a baptismal water ceremony but it would've been so much simpler to have just used one of the "baptismal" words. I think that while a metaphor is involved, the imagery is that of a good bath and that by referring to the concept of "body" he's referring to "all that a person is"—the entire person. Of course, the writer is actually referring to the recipients of the letter and himself. So he says "bodies" rather than "body." And "pure water" is possibly to be understood as another way of referring to the blood of Jesus the pure one, the writer having just referred to the blood of Jesus, the Christ in that verse 19. In fact the person of Jesus is the dominant feature of verses 19, 20, and 21 In verse 20 it says that he "opened for us a new and living way." And verse 21 refers to him as "a great priest over the house of God." It would be strange if a water ceremony in verse 22 were spoken of as though it had "cleansing properties" in itself.

GB: I guess one could argue that the phrase "bodies washed with pure water" though a metaphor, has as a backdrop, the baptismal water ceremony. Though as you've suggested, the use of the word "pure" seems to undermine that idea.

TS: I think so. Can we now turn at last to Matthew 28:19?

GB: Absolutely.

Matthew 28:18-20

TS: Well, we really need to see the verse in its setting and in all fairness we need to look at verses 18 and 20 as well as 19. They read something like this—"And Jesus came and spoke to them saying, 'All authority has been given to me in heaven and on earth. Going therefore, make disciples of all nations, baptizing them in the name of the Father and of the Son and of the Holy Spirit, teaching them to observe all that I've commanded you, and lo, I am with you all the days until the close of the age.'"

GB: Why did you refer to "going" rather than "go," as a translation that I have has it?

TS: Just to point out that the only straightforward imperative in the text is, "Make disciples of all nations." "Going," "baptizing" and "teaching" are all participles. They "hang off" that imperative—"Make disciples of all nations." It's true that an aspect of the imperative carries over to the participles, those things having to be done as well, but the thrust of what they—the "them," the eleven disciples—have to do, is to make disciples of all nations.

GB: So, if I understand you correctly, the emphasis is on making disciples but, if I might add, also on the idea that they will come from all nations. And in order to do this they will have to "go"! The nations are beyond Israel. To reach them requires getting up and going!

TS: Yes.

GB: I've noticed when reading Matthew, you might have mentioned it earlier, that even though it's a very Jewish Gospel every now and then people who are not Jews come into the picture—the Magi, a centurion and his servant, two demon possessed men, probably gentiles, a Canaanite woman and her daughter, the nations referred to in the parable of the sheep and the goats, and the centurion at the crucifixion. It looks like right at the close of the Gospel, where Matthew is reporting on the final words of Jesus, important words, readers, originally, probably mainly Jews, are being reminded of how important the "nations" are. Jewish readers might have found this a little difficult to stomach!

TS: I'm interested that you've picked up on both the importance of "the nations" and how this reference to "the nations" might have been difficult for some Jewish folk to cope with. I don't know if you've also noticed that at the end of Matthew's Gospel there are a number of references to "Galilee"—some women at the cross had followed Jesus from Galilee, after the resurrection of Jesus from the dead an angel told some women to tell the disciples that Jesus would see them in Galilee, later Jesus himself said much the same thing to the women and finally Matthew mentions that the eleven disciples met with Jesus on a mountain in Galilee where he gave his final instructions. Given that there is a text in Isaiah that refers to "Galilee of the nations," Matthew might have been indicating the importance of the nations, to his Jewish readers, simply by his references to Galilee. Anyway, what you've raised is important not only for appreciating how some readers might react but also for understanding some of what Jesus himself is saying here. If we don't keep in mind this focus by Jesus on, "Make disciples of all nations," we could well misunderstand other elements of what Jesus said.

GB: I know that this sounds like a rather simple question, the answer to which I'd have thought was rather obvious, but just in case I'm missing something, what do you think is essentially involved in a person becoming a disciple? What exactly is meant by the term "a disciple"?

TS: Well, one way of thinking about *becoming* a disciple of a teacher, and Jesus was certainly a teacher and more, is to consider what it means to become a follower of that teacher. That's what a disciple is—a follower. It would mean learning about that person, learning from that person and being committed to him and to what was learnt from him.

GB: And of course the eleven disciples were disciples of *Jesus* and those who would become disciples in the future would become disciples of *Jesus*. They wouldn't be the disciples of anybody else. Although the eleven had learnt, and any future disciples would learn, much about God the Father and even the Holy Spirit, from what the Son, Jesus, had taught, if anyone were to become a disciple in the future it would only make sense to say, that they would become a disciple of Jesus. He was the teacher! He is the one whom God had sent into the world, as a man, to gather disciples around him and to die for them and for others. I've learnt so much from him myself.

TS: You have indeed! And what you've just said ties in with what Jesus said when he began to give these final instructions—"All authority has been given to *me*"—and also with what he said later on—"Teaching them to observe all that *I* have commanded you." These last words are essentially not about the Father or the Holy Spirit. They are about the Son. Even the *very* last words, as recorded in Matthew—"And lo, I am with you all the days until the close of the age"—are about *him*. I suspect that the focus that Jesus places upon himself in these verses is sometimes lost. And the command that Jesus gave to the eleven was for them to make disciples of all nations—disciples of *him*. To do this they would need to go, they would need to "baptize" and they would need to teach. All these things are required in order for disciples of him to be made from all nations.

GB: Is there any significance in "going" being placed before "make," but "baptizing" and "teaching" being placed after the command to "make"? As you mentioned a moment ago his disciples would need to go in order to make disciples of all nations, but is it that that the actual business of making disciples has to do with "baptizing" and "teaching"? So, the "baptizing" and the "teaching" elements are left until after the reference to "make." Is that it?

TS: Yes, I think so. The "baptizing" and "teaching" explain what's involved in "make disciples," without losing sight, of course, of that aspect of the command—"of all nations."

Matthew 28:18-20

GB: For me, the reference to "the Holy Spirit" stands out a little. In spite of what I just said a moment ago, I don't recall Matthew's Gospel saying all that much about the Holy Spirit. Of course, John in his Gospel refers to the Holy Spirit many times.

TS: I understand what you're saying, although Matthew's Gospel does have more to say about the Holy Spirit than we might appreciate from first impressions. He specifically mentions "the Holy Spirit" or "a holy spirit," to be identified surely as "the Holy Spirit," five times and on at least five other occasions he refers to "the Spirit," where again, the reference, in effect, is to "the Holy Spirit."

GB: But surely Matthew makes many more references to God, specifically God as Father.

TS: Yes. That's correct. I think there are more than forty such references and almost always, if not always, God is referred to as "Father" by Jesus himself.

GB: Another matter. I find it strange that only Matthew's Gospel makes mention of this command to make disciples of all nations.

TS: Well, the other Gospels, one way or another, do make references to the gospel being proclaimed outside of the Jewish world but perhaps not in as pointed a way as it's made in Matthew. Maybe it's referred to in a more pronounced way in Matthew because, being a Gospel more directed towards Jews than the other Gospels, that message needed to be made that much more obvious.

GB: Still, one would've thought that the requirement to be baptized being so important would've been mentioned in all four. It's only referred to in Matthew. It's one of the last things that Matthew mentions. It is one of the last things that Jesus said before he left his disciples. It has to be important.

TS: I take your point. However there are other important matters that are not referred to in all Gospels—the virgin birth of Jesus, for example. Details of his birth are only given in Matthew and Luke.

GB: You're right. But still, Jesus is saying that part of becoming a disciple is to be baptized, if I understand him correctly. I realize that knowing about the virgin birth of Jesus is exceedingly important and that a new disciple would need to learn that fact about Jesus in due course. But surely, being baptized is something a new disciple would need to know about from almost the very beginning of his being instructed. . . . And now I am becoming anxious again about the fact that I am not baptized!

TS: Please don't be anxious. As I've said before, you don't need to be. Just be patient for a little longer. . . . I think it's about time now that we began to look more closely at that part of what Jesus said, that is, his reference to, "baptizing."

GB: It seems simple enough.

TS: Well, for starters, did you notice that it's not a command to be baptized?

Part 2: Baptism

GB: What? ... Oh, I see what you mean. I've always read it as Jesus saying that we all needed to be baptized. And I still think that that's what's implied. But, technically, you're correct. It really is a matter of what the disciples were being instructed to do. They needed to baptize others. Yet as I say, I think it implies that we all need to be baptized, well, all those who wish to become disciples.

TS: Maybe. However if it really is a requirement that everybody who wants to become a disciple needs to be baptized, one might have thought that Jesus somewhere would've said just that. Surely such a command is more to the point than one that instructs those who already are his followers to baptize others.

GB: Hmm. I realize that not everybody who decides to become a disciple can be baptized. A person might decide to become a follower of Jesus just before they die and there is no time or opportunity to be baptized. The thief who was crucified alongside of Jesus, who turned to him, is an obvious example. But surely, God would overlook such situations. As the saying goes, they are simply exceptions that "prove the rule."

TS: Maybe, maybe not. I am asking you to be very patient and again not to be anxious. ... I know we've only begun to focus in on that verse 19 and I know that the day is still young but I am going to suggest that we call it quits. I think you, well both of us, need a break. But could we meet again tomorrow? I don't want you to be worried about your relationship with God.

GB: Tomorrow would be fine. And I know that my safety is in God's hands. I simply want to do the right thing.

TS: I understand. Tomorrow it is.

Matthew 28:18-20

EXPLANATORY NOTES: DAY 10

In discussing Heb 10:22 (NIV and NAG) TS could've mentioned *The Didache* where reference is made to the preference of running water over cold water and to cold water over warm water, for use in the baptismal rite. See *The Didache*, section 7. The text can be found in English in Stevenson, *A New Eusebius*, 7.1–3, 126. TS does refer to *The Didache* and these different types of water during Day 13. Ferguson in *Baptism*, 63–64 refers to the tractate Mikwaoth of the Mishnah, chapter 1 which distinguishes "six grades among pools of water according to their degree of purity." Such texts indicate the importance that was placed on the purity of the water for ritual washings, at one time, but no such idea is associated with the water baptismal ceremony in the New Testament.

Another text that some people believe refers to baptism but in which the words "βαπτιζω" and "βαπτισμα" do not occur is John 3:5. Jesus speaking to Nicodemus says, "Truly, truly I say to you unless a person is born of water and the Spirit he cannot enter the kingdom of God." (NIV). However, this verse does come up for discussion on Day 13, a few days later.

The references in Matt to the Magi, a centurion and his servant, two demon possessed men, a Canaanite woman and her daughter, the parable of the sheep and the goats, and the centurion at the crucifixion can be found at Matt 2:1–12, 8:5–13, 8:28–34, 15:21–28, 25:31–46, 27:54 (NIV) respectively.

The references, mentioned by TS, to "Galilee" towards the end of Matt, can be found at Matt 27:55, 28:7, 10, 16 (NIV), and the text which mentions "Galilee of the nations" is Isa 9:1 (NIV).

The Gospel apart from Matthew that's quite explicit about the need for the gospel message to be preached beyond the Jewish world is Luke. Luke records how Jesus, after his resurrection, explained to his disciples that, "repentance and forgiveness of sins should be preached in his name to all nations."—Luke 24:47 (NIV).

The five references in Matthew that speak of "the Holy Spirit" or "a Holy Spirit" are Matt 1:18, 20, 3:11, 12:32, 28:19 (NIV). The five instances where the "Spirit" is mentioned in Matthew's Gospel, where in effect the reference is to "the Holy Spirit," are found in Matt 3:16, 4:1, 12:18, 28, 31 (NIV). Twice the reference is to "the Spirit of God," twice the reference is to "the Spirit" and once the reference is to "my Spirit," these last words occurring in a quote from Isa 42:1 (NIV).

Day 11

More on Matthew 28:18–20

This is the day when TS and GB begin to consider in earnest the phrase in Matthew 28:19 "baptizing in the name." The discussion is complicated and both TS and GB need to keep their wits about them. They look at various prepositions used in association with "baptizing" and, separately, "the name," both inside and outside of the New Testament. They consider "in the name," particularly "in the name of the Lord" as a concept. They then turn to the four occurrences of "baptizing in the name" in the New Testament where the reference is to Jesus. Frustratingly perhaps, the day then comes to a close.

TS: Hi. At last the crucial clause—"Baptizing them in the name of the Father and of the Son and of the Holy Spirit"—that's what our attention will be on today! And with an even narrower focus we ought to look initially at the phrase, "in the name."

GB: What's the preposition used and is it unusual? Is there one? If there is, is it the one normally used when immersion in a watery medium is in mind or is it different because a watery medium is not mentioned or is it what it is because it governs "the name"?

TS: I'm a little amazed at the questions you've just asked, though perhaps I shouldn't be! Fancy homing in on the preposition used! I didn't anticipate that you would want to look at such detail. However, that's exactly what I was planning to do. But I should point out from the start that I don't think that we are going to learn very much.

GB: Why is that?

TS: Well, for starters, even though there *is* a preposition in our phrase, there aren't all that many instances, particularly outside of the New Testament, where a preposition is used in association with "βαπτιζω." Furthermore when we look at all instances both inside and outside of the New Testament there isn't much consistency in the use of prepositions in association with either "βαπτίζω" or "the name," at least not up until the beginning of the second century CE.

GB: None the less, I'm interested. What do we know?

TS: You're asking a lot! Often the verb "βαπτίζω" is simply followed by the noun for the medium, into which the immersion occurs or doesn't occur, the noun being in the dative case. However when it *is* accompanied by a preposition, that preposition is either "ἐν" (*en*), "ἐπι" (*epi*) or "εἰς" (*eis*). Outside of the New Testament and up until the first century BCE, we have only two examples where a preposition is used and it's "ἐν" in both instances. From the first century BCE until the end of the first century CE, again restricting our observations to examples outside of the New Testament, we have twelve examples where a preposition is used. In one case the preposition is "ἐν." In all other instances it's "εἰς" and in one of these cases the "immersion" involved is of a metaphorical nature. Perhaps there was a change in usage over time. It's simply difficult to tell. On the basis of the evidence available we could suggest that in the case of the literature external to the New Testament when a preposition is going to be used, and when the object of the preposition is a locality or place, such as a swimming pool or a river, then "ἐν" is the preferred preposition of choice, but when the actual medium, say water, is in view then "εἰς" is the more appropriate one to use. Yet the evidence is so limited it's difficult to be confident about the validity of such a generalization. I suppose one thing we could say is that "εἰς" with the sense of "into" would certainly not be inappropriate when the medium is, say, water.

GB: What about in the New Testament itself?

TS: In the text in which we're interested the preposition is "εἰς." In the New Testament "εἰς" in association with "βαπτίζω" occurs eleven times. "Ἐν" and "ἐπι" occur in such an association fifteen times and once respectively. Of the fifteen times that "ἐν" accompanies "βαπτίζω," the preposition is followed by the Holy Spirit six times, by water four times—notice here that "ἐν" is associated with water as the medium!— by a locality of one sort or another four times, and by "the name" once. That last instance can be found in Acts chapter 10, verse 48.

GB: Given that "εἰς" is the preposition used in Matthew 28:19, I take it that we are more interested in the combination "βαπτίζω" and "εἰς" as found both in that text and elsewhere throughout the New Testament.

TS: Sure. As I said, the combination occurs eleven times in the New Testament. "Εἰς" following the verb "βαπτίζω" occurs once where the object is the death of Jesus—"his death," once where the object is "one body" and once where the object is "what" as part of a question—"in what . . . ?" Three times the object is the actual name of a person, the name being Christ Jesus, Christ, or Moses. Five times the preposition is followed by "the name of." Those five instances can be found in Acts 8:16, 19:5 and 1 Corinthians 1:13 and 15 and of course our text.

GB: It's complicated isn't it?

TS: I did say that I thought looking at the preposition wouldn't be all that helpful and that's partly because there is no simple pattern. I think all I can say at this point is that with respect to Matthew 28:19 the idea that "εἰς" has the sense of "into" seems reasonable. It could be that in the New Testament the preposition is determined either by the particular grammatical construction of the verb "βαπτιζω" or the particular object governed by the preposition or both. Or it could be that it's determined at the whim of the author. I really don't know. It's not helpful that none of the grammatical constructions of the verb "βαπτιζω," when accompanied by "εἰς," are duplicated when the verb is accompanied by "ἐν." And the grammatical construction of "βαπτιζω," when the preposition is "ἐπι," is different to any of those where the preposition is "εἰς" or "ἐν."

GB: Okay. It *is* complicated. My next question however, is what about simply the phrase "in the name"? What do we know about the usage of that phrase in the Greek-speaking world, in or outside of the New Testament, whether or not it's associated with the verb "βαπτιζω"?

TS: If you insist. But we mustn't spend too long on this. And to save time could we restrict your question to the Greek phrase that contains the preposition in our text—"εἰς το ὄνομα"—generally translated "in the name"?

GB: Okay. But I simply want to make sure that we know, in so far as it's possible, what Jesus was really getting at in Matthew chapter 28.

TS: Actually, the truth is there are very few examples available of "εἰς το ὄνομα" in the Greek literature outside of the New Testament, at least up until the beginning of the second century CE, so could we first give some attention to the phrase "in the name" as we find it in the Hebrew Scriptures? That is, let's first look briefly at the Hebrew concept "in the name" but particular where the reference is to God. After all, almost all, if not all, of the writers of the New Testament were Jews who came from a Hebrew-speaking background, even if they couldn't speak Hebrew fluently themselves.

GB: Sure. I understand.

TS: There are a few words we could focus in on but "בְּשֵׁם" (*beshēm*), meaning "in the name" or similar, and its associate "וּבְשֵׁם" (*ūbeshēm*), which simply means "and in the name" or similar, are the most relevant ones. On about 50 occasions one of these words is found where the reference is to God. The various contexts refer to such as "glorying in the name," "speaking in the name," "calling on the name," "help being given in the name," "trusting in the name," "serving in the name," and "being named in the name."

GB: Am I right in suggesting that "the name" in those contexts not only refers to his actual name but perhaps even more to the point, his very being, who he is, all that he is or something particular about who he is? That is, whatever the context, the essence of "in the name" is that whatever is being said or done is being said or done very much with respect to him.

TS: I think so. We could look at his actual name and what that meant but I think you've got the essential point. It wasn't just his name that was being appealed to it was what was behind that name—the very character of God or some specific aspect or aspects of his character. There is an interesting text in one of John's epistles in the New Testament where some believers are spoken of as having done something "for the sake of the name." The reference is almost certainly to Jesus but the expression "the name" was appropriate for and good enough for, indicating that the very person of Jesus was in mind, without actually mentioning his name as it were.

GB: As you say, interesting.

TS: But now to the Greek literature external to the New Testament! Using the *Thesaurus Linguae Graecae* I am only aware of two occurrences of "εἰς τὸ ὄνομοα" up until the beginning of the second century CE. One is in a work by Plato where he discusses the construction of words—a very philosophical type of discussion—we won't go into that—and the other is in a book called 2 Maccabees, which can be found in the *LXX*, the *Septuagint*, where the text speaks of blasphemy against the Lord's name.

GB: I can see why you thought we should consider some Hebrew material. There really isn't anything much to go on in the Greek literature external to the New Testament is there! Well then, what about the references to "εἰς τὸ ὄνομα"—you see, I am becoming more and more familiar with Greek pronunciation—in the New Testament?

TS: There are eleven such instances—four being associated with the verb "πιστευω" (*pisteuō*) the combination having the sense of "believing in the name." All four can be found in the writings of John and all refer to Jesus in one way or another. There is one instance that conveys the sense of "indicating in the name" and another that has the sense of "gathering in the name." "The name" in both of these cases also relates to Jesus. On five occasions the associated verb is "βαπτιζω." I mentioned that just a moment ago. In addition to the occurrence in Matthew 28:19, as I pointed out, there are the two instances in Acts and the two in 1 Corinthians. The two texts in Acts—Acts 8:16 and 19:5—both refer to people being "baptized in the name of the Lord Jesus." In 1 Corinthians 1:13 Paul asks the question, "Were you baptized in the name of Paul?"—we looked at that verse on Monday—and in verse 15 of the same chapter, Paul denies that except for a few exceptions, none of the Corinthians "were baptized in my name." Though I did refer to that text, I didn't discuss it in any detail last Saturday when we were looking at the noun "βαπτισμα," as I thought it was probably a reference to a literal water baptism.

GB: I know that you thought that the text of 1 Corinthians 1:13 was a problematic one, but overall, doesn't it seem fairly obvious that "baptized in the name" wherever it occurs refers to a literal water baptism just as Paul's reference to "baptized in my name" probably does?

TS: I think that's correct, but only as a general rule. And with respect to that 1 Corinthians 1:13 text I did say that I was inclined to think that it *did* refer to a literal water baptism. . . . I think that now we should try to come to some understanding of what "in the name" means when it's in association with "βαπτιζω," regardless of whether we think that all such instances relate to a literal water baptism or not.

GB: I'd have thought it meant something like, "coming under the authority of" that person. In the two cases in Acts located in chapters 8 and 19, even without looking at the context, it seems to me that the phrases used would've meant ostensibly coming under the authority of Jesus and all that that implied—wanting to serve Jesus and wanting to learn more about him. The ceremony itself—I'm guessing that there was a ceremony, perhaps the word "ceremony" is not the best word to use—probably would've conveyed the idea that the person being baptized was radically changing the direction of his or her life. He was dying to an old way of life and rising to a new way of life. It probably would have also conveyed the idea that the person was being made clean. Given that repentance was supposed to accompany such a baptism, the cleansing would most likely have been understood as a cleansing from sin.

TS: Well said! And it won't hurt us to keep in mind, as we ponder our Matthew text, the notion of "in the name" when that name referred to God in the Old Testament. After all, as I've said, almost all, if not all, of the writers of the New Testament were Jews and they would have been very familiar with their Hebrew Scriptures, even if they gained their understanding of those Scriptures, when they were read or when they heard them read in *Aramaic*, the common language of their world or even as they read or heard them read in a *Greek* version. There, in their Scriptures, the sense of "in the name of the Lord," or more strictly, "in the name of Yahweh"—something sounding like, "Yahweh," was God's personal name, though generally it was not pronounced—the sense was something along the lines of "with respect to who he is" or "with respect to some aspect or aspects of who he is." That was my feel for how the Hebrew words we discussed were to be understood and I think you agreed.

GB: Yes, I did.

TS: And we can't separate what he's said and what he's done from "who he is"!

GB: And I guess the same applies to the notion of "in the name" when the reference is to the Lord Jesus. And he is being identified, in that title, in part, as to who he is—he is Lord! We can't separate his words or his actions from who *he* is, either, can we?! And coming under his authority entails some recognition of who he is. And his actual authority and who he actually is go hand in hand. They are bound together in what his name signifies. . . . All of which reminds me of a question I've had in the back of my mind. What is the significance of there being only one reference to "the name" in

More on Matthew 28:18-20

the phrase "in the name of the Father and of the Son and of the Holy Spirit"? Why wouldn't Jesus have referred to "the name of the Father," "the name of the Son" and "the name of the Holy Spirit"? Has it got something to do with the oneness of God?

TS: I think it does, though I admit, the expression strikes us as a little odd. It could be that we're meant to understand the text as though the "name" is in fact repeated for all three. But alternatively, and in my view, more likely, the idea being conveyed is that there is in essence only the one name. From a Jewish point of view, from a proper point of view, there is only one God. You thought the way the phrase was expressed had to do with the oneness of God. I think you're correct.

GB: That is, the "one name" is consistent with the Jewish, and as you say, proper, understanding of the nature of God. It would be important for Jewish readers to see that point wouldn't it!

TS: Absolutely! And of course, from a Gentile perspective, if you only spoke about the Father, the Son and the Holy Spirit as separate persons, then it would seem that you were talking about three gods, three deities. The idea that there might be three Jewish gods, even if they were related, wouldn't cause the pagan world any problems, of course, since the prevailing view in that world was that there was a multiplicity of gods. I think that Jesus speaks of the one name because indeed there is only one God though there are three distinct persons, as we sometimes refer to them. And of course having one name implies that they work together in unity with each other. And Jesus by using the words, "the name" and only once, focuses on that unity. The disciples coming from the pagan world should understand at the outset, that there is one God, one God alone, though there is the Father and the Son and the Holy Spirit.

GB: I know that God has revealed himself in various ways. And I understand him as the Father and the Son as his Son and the Holy Spirit as his Holy Spirit, but I still find it difficult to get my head around what God being a triune God really means.

TS: Join the club! Let's move on. I wonder if we could now have a closer look at Matthew 28:19.

GB: I know I've been asking fairly specific questions that perhaps in the end aren't all that important, and I know that we agreed to only look at "in the name" when the preposition was "εἰς" but how often do we come across the phrase "in the name" when the preposition is not "εἰς"?

TS: In the Greek literature, external to the New Testament, up until the beginning of the second century CE, we can locate forty instances of "ἐπι τῳ ὀνοματι." Most of them can be found in that Greek translation of the Old Testament and other literature, called the *LXX*, the *Septuagint*. I don't think there is much point in going into the detail of how the phrase is used there or elsewhere. After all, the preposition we are really interested in is "εἰς."

GB: I know I'm being a little difficult but how often does "ἐπι τῳ ὀνοματι" occur in the New Testament?

TS: You're not being difficult. It's what I'd call "wanting to have some sort of feel for things around the edges"! The phrase occurs fourteen times in the New Testament. All except one of these refer to Jesus in one way or another, with one account referring to being *baptized in the name* of Jesus Christ. It occurs in that famous speech of Peter's given on the day of Pentecost, in Acts 2:38.

GB: And what about where "ἐν" is the preposition?

TS: You don't give up do you! The phrase "ἐν τῳ ὀνοματι" can be found only four times in the Greek literature outside of the New Testament, up until the beginning of the second century CE but it occurs twenty nine times in the New Testament. On twenty three of these occasions the reference is to Jesus with Acts 10:48 recording Peter commanding that Cornelius and his company be *baptized in the name* of Jesus Christ. By the way, notice in this instance and in the one in Acts 2:38 where Peter delivers his speech, how Jesus is identified as the Christ. The actual name used, conveys something about who Jesus is.

GB: I see what you're saying. But if you'll still allow me to go on about these other prepositions, it is interesting that *both* "ἐπι" and "ἐν" are used in the book of Acts in connection with "baptizing" and "the name." And of course, that's also true with respect to "εἰς" as you've already mentioned.

TS: True. It's a bit of a puzzle to me as to why in any instance one preposition is used and not another. Perhaps Luke, the author of Acts, felt free to use either "εἰς," "ἐπι" or "ἐν" in connection with "baptizing" and "the name" at any time. By way of reminder, on two occasions, it is "baptizing in, 'εἰς,' the name of the Lord Jesus" and once each "baptizing in, 'ἐπι' or 'ἐν,' the name of Jesus Christ." It's difficult to argue that the different prepositions in these texts convey something different. In the case of Acts 8:16 and 19:5, where "εἰς" is found, the actual "baptizing" words used are—"βεβαπτισμενοι" (*bebaptismenoi*) and "ἐβαπτισθησαν" (*ebaptisthēsan*) respectively. In Acts 2:38 it is "βαπτισθητω" (*baptisthētō*) and in Acts 10:48 the word is "βαπτισθηναι" (*baptisthēnai*), with the prepositions used being "ἐπι" and "ἐν" respectively. There may be a reason in each case why one preposition is used and not another but I don't know what such reasons would be.

GB: Why do you think that sometimes people were baptized in the name of Jesus Christ and on other occasions they were baptized in the name of the Lord Jesus?

TS: I'm not sure. . . . I haven't looked into it but different circumstances could've meant that a different reference to Jesus was appropriate—"Jesus Christ" or "the Lord Jesus." Alternatively it may be that we're making too much of the difference. Luke may have felt free to use either title when reporting on a particular event, just as perhaps he felt free to use different prepositions.

More on Matthew 28:18-20

GB: Fair enough.

TS: There is an intriguing account in Acts chapter 19 where Luke records that some itinerant Jewish exorcists, having seen some extraordinary things done by Paul, decided to pronounce the name of the Lord Jesus over some people possessed by evil spirits. Their words, as given by Luke, were "I adjure you by the Jesus whom Paul preaches." They were unsuccessful and what they tried to do worked out to their own detriment. However it's interesting that though Luke wrote that they decided to pronounce the name of the Lord Jesus, in the actual words that Luke used to express what they said, the reference is only to the name, "Jesus." Perhaps Luke wanted to convey the idea that they did not really understand that Jesus was Lord or Christ. And of course, in reality, they may only have used the name, "Jesus," but identified him in their own minds as the Jesus whom Paul proclaimed. Of further interest is the fact that in what Luke records what they actually said, no preposition is used in conjunction with the word "Jesus." The word "Jesus" simply occurs in the accusative case. Furthermore, as I've indicated, the word, that is, the Greek word for "name," doesn't occur in Luke's report of what they said.

GB: Anyway, it's clear that there are four texts in the Acts of the Apostles were people were baptized either in the name of the Lord Jesus or in the name of Jesus Christ.

TS: And these four texts are the only references in the entire New Testament to "being baptized in the name," where the sole reference is clearly to Jesus. The only other references to "being baptized in the name" are the two in 1 Corinthians 1:13 and 15 where Paul's name is in view, which texts we've already mentioned, and the Matthew 28:19 text, the text of our ultimate focus!

GB: I know that you said that looking at the prepositions wasn't going to be all that helpful but I feel better for having covered the field, as it were. And I think examining the notion of "in the name of" has been both important and helpful.

TS: I agree. I was hoping that today we could have finished up with Matthew 28:19 but it's really too late now to draw things to a conclusion. What we did today was okay though. The next time we meet, I promise that that day will see us come to the end. Could we give tomorrow a rest and meet again on Friday?

GB: Sure, Friday is fine.

Part 2: Baptism

EXPLANATORY NOTES: DAY 11

The two instances located in the Greek literature up until the beginning of the first century BCE where "βαπτιζω" is followed by "ἐν" can be found in *LXX*, 4 Kgs 5:14; *LXX*, Isa 21:4.

The one instance located in the Greek literature for the period first century BCE to first century CE where "βαπτιζω" is followed by "ἐν" can be found in Josephus in *Josephus II*, Book I, 437, line 12, 206–07.

The eleven instances located in the Greek literature for the period first century BCE to first century CE where "βαπτιζω" is followed by "εἰς" occur in works authored by, Josephus (twice), Plutarch (three times), Strabo (once), Heron (four times) and Soranus (once). The authors where the instances can be located are as follows. In each case the object governed by the preposition "εἰς" is also given.

Josephus in *Josephus VI*, Book X, 169, line 2, 252–53—the object of the preposition is "sleep."; Josephus in *Josephus II*, Book II, 476, line 4, 508–09—the object of the preposition is "his own neck."; Plutarch in *Plutarch's Moralia II, On Superstition*, 166, section A, line 6, 460–61—the object of the preposition is "the sea."; Plutarch in *Plutarch's Moralia IV, Greek and Roman Parallel Stories*, 306, section C, line 4, 262–63— the object of the preposition is "his blood."; Plutarch in *Plutarch's Moralia XII, Beasts are Rational*, 990, section E, line 1, 520–21—the object of the preposition is "Lake Copais."; Strabo in *The Geography of Strabo V*, Book XII, chapter 5, section 4, line 7, 472–73—the object of the preposition is "it" (Lake Tatta); Hero in *Pneumatica*, Book 1, chapter 2, line 31—see *Thesaurus Linguae Graecae* for the Greek word, "βαπτιζομενον" (*baptizomenon*) and a translation of the text in Greenwood and Woodcroft, *The Pneumatics of Hero of Alexandria*, "Theorem" 1, "The Bent Siphon," 11–14—the object of the preposition is "the water."; Hero in *Pneumatica*, Book 1, chapter 5, line 42—see *Thesaurus Linguae Graecae* for the Greek word, "βαπτιζεσθαι" (*baptizesthai*) and a translation of the text in Greenwood and Woodcroft, *The Pneumatics of Hero of Alexandria*, "Theorem" 4, "Siphon which is Capable of Discharging a Greater or Less Quantity of Liquid with Uniformity," 17–18—the object of the preposition is "the water."; Hero in *Pneumatica*, Book 1, chapter 16, line 4—see *Thesaurus Linguae Graecae* for the Greek word, "βαπτιζομενου" (*baptizomenou*) and a translation of the text in Greenwood and Woodcroft, *The Pneumatics of Hero of Alexandria*, "Theorem" 15, "Birds made to Sing and be Silent Alternately by Flowing Water," 31–32—the object of the preposition is "the water."; Hero in *Pneumatica*, Book 1, chapter 38, line 35— see *Thesaurus Linguae Graecae* for the Greek word, "βαπτιζομενον" and a translation of the text in Greenwood and Woodcroft, in *The Pneumatics of Hero of Alexandria*, "Theorem" 37, "Temple Doors opened by Fire on an Altar," 57–58—the object of the preposition is "the water."; Soranus in *Gynaeciorum* Book 4, chapter 11, section 5, line

More on Matthew 28:18-20

3—see *Thesaurus Linguae Graecae* for the Greek word "βαπτίζειν" and a translation of the text in *Soranus' Gynecology*, 193—the object of the preposition is "the embryo."

TS mentions that in one of these eleven instances, the "immersion" is of a metaphorical nature. It is found in the first text of the list given above. The usage is by Josephus and the reference is to a certain Gadalias having sunk into a drunken sleep.

The eleven instances in the New Testament where "βαπτιζω" is followed by "εἰς" occur in Matt 28:19; Acts 8:16, 19:3, 5; Rom 6:3 (twice); 1 Cor 1:13, 15, 10:2, 12:13; Gal 3:27 (NAG). The forms of the verb present in these eleven instances are—"βαπτίζοντες" (*baptizontes*), "βεβαπτισμενοι" (*bebaptismenoi*), "ἐβαπτίσθητε" (*ebaptisthēte*), "ἐβαπτίσθησαν" (*ebaptisthēsan*), "ἐβαπτίσθημεν" (*ebaptisthēmen*), "ἐβαπτίσθημεν," "ἐβαπτίσθητε," "ἐβαπτίσθητε," "ἐβαπτίσθησαν," "ἐβαπτίσθημεν," and "ἐβαπτίσθητε" (NAG) respectively.

The fifteen instances in the New Testament where "βαπτιζω" is followed by "ἐν" occur in Matt 3:6, 11 (twice), Mark 1:4, 5, 8; Luke 3:16; John 1:26, 31, 33 (twice), 3:23; Acts 1:5, 10:48, 11:16 (NAG). The forms of the verb present in these instances are—"ἐβαπτίζοντο" (*ebaptizonto*), "βαπτίζω," "βαπτισει" (*baptisei*), "βαπτιζων" (*baptizōn*), "ἐβαπτιζοντο," "βαπτισει," "βαπτισει," "βαπτιζω," "βαπτιζων," "βαπτιζειν" (*baptizein*), "βαπτιζων," "βαπτιζων," "βαπτισθησεσθε" (*baptisthēsesthe*), "βαπτιθηναι" (*baptisthēnai*), and "βαπτισθησεσθε," (NAG) respectively.

The one instance in the New Testament where "βαπτιζω" is followed by "ἐπι" occurs in Acts 2:38 and the form of the verb is "βαπτισθητω" (*baptisthētō*) (NAG).

Of the eleven instances in the New Testament where "βαπτιζω" is followed by "εἰς," one instance is with reference to the death of Jesus—Rom 6:3, another to "one body"—1 Cor 12:13 and another to "what" occurring in a question being asked—Acts 19:3. Three times the reference is to a person actually named—Rom 6:3; 1 Cor 10:2; Gal 3:27, and five times the reference is to "the name"—Matt 28:19; Acts 8:16, 19:5; 1 Cor 1:13, 15 (NAG).

1 Cor 10:2 is an interesting verse in that while the baptizing is into ("εἰς") Moses, the text continues with in ("ἐν") the cloud and in ("ἐν") the sea (NAG). It could be judged that "ἐβαπτίσθησαν"—the actual form of "βαπτιζω" in the text— uses one preposition with one object and a different preposition with two other objects. It was decided to refer only to the baptizing into Moses in the analysis. The text was referred to during the discussions of Day 9 and is mentioned again in the Explanatory Notes for that day.

In the New Testament, of the fifteen instances where "βαπτιζω" is followed by "ἐν," there are six occurrences where the object is "the Holy Spirit"—Matt 3:11; Mark 1:8; Luke 3:16; John 1:33; Acts 1:5, 11:16, four where the object is "water"—Matt 3:11; John 1:26, 31, 33, four where the object is a locality—Matt 3:6; Mark 1:5 (in both of these texts the object is the river Jordan); Mark 1:4 (the locality is the wilderness); John 3:23 (the locality is Aenon) and one where the object is "name"— Acts 10:48 (NAG).

Part 2: Baptism

The text where mention is made of "for the sake of the name" that TS referred to is 3 John 7.

The two instances of "εἰς τὸ ὄνομα" in the Greek literature external to the New Testament, up until about the beginning of the second century CE can be found in *LXX*, 2 Macc 8:4; Plato, *Plato IV, Cratylus*, 427, C, line 6, 146–47.

TS made reference to the two Hebrew words "בְּשֵׁם" (*beshēm*) and its associate "וּבְשֵׁם" (*ūbeshēm*). In the Old Testament "*beshēm*" in association with the name, meaning God's name, can be found in Gen 4:26, 12:8, 13:4, 21:3, 26:25; Exod 33:19, 34:5; Deut 18:5, 7, 20, 22, 21:5; 1 Sam 17:45, 20:42; 2 Sam 6:18; 1 Kgs 18:24, 32, 22:16; 2 Kgs 2:24, 5:1; 1 Chr 16:2, 10, 21:19; 2 Chr 18:15, 33:18; Ps 20:7, 33:21, 105:3, 118:10, 11, 12, 26, 124:8, 129:8; Isa 50:10; Jer 11:21, 26:9, 16, 20, 44:16; Joel 3:5; Amos 6:10; Mic 4:5; Zeph 3:9, 12; Zech 13:3 (IHG)—a total of forty six times. The name of God is specified as, "Yahweh" in all but four of these instances. "*Beshēm*" (IHG) is found nineteen times with reference to other gods, people or places. "*Ūbeshēm*" in association with God's name, in the Old Testament, is found in Ps 20:5, 116:4, 13, 17; Isa 44:5 (IHG)—a total of five times. In all but one of these instances, the name of God is again specified as "Yahweh." "*Ūbeshēm*" (IHG) is only found once where the reference is not to God.

Concerning the eleven instances of "εἰς τὸ ὄνομα" to be found in the New Testament, the four associated with the verb "πιστευω" are located in John 1:12, 2:23, 3:18; 1 John 5:13, the one associated with "indicating" occurs in Heb 6:10, and the one associated with "gathering" can be found in Matt 18:20 (NAG).

The episode of the Jewish exorcists attempting to pronounce the name of the Lord Jesus over certain people who had evil spirits is located in Acts 19:11–16.

Day 12

The Conclusion to Matthew 28: 18–20

The discussions that TS has had with GB over a number of previous days have obviously been intended by TS to lead to a particular understanding of Matthew 28:19. On this day, TS tries to pull together a number of those ideas previously discussed by asking GB a series of questions. Finally, TS produces an expanded paraphrase of verses 18 to 20 for GB's consideration.

GB: Hi. Last night, thinking about what we had discussed the other day, something struck me as odd. The text, Matthew 28:19 refers to baptizing in the name of the Father and of the Son and of the Holy Spirit. Yet in the Acts of the Apostles the reference is only to people being baptized in the name of Jesus Christ or the Lord Jesus. What do you make of that? I can understand that Luke may have felt free to use one title or another but surely at least on one occasion he would've reported that a person was baptized in the name of the Father and of the Son and of the Holy Spirit.

TS: What do *you* make of it? I've heard it argued that although in Acts there are only references to people being baptized in the name of Jesus Christ or in the name of the Lord Jesus, the baptisms were actually carried out in association with references, of one sort or another, to Jesus as well as to the Father and the Holy Spirit.

GB: How can anyone say that? I know that in each of the four situations there is some reference to the Holy Spirit, although in the account in Acts chapter 10 it's clear that the Spirit had not yet been given to those who had already been baptized. We discussed the importance of the giving of the Spirit in those baptismal situations a few days ago. But I don't recall any mention of God the Father, as Father, in connection with any of those baptisms.

TS: Your recollection is spot on. I don't think the argument has many legs. We will need to deal with the oddity that you've raised, by some other means.

Part 2: Baptism

GB: Well, however we solve the problem, on those four baptismal occasions there is only direct reference to the name of "Jesus the Christ" or "Jesus the Lord"—if that way of putting things is okay. That's correct isn't it?

TS: Absolutely.

GB: And when you think about it, that there *are* only references to "Jesus the Christ" or "Jesus the Lord" is consistent with the overall focus on Jesus that we find in our Matthew 28. All authority has been given to *him*. Disciples of all nations are to be made and obviously they will be disciples of *him*. And, they're to be taught to observe all that *he, Jesus*, commanded the original group of disciples to observe.

TS: That's correct. You're making an important point. And now, let me ask you three simple questions. First question—"What will disciples need to be taught if they are to come from all nations?"

GB: That's not a simple question but I'll give it a shot. They will need to be taught a great deal. Since most of them will not be Jews they will have very little understanding of God. Even for Jews, their understanding of God as Father, as Jesus revealed him to be, would've been quite limited. And then, the whole idea of there being a Holy Spirit would've been quite foreign to almost everybody. If I understand things correctly, the idea of there being "*the* Holy Spirit" doesn't seem to have been around until the coming of Jesus. And of course they would need to be taught many, many things about Jesus, the Lord Jesus, Jesus the Christ—all those things he taught the original disciples, all those things that he did, his relationship as Son with the Father, his coming into the world, his death, his resurrection, his departure and his coming at the end of things as Judge. You may have guessed it, but I've had at the back of my mind that part of Matthew 28:19 that refers to "in the name of the Father and of the Son and of the Holy Spirit."

TS: Not a bad answer! Second question—"Imagine that you read Matthew in one sitting from beginning to end, to find almost at the end of the Gospel that Jesus commanded his disciples to carry out a water ritual, when they made other disciples. Is that what you would have expected?"

GB: I think your question is loaded and it's not an easy one to answer without some bias. . . . If you have already read Matthew a few times you already have a sense of what most of his final words as recorded in Matthew mean. I've now read it a number of times. However, I'll try to imagine that I've only just read the Gospel from beginning to end in one sitting and for the first time. In my imagination, having just finished reading the Gospel I might be thinking particularly about the last few chapters. I'd be reflecting on that lengthy diatribe uttered by Jesus against the Pharisees and the Scribes and their hypocrisy, his reference to the destruction of the temple and the dreadful times to come, his coming in the future and the need to be vigilant, the parable of his judging the nations, and then of course the Last Passover Meal, his prayer

The Conclusion to Matthew 28:18-20

in the garden of Gethsemane, his betrayal, arrest, trial before the Sanhedrin, Peter's denial, his awesome death, his wonderful resurrection. . . . Come to think of it, a reference right at the last to a water ritual does seem a little odd!

TS: What a good memory you have! I wish that my memory was as good as yours. Third question—"Remember Paul's letter to the Galatian believers. If Jesus really did issue a command about a water ritual, and I know almost everybody thinks that that's the case, might you not expect Paul to have referred to it in his Galatian letter, as an exception to what he was saying? I know I've raised this matter with you before but I think it's important. Does the idea that fundamental to becoming a disciple is the requirement to be baptized in a water ceremony? Does that idea seem to be at odds with what Paul wrote to the Galatians and even at odds with the gospel message itself?"

GB: You've really asked two questions there but I can see how they're related. I am a little unprepared for where I think your questions are going. However, as far as Galatians is concerned, if being baptized was a well-accepted aspect of becoming a disciple of Jesus, then to nominate baptism as an exception to what Paul said in that letter might seem unnecessary. After all, in the letter he was dealing with an ancient Jewish rite, that of circumcision, not a new ceremony. But to be honest, if there had been no reference to a water ritual of baptism at the end of Matthew *that* would not have surprised me and such an absence would've seemed to be entirely consistent with Galatians, I must confess. But there must be something wrong here. Something I'm not seeing. The reality is that there *is* a reference to the water ritual of baptism and although it doesn't explicitly say that disciples must be baptized, the implication of what Jesus *did* command is that they should be. If the disciples are commanded to baptize new disciples, then people who wish to become disciples should be baptized! Unless, unless . . .

TS: Let's hold your "unless" there. Let me continue. In Matthew's Gospel there is really only one setting prior to Matthew 28:19 where a water ritual of baptism is mentioned.

GB: When John is baptizing in the Jordan.

TS: Yes. The ministry of John, which centered on his baptizing people, is covered in chapter 3 of Matthew. However, in that chapter two types of baptisms are mentioned. Of course, one is with respect to John who baptizes with water. Five times the verb is used in this connection and the preposition "ἐν" is involved twice, the object being "water" once and the "river Jordan" once. No other preposition is involved. The second type of baptism is the baptism with the Holy Spirit and fire. The verb is used only once in this connection and it is again accompanied by the preposition "ἐν" with the objects being the "Holy Spirit" and "fire." . . . I don't think we need to discuss what John was referring to when mentioning "fire." The reference has got to be significant but a discussion on that matter will side-track us too much. . . . "Βαπτιζω" is used in the first type of baptism to describe a literal physical immersion carried out by

John. In the second type of baptism "βαπτίζω" refers to a metaphorical immersion to be carried out by Jesus. By the way, the noun "βάπτισμα" occurs twice in Matthew once in chapter 3 and once in chapter 21. On each occasion it's a reference to John's baptism. Though the word "βαπτίζω" occurs six times in chapter 3, those two types of "immersing" are the only types referred to in that chapter and they are the only ones you come across before meeting up with "immersing" again in Chapter 28.

GB: Is there any significance that whereas "ἐν" is used by Matthew in those two types of baptizing in chapter 3, in chapter 28 the preposition he uses is "εἰς"?

TS: In the light of what we discussed a couple of days ago about the various prepositions and their use in association with "βαπτίζω" I'd be reluctant to say that there's any special significance especially in the choice of "εἰς." Luke may have felt free to use one preposition or another and Matthew likewise. Having said that, it's true that in every reference in the New Testament to being baptized in the Holy Spirit the preposition "ἐν" is used and that could be for good reason. And it's true that in the New Testament "ἐν" is also commonly used with "βαπτίζω" when the baptizing is in water or the river Jordan but "εἰς" is used five times when the object of the preposition is "the name." It may be that for Matthew to use "εἰς" in chapter 28 but "ἐν" in chapter 3 *could* be significant but as I've indicated I don't think we should stake too much on that. I don't think it matters much. . . . Perhaps now, the most important question to consider is, I know this is a fourth question, "In chapter 28 is the reference to "immersing" a reference to a literal physical immersing or a metaphorical immersing?" Although I am somewhat reluctant to put it this way, on the sole basis of what Matthew has recorded earlier, there is a fifty-fifty chance that it's metaphorical. I think I may have anticipated your "unless."

GB: You have! I was going to say, unless, the baptizing in Matthew 28 is a metaphorical baptizing. Surely however, in response to your last question, almost everybody thinks Matthew 28:19 *is* a reference to a literal, physical water immersing!

TS: But whether they do or not, if we are simply trying to sort out the truth shouldn't we at least consider the possibility that the reference *is* to a metaphorical immersing? The questions I've been asking were designed to help us consider that possibility. In fact, all of that information I was trying to convey about the metaphorical usage of "βαπτίζω" and "βάπτισμα" both inside and outside of the New Testament was intended to lead to the suggestion that a metaphorical understanding of "βαπτίζω" in Matthew 28:19 was a real possibility. And with all of that discussion about what "make disciples of all nations" would entail and through all of that rather wearisome discussion concerning "in the name" I was also hoping that we could have a better understanding of what Matthew 28:19 could mean, *particularly* if "βαπτίζω" were to be understood metaphorically. I was also trying to lay a foundation that might anticipate questions or even objections that you might have had or might have in the future. Remember that "make disciples of all nations" would entail teaching people a great deal

The Conclusion to Matthew 28: 18-20

about the one God—the Father and the Son and the Holy Spirit and remember that "in the name" can mean, "with respect to all that a person is, all that a person stands for, or with respect to some important aspect or aspects of that person."

GB: I remember and of course you were trying to steer my thinking in a particular direction! . . . Well, given your approach, how might Matthew 28:19 read?

TS: If I could paraphrase and expand verses 18 to 20, with a metaphorical understanding of "βαπτιζω" and a certain understanding of "in the name" and a view of what "make disciples of all nations" would entail, I think it would read something like this—*"And Jesus came and said to his eleven disciples, 'I have been given absolute authority by my Father, over all affairs, whether they be heavenly matters or earthly ones. Consequently, I am now giving you an instruction, which you must understand carries that authority. It is the last instruction that I will give you and it relates to what you must do, now that I am soon to depart from you and now that you will be engaged in that ministry for which I have prepared you. You won't be able to stay in or around Jerusalem, Judea or Galilee. Of course you will have a ministry in your homeland but as difficult as it is for you to comprehend, you will need to go further afield. What I demand of you is that you are to make disciples. They will be my disciples just as you are my disciples. You are to make disciples from among all nations, and this of course includes the Gentiles themselves. They will have to be taught a great deal. They will know so little. Swamp them, engulf them, envelop them, immerse them in who the Father is, who the Son is, who the Holy Spirit is, while helping both Jew and Gentile alike to understand that they, Father, Son and Holy Spirit, are one. They are one in purpose and one in being. But don't just educate them, as it were. Teach them that they need to observe, to embrace all those things that I commanded you to observe. Do all that I have just told you and then they will truly be my disciples as you are my disciples. And I know that I am going away and you may think that you are going to be on your own to carry out this ministry. But you won't be. I am with you now and I will always be with you. I promise to be with you as long as this present age lasts. Never fear."*

GB: That's extraordinary! When you put it that way it all makes sense. It would also explain why the baptisms recorded in Acts refer to the name, "Jesus the Christ" or "Jesus the Lord" and not to the name, "the Father and the Son and the Holy Spirit." Until today I've never thought of those closing words in that way. . . . This has been a wonderful day. Better than the day before! This is such a different way of understanding the reference to "baptizing." However I still need to think about it. Do you mind if we have another break for a couple of days? I do want to get back to you on this, but perhaps I should think seriously about why you could be wrong. It wouldn't worry you if I came back with some objections, if I can think of them, would it?

TS: Not at all! Would Monday be too soon?

GB: No, Monday would be good. See you then.

Part 2: Baptism

EXPLANATORY NOTES: DAY 12

Robinson in "Towards a definition of baptism," questions the notion that the "baptism" of Matt 28:19 is a reference to a water rite, suggesting that it could be a reference to a "baptism of judgement."

Knox in "New Testament Baptism" in *Broughton Knox*, 263–309, believes that "Jesus' reference to baptism in the great commission is purely metaphorical" and that "'to disciple,' 'to baptize' and 'to teach' are (in Matthew 28:19) synonyms."

In Matt, "βαπτίζω" is used in association with the preposition "ἐν" in 3:6, 11 (twice) (NAG). One of the usages in verse 11 refers to being baptized with the Holy Spirit and fire and the other refers to being baptized in water by John with the usage in verse 6 referring to being baptized by John in the river Jordan. The usage of "βαπτίζω" without an accompanying preposition, all usages relating to John's baptism, can be found in 3:13, 14, 16 (NAG).

In Matt the noun "βάπτισμα" can be found in 3:7, 21:25 (NAG). Both instances refer to John's baptism.

As mentioned in Explanatory Notes: Day 11, in the New Testament, "βαπτίζω" is followed by "ἐν" with the object being the "Holy Spirit" six times, the instances being found in Matt 3:11; Mark 1:8; Luke 3:16; John 1:33; Acts 1:5, 11:16 (NAG). In those same notes mention is made of the four times that "βαπτίζω" is followed by "ἐν" and has the object "water"—Matt 3:11; John 1:26, 31, 33, together with the two instances where "βαπτίζω" is followed by "ἐν" and has the object the river Jordan—Matt 3:6; Mark 1:5 (NAG). Similarly in Explanatory Notes: Day 11 reference is made to the five instances in the New Testament where "βαπτίζω" along with "εἰς" is followed by "the name"—Matt 28:19; Acts 8:16, 19:5; 1 Cor 1:13, 15 (NAG).

In the New Testament "βαπτίζω" is followed by "water" with that noun being in the dative case but without there being a preposition, four times, the instances being found in Mark 1:8; Luke 3:16; Acts 1:5, 11:16 (NAG).

Day 13

Objections Considered

Though impressed with the paraphrase that TS had provided for Matthew 28:18 to 20, on Friday, GB, after talking with friends, raises a number of objections. One relates to what the early Christians might have thought those verses meant. In response to this matter TS takes the opportunity to go into some detail about the baptismal beliefs and practices that were around in those early days. GB is intrigued with the variations in practice that existed and surprised at some of the associated beliefs.

TS: Hi there. Well, have you come up with some objections to understanding Matthew 28:19 metaphorically, in the way I tried to outline?

GB: I've thought a lot about what Matthew 28:19 might mean and I've talked to a few people. I've decided not to worry about keeping our conversations confidential. . . . I'm not saying you're wrong, but I've thought of a few questions.

TS: Okay. What's your first one?

GB: How do you know that "βαπτίζω" in Matthew 28:19 is metaphorical? Aren't you simply looking for another way to interpret the text?

TS: A good one. For starters, when "βαπτίζω" is used metaphorically in the Greek literature external to the New Testament, the writer never announces that the usage is metaphorical. Of course, one can tell when a simile is involved, by the presence of "like," "as" or an equivalent. But the vast majority of abstract usages in that literature are metaphorical in nature. The context indicates whether or not a metaphorical usage applies. Similarly, in the New Testament, it's the context that gives the clue, if there is an obvious clue, as to whether or not a metaphor is involved. In the case of Matthew 28:19, we've become so conditioned to seeing it as referring to a literal water baptism that the idea that it could be metaphorical tends to elude us. The same problem has occurred with our understanding of 1 Corinthians 15:29 where traditionally translations refer to "being baptized on behalf of the dead."

GB: I suppose the fact that there's been a tendency since ancient times to transliterate "βαπτιζω" and "βαπτισμα" in the New Testament to "baptize" and "baptism" or similar in other languages, hasn't helped either.

TS: I'm sure that's the case. But let me continue. I really think it's important to point out to people, what you've already become quite aware of, that there is no evidence in the Acts of the Apostles that anyone ever carried out a literal water baptism in the name of the Father and of the Son and of the Holy Spirit. This should warn the reader that the reference in Matthew 28:19 might not be a reference to a literal water baptism. As an alternative one should at least consider the possibility of a metaphorical usage. Furthermore, as I think we mentioned earlier on one of our days, a Greek reader or listener coming to the New Testament documents in the first century without being acquainted with Christian customs, would almost certainly find it odd that in the New Testament "βαπτιζω" was mainly used in connection with a religious ceremony. I'm using the words "religious" and "ceremony" in the way that perhaps he would see things. Furthermore, he would not be surprised to find metaphorical usages here and there even if that would not be the way he would describe them. As I indicated earlier and as you yourself became aware, about thirty of the one hundred or so known instances from early times up until the end of the first century CE are metaphorical. Furthermore, only one or at the very most only three or four relate in any way to a religious ceremony. My question to others is "What makes *you* think that "βαπτιζω" in Matthew 28:19 refers to a literal water ceremony?"

GB: But putting aside the Greek speaker of the first century CE who would be unfamiliar with Christian customs, the practice of "baptism" as a religious rite or ceremony is a very common one in the book of Acts. And there are other references to the practice of "baptism" in that same sense in the Gospels. And in the second chapter of the Acts of the Apostles Peter actually commands that people be baptized.

TS: I am not denying the extent to which baptisms are recorded both in the Gospels and in the Acts of the Apostles. Nor am I in any way or to any extent decrying their great value. As we discussed earlier, John the Immerser, for example, carried out many baptisms "of repentance for the forgiveness of sins." He was known as "the Immerser"! Somehow or other God directed him to baptize. He received his name from that practice which, to begin with, was peculiarly his. Later, during the ministry of Jesus, the disciples of Jesus baptized people, at one stage, baptizing even more than John the Immerser. Then of course, after Jesus went to the Father, Peter and others, as recorded in the Acts of the Apostles, baptized many, many people and not only Jews. In 1 Corinthians, Paul happens to indicate, while being concerned about factionalism, how the early believers in Corinth had been baptized. It was then, and today can be, a wonderful ceremony in which to be involved, both for those being baptized and for

Objections Considered

those who look on. I suggested earlier that the practice had become so common that when the Ethiopian Eunuch wished to become a believer, at the same time, he also wanted to be baptized, as though to experience baptism would be a natural thing.

GB: Well, it's understandable then that people should think that the reference in Matthew 28:19 is a reference to a literal water baptism.

TS: Yes and no. Almost all people of today certainly make that assumption and probably partly so because they're influenced in their judgement by the extent to which literal water baptisms are referred to in the Acts of the Apostles, in particular. But would the early readers of Matthew have come to the same conclusion? We need to recognize that Matthew and the Acts of the Apostles are quite separate documents. They stand independently of each other. To a large extent, Matthew has to be understood from its own perspective. Now if Luke had recorded something like Matthew 28:19 we might be tempted to think differently since Acts simply follows on from Luke and is Luke's document. We might have understood the relationship between what is called the Great Commission and the practice of baptism as recorded in Acts to be a close one. But Luke didn't record the Great Commission. In fact only Matthew makes reference to it. Furthermore, and I know I mentioned it again only a moment ago, in the Acts of the Apostles there is no evidence of what is commonly called the Trinitarian baptismal formula, I am sure you know what I mean, ever being used. Matthew 28:19 stands out as different to anything recorded in the Acts of the Apostles and different to anything recorded about baptism anywhere else in the New Testament. Don't worry! I will refer to Peter's address in chapter 2 of the book of Acts, later on. I won't forget.

GB: Now that you've again mentioned the "Trinitarian formula," don't you think that what Matthew records concerning the real water baptism of Jesus, betrays a Trinitarian theme? Jesus is being baptized, the Spirit descends upon him, as or like a dove, and God the Father speaks from heaven declaring that this is his Son with whom he is well pleased. The record of this event is located very near the beginning of the Gospel. Isn't the mention of the Son, the Father and the Spirit, at the beginning of his Gospel, being mirrored by Matthew at the end of his Gospel? Aren't the two accounts like parentheses? I have to be honest. I didn't think of this myself. The idea was suggested to me by one of my friends with whom I talked yesterday.

TS: That's interesting. I hadn't really thought of that. Hmm. Of course, God is not mentioned at the baptism of Jesus, as the Father. And there are other places in Matthew where there is some mention of the Father, Son and Holy Spirit, but not exactly by the use of those names or titles. In Matthew 10:20 Jesus speaks about the Spirit of your Father—admittedly it's not a direct reference to the Father, as the Father of Jesus. Then again, in Matthew 12:18 Jesus, quoting from Isaiah chapter 42, speaks of God and his servant, his beloved, upon whom he will put his Spirit. And later in that twelfth chapter of Matthew it's recorded that Jesus, speaking of the matter of blasphemy against the Spirit, says, "If it is by the Spirit of God that I cast out demons, then the kingdom of God has come upon you." You could even have referred to the account in Matthew, earlier than the baptism of Jesus, where it's recorded that Mary had become pregnant with him, the one to be named Jesus, by means of the Holy Spirit, or literally, "a holy spirit." The fact that the three, the Father, the Son and the Holy Spirit are mentioned in one way or another here and there throughout Matthew is perhaps not unexpected. I think I'll just leave it at that. By the way, I know I referred to the Trinitarian formula but the idea of there being a formula can be misleading. It makes what Matthew reports what Jesus said to be too formalistic, too legalistic.

GB: I take your point. My next question concerns baptismal beliefs held by early believers who came along after New Testament times. Did they think that Jesus commanded people to be baptized, or at least, that in the New Testament there is an explicit command by Jesus given to his original disciples to baptize people?

TS: I think that many, if not most, probably did, though it's difficult to tell exactly what is being said in some cases. And in most instances we're being informed about baptismal practices being carried out at the time of writing, not directly about what it was believed that Jesus said. Justin Martyr, writing in about the middle of the second century CE, in what is generally called his *Apology 1*, refers to people receiving a washing with water "in the name of God the Father and Lord of all and of our Savior Jesus Christ and of the Holy Spirit." Whether or not he's referring to that expression being uttered over a person being baptized at the moment of baptism is difficult to know. He follows this statement with "Over him who chooses to be born again and who has repented of his sins, there is pronounced the name of God the Father and Lord of all." During the baptismal ceremony at the time of the baptism, there may have been a reference only to the name of the Father or to the name of all three or indeed both types of statements may have been made. It's just difficult to tell what actually was said and we don't have an explicit word here about Jesus commanding this or that.

GB: What about other early Christian writers?

TS: There are references to a baptizing in water, in the name of the Father and of the Son and of the Holy Spirit in what is called *The Acts of Peter*. It's believed that the document was written late in the second century CE. There is another document, called *The Didache* where there is a directive to baptize in the name of the Father and of the Son and of the Holy Spirit in running water. Further advice is given in the case where running water is not available. In that situation the water should be cold but if not cold then warm. Then, if neither cold nor warm water is available, water should be poured on the head three times in the name of the Father and of the Son and of the Holy Spirit. There seems to be a gradation of what is considered desirable. At the top of the list, an amount of running water sufficient to enable full immersion seems to be the most desirable. Next, the same situation, but with "still" cold water being used. Thirdly the same situation but using "still" warm water and fourthly, where water enabling full immersion is not available, water should be poured three times on the

Objections Considered

head. Some argue that *The Didache* was written late in the first century CE, others that it was written in the second or even third centuries while there is also some contention that various sections were written at different times.

GB: Pouring water on a head three times is interesting. I guess that that was to reflect the three persons.

TS: I suppose so. The idea that something had to be done three times however doesn't seem to have been uncommon. In a strange story told about Paul in a work called *The Acts of Paul and Thecla*, perhaps written late in the second century, Paul is supposed to have immersed a lion that wished to be baptized, three times.

GB: Weird! Is there any evidence that some people baptized only in the name of Jesus or the Lord Jesus or Jesus Christ?

TS: An interesting question. In fact in the story of Paul baptizing the lion, just referred to, Paul baptizes the lion three times in the name of Jesus Christ. In that same work, a woman, Thecla, is supposed to have baptized herself, just before her death in an arena, with the cry, "In the name of Jesus Christ, I baptize myself on the last day (of my life)." In *The Shepherd of Hermas*, a work written, perhaps early in the second century, there is a reference to a person in baptism, bearing the name of the Son of God. Even in *The Didache* there is a reference to those baptized in the Lord's name.

GB: Are there two different traditions here?

TS: I think we're getting somewhat off the track, but yes, some have argued that probably the so-called formula referring to the trinity was first used in Syria, perhaps where Matthew's Gospel first circulated, but that in the West, the "formula" only came to be acceptable in the eighth century or thereabouts. Indeed it's been claimed that it wasn't even until many centuries later than this that the expression referring to the three persons of the trinity became the accepted formulation throughout most of the world.

GB: Do you think people were being torn between the expressions used in the Acts of the Apostles and what is reported in Matthew 28:19?

TS: I don't know. But it's a possibility. However, the evidence we've just perused does suggest that some did not take what Jesus said in Matthew 28:19 completely at face value, even if the text was understood to be a reference to water baptism. But back to your original question! Did early believers, post New Testament times, did they think that Jesus actually commanded his disciples to baptize people? As I said, I think so, though there aren't many references by early writers indicating that they explicitly understood that Jesus commanded such. However, Irenaeus in his work *Against Heresies*, probably written in the late second century, explicitly connects the Matthew 28:19 text with the idea that the disciples were given "the power of regeneration" by Christ. His reference to "regeneration" fairly clearly indicates that he had water baptism in mind.

And Tertullian, early in the third century, in his work, *On Baptism* links "the necessity of baptism" to what Jesus said in that same text.

GB: Why do you think that a reference to "regeneration" implies that Irenaeus had a water baptism in mind?

TS: Well, it was his belief that being baptized was connected with being regenerated, being born again! It's intriguing to find so many of the early Christian writings, when referring to water baptism, associating the rite with "being born again." I suppose they could appeal to texts such as the one recorded in Titus, a letter written by Paul to a fellow of that name—"He (God) has saved us by the washing of regeneration and renewal of the Holy Spirit." The word translated "washing" might have suggested to some that Paul had in mind at that point, "water baptism." Then there's the word, "water" in the statement that Jesus made to Nicodemus, as recorded in chapter three of John's Gospel—"Unless a man is born of water and of the Spirit, he cannot enter the kingdom of God." Irenaeus seems to have taken the Greek word for "water" there to be a reference to "water baptism." This understanding dominated the thinking of many of the early and even later Christian writers when it came to their understanding of salvation.

GB: Meaning that undergoing the rite or ceremony was essential for salvation?

TS: Yes. Some today have the same view. I mentioned that earlier.

GB: I understood that when Jesus said, "Unless a man is born of water and of the Spirit" he was referring to firstly being born physically and secondly being born spiritually. Nicodemus had asked the question, "Can a man enter his mother's womb a second time and be born?" and Jesus took up his reference to being born of a woman by making a reference to being born of water, that is, the "waters" associated with the beginning of a physical birth. At least that's what I think Jesus was referring to.

TS: I think that that perspective makes more sense than the other. Jesus follows these words, with "That which is born of the flesh is flesh and that which is born of the Spirit is spirit." I don't think what Jesus says has anything to do with baptism. It's interesting that in the previous verse the Greek doesn't have any definite articles—it's simply "of water" and "of spirit"—although we tend to translate the last part—"of the Spirit." But in the verse just mentioned there are two definite articles—"the flesh" and "the Spirit." I suspect that the way John is reporting what Jesus said has Jesus contrasting firstly "water" with "spirit"—small "s." But that sort of understanding would only be on the surface of what he is getting at. While his reference to "water" would still be a reference to the physical entity, water, the "spirit" was ultimately a reference to the spiritual entity, the person, "the Spirit." I think John makes it clear that Jesus is indeed referring to "the Spirit" when he then compares being born of "the flesh" with being born of "the Spirit." However, understanding the significance of the presence or absence of the definite article in Greek is tricky!

GB: Are there any references in the Old Testament where the two terms, "water" and "spirit," are closely connected?

TS: Now that you mention it, there is a passage in the book of Ezekiel that links the two terms together. I think it's in chapter thirty six. Wait a minute. I'll just look it up. . . . Here it is. It's God speaking. He says, "I will sprinkle clean water on you and make you clean from all your idols"—verse 25, then, "I will give you a new heart—verse 26 and then, "I will put my spirit within you"—verse 27. Jesus did say to Nicodemus that he should have known what he, Jesus, was talking about. Perhaps Jesus was making a reference to something like that passage in Ezekiel. Anyway, surely the reference to "water" there is metaphorical and whether Jesus was making a reference to the Ezekiel text or referring to the birth of a baby, I don't think he was making any reference to a water rite.

GB: I agree. And I guess that when Paul wrote to Titus about, "washing," "regeneration" and "renewal" he was probably referring to "cleansing from sin," "becoming an entirely new person" and "being transformed by the working of the Holy Spirit," respectively—somewhat reflective of the Ezekiel texts. Again, nothing to do with a water rite.

TS: I think you're right.

GB: Anyway, back to my concerns! In spite of what you think Jesus is saying in Matthew 28:19, it appears that most, if not all, of these early Christian writers probably thought that Jesus commanded that an actual water rite be performed, whether or not there was agreement about what should be said or indicated in such a ceremony.

TS: Yes, I think you're right. But before we decide that their understanding must be the correct one, we must keep in mind what some of their understandings were. Firstly we've already mentioned that some thought that undergoing the ceremony or ritual was associated closely with being "born again." The writer of *The Shepherd of Hermas*, along with many others, similarly believed that a literal water baptism was essential for salvation. In another work, *The Epistle of Barnabas*, perhaps written in the second century, the view is expressed that the ceremony brings with it the forgiveness of sins. In *The Shepherd of Hermas* however, forgiveness is restricted to the forgiveness of past sins. In a document, *The Gospel of Nicodemus*, compiled perhaps around the fifth or sixth century from earlier works, reference is made to certain dead people—righteous people—having been baptized by Jesus. The implication is that those dead people needed to be baptized. It was essential. There is a similar sentiment expressed in *The Apocalypse of Peter*, perhaps written early in the second century, and *The Epistle of the Apostles*, possibly composed in the mid-second century. Fasting prior to baptism is seen to be a necessity in a work entitled, *The Acts of John*, perhaps written in the latter half of the second century. The same is held to be true according to Justin Martyr in his *Apology 1*, written in the middle of the second century, and also according to

The Didache. Clement of Rome in his *2 Clement* seems to refer to baptism as a "seal," perhaps the idea being that at one's baptism one is sealed with the Holy Spirit. In *The Shepherd of Hermas* the claim is made that in the ceremony a person is sealed with the name of the Son of God. Justin Martyr in his *Apology 1* seems to refer to baptism as "enlightenment" although he may have viewed the enlightenment as having occurred as a consequence of the instruction received concerning Christ. Writing early in the second century, Ignatius in *To the Smyrnaeans*, a letter to people called the Smyrnaeans, stipulates that only a bishop or someone approved by such should perform baptisms. He's probably mainly concerned with the matter of order. The lion in *The Acts of Paul and Thecla*, after being immersed three times, speaks to Paul and says "Grace be with you."

GB: Wow! . . . I was going to suggest that given that these writers wrote relatively close to the time when Matthew's Gospel was written, that their view, apparently being that Matthew 28:19 refers to a water ceremony, is more likely to be correct than the view you're offering. However I am now somewhat reluctant to make that suggestion. What is particularly worrying to me is not so much some of those things you've just mentioned and the great variety in beliefs that were around at the time, but what appears to be an extraordinary emphasis on the necessity of undergoing the rite in order to obtain salvation.

TS: Don't get me wrong. The authors weren't denying that there was a role for "faith," the necessity of the grace of God, the reality of the cross of Christ—his death for sinners, and the power of his resurrection. It's just that as part of the theological mix there was this notion of the absolute necessity of undergoing a water rite. If you understood Matthew 28:19 as a demand that a water rite be practiced, then perhaps it's understandable that you also saw the undergoing of this rite as necessary for salvation. To be fair it's also true that in these writings, the rite is associated with repentance—a turning from the past towards the beginning of a new life of righteousness. One of the problems that arose however was the question of what sins were forgiven. Were only the sins before being baptized forgiven? As I said, that's a view expressed in *The Shepherd of Hermas*. If so, what could be done about sins committed after baptism? And what of those who "fell away" and then wished to return to the faith? Could, should, a person be baptized a second time? These were matters that for the early Christian writers sometimes assumed immense importance.

GB: From what you've said, it's obvious that in those early days there wasn't one simple view, acceptable to all, as to what should be said, what should be done or what happened at a baptism.

TS: Yes, and of course it's the same today. One thing that does seem to have been the norm, however, was the requirement for the person wishing to be baptized to undergo some form of instruction. I mentioned such instruction when referring to Justin Martyr's view of enlightenment.

GB: What was involved?

TS: They were instructed in many matters, particularly about the need for repentance. An example of such instruction is given in considerable detail in a work entitled, *The Apostolic Tradition*, ostensibly written by a certain Hippolytus of Rome in the early part of the third century. Though there is dispute about authorship and the authenticity of certain parts, it's worth some consideration. In one section there is a reference to candidates for baptism being asked three questions. The first relates to faith in God, the second to faith in Christ and the third to faith in the Holy Spirit. Each time after answering, "I believe" the candidate's head was dipped under the water. One could interpret this practice as suggesting that something like, "being immersed into, being taught all that pertains to, the Father and the Son and the Holy Spirit"—what I am suggesting is part of the kernel of Matthew 28:19—was in the minds of those who introduced the practice and those who continued the practice!

GB: Could it have been that when Jesus uttered those words recorded in Matthew 28:19 that he had in mind his disciples both immersing people by means of a literal water baptism and immersing them in who the Father, the Son and the Holy Spirit is by instructing them?

TS: I suppose he could have but there would still appear to be an inconsistency between what is recorded in the Acts of the Apostles and what is recorded in Matthew. In the Acts of the Apostles, whatever information people were given prior to being baptized, and that varied depending on the circumstances, the baptism itself focused on Jesus. People were immersed by means of a water baptism in his name, well either the name "Jesus Christ" or "the Lord Jesus," regardless of whether we understand these words to have been formally recited at their baptism or alternatively, words that simply indicated what that baptism signified.

GB: By that last statement you meant that either those words were used when people were being baptized or that those words simply indicated that the people being baptized were associating themselves with this Jesus as the Christ or as the Lord?

TS: Yes. Sorry that I didn't make that clearer. By being baptized in the circumstances as recorded, people were indicating that they were now associating themselves with Jesus but whether those actual words, "in the name of Jesus Christ" or "in the name of the Lord Jesus" were recited at the baptism is the question. I think, and most people seem to agree, that those actual words, of course in another language—not English—were in fact used! When Peter addresses a cripple, begging at the temple entrance, he says "In the name of Jesus Christ of Nazareth, walk." It appears that he uses "in the name of Jesus Christ" directly in speech.

GB: Okay. I mentioned that although I was thinking of raising the objection that surely these early writers would know better than us on how to interpret Matthew 28:19, their heavy reliance on the rite for salvation, put me off. But I've also been thinking of that letter that Paul wrote to the Galatians. You mentioned that he probably wrote it only a few years after they had first heard the Gospel. If the Galatians in just a few years were getting it so wrong, why should I think that people, decades, even a century or more removed from the writing of Matthew's Gospel, would necessarily get it right? And the more I think about it, even though, according to you they would've appealed to the grace of God, I think that they were really undermining the grace of God. I wonder if some of those writers had ever seriously reflected on Paul's letter to the Galatians, his letter to the church at Colossae or his letter to the church at Rome.

TS: I guess we all have a hunger for relying on what we do—a desire to perform something or other to win God's approval—rather than to have to admit our need for dependence on God alone, his mercy and his abundant grace, his overwhelming kindness.

GB: We took a long time dealing with the last objection!

TS: Yes. And perhaps we should call it a day. Today has been a Marathon. See you tomorrow? Would that be okay? Oh and by the way I haven't forgotten that we should look at what Peter said on the day of Pentecost.

GB: Neither have I. Tomorrow it is!

Objections Considered

EXPLANATORY NOTES: DAY 13

References to the name or names invoked in early Christian baptisms can be found in Ferguson, *Baptism*, page numbers in parentheses, as follows—Justin Martyr, *Apology 1*, 61.3, 13. (239); *The Acts of Peter* V (228); *The Didache*, 7.1, 3 (202–03); *The Acts of Paul and Thecla* (230–31); *The Shepherd of Hermas*, 3.3, 7 (215).

Whitaker in "The History of the Baptismal Formula," writes "It is a fact . . . that the literature of the Latin Church provides no clear and incontestable reference to our modern formula earlier than *De Cognitione Baptismi* of Hildephonsus of Toledo, which was written at some date before his death in 667; and the earliest Roman reference is in a letter written by Pope Gregory in the year 726."

Duck, in *Gender*, in chapter 6: "The History of the Baptismal Formula," 123–37, writes "Only after eight centuries of the Christian Era was the baptismal formula 'in the name of the Father and of the Son and of the Holy Spirit' used in Christian baptisms throughout the world. Almost as many centuries passed again before the Western church explicitly required the formula." She also believes that the Syrian churches were probably the first to baptize with a declarative Trinitarian formula and that Matthew and *The Didache* were probably written in Syria. She accepts as possible the proposition that what she calls the Syrian formula may have travelled to the West by way of Alexandria into Spain but not before the year 538. She also claims that the evidence is such that the first time the formula is used liturgically in Rome is in the year 726.

References linking the practice of water baptism with Matt 28:19 can be found in— Irenaeus. *Against Heresies*. Book III, 17.1—see also Ferguson, *Baptism*, 307, and Tertullian, *On Baptism*, 13—see also Ferguson, *Baptism*, 339 and http://www.newadvent.org/fathers/0321.htm.

Ferguson, *Baptism*, (page numbers in parentheses) attests to an association of water baptism with regeneration in the writings of Irenaeus (304–07), Justin Martyr (240), and Clement of Alexandria (309–11). The references he cites include—Irenaeus, *Against Heresies*, Book I, 21.1, Book III, 17.1, Book V, 15.3; Irenaeus, *Fragment* 34; Irenaeus, *The Demonstration of the Apostolic Preaching*, Demonstrations 3, 7; Justin Martyr, *Apology 1*, 61.1; Clement of Alexandria, *Paedagogus*, Book I, chapters 6, 12.

The texts, "He has saved us by the washing of regeneration and renewal of the Holy Spirit" and "Unless a man is born of water and of the Spirit, he cannot enter the kingdom of God" can be found in Titus 3:5; John 3:5 (NIV) respectively.

Carson, in *The Gospel According to John*, 191–95, discusses several understandings of the phrase, "born of water and the Spirit" as it occurs in John 3:5.

References to various beliefs, held by early Christians, associated with baptism can be found in Ferguson, *Baptism* (page numbers in parentheses)—*The Shepherd of Hermas*

(215–19), *The Epistle of Barnabas* (213–14), *The Gospel of Nicodemus* (106–07, 226–27), *The Apocalypse of Peter* (225), *The Epistle of the Apostles* (225–27), *The Acts of John* (232), Justin Martyr (239, 241), *The Didache* (202), Clement of Rome in *2 Clement* (207–08), Ignatius, *To the Smyrnaeans* (209), and *The Acts of Paul and Thecla* (231).

The passage that TS cites from *The Apostolic Tradition* can be found in section 20.12–18. See also, Ferguson, *Baptism*, 327–33.

The reference to Peter addressing the cripple outside the temple can be found in Acts 3:6 (NIV).

Day 14

More Objections Considered

GB is not absolutely convinced that TS's understanding of Matthew 28:19 is correct and raises even more objections. One relates to what the reformers thought. Another concerns the way that baptism in the Acts of the Apostles seemed to be treated as a necessity. Of particular interest to GB is what Peter said on the Day of Pentecost.

TS: Hi. I enjoyed yesterday's session. I know we got off the track a little but I thought we had a profitable time. Have you got any other objections to the idea that "βαπτιζω" in Matthew 28:19 might be correctly understood metaphorically?

GB: Well, yes, one in particular. It's sort of related to the last one—about early Christians getting it wrong. I've learnt from my friends that when the reformers came on the scene, from time to time, they relied on what some of those early Christian writers said in order to back up their claims.

TS: I think they believed they had to do that in order to undercut some of what later people, popes and others, had declared to be the truth and what was being pronounced as the truth in their own age, They wanted to argue from Scripture of course but if they could convince people that their views coincided with those held by early Christians then that would add credence to their own position.

GB: I can understand that. And the reformers, under the good hand of God, were so significant in delivering us from what they rightly saw as man-made religion and a reliance on works rather than trusting Christ alone. How come they also didn't understand baptism correctly, if what you're suggesting is indeed correct?

TS: I don't think that baptism was one of the main concerns of the reformers, though they certainly found themselves needing to justify the baptism of infants. And anyway, sometimes we expect far too much of them. What they did was extraordinary as it was. They had to battle against a large number of opponents. There was so much theological and political opposition. To argue against practices and beliefs that had been embedded for centuries in their Christian world was to stand out as a type of revolutionary. Understandably, many people thought that they had to be wrong. Recognizing how great their difficulties were, why should we imagine that they "got it all right"? And of course they didn't. They couldn't even agree with each other! And of course once they went public—they could not avoid going public—it would've been very difficult for them to have changed their basic positions, particularly those they had strongly held to, to begin with.

GB: That's a difficulty we all experience, even if "going public" means, simply "letting your friends know."

TS: And, similar to what we can experience in our world, the more that each reform "group" entered into debate the more likely it would've been that the members of that "group" would've become more settled in their thinking that they had the truth. However, the extent to which they disagreed with each other should've made them somewhat cautious. Perhaps for some it did. Yet, for example, in the matter of the significance of the "Eucharist," "Holy Communion" or the "Lord's Supper," various names for what some would say were supposed to be the same thing, the reformers Luther, Calvin, Zwingli and those that followed them, sharply disagreed. And there was a group called the Anabaptists who were persecuted, in part, because of their insistence on adult baptism, a baptism involving a re-baptism for those who had been baptized as infants. The "ana" of "Anabaptist" signifies, "again"—the reference being to "being baptized again."

GB: And that was regarded as a particularly bad thing?

TS: Yes, obviously. The name "Anabaptist" was given to a complex group of people whose individual beliefs differed enormously though the need for "adult baptism" was a belief held in common. I think that the opposition to them was as great as it was because they were regarded as extremists. By and large the mainstream reformers existed in a society that was regarded as Christian and it seems that a prevailing view was that infants came into that Christian society by means of baptism. I mentioned something like this in our earlier discussions. Baptism was regarded as a necessity for entrance into that society. And relying on early Christian thinkers who wrote in the first few centuries after Christ, in my view, didn't help either. We live in a very blessed set of circumstances. We have the intellectual and religious freedom to investigate the truth for ourselves without the sort of pressure on us that they had to endure. And we have access to more manuscripts of the Scriptures, and I think a better understanding of the Greek and Hebrew languages. Some documents available to the reformers may now be lost to us but overall I'd have thought that we have far more information on a range of relevant matters associated with the ancient world.

GB: It seems to me, that given our greater knowledge and the easy access to sources that the modern computer age provides, we owe it to ourselves and others to work very hard at trying to sort out error from truth, being cautious not to become over-confident, knowing how prone we are as sinful human beings to want to glorify ourselves. The reformers wanted to rely on Scripture as the final source for truth and we must do the same!

TS: That's obviously the way to go. For theological and historical reasons we *must* examine our beliefs and practices from time to time, in the light of Scripture, more often than we tend to do. Theologically, we understand that we are sinful and get things muddled. Historically, we learn that we often get things wrong despite the best of motives. We're not only sinful but also simply deficient in knowledge and lacking in the wisdom to know how best to deal with various issues. Certainly we can be grateful to God for teaching us the fundamental truths concerning the person and work of Christ, his birth, death, resurrection and coming again. But we can never guarantee that we've "got everything right."

GB: And don't I know it. Now, as I mentioned yesterday, I've been talking to a few people about what we've been discussing and one of them said "Why would God allow us to be wrong in our understanding of Matthew 28:19, if indeed we're wrong, for such a long time?" How would you reply to that?

TS: One could've asked the reformers the same question. And presumably that question was asked as a counter to some of the reformation claims. God hasn't guaranteed that errors are only ever around for short periods of a time. Short time or long time, errors when discovered need to be understood as such. Or to put it another way, we should always be open to being corrected for our own sakes, for the sake of those who are influenced by us and for the cause of the glory of Christ. There is no satisfactory substitute for the truth. Error, one way or another, subtly or not so subtly cloaked as the truth, significant in its effect on our lives or not thought to be all that significant, should give way to the truth. And God has determined that we're under obligation to search for and pursue the truth.

GB: But how come when we do get things wrong that we later often have great difficulty recognizing that we are in error? I know I can come up with some answers to my own question, even from my own experience, but what do you think?

TS: I suspect that there are a number of reasons why it's difficult for us to admit we've got something wrong. For starters, it can be humbling, even to admit to ourselves, that we were wrong. This is particularly so, if for a long time we've held on to a belief that we've regarded as important. It's even more difficult to change our views if we've gone public on the issue. We mentioned that a moment ago. Then, forgetting about the general public, there are our friends. You also mentioned them. We don't normally want to be seen to be different to them. We don't want to be offside with them. We might think we could lose their friendship or support. And even when we try to counteract these types of influences, once we've become used to a certain way of thinking, we might find it "implausible" that an alternative could be correct—implausible for lots of reasons—too many others believe to the contrary, we've become used to how to understand particular texts of scripture or we've lived much of our life in accordance with a particular tradition. The idea that something is implausible is an intellectual problem.

GB: I hadn't thought of the notion of plausibility. "Implausibility" is something you can't put your finger on easily but it's sometimes there in the back of your mind when you're considering what you regard as an "odd" position.

TS: Yes. Polanyi, a physical chemist and a philosopher of science gave some prominence to the matter of plausibility in some of his writings. He even cited a case in his own field. He had a particular theory about the nature of certain chemical reactions involving a solid surface. The theory that he proposed was rejected by the relevant scientific community and later he argued that it was right to do so because his theory was, he considered understandably, regarded as implausible, by that community, at that time. It needed the passage of many years before what had once been regarded as implausible then became plausible. Opponents to his perspective needed time for new information to become available before they were willing to concede that his understanding rather than the older prevailing one was more likely to be "correct."

GB: I suspect that your particular view is likely to run into the same problem but hopefully some of the information you "have up your sleeve" might help. One last question! At least I think it will be my last question. Putting Matthew 28:19 to one side, Peter commanded people on the day of Pentecost to repent and be baptized. Why wouldn't that command still hold sway today? You did say you were going to discuss that speech of his.

TS: Correct. However, we might consider not only Acts 2:38, the text you're referring to, but Acts 10:48 and 22:16 as well.

GB: Acts 10:48 and 22:16? I'm pretty sure you've mentioned the first text before, maybe both of them. Let me check. . . . The first refers to Peter commanding Cornelius and his group to be baptized. Yes we did discuss that text. . . . The second refers to Paul recalling how Ananias told him to rise and be baptized. I think you've mentioned that once or twice. I can see how they're similar to what Peter said on the day of Pentecost, "Repent and be baptized." They each involve commands.

TS: It's interesting that the translations you've just referred to have this note of command built into them, isn't it?

GB: Well, they obviously seem to be commands. Take Acts 10:48 for example. Peter commanded Cornelius and his group to be baptized.

TS: The Greek word translated "commanded" there is "προσέταξεν" (*prosetaxen*). It certainly can mean "commanded" but "enjoined" is also a possibility. Having asked the rhetorical question, "Can anyone forbid water for baptizing these people who have received the Holy Spirit as we have?" it would not be odd if Peter then "enjoined" them, "invited" them to be baptized. The translator has the option to translate the word one way or another.

GB: What about Acts 22:16?

TS: Here the relevant Greek word is "βαπτίσαι" (*baptisai*). In Acts 9:18 where Paul's baptism is first reported on, as told by Luke himself, it simply says that "Paul rose and was baptized." In Acts 22:16 Paul himself reports that Ananias said to him "Rise, be baptized and wash away your sins, calling on his name, the Lord, the Righteous One." "Be baptized" and "wash away" are *both* imperatives. "Rise" is a participle that "hangs off" the imperatives. From what I've said earlier you would understand that I don't believe that the action of his being baptized washed away his sins. He was cleansed as a result of his "calling on his name," that is, the name "the Lord." Of course being baptized could be understood symbolically as a thorough washing—a cleansing ceremony—and so his baptism could readily be associated with the idea of the washing away of his sins.

GB: I agree but surely he was called upon to undergo baptism!

TS: Yes, but "called upon" doesn't have the same "strength" as "demanded." Did you mean to say "called upon"?

GB: I did, sort of, but perhaps I wasn't really thinking. By phrasing it that way I realize that an imperative can vary in its "strength." I take it that this is true in Greek as well as in English?

TS: Well, the imperative mood in English usage and in Greek usage is not the same, but variation in "strength," as you put it, is possible in both. The imperative "ἀπόλυσαι" (*apolusai*)—"wash away," the other imperative involved, doesn't imply that Ananias was commanding Paul "You Paul, wash away your sins." It more likely has the sense of "Paul, have your sins washed away by calling on his name." Both "βαπτίσαι" and "ἀπόλυσαι" in Acts 22:16 can be understood in such a way that a strong sense of "demand" is not entailed.

GB: I get the point. By the way I notice that like the four instances in Acts of people being baptized in the name of "Jesus the Christ" or "the Lord Jesus," calling on the name here, also refers to Jesus, but here the title used is simply, "Lord." There is certainly no reference here, as with those four texts, to an expression involving all three persons of the trinity!

TS: No. Quite right.... Let's now have a look at Acts 2:38. You've raised it but I said I would get around to it. As with Acts 22:16, an imperative is used—"βαπτισθήτω" (*baptisthētō*). What is interesting is that while the "repent" of "Repent and be baptized each one of you" is second person plural, the "be baptized" is third person singular. The sense seemingly being conveyed is that the crowd is in mind with respect to "repent"—they are all being told to repent, but that each individual member of the crowd is in mind with respect to "being baptized." The "each one of you"—"ἔσκατος ὑμῶν" (*eskatos humōn*)—that follows "βαπτισθητω" confirms that idea. Peter makes this statement in response to the question asked by the crowd—"Brothers, what shall we do?" He gives them the answer—"Repent all of you and be baptized each one of you."

GB: Well, you must admit that repentance was absolutely necessary. Doesn't that mean that "being baptized" was also a necessity?

TS: Yes and No. One of course would answer "yes" without any "no" if, in spite of everything we've talked about, one thought that God places at least one ceremony, if not more, in the category of "must do." Yes, even in spite of Galatians. Let me explain why I think the answer is "Yes, it was necessary." from a different point of view, without claiming that it was *absolutely* necessary. John the Immerser and the disciples of Jesus had baptized many people. There is no evidence that others had done what they had been doing. In other washing ceremonies, people immersed themselves. Furthermore, theirs was basically a one-off baptism unlike most other "washings." And now, remember how in John's case many came from Judea and Jerusalem to see him. "Multitudes were baptized by him." Zechariah, his father, had been told, "He will turn *many* of the sons of Israel to the Lord their God." And what John said to people is summed up in the Gospels in the statement, "Repent and be baptized for the forgiveness of sins." Later on, the disciples of Jesus were baptizing even more people than John was baptizing. Baptism was a feature of the ministry of the believers. It was automatic therefore that on the Day of Pentecost that Peter should utter very similar words. Baptism, a unique ceremony had become the accepted ceremony to accompany one's repentance. That's why I think the answer is "Yes, it was necessary." while holding back on stating that it was *absolutely* necessary. The ceremony, such a distinctive and highly symbolic ceremony, had become the hall mark of a person's repentance, like a badge, both in the ministry of John and the ministry of the disciples under Jesus, the one who came after John. It was to continue as a distinctive and wonderfully symbolic ceremony accompanying the repentance of those who would now become the followers of Jesus in the apostolic age. You became a believer? You were baptized! Although perhaps we should note that not every account in the book of Acts of a person believing is followed by a mention of their being baptized.

GB: Yes and I see what you're saying.

TS: It's a little like the situation of a man who has been going out with a woman for some time but who hasn't got around to proposing. His friend says to him, "Make up your mind, marry the girl and have a wedding." Having a wedding is customary in our world, no matter how complex or simple the affair. However, the marriage is what is fundamental. The wedding is customary. Is the wedding a necessity? "Yes." says anybody who values customs both for themselves and others. And what had become an established custom—that of "baptism"—was no exception. The answer has to be "Yes, it was necessary." What can look like a demand can in fact be more like a call to conform to a well-known, distinctive and very significant custom.

GB: And so in what way can the answer be "No."? I think you are going to say "No" to the idea that it was or is *absolutely* necessary.

TS: Yes. The answer has to be "No," for example, for the person who has no opportunity to be baptized, like the thief who died alongside of Jesus but who asked to be remembered by Jesus when Jesus would take possession of his kingdom. I think we've mentioned that before. The answer could also be "No." for the person who doesn't understand the custom or who considers that in being baptized others will badly misunderstand the Gospel for whatever reason. A person who is in the position of baptizing others might also say, "No." if he considers that the custom is being abused, misused or misunderstood. However for Peter on the Day of Pentecost there were no such problems. But, in the final analysis the answer can be "No." because being baptized, undergoing a ceremony, is not fundamental to the gospel, just as having a wedding is not fundamental to being married.

GB: What do you mean by the custom being abused, misused or misunderstood?

TS: The sort of thing that Paul meant when he wrote 1 Corinthians. At the beginning of that letter he makes a strong appeal to the believers that "by the name of our Lord Jesus Christ" they all be in agreement, that they be united in the same mind and judgment and that there should be no divisions amongst them. As evidence of what, to the contrary, seemed to be happening, he referred to what had been reported to him—namely, that they had been quarreling with each other. "One is saying I am of Paul, another, I am of Apollos, another I am of Cephas, and another, I am of Christ." We talked about this text a few days ago.

GB: Yes I remember.

TS: Paul then asks, rhetorically, "Is Christ divided? Was Paul crucified for you? Or were you baptized in the name of Paul?" Having mentioned the matter of being baptized, and as I tried to argue, it's just possible that he might not have been referring to literal water baptism at this point, rather the idea of being thoroughly instructed in his teaching, he then says, "I am thankful that I baptized none of you." I think he's certainly referring to a literal water baptism in this last remark.

GB: But he did say that he had actually baptized some.

TS: Yes, in his thorough going honesty, he goes on to say "Except Crispus and Gaius." And then, as if he just at that point remembered, he says, "I also baptized the household of Stephanas." Next, to indicate how he's trying to recollect exactly whom he had baptized, he says, "Beyond that, I do not know whether I baptized anyone else."

GB: He's really trying to distance himself from having baptized people, isn't he?

TS: Yes, though he's not speaking disparagingly of the water ceremony itself.

GB: Is he simply saying that he didn't baptize many so that only very few involved in those factions would be able to claim that sort of link with him?

TS: Well, in part, yes. But his argument wouldn't have had much strength if he didn't think that it would also have been helpful if others, like, Cephas and Apollos, could also say the same sort of thing. Or, at least, like him, distance themselves from the idea that being baptized was a fundamental issue.

GB: You think it's fairly clear that Paul was indicating that he didn't think that being baptized was all that important?

TS: I suppose that if the circumstances had been different, Paul wouldn't have written anything about his being thankful that he had baptized only a few. However, look at how he concluded this part of his letter, "For Christ did not send me to baptize but to preach the gospel, and not with eloquent wisdom, lest the cross of Christ be emptied of its power." Preaching the gospel, the gospel of the cross of Christ, was what was essential, not baptism.

GB: I think someone I was talking to me said that Tertullian in his work, *On Baptism* had a response to those who appealed to this text.

TS: Tertullian was not the last or probably the first who found that he had to make some response to what Paul says here. Tertullian seems to argue that Paul, though concerned with what was happening at Corinth, in lining up preaching against baptizing, was merely indicating that preaching comes before baptism. I really don't think that that's the plain reading of the text. I am not saying that Paul is opposed to the custom of baptism but that he's indicating its lesser importance compared to the preaching of the gospel. But additionally and more importantly, I am arguing that he distances himself from the custom in such a way that makes it clear that he does not regard it as an absolute necessity. If he had regarded it as a necessity, surely he could not have said what he did. He would've found some other way of arguing against the divisions about which he was so concerned.

GB: Okay, I understand what you're saying. These days, I haven't really believed that baptism was an absolute necessity, though I may have had some doubts, but I thought I'd mention the issues that some of my friends raised with me. I think the message of Galatians makes it fairly clear. Whatever customs we have, even ones that have arisen historically under the good hand of God, they are customs. They have no advantage in themselves. It's the grace of God that counts and faith must be our response. It's the fruit of the Spirit that God desires, not our conformity to this or that so-called "regulation." Why don't people read and ponder Galatians and Colossians and yes, Romans as well, and indeed all of Scripture more and more? I said something like this earlier.

TS: I wish there were many people who could hear what you're saying. . . . Well now, have you decided what to do with regards to being baptized yourself?

GB: I am pretty sure of my decision. But I'd like to think about the matter, at my leisure, just one more day. I'll tell you what I decide tomorrow.

TS: Okay. See you then.

PART 2: BAPTISM

EXPLANATORY NOTES: DAY 14

There is a multitude of works devoted to the reformers, their emergence, their thinking, including their ideas on baptism, how they operated, and their opposition. One could consult an older work like, Grimm, *The Reformation Era*, a somewhat more modern one, such as, McGrath, *Reformation Thought*, a more recent work like, MacCulloch, *Reformation*, or Woodbridge and James, *Church History*.

For an interesting account of how baptism, according to the rites of the Church of England, should be understood and how the practices and beliefs associated with it are reformed, see Robinson, "The Doctrine of Baptism."

For a work that discusses how the early reformers used the Early Fathers, sometimes referred to simply as the Church Fathers, in their debates over the Eucharist, see Chung-Kim, *Inventing Authority*.

Arnold in "Reformation Men" provides a short statement on the Anabaptists.

Polanyi writes of the importance of "plausibility" as a concept involved when accounting for the acceptance or otherwise of an idea as scientific in "The Republic of Science" and "The Growth of Science in Society."

There are a number of references in Acts to a person or persons believing without there being an accompanying statement that they were baptized. See Acts 13:12, 48 (NIV) for two examples.

Dunn in "Baptism." is prepared to speak of Paul deemphasizing baptism in his (Paul) stating that Christ did not send him to baptize but to preach the gospel, 449–50.

For Tertullian's argument against those who claimed that Paul in making the statement that Christ did not send him to baptize, indicated that baptism was not a necessary rite, see Tertullian, *On Baptism*, 14. Reference to this matter can also be found in Ferguson, *Baptism*, 339–40.

Day 15

Decision Day

GB finally resolves what to do about being baptized. TS is concerned that GB take into account four principles in thinking about what should happen but warmly supports his decision. He gives him some advice about what he might say to his pastor and encourages him to invite neighbors and friends to witness the occasion.

TS: Well, what have you decided?

GB: I want to be baptized.

TS: I'm glad, although I feel I must ask why you want to be baptized.

GB: It's hard to put my finger on it exactly. I am now pretty well convinced that it isn't mandatory. However, I really do want to be baptized. It's a great ceremony. The symbolism in it is great and being part of that symbolism is very humbling.

TS: What do you see as the symbolism?

GB: Oh, much along the lines we talked about. It is dying and death to one's old life. It's an abandonment of all that's utterly pagan—living without Christ, living as though all that mattered was oneself, one's worshipping of oneself. And then there's the coming back from the dead. Coming into an entirely new life, a splendid life, a life that's God directed, God focused, Christ glorifying. But also I see the cleansing side of things. Before God, I was utterly unrighteous, thoroughly contaminated, unclean through and through. Then having been thoroughly washed, at the deepest roots, I am now thoroughly cleansed. The contrast between "death" and "unclean through and through" on the one hand and "life" and "thoroughly clean" on the other hand is world dividing, if I can put it that way.

TS: But you have already died with Christ. You have already been raised with him. You have already been washed clean. The Spirit of God already abides in you. You may not

Part 2: Baptism

be precisely aware of when God shed his grace upon you but from what you explained to me earlier, it was a reasonable time ago. Why would you want to be baptized now?

GB: Well, I've never experienced being part of that ancient custom, that God approved custom, that wonderful picture of the reality that God has wrought in me, yes, what God brought about in me roughly a year ago now. But I know what you mean. I think I will need to tell my pastor that I'd like him, as part of the ceremony, to declare that I had become a believer many months beforehand. Perhaps I could say that myself. I don't want people thinking that I've only just become a believer. That would be a lie and not to the glory of God.

TS: And, would you like your pastor to indicate to others that what you will be doing will not be the same type of thing that happened at the day of Pentecost. That is, that you are not repenting at your baptism, but rather that you repented some time ago.

GB: I don't think that will be necessary. That should be obvious. Perhaps I will be allowed to explain to people exactly why I want to be baptized, just as I've explained it to you.

TS: I hope your pastor will understand your point of view.

GB: I think so. He's a very thoughtful and caring sort of person and he does want to base his beliefs and practices on the Scriptures.

TS: Well, I said it earlier. As long as what you do is helpful, especially to you but also to anybody else who will be there, as long as what you do is not misleading, and I am sure you don't want it to be, as long as some historical precedence that can't be justified is clearly not being claimed, and finally, as long as you don't see it as mandatory and that you don't give that sense to others, I am sure you will have God's blessing in abundance. What do you suspect your pastor will think about the matter of baptism being mandatory or not?

GB: I'm not quite sure. Should I raise the issue?

TS: It might be difficult to avoid it. But whether it's raised by him or not, I think for your own sake and for his you ought to bring your views out into the open. . . . Who are you going to invite to come along to your baptism?

GB: I've thought about that. I'd like to invite a lot of people—some friends, some relatives, some of the people with whom I study, some of my fellow teachers. I haven't seen my fellow students or most of my teaching colleagues for a few weeks but I'll be meeting up with most of them again on Monday. I've been on vacation, as you know. How otherwise could I've spent all this time chatting with you! I might even invite the neighbors on the left of my house and the family across the road. I've been pretty friendly with both over recent years, although come to think of it the lady across the road is a Catholic. I'm not sure she'd come.

TS: Give her a try, she might. What about the neighbors on your right?

Decision Day

GB: Oh, they're Muslims. I don't think they'd come.

TS: You never know. They might come and for any number of reasons—perhaps just out of curiosity. I'd make any invitation as warm and as welcoming as you can. See if your pastor can have the ceremony at a convenient time for all those you'd like to invite and see if he could make it not last too long. He will probably have a set service in mind but he could be a little flexible. You could even have a morning or afternoon tea or even a light lunch afterwards, depending upon the time of day involved. At the ceremony he'll need to make some sort of a speech, explaining what it's all about and I hope he will emphasize the grace of God at work in you through the Lord Jesus Christ, rather than the ceremony itself.

GB: Yes. I must keep that in mind myself. It's not all about me. It's fundamentally all about him, my Lord.

TS: Would you like him to use a phrase, something like, "in the name of the Lord Jesus" or "in the name of Jesus Christ" or one where reference is made to the Father, the Son and the Holy Spirit?

GB: I don't really mind. I'll think about that. I suspect having the words, "in the name of the Lord Jesus Christ," wouldn't be a bad idea!

TS: Please let me know if you have any difficulties with your pastor, particularly concerning your view that the ceremony isn't something you have to do. I don't know what I could do, but I'd be happy to have a chat with him, if he were happy with that. I'd promise that it wouldn't be a long chat. I wouldn't try to persuade him of anything. I'd just try to explain your point of view, what I think is your point of view.

GB: I know I haven't spoken in a straightforward sort of way, but yes I really don't think it is mandatory and I'm not trying to hedge my bets by being baptized, although I think deep down, from time to time I do have a doubting twinge. It's not easy now having so many keen loving Christian friends, most of whom probably do think it is necessary, and my having a different view.

TS: I understand. I think when I first started to think about these issues, I was somewhat worried that I was almost on my own. I was helped by a few very good, hardworking, very thoughtful and scholarly believers who themselves were willing to try and see things afresh, to reexamine the Scriptures, almost starting from scratch, having very few presuppositions.

GB: Thanks for telling me that. I've tended to see you as someone who had always had the views you do have, although of course that wouldn't be true. . . . I hope *you* will come to my baptism.

TS: Of course I will, if at all possible. Just let me know when and where. And don't forget, if I can be of any help in any way, in the future, I'm just at the end of an email.

One day, perhaps when you next have a vacation we can look at that other problem of yours, the one concerning the Lord's Supper, as you probably refer to it.

GB: Don't worry. I haven't forgotten. I think the pastor will want to talk to me about that anyway. But again, I want to take my time. I want to be able to live with myself in all good conscience.

TS: You've done pretty well so far. . . . Well, I guess that's it for today. Thanks for your honesty. See you at your baptism or sometime in the future— at your convenience. Cheers for now and all the best as you talk with your pastor.

Author's Comments

GB was baptized about a month later. He was able to convince the pastor to convey to those present all those things that he thought important. The pastor was somewhat worried about GB's view that baptism was not mandatory but after some discussion agreed to a statement being made by GB that he did not believe that it was necessary for *salvation*. The pastor pointed out that there could be members of his church who would take a different view to this but that he didn't agree with them. The pastor was also happy to baptize GB in the name of "The Lord Jesus Christ." His baptism was by immersion in what looked like a very large bath that they have at his church.

Interestingly, the neighbors on his left did not come but the lady from across the road did and both the Muslim man and his wife came as well. Lots of his friends came. Even some from what some would say was a very liberal church. He was delighted. You couldn't keep the smile off his face. But his greatest joy was simply declaring what this Lord Jesus Christ had done for him. I don't think anybody that day could go away without pondering anew or for the first time on the amazing love of God and the deliverance he promises from the judgment to come.

The pastor did raise the matter of GB participating in the Lord's Supper at the very next time it was celebrated in their church. He was a little taken back when GB explained to him that he wouldn't until he was very clear in his own mind what it was all about. Explaining again to the pastor his past close association with ceremonies as part of his cult world somewhat helped the pastor to understand his hesitancy.

A few months later GB contacted TS by email, attempting to arrange a further series of meetings. TS had been hoping that GB would contact him again, being very aware that the Lord's Supper was still one of GB's concerns.

PART 3

The Lord's Supper

Day 16

What they Call it, what they Believe and what they Do

GB is familiar with the service of the Lord's Supper as conducted in his own church—what they do and what they believe. He is also aware that other churches, other denominations, do things differently and think differently about the significance of what they are doing. Today he simply wants TS to give to him as broad a picture of the situation as possible. He wants to know more about, what he considers to be, the "mine field" in which he is now prepared to walk.

TS: Thanks for the email. I was wondering how you were going. From what you said I see you are on vacation again! Oh to be a schoolteacher!

GB: I enjoy teaching. It's one of the best jobs I've ever had. The breaks between terms aren't bad either! By the way, is it still okay for us to meet at your house on a regular basis?

TS: It's okay with me if it's okay with you. . . . Well, it's been some time since we last talked. But now it's the matter of the Lord's Supper. What's the problem or problems from your perspective?

GB: I've continued to do a lot of reading and thinking. I'm beginning to become very familiar with various sections of Scripture and I think God has been kind to me, giving me a very good pastor who is also a good teacher. I don't have any significant problems. It's just that I'm aware that Christians have so many different ways of seemingly doing the same thing. And they have different names for what they do. And I'm aware that there are some fundamental differences in what they believe about what our pastor calls the Lord's Supper. Also he's a little concerned that I haven't yet participated in the ceremony. He thinks it's a very important ceremony and still wonders why I've declined to take part, though I've tried to explain my aversion to being involved in ceremonies. I don't want to offend anyone, except, you know me, I'm reluctant to do anything unless I am quite sure I know what I am doing and for what reason.

TS: I understand, though you are, I hope you don't mind my saying this, you are a little unusual. Most people just automatically celebrate the Lord's Supper or Holy Communion, in whatever church they find themselves and without any questions being asked about why their church does it this way or that way and what its members believe about it. I think your questioning mind and your cautious approach is to be commended. Where would you like to begin?

GB: Well, what about a brief run down on three things—what various Christians do, what they call it and what they believe about what they're doing? Any order will do.

TS: Sure. But those three items constitute a big subject and I can't profess to know much about the various practices. Why don't you search the internet some time? That might help. Let's start with what they call it. That's the simplest of the three issues. Some of the terms you'll come across are the Mass, the Eucharist, the Holy Eucharist, Holy Communion, the Breaking of Bread, the Divine Liturgy, the Holy Sacrifice, and of course, the Lord's Supper.

GB: I know that Roman Catholics believe in something called "transubstantiation." It has something to do with the bread and wine turning into the body and blood of Christ doesn't it?

TS: Yes. They believe that it's during the Mass, when the bread and the wine, sometimes called "the elements," are prayed over in a special way by a priest, that that occurs. The bread and the wine still have the appearance of bread and wine but they believe they have become something quite different—the body and blood of Christ. The Eastern Orthodox Church has a similar view although what happens to the bread and the wine is often referred to as "a mystery." In fact many churches refer to what happens at the service as a mystery. Lutherans believe, that in some sense, but not by means of "transubstantiation," the bread and wine have also become the body and blood of Jesus.

GB: The word, "Eucharist" has something to do with "thanksgiving," doesn't it?

TS: In origin it's a Greek word, conveying just that. In Roman Catholicism it's people being thankful as they partake of the actual body and blood of Jesus. In fact the body and blood are themselves spoken of as "The Eucharist." Lots of people refer to the ceremony as the Eucharist, even some from the Church of England, otherwise known as Episcopalians or Anglicans. But you can see how the use of the term varies.

GB: What do Anglicans, I'll refer to them as Anglicans, what do they believe?

TS: In one of their thirty nine articles, it says that in the Lord's Supper people partake of the body and blood of Christ, but that his body is taken and eaten in a heavenly and spiritual sense and that the means by which his body is received and eaten is by faith.

GB: So a number of Christians believe that in some sense they are actually receiving the body and blood of Christ?

TS: Well, yes, but to believe that the bread and wine have been changed into the body and blood in a literal, physical sense is one thing. To believe that when you partake of the bread and wine you're partaking of his body and blood in a spiritual sense is a very different thing, even if you have some notion that what you're doing is a mystery.

GB: Yes, I can see that. And I can understand how such beliefs make the ceremony very, very special.

TS: Well, even those like the Baptists and the Brethren who simply see the bread and wine as symbols representing the body and blood of Christ, regard the ceremony as very important and meaningful. I'd have thought that almost all, if not all Christians, whatever their view of what happens during the ceremony, believe that they should quite seriously reflect on the death of Christ and its relevance for them whenever they celebrate the Eucharist or whatever they call the ceremony.

GB: Is there any significance in the ceremony involving a number of people? That is, if the ceremony only involved one person would there be something not quite right about it? I think I've come across that sort of idea somewhere.

TS: Many would see that in the ceremony itself, the believers who are participating are being visibly united with each other. Some think that in the ceremony all of God's people, wherever they are, even if that's understood to include something like those who are existing in the heavenly realm, are being united. Perhaps people argue for this position by appealing to the idea that through the death of Christ all who are his have become one.

GB: I know that the way the ceremony is conducted varies. Is there much variation?

TS: Well it can vary within the one church and it certainly varies among churches or denominations. At one extreme, in a particular church or denomination, the liturgy can be quite fixed and doesn't vary from week to week or however frequently the service is conducted. Certain things have to be said or sung, only certain types of people can perform various duties and so on. At the other extreme, in other churches or denominations the service can be quite informal and conducted along different lines from week to week. However the reality is that most churches tend to adopt certain customs and conform to those customs regularly. An important feature, for many churches, is addressing God and even physically approaching God in what would be regarded as the appropriate manner beforehand. An important element in the so-called preparation required before taking part in the Eucharist or whatever it's called, is the confession of sins—that is, sorting out things with God before participating in the ceremony. Making sure that one is right with one's fellow man, before coming to the service, can also be an important feature of that preparation. Some people believe you should fast before taking part.

GB: But isn't it also true that the way the bread and wine is distributed differs from one church or denomination and that what the actual bread and wine is made up of can also be different?

TS: Yes, that's correct. For some, the bread is dipped in the wine and using a spoon the moistened bread is then placed inside the mouth with care being taken not to touch the lips and other parts of the mouth. Others only allow the bread to be taken. Sometimes the bread is placed on the hand. Others allow the bread to be taken from a plate. And for some the bread is in the form of a wafer or comes in small cubes. In some cases the bread has to be leavened bread but in others it must be unleavened bread. Some have a tradition of breaking a loaf of bread across the middle, while others break off the ends of a loaf. Some only have fermented wine, others only unfermented grape juice or similar. In some cases there's a choice.

GB: How often do the various churches celebrate Holy Communion or whatever one calls it?

TS: Some, very rarely, only a few times per year. It partly depends upon how important the ceremony is considered to be and what are thought to be the benefits conveyed by taking part in the ceremony. Where it's thought that those who participate are significantly enriched, either spiritually or physically or both, then understandably, the more often one participates, the better off one is. In this case, it might be considered valuable to take part in the ceremony once a week or even once a day.

GB: And I think you mentioned some time ago that many refer to the ceremony, by whatever name it's called, as a sacrament, but only as an ordinance, by others.

TS: Well, almost everybody can refer to it as an ordinance, in the sense that they believe that it's been ordered by Jesus. Those who believe that as a direct consequence of the nature of the ceremony itself—what is said what is done, what happens—special benefits being conveyed upon those who appropriately participate—also tend to refer to it as a sacrament. And so one can understand why in that case it is thought that something of a special spiritual "mystery" is involved. And if it's a spiritual mystery you can appreciate some people believing that if anyone comes to the service with an inappropriate frame of mind, then the extent to which such benefits are bestowed are limited. In fact in certain circumstances, where the person comes with a sinful mindset, it is thought that the consequences could be quite dire. And of course those who see the service as being simply symbolic, though powerfully symbolic, only see it as an ordinance, though they may not use that term. Baptists, Brethren and Seventh Day Adventist folk, for example, see what they do as conforming to something that Jesus demanded and as highly important but they do not see themselves as being involved in a sacrament.

GB: And if I remember what you said when we were talking about baptism, neither the Quakers nor the Salvation Army would see it as an ordinance or a sacrament.

TS: True, although they would probably not be concerned if any of their followers participated in a Eucharistic type of service conducted by someone else.

GB: . . . Well, what you've told me hasn't been too much of a surprise. It's clear that like baptism, the practices and beliefs associated with a Eucharistic ceremony vary enormously. There's even a multiplicity of names for the ceremony! Which all highlights my problem. What am *I* supposed to believe? What practice should *I* get involved in? I think I've already made up my mind but I'd appreciate our talking some more about the issues and in particular I wouldn't mind hearing what you yourself think.

TS: Why don't we call it quits for now and take up the subject again tomorrow if that's okay with you. Oh, and as I said earlier, I don't claim to be all that knowledgeable in this area. I am sure that practices and even beliefs can vary enormously even within denominations and the various church groups. So please don't quote me, particularly with respect to details.

GB: No problem. You've given me a general idea and that was all I asked for. Tomorrow? Yes, that's fine. See you then.

TS: Okay. Cheers!

PART 3: THE LORD'S SUPPER

EXPLANATORY NOTES: DAY 16

For an understanding of various beliefs and practices concerning "The Lord's Supper," "Holy Communion," "The Eucharist" the reader could consult the Internet, using these titles as well as others such as "The Divine Liturgy" and "The Holy Sacrifice." The Internet site—en.wikipedia.org/wiki/Eucharist could serve as a general introduction, though one might question much of what is said there concerning the general biblical basis for the practices detailed. As an alternative or additionally, the reader could search for the practices and beliefs of various denominations or church groups, individually.

Of the thirty nine Articles of the Church of England, the one that relates to the nature of the body of Christ in the Lord's Supper, is number twenty eight, entitled, "Of the Lord's Supper."

Day 17

The Last Passover Meal

In discussing the Last Passover Meal TS describes what the meal was probably like and goes into considerable detail about what each of the Gospels record and how they compare. He also reflects on what Paul records in his 1 Corinthians letter about the same event. It appears that he wants GB to become familiar with the details of what is recorded in order to discuss the significance or otherwise of those details sometime in the future.

TS: Hi there. Today I think it would be helpful if we looked at what is sometimes referred to as the Last Passover Meal, that is, the Passover meal that Jesus had with his disciples just before he died. Whatever we think about the Lord's Supper it has its origins in that meal.

GB: I take it that the Last Passover Meal is the same as the "Last Supper"?

TS: Yes. There are some who believe that that "Last Supper" was held a day earlier than was normal for a Passover meal. However, I don't think the arguments for that position are all that compelling. Besides for our purposes it's sufficient to recognize that in terms of its nature it was a Passover meal, whenever it was held.

GB: I take it that such meals had a set structure.

TS: Well to a large extent. However, there is some evidence that in Jesus' day there were disagreements over some specific matters to do with the meal, so presumably there wasn't a rigid uniform pattern that everyone followed at every Passover meal.

GB: The meal was partly divided into sections by the drinking of wine at certain points, wasn't it?

TS: Yes, one could understand it that way. You've obviously done some reading in the area!

GB: Only a little.

TS: Well, a fellow called, Joachim Jeremias—have you heard of him?

GB: No. Sorry, I haven't.

TS: Well, he's written about what he thinks the overall structure to the meal was. Although his analysis is in no way crucial for our purposes, it still might be of some help to consider what he thinks Passover meals were like at the time.

GB: Sounds good.

TS: According to Jeremias, the meal began with what he describes as a word of dedication. This involved a blessing of both the day and a cup of wine. People then partook of a preliminary dish, like an entrée, consisting of some herbs and a type of sauce made from fruit. The main meal was then served but not eaten. This preliminary stage was then followed by the Passover liturgy. This began with what was called the Passover *haggadah,* which was a meditation on the Passover in Aramaic. The *haggadah* was then followed with the first part of what was called the Passover *hallel* and this involved the singing of a specific Psalm or Psalms in Hebrew. This was followed by a second cup of wine. The main meal was then begun with a grace being said over unleavened bread. That meal consisted of the Passover lamb, the unleavened bread, some bitter herbs, a fruit puree and some wine. This main course was then followed by another grace spoken over a third cup. The conclusion to the meal consisted of the second part of the Passover *hallel*—other specific Psalms being sung in Hebrew—with praise being offered to God over a fourth cup.

GB: I know that these meals were supposed to be in accordance with what God commanded the people of Israel through Moses and that they were to celebrate the Passover meal on a yearly basis. In that instruction, which I found in the book of Exodus—I've been doing some reading on the Passover—reference is made to having a lamb at these meals and having only unleavened bread. However, I don't recall any reference to wine.

TS: The Exodus account also refers to the use of bitter herbs, which, as I've explained, did have a part to play in Passover meals in Jesus' day. But you're right. There's no mention of wine in the instructions recorded in Exodus.

GB: I don't suppose that's important although Jesus refers to that aspect of the meal when he speaks of his blood.

TS: I think that what we have at the time of Jesus is a fairly highly structured formal meal, with some variation here and there, one that had developed from the less formal meal outlined in Exodus. The drinking of wine at four or so different points had obviously become an established part of the meals as celebrated by Jews in the first century, and probably in even earlier times.

The Last Passover Meal

GB: The meal was meant to remind the Jews of that ancient meal eaten in haste by the Israelites on the eve of their departure from Egypt, many, many centuries before, wasn't it? It meant looking back on the past, remembering how God had delivered his people from slavery under the Egyptians and how he had saved their firstborn sons from death, unlike what happened to the firstborn sons of their masters. I remember reading how, for the safety of their firstborn sons, those fleeing from Egypt had to slay a healthy year old lamb and display its blood on the door frames of their houses.

TS: Yes. In the time of Jesus the lamb had to be taken to the temple and killed the day before the day of the Passover meal with the roasted lamb being eaten that night, the beginning of the new day.

GB: The part that the lamb played in the meal was central wasn't it? And, if I understand what you've said correctly, in Jesus' day, as seems was the case originally, it appears to have been the essential component of the main part of the meal.

TS: Yes. And according to Jeremias that part of the meal was introduced by a grace being said over the unleavened bread and finished with a second grace being said over a cup of wine—the third cup. The grace before and the grace afterwards acted like quotation marks, together encompassing the sacrificial lamb.

GB: I suppose that normally the meal was celebrated within a family, as on the first occasion.

TS: I'm sure. But with respect to Jesus, in the last couple of years of his life, his family, as it were, consisted of himself and his disciples. And the custom with Passover meals, as with ordinary meals, was that the head of the family presided over such meals. In the case of the disciples, that head would've been Jesus. He would've been in control of the meal. That he recited a blessing over the bread, that he broke the bread and that he handed a piece to other members of his "family," as the Gospel accounts have it, all of those actions would presumably have been in accordance with that custom.

GB: From what I remember, the details of what actually occurred at that Last Passover Meal are only recorded in Matthew, Mark and Luke.

TS: Well not really. Though I think I know what you're getting at. John's Gospel doesn't mention what Jesus said about his body and blood, but Paul in 1 Corinthians also makes reference to what Jesus said about the bread and the wine, along with the three Gospels you mentioned. John in his Gospel gives far more detail about other matters, for example, the washing by Jesus of his disciples' feet and the teaching of Jesus about the Holy Spirit. I think we're meant to understand, from John's Gospel, that the actual meal involved Jesus speaking a great deal, perhaps when the main part of the meal had concluded. This would be similar to the way that Greco-Roman formal meals were conducted. The main meal was followed by after-dinner conversations or other activities. I am not suggesting that Passover meals at the time of Jesus closely mirrored such meals but simply that there might have been some similarities.

Part 3: The Lord's Supper

GB: Sorry. Yes, I was thinking only about what Jesus said about the bread and the wine as recorded in the Gospels. I hadn't forgotten about Paul's contribution at all. It's what Jesus said about the bread and the wine, wherever it's recorded, that most interests me. However, before we go on, it was at that meal that there was some discussion about the betrayal of Judas, wasn't it?

TS: Yes. I don't think you would call it a discussion though. It seems that the disciples and Jesus were reclining, each probably using his left arm as a prop. John may have been to the immediate right of Jesus with Judas to his immediate left. During the meal Jesus announced that one of the disciples would betray him. There must have been astonishment all round. Peter seems to have asked John to discreetly ask Jesus who that person actually was. It may have been only John or perhaps both Peter and John who heard Jesus say something to the effect that it would be the one to whom he would give a piece of bread that he had dipped in a dish. Alternatively he could've meant that it would be the one who would be dipping a piece of bread in the same dish roughly at the same time as himself. We understand that it was customary to pass a bowl of stewed fruit, the fruit puree, from person to person and that people would dip some bread into it before passing it on. Additionally, a person might dip a piece of bread into the dish on someone else's behalf and pass the bread to that person. In the case of this Passover meal we can't really be exactly sure as to what happened and who heard.

GB: Sorry about this sidetrack. I was just interested. Back to what Jesus said about the bread and the wine.

TS: No problem. The accounts given by Matthew and Mark are very similar. Matthew writes, "As they were eating, Jesus took bread and said, 'Take eat, this is my body,'" followed later by, "And he took a cup, and when he had given thanks he gave it to them, saying, 'Drink of it, all of you; for this is my blood of the covenant, which is poured out for many for the forgiveness of sins.'" Mark refers to what Jesus said slightly differently, perhaps the main difference being that he omits mentioning "for the forgiveness of sins." It could be that the reference by Jesus to "many" was an indication that what he would do would be for more than just the Jews.

GB: And Luke?

TS: Luke is a little more complicated. All three Gospels record that Jesus broke bread and that later after the meal, they drank wine. Matthew and Mark record that upon that wine being drunk Jesus said something along the lines of his not drinking the wine again until the arrival of the kingdom of God. By that I take it he was referring to his not drinking wine again until the time when the feast for the Messiah would come, at the end of the age. The concept of a Messianic feast was one held by many a Jew at the time and it had its roots in the Old Testament. Luke referred to Jesus saying something very similar but before the breaking of bread. In fact Luke records Jesus at the beginning of the meal saying, "I have eagerly desired to eat this Passover with you before I suffer." He then follows this with Jesus taking a cup, giving thanks and instructing the disciples to take it, saying that he will not drink wine again until "it finds fulfillment in the kingdom of God."

GB: Does this mean that Luke is in disagreement with Matthew and Mark?

TS: No, well, not necessarily. I think the three Gospels taken together give us the following picture. Jesus is quite disturbed, understandably so, as events around his life come to a conclusion. I am sure he's not saying that he's looking forward to this meal because it will prove to be a happy occasion! I believe that he's indicating that he's anxious for events to unfold and considers that the Passover meal will be a very opportune moment to better explain the significance of his coming death. He begins the meal by saying something of this and then proceeds to take the first cup. At this point he explains he will never drink with them again until it—I think by "it" he means the Passover—will have had its significance brought to a conclusion with the coming in of the kingdom of God in all its completeness. That's my understanding of the sort of thing Jesus was getting at. Anyway, we're dependent entirely on Luke for this part of what happened. Later on, when giving thanks over the third cup, Jesus again refers to his never drinking wine with them until that time when he drinks again—when the kingdom of God has finally come. Matthew and Mark are the ones who record this part of what Jesus said at this point. At least that's one way of reconciling the accounts. His departure is overwhelmingly on his mind. It's quite conceivable that he should say similar somber things at different times during the meal. It's also quite possible that Jesus himself did not partake of any wine during the meal or at least any wine after the first cup.

GB: But it's Luke who records the words about remembering, isn't it?

TS: Certainly. As with Matthew and Mark, Luke records Jesus referring to his body, when giving thanks over the bread which, I take it, occurred before the main part of the meal during which the sacrificial lamb was consumed. And all three refer to his blood, when, again as I understand it, Jesus gave thanks over the third cup. However, in the Gospels, it's only with reference to the bread that it's recorded that Jesus says, "This is my body, given for you, do this in remembrance of me." And these words occur only in Luke.

GB: But surely he said something similar when referring to the wine—presumably the wine of the third cup?

TS: In Paul's account, there is such a reference, but not in Luke's. With respect to that cup Luke simply records that Jesus said to them, "This is my blood of the covenant, which is poured out for many." In fact, there are some textual problems associated with Luke's Gospel concerning what Jesus said about both the bread and the wine. There is some considerable evidence that Luke originally omitted any reference by Jesus to his body being given for them, and any reference to the cup and the blood.

That is, there is some significant evidence that indicates that what Luke originally recorded went something like, "And he took bread and when he had given thanks he broke it and gave it to them, saying this is my body," followed by, "Behold the hand of him who betrays me is on the table." You see, there are manuscripts that contain only part of what we normally consider to be the text.

GB: But in Paul's account, as well as in Matthew's and Mark's it is fairly clear isn't it that Jesus did make a reference to both his body and blood?

TS: Yes, and so I don't think we should concern ourselves too much with what Luke did or did not record. Except perhaps to point out the obvious—that even if we do accept what we can refer to as "the longer account" in Luke—it would be of the four Gospels, only Luke's that makes a reference to "Do this in remembrance of me." and then only with respect to the bread. We make a great deal of what Jesus said and so we should, but it should be recognized that of the four Gospel writers, at best, only Luke in his Gospel considered it appropriate to mention Jesus saying, "Do this in remembrance of me."

GB: Well then, what about looking at what Paul said. There's no problem with the relevant text in 1 Corinthians is there?

TS: No, except for one significant matter of translating the text that I'll refer to down the track. What Paul wrote and what Luke may well have recorded concerning what Jesus said at the Last Passover Meal is pretty similar. However, there are some interesting differences.

GB: They being?

TS: Paul says that he had received certain information from the Lord that he had passed on to the Corinthians, and this information concerned what Jesus said at that Last Passover Meal about his body and blood. What exactly he meant by "received from the Lord" I'm not sure. He could've meant that the Lord Jesus had given him this information by some direct, though extraordinary means or alternatively, indirectly, via one of the disciples. I really don't know. What *is* important, however, is that he is reminding them of what they've already been told and indicating that this information is absolutely trustworthy. It comes from the Lord.

GB: Are we going to look at why Paul needed to remind the Corinthians of what Jesus said?

TS: Yes. We will certainly need to, but later on. For now let's be clear about what Paul wrote at this point in his letter. It goes something like this, "The Lord Jesus, on the night when he was betrayed, took bread and when he had given thanks he broke (it) and said, 'Take, eat, this is my body which is given for you. This do in my remembrance.' Similarly, also, (he took) the cup after supper, saying, 'This is the new covenant in my blood. This do as often as you drink (it) in my remembrance.'" You'll notice by how I recited this that in order for the text to make sense in English, we need to supply some words that are not in the Greek.

GB: You're also being somewhat literal here as well, aren't you?

TS: I guess I am being a bit pedantic. More importantly, I want to point out that there really isn't any good manuscript evidence that Jesus referred to his body being broken, though some manuscripts and so some translations contain such a phrase. Also I thought I'd refer to, "This do" rather than "Do this," since that's the order of words in the Greek and we may find this order to be relevant when we later discuss in somewhat more detail what it's claimed that Jesus said. Furthermore, I've tried to make it clear that Paul, in the Greek language of course, is reporting that Jesus said, "as often as" or "whenever" only with respect to the cup. I don't think anything really hangs on this but I'm trying to point out the extent and the limits of what Paul reports that Jesus said.

GB: You also refer to "my remembrance" rather than "remembrance of me."

TS: I don't think that's all that important either and although, as you say, I am being rather literal, I suspect that by referring to, "my remembrance" we have a better "feel" for what Jesus was saying. By the way did you notice the stylistic somewhat formal character to what Paul reports, in the beginning of his account, with his words, "On the night when he was betrayed"? I suspect that what he's reporting is a statement that has already been appealed to a few times by others in different contexts and on different occasions. What he reports could be somewhat creedal in character.

GB: No I hadn't picked that up. But yes, interesting. You could be right. However, overall, what we have in 1 Corinthians is reasonably similar to what we find in Luke isn't it? Although you said, and it's fairly obvious now, there are some differences. I asked you what they were, but then also asked some other questions!

TS: I was going to make the differences fairly explicit. Just for the sake of clarity. If we accept the longer reading in Luke, the accounts are reasonably similar. However, with respect to the differences, Luke does not record words of remembrance for the wine and only Paul refers to "as often as" or "whenever" even if only with respect to the cup. I think these differences show that while Paul may have been appealing to a somewhat set formula, Luke, almost certainly writing later, may not have. However, I really don't know why the differences exist. I'm simply guessing.

GB: Well, regardless, it seems fairly clear what Jesus meant by those remembrance words uttered at the Last Passover Meal. What do you think?

TS: Why don't we leave that question until tomorrow? Would that be okay?

GB: Sure. A bit of a sudden end to the discussion! However, I realize that it's getting a little late. See you tomorrow then.

PART 3: THE LORD'S SUPPER

EXPLANATORY NOTES: DAY 17

For a view that the Last Supper of the Gospels is not to be identified with a Passover meal, see Smith, *From Symposium to Eucharist*, 4.

I am indebted to Maurice Casey for information that Passover meals held during Jesus' day were not of a uniform nature.

The work written by Jeremias that TS referred to is *The Eucharistic Words of Jesus*.

Jeremias's view of the nature of the Passover meal in the time of Jesus can be found in that work, 84–88 with additional information being provided on 55 note 1. In that note Jeremias points out that the schools of Shammai and Hillel differed as to which Psalms constituted the first and second parts of the *hallel*.

Accounts of the Last Passover Meal and what immediately preceded it can be found in Matt 26:17–30; Mark 14:12–26; Luke 22:7–23; 1 Cor 11:23–25 (NIV).

An interesting discussion of the circumstances applying when Jesus predicted his betrayal during the Last Passover Meal can be found in Carson, *The Gospel according to John*, 470–76.

One of the clearest references in the Old Testament to a feast that God would hold at the end of all earthly things can be found in Isa 25: 4–9 (NIV).

The textual problems concerning what is recorded in Luke's Gospel about what Jesus said at the Last Passover Meal regarding his body and blood can be found in the Nestle-Aland. *Greek-English New Testament*, 233.

Day 18

"This Do in Remembrance of Me"

On this day TS focuses on what Jesus meant by "This is my body," "This is my blood" and "Do this in remembrance of me." Understandably, TS considers that in any determination of their meaning, it is essential to keep in mind the context in which the words were uttered.

GB: Those words, "Do this in remembrance of me," they have got to be among the most important words that Jesus uttered at that Last Passover Meal."

TS: Well I guess so, though I wouldn't dismiss any of the words that Jesus said on that occasion as unimportant, whether recorded in the Synoptic Gospels, that's Matthew, Mark and Luke, or in John's Gospel, or in Paul's 1 Corinthians letter.

GB: True.

TS: However, the words you mentioned happen to be exactly the words I wanted us to think about today!

GB: Good!

TS: The big question is, "What exactly did he mean when he said that?" For me, in attempting to answer the question, it's important to keep in mind that the Passover meal was a remembrance event. It wasn't novel of Jesus to speak of remembrance. What was entirely new, at least from the disciples' point of view, was Jesus attaching that remembrance to himself. The meal was designed to help people recall how in the past God had delivered his people from slavery and how he had preserved their firstborn sons from the angel that brought death to the firstborn males of others. And what was the most important thing that the Israelites had to do at that first Passover meal? What did God require from them if their children were to be saved?

Part 3: The Lord's Supper

GB: The killing of a lamb and the placing of the blood of that lamb around the doorways of their houses.

TS: Yes. No firstborn in an Israelite family needed to die. Only a lamb!

GB: And when Jesus uttered those words "Do this in remembrance of me," he is making his disciples focus upon himself and his death, as the means of salvation for *them*.

TS: Exactly. And we need to keep in mind, if our understanding of what happened at that Last Passover Meal is correct, when it was, during the meal, that he broke the bread and referred to his body. It was just before the beginning of the main part of the meal where the roasted lamb, the lamb that had previously been sacrificed, was to be eaten. And when he offered the cup to drink and referred to his blood, it was at the conclusion of that part of the meal. His words concerning his body and blood encompassed the eating of the sacrificial lamb.

GB: And the real significance of that? I think I see it.

TS: Well, for a Jew, there was something quite substantial about death when the blood had been drained from the body. The life of the body was perceived to reside in the blood. The blood separated from the body bespoke of death. Jesus separates the reference to his blood from the reference to his body. This is a very pointed way for Jesus to refer to his death. So I think that what we have at the Last Passover Meal is Jesus drawing attention to his death not simply by means of first speaking of his body and then secondly by referring to his blood, but by referring to both, each being separated by the main part of the meal consisting of the slain lamb. The sacrificed lamb reminded the Jew of God's salvation brought about long ago. And, having bracketed the main part of the meal, which featured the sacrificial lamb, with words that taken together referred to his death, Jesus pointed to his own death as the means of salvation for them—indeed for many, as Matthew and Mark record.

GB: Of course, I knew that Jesus was referring to his own death. However, I must confess I had never seen the significance of what he said about his body and what he said about his blood, being remarks separated by the meal of the sacrificed lamb, as together pointing to his death. But that seems more than plausible. The remarks made either side of the meal of the lamb spoke of his death and the sacrificed lamb itself, spoke of his death. In fact it says somewhere in the New Testament that Jesus was our Passover lamb, doesn't it?

TS: Yes. Paul in chapter 5 of 1 Corinthians writes, "Christ our Passover lamb has been sacrificed for us." He may well have had the Last Passover Meal in mind. . . . But those remarks that Jesus made about his body and his blood, do you think they were literal references to his body and blood?

GB: Well yes, but not in the sense that the bread was actually his body and that the wine was actually his blood. He was, however, talking about his real death, his body and his blood, but he used the bread and the wine, in the special circumstances of that Last Passover Meal, to draw attention to his death as being the great salvation event.

TS: For me it's difficult to think otherwise. The disciples, along with other Jews, came together each year to celebrate the Passover. Presumably, the disciples and Jesus, together, had done that at least on two occasions prior to their taking part in that Last Passover Meal. But at this meal Jesus said some things that he had never said before and as it eventuated, though he knew about it, he said those things just a few hours before he actually died. He declared that his death was the great salvation event and that the blood, his blood, was the blood of the new covenant—the new contract that God would make with his people. He was probably alluding to the new covenant that the prophet Jeremiah had spoken about. You can find a reference to that new covenant in chapter 31 of his book. With the death of Jesus the new age was arriving. With his blood being shed for the forgiveness of sins, a greater deliverance than that historical deliverance of many years before was now made possible.

GB: Very sobering. One needs to sit back and reflect for a while. . . . How wonderful of God but how costly! . . . Is there any significance in Jesus breaking the bread? That is, was that act referring to his body being broken?

TS: I really don't think so. We ought to look closely at that matter later, when I'm hoping that we can consider passages in the Acts of the Apostles that refer to the breaking of bread. Suffice it to say, at the moment, that I'm pretty sure that in those days people often baked bread in the form of loaves rather than small buns—though they probably did both. It's an economical way of doing things. To distribute the bread one had to break pieces off the larger loaf. Sometimes people baked bread in the form of what we might describe as cakes or types of fancy bread. There was however, nothing special about the act of breaking bread. If you wanted to eat a piece of bread, you normally had to break a piece off a loaf. Also, as I've already mentioned, in accordance with the best manuscript evidence, Paul, in referring to what he received from the Lord regarding "the night on which Jesus was betrayed," does not include the phrase, "broken for you."

GB: Come to think of it, I remember that John in his Gospel seems to make a point of the body of Jesus not being broken. I am fairly sure that he wrote that the fact that his body had not been broken was a fulfillment of a portion of Scripture—something from one of the Psalms.

TS: That's right.

GB: But back to the matter of what Jesus meant by his reference to the bread and his body and to the wine and his blood. What do you think the *disciples* understood by what he said?

TS: I don't know for sure. I find it very hard to believe that they would've thought that the bread was literally his body and the blood literally his blood. Jesus was inviting them to eat the bread and to drink the wine. For them to imagine that this was an invitation literally to eat his body and to drink his blood seems inconceivable. Surely they would've understood that idea to be an act of cannibalism. I know that some people think otherwise today, that is, that in some important sense he really was referring to the bread as his body and the wine as his blood. However, it seems to me that it's too easily forgotten that Jesus often used powerful, colorful, and sometimes disturbing images in his teaching and his rebukes. Consider—"I am the light of the world," "You brood of vipers," "My yoke is easy, my burden is light," "I am the true vine and my Father is the gardener," and "You are like unmarked graves which men walk over without knowing it." Why wouldn't we consider what he says in this instance, as powerful imagery? Why would we believe that he was claiming that the bread was literally his body and that the wine was literally his blood?

GB: I don't know. Is there a hankering inside of us to want to create the mysterious?

TS: Maybe. Anyway there's enough about the Godhead that's difficult to comprehend as it is, without looking for something else. Perhaps people are attracted to the idea that they are really taking on something of Jesus himself when they eat the bread and drink the wine at Communion. There is of course, a reality to the idea that God can give us something of himself—he gives his Holy Spirit to those who repent and trust in him. In fact he not only comes to his people but he dwells within them. His Spirit does not pay us a visit from time to time, coming as a result of our partaking part in a ceremony. Believers already have the Spirit of Christ abiding within them. No wonder that Jesus could say at the end of Matthew, without appealing to any ceremony, "And, Lo, I am with you until the end of the age."

GB: Thinking about what the disciples might have understood by what Jesus said, they really didn't seem to recognize that Jesus was going to die and that only by his death would salvation be possible for anyone. Surely they wouldn't have understood that all of God's purposes for the salvation of humankind had always revolved around his Son who had now finally come to this earth as a man with the express purpose of dying for sinful mankind. I doubt that at this time they would have thought that he was the righteous one about to die for the unrighteous so that the unrighteous could be reconciled to God. I can't imagine that they had come to the conclusion that the sacrifice of an animal had never dealt with sin, that such sacrifices were only pictures of what was needed and that they found their fulfillment in that ultimate sacrifice of Jesus, the Son of God. I guess it would only be in retrospect that the disciples would appreciate that Jesus was referring to his death as the ultimate salvation event to which the original Passover of yesteryear had pointed.

TS: . . . Again, I am astonished and realize that I shouldn't be. You've obviously read and thought a great deal about these matters. And I think you're right. It was only after his resurrection that we find Jesus, as recorded in Luke's Gospel, explaining to the disciples about the necessity of his death and relating that death to the forgiveness of sins. So, my guess is that what Jesus said on that Passover night was basically mystifying. Perhaps they had some idea of what Jesus was saying but without it making much sense!

GB: But what was Jesus trying to convey by having them eat the bread that he said was his body and drink the wine that he said was his blood? I mean, what was the actual eating and drinking meant to signify? I *can* guess.

TS: My take on it is along the following lines. Eating and drinking is what is necessary to sustain life. However the bread and the wine, what was to be eaten and what was to be drunk, to which Jesus referred, were special. They were part of the Passover meal. The meal was in memory of that great deliverance that God had brought about for his chosen people in the past. It was life-giving deliverance. Now, by Jesus referring to eating that bread that was symbolically his body and drinking that wine that was symbolically his blood, he was presumably saying that it was his death that would enable them to live, live in a very special way—that participating in his death symbolically depicted by the eating of that bread and the drinking of that wine, would give them life, life that belonged to the end of the ages. Quite possibly they didn't have much understanding of what Jesus was saying on the occasion, as we've already said, but later they must have seen the significance. Jesus was indicating "You need my death, in order to have life." Or, to put it another way, "You need to be caught up in my death in order to have that life before God which lasts."

GB: That is, it wasn't so much that they were taking on Jesus. Rather they were taking on his death!

TS: Well, to "take on" Jesus, to use your words, is actually to "take on" his death. It is also to "take on" his resurrection. Paul expresses that sort of thing in his letter to the churches at Rome.

GB: Hmm. . . . I guess one of the odd things about what Jesus said was that although he was pointing to his death and how necessary that death was for life, the life that counts, he hadn't yet died.

TS: I understand what you mean. However it was less than twenty four hours before he would die. And, from all that we know, he had never said that sort of thing at earlier Passovers. At this Passover meal his death was imminent, though his disciples probably did not realize that, even though they did have significant concerns about his safety.

GB: All that you've just said makes a lot of sense, at least to me. But as you point out, at the time, it might not have made much sense to his disciples. Yet, regardless of what they thought Jesus was saying, it would've been reasonably clear to them that he was giving them a type of command when he said "Do this in remembrance of me."

TS: Even though of all the Gospels only Luke records Jesus saying these words and only with respect to the bread and then only if we accept the longer reading, it is still clear from what Paul recounts that Jesus made this statement or gave this command in connection with both the bread and the wine. And although Paul has Jesus saying "ὁσάκις" (*hosakis*), meaning "whenever" or "as often as," with respect to the wine only, let's assume that Jesus also said the same thing in connection with the bread. However, it doesn't really matter if that assumption is false. Surely the sense of "whenever" would not have been limited to the wine only. And of course Jesus almost certainly wasn't speaking in Greek. Presumably he would have spoken in Aramaic, his native language. Paul was just giving the Greek equivalent.

GB: I understand.

TS: And now, in trying to work out what Jesus meant by those words of remembrance, let's keep in mind the actual occasion upon which those words were uttered.

GB: The Last Passover Meal!

TS: So then, the natural understanding of the statement would be, "Do this now and whenever you celebrate Passover," wouldn't it?

GB: . . . I guess so. However, that's not the way most people understand the command. People celebrate Holy Communion once every few months, once a month or once a week. I know, as you pointed out, *some* probably think it's important to have Communion every day. Are you suggesting that what Jesus was saying was that they should remember his death just once a year?

TS: Well yes and no. It seems obvious, that for any disciples celebrating Passover in the future, they would do so with a radically new understanding. It had always been a remembrance ceremony celebrating God's salvation in the past but now it would be a remembrance ceremony celebrating God's greatest of all salvation events made possible through Jesus. They could never see Passover simply in the old way again. Their Lord had died for their salvation. His death was the salvation event of which all other salvation events were simply reflections, as powerful as they were. And of course they would often, perhaps very often, certainly not just once a year, remember that Jesus had died for them without the need to participate in any ceremony. How could they forget? Surely, they would often reflect on that awesome event and what it meant for them.

GB: I understand that. But what would Gentile Christians do—those who had never celebrated Passover?

TS: I don't know if in the very early days they did anything. Most, if not all, probably didn't celebrate any of the Jewish festivities. Nonetheless, in time, we know that some began to formally remember the death of Jesus on an annual basis and at the same time that Jews began to celebrate Passover. However, other Christians wished to distance themselves from anything Jewish and at a Council in Antioch Syria, in the fourth century, there was a declaration that anyone who celebrated the death of Jesus at the same time that the Jews celebrated Passover was to be considered alienated from the church. And I suspect that today, hardly anyone would think that when they remember in a special way the death of Jesus at Easter that they're involved in a Passover Festival.

GB: Are you suggesting that only those early believers who were Jews formally responded to the command "Do this in remembrance of me." and then only with respect to the Passover Festival, even though they now understood Passover in a new way?

TS: I don't really know what happened in those very early days. There is however, some evidence to that effect but to what extent this or that practice was widespread is very difficult to tell. What I'm fairly confident about is that there is no historical evidence that anyone in those early days understood "Do this in remembrance of me." to mean that Jesus was saying that his followers should remember his death in a special way every time they had a meal.

GB: But don't the words—"Do this whenever you drink it." imply that at any meal, and now I'm beginning to find myself having to express something I'm not all that happy with—whenever we have wine at a meal—the "it" would be a reference to the wine.... Sorry this doesn't seem right.

TS: It's the word "it" that's causing you the problem isn't it? Actually, there's no word that we would translate "it" in the text. So one could understand, "Do this as often as you drink" to refer to whenever one drinks, whether at a meal or not. But Paul had just quoted Jesus saying, "This cup is the new covenant in my blood." The Passover reminded Jews of the way God had delivered his people from slavery—the necessary precursor to his establishing his covenant with them at Sinai—the old covenant. What Jesus said really does connect with the Passover, not with everyday meals and not whenever one has a drink of wine.... I notice that you were careful not to apply the "whenever" phrase to the eating of the bread. I think that it's okay to apply it to the bread, as I was suggesting, though it's interesting that it doesn't occur in the text. And, I think that it's okay, even though Paul's introduction "In the night that he was betrayed" ... might suggest, as I mentioned yesterday, that what Paul recalls had become or was becoming a well-known statement as to what happened and what was said on that occasion. On the other hand, if what Paul says is fresh from his pen or his scribe's pen, as it were, I would have thought that he doesn't think it necessary to adopt a very neat expression that has parallel clauses for both the bread and the wine. By the way, I don't know of anybody who thinks that whenever a believer drinks, he or she should begin to reflect on the death of Jesus. But who knows? There could be such people.

GB: Maybe. However, regardless of all that you've been saying, don't we have evidence that the Corinthian Christians met once a week and celebrated the Lord's Supper?

Part 3: The Lord's Supper

Doesn't that suggest that they thought they ought to remember the Lord's death at a ceremony a little like the Passover or somehow or other reflective of the Last Passover Meal and on a weekly basis? And many if not most of these Corinthians were Gentiles! Why wouldn't we do something similar, even if not on a weekly basis, and see it as obeying a command of the Lord?

TS: Can we leave a discussion on the Lord's Supper, as it's referred to in the Corinthians letter, until later? Which means, I'd rather leave your last questions unanswered or at least without comment, for the moment. I'm sorry. I promise that I won't forget. We really do need to consider a number of things yet, but if we do so, as it were, all at once, I think we'll become confused.

GB: Well, I suppose we can move on to something else. You seem to have a route mapped out for us that we should follow, whenever we talk! Don't misunderstand me, I'm not complaining. I don't mind what you do.

TS: I'm sorry. I do have a number of matters in mind that I think we need to reflect on but I have to admit that I'm not quite sure of the order in which they should be considered. I'm trying to be as helpful as I can. . . . At this point I want us to move onto something that's a little unusual, a little odd, though it's still connected to what Jesus said at that meal.

GB: Okay. Let's go there.

TS: Yes, but not right now. I think we need a break. It's been a long enough day as it is. What I'd like for us to consider next, could also be more than a little complicated. Would meeting again tomorrow be okay?

GB: Sure.

TS: Then tomorrow it is!

"This Do in Remembrance of Me"

EXPLANATORY NOTES: DAY 18

The idea that the life of an animal is intimately associated with its blood is clearly expressed in Lev 17:10–14 (NIV) where it's also stated that, for both Israelite and the resident alien, eating blood is forbidden.

The quote made by TS—"Christ our Passover lamb has been sacrificed," comes from 1 Cor 5:7 (NIV) and Jeremiah's reference to the new covenant, to which TS also referred, can be found in Jer 31:31–34 (NIV).

Though TS indicated that he wanted to discuss the matter of "breaking bread" later, it might be helpful to note the following even at this point.

Using IHG, a survey of the Old Testament gives the impression that bread was normally cooked in the form of loaves. The following information may also prove of interest to the reader—The word, "*lechem*" (לֶחֶם) occurs 287 times in the Masoretic text of the Old Testament and is found in thirty of its books. See IHG. It ordinarily refers to bread but is often understood to mean more generally "food." This is an indication of the extent to which bread was part of the diet of the ancient Israelite. Additionally there are specialist words meaning "leavened" or "unleavened" often translated "leavened bread" or "unleavened bread." There are a few words, occurring only from time to time that seem to refer to different varieties of bread that we might understand to be in the form of something like buns or cakes. See IHG. On a number of occasions "*lechem*" is mentioned in association with "water,"—see IHG—the phrase seemingly being an idiomatic or summary expression for the basics required in order to live. See the text for Day 21 where TS speaks of matters concerning bread when conversing with GB.

The statement made by TS that baking bread in the form of loaves was a common way of making bread in the ancient world, generally, without limiting it to the ancient Israelite, is more of a guess on my part rather than a claim based on hard evidence.

In the Old Testament there are a few references to "pieces of bread." For example—Gen 18:15; Judg 19:5; 1 Sam 2:36, 28:22; 1 Kgs 17:11; Prov 28:2; Ezek 13:19 (IHG) and one poignant reference to the breaking of bread—Jer 37:21 (IHG)—little ones ask for bread but no one breaks bread for them.

In the *LXX*, Jer 17:7 there is the statement, "There shall be no bread broken in mourning" and references to pieces of bread or bread that has been broken are to be found in the *LXX*, Ezek 13:19.

John 19:31–36 (NIV) records how the legs of Jesus were not broken and that this was in fulfillment of Scripture. The passage of Scripture that John appeals to is Ps 34:20.

The examples of the use by Jesus of "powerful, colorful and sometimes disturbing images" that TS refers to can be found in John 8:12; Matt 12:34, Matt 11:30; John 15:1; Luke 11:44 (NIV), in that order.

Part 3: The Lord's Supper

That Jesus said that he would be with his disciples until the end of the age is recorded in Matt 28:20 (NIV).

The passage in Luke that TS was referring to that records Jesus explaining about the necessity of his death and linking that death with the forgiveness of sins is Luke 24:45–46 (NIV).

TS was referring to Rom 6:3–4 (NIV) when he said that Paul in a letter to the churches in Rome had the notion of something similar to the "taking on" of Jesus, terminology used by GB.

Concerning Easter, Canon I of the Synod of Antioch in Syria held in 341 CE made it clear that some Christians were celebrating Easter at the same time as Jews celebrated Passover. This practice was condemned in that Canon.

Such a practice may have begun as early as the second century or even the first century. In a list of those who had died in Asia who had observed the fourteenth day of Nisan—the day Jews began their celebration of Passover—as the appropriate day to remember the death of Jesus, Polycrates, quoted by Eusebius, names first of all the disciples of Philip and John before next referring to Polycarp. See *Eusebius, Ecclesiastical History*, Book V, chapter 24, 2–6 in Stevenson, *A New Eusebius*, 148. Assuming the accuracy of what is detailed in that account, the information could be understood to indicate that some Jews, who had become Christians, were now celebrating Passover but in a new light. Given that some disciples of Philip and John might also have been Gentiles it could be assumed that something like Easter might have had its beginnings for Gentiles at around this time.

It is not clear to what extent in the very early days Jews and Gentiles held some customs in common. However, Ignatius of Antioch, writing around the turn of the first century, indicates that some Christians were living in accordance with some Jewish practices, by his denunciation of such behavior. He wrote—"If we continue to live until now according to Judaism, we confess we have not received grace."—Ignatius, *To the Magnesians*, 8.1, 118; "Those who lived in old ways [but now have] come to newness of hope, no longer keeping Sabbath, but living in accordance with the Lord's day."—Ignatius, *To the Magnesians*, 9.1, 123; "It is ridiculous to profess Jesus Christ and to Judaize; for Christianity did not believe in Judaism, but Judaism in Christianity."—Ignatius, *To the Magnesians*, 10.3, 126; "But if anyone expounds Judaism to you do not listen to him."—Ignatius, *To the Philadelphians*, 6.1, 200.

The terms of the covenant that God established with his people at Sinai and their response to God's promises can be found in Exod 19:3–8 (NIV).

Given that the Salvation Army does not conduct services of the Lord's Supper, it is interesting to consider what any of their number believes concerning what Jesus meant when he said, "Do this in remembrance of me." An unknown author in an issue of *The War Cry*, 7 and the Army Salvationists Layton in *The Sacraments and the Bible*, 44 and

Kew in *Closer Communion,* 19 suggest that Jesus could've been referring to what his disciples should do at the Last Passover Meal and what any of his disciples should do at future Passover meals.

The idea that the Corinthian believers met together weekly is based on the text in 1 Cor 16:2 (NIV) where Paul writes, "On the first day of the week each of you is to put aside and store it up as he may prosper."

Day 19

"You are Doing This in Remembrance of Me"

What TS proposes that he and GB should consider today is a very unusual understanding of what is otherwise a well-known statement made by Jesus. The evidence he proposes for his suggestion is not compelling though he does not believe that it can be easily dismissed. However, he does not consider his suggestion as crucial for the case he will ultimately endeavor to make.

TS: Hi. I'm glad you're persevering.

GB: It's not a matter of persevering. I enjoy what we're doing. But what you're planning to do today seems a little mysterious.

TS: Not mysterious, just complicated. I hope not too complicated. Let me begin by pointing out that the Greek for "Do" in "Do this in remembrance of me" is "ποιειτε," *(poieite)*. This is the form when one wishes to say, "Do," as in the imperative mood, second person, plural. It's also the form when one wishes to say, "You are doing," as in the *indicative* mood, second person plural.

GB: And?

TS: Well, it's possible to translate what Jesus said, either as recorded in Luke or in 1 Corinthians, as, "You are doing this in remembrance of me."

GB: But, what would that mean?

TS: It would partly depend on what the "this" actually refers to. In Luke it would seem that its immediate reference is to the eating of the bread that was distributed just prior to the main course. In 1 Corinthians where we have two such statements, it would seem that the first reference is to the eating of the bread, as with Luke, and the second to the drinking of wine. However, recognizing that in 1 Corinthians the two "this" statements, considered together, embrace the main course, the words could also be understood to refer to the Passover meal as a whole. We sort of touched on something of this yesterday. In which case, Jesus would be saying that their taking part in the Passover meal as a whole was an actual remembrance, in itself, of his death. Participating in the meal had been a remembrance of God's great salvation act in the past. Now the disciples were to see it as a remembrance of the greatest of all God's great salvation acts, an act yet to occur. "You are doing this in remembrance of me." *You are taking part in this Passover meal right now in remembrance of me.*"

GB: But what about Paul's report of Jesus saying "Do this as often as (whenever) you drink it in remembrance of me"? Surely "whenever" refers to future occasions and so "Do this" has to be understood as an imperative!

TS: Not necessarily so. Translate the text simply as follows—"You are doing this, whenever you drink it, in remembrance of me." If understood to be in the indicative mood, "ποιειτε" together with "ὁσακις," the "whenever" word, would mean that whenever they had been celebrating Passover they had been doing so in remembrance of Jesus. That is, Jesus could've been indicating that even though the disciples and others before them had never understood the Passover meal to be associated with *him* it *did* indeed have to do with him. Jesus could've been implying that in the mind of God, given that his great redemptive purposes were being fulfilled in his Son, Jesus, the Passover, in an important sense, from an important perspective, had always been about him. And it was about him now. The "old covenant" was being understood as an inevitable forerunner of the "new covenant." Remember how Jesus made a reference to the new covenant, quite possibly having something Jeremiah said about a new covenant, in his mind. We mentioned that yesterday. The "old covenant" has its fulfilment in the "new."

GB: That sounds like very powerful theology! I've never understood the words of Jesus to imply that! I am seeing the "whenever" in an entirely new light. But why is there no mention of "ὁσακις" in Luke or why in 1 Corinthians is it mentioned only with respect to the cup?

TS: In response let me first say something about Luke's reference to Jesus saying either "Do this in remembrance of me" or "You are doing this in remembrance of me."

GB: Go ahead.

TS: That Luke records Jesus saying either of those sets of words at the beginning of the main course may be thought of as Luke seeing it as introductory to the main course and hence to be understood as having some application to the Passover meal as a whole. It's possible that Paul, if he wasn't simply reciting an already formulated statement, was trying to do something similar but by using a different technique. Luke records Jesus as saying whatever he actually said, only once, and at the *beginning* of the main meal whereas Paul records Jesus saying "whenever" only once, but at the *end* of the main meal. Paul may have considered that the word "whenever," along with its accompanying words, drew the meal to a conclusion and being a conclusion, just like Luke's introduction, it also applied to the Passover meal as a whole.

GB: That makes some sense but it's only speculation isn't it.

TS: Sure. But let me continue. I think that Paul's use of the word "ὁσακις" probably had an additional function. My guess is that it was important for him to mention "whenever" when quoting the words of Jesus and to mention the word almost at the end of the quote, given what he wished to say more directly to his readers or hearers. He wanted to link the words of Jesus with what he wished to say to *them*. Paul wanted to say, "whenever" to the Corinthians. I'd like to look at that matter a little later. Back to Luke. Why he didn't mention "whenever" at all, I don't really know. As a suggestion, perhaps it was simply that he didn't see the need for it. It's possible that he considered the statement "You are doing this in remembrance of me," if that's what Jesus said, as striking enough on its own. Of course perhaps we should recall that originally Luke's Gospel might have made no reference whatsoever to any remembrance words of Jesus.

GB: That Jesus said, "Do this," rather than "Eat this" or even "Drink this," assuming the imperative mood is the case, although in 1 Corinthians it's clear that the second imperative "Do this" has to do with drinking, seems to me a little strange. Do you think that his use of the word "do" might bear on what you're suggesting?

TS: It might have some relevance, though I think it could be simply understood as Jesus indicating that overall his words were meant to refer to the main course and hence to the Passover meal as a whole. The somewhat indefinite character of "do" might have been his way of having the focus on the bread and the wine broadened so that they were seen together as embracing the main course and so relating to the Passover meal in its entirety.

GB: What still seems a little odd to me, I mentioned this yesterday, is that even if Jesus said "Do this in remembrance of me" and that it was his death that was primarily the subject of that remembrance, he hadn't yet died. Of course he was very soon to die, as you've said, but "remembering," strictly speaking, has to do with the past. Perhaps what I'm raising is of no significance.

TS: I think that's probably the case. However, if we understand that what Jesus said was "You are doing this in remembrance of me," that oddity, although I think it *is* of little significance, seems to disappear. The Passover meal has always been a remembrance event and it has always been about him.

GB: I must say that I can't imagine many people seeing "ποιειτε" the way you do. Your view is hardly a common one is it?

TS: No, it certainly isn't a common view. I know of only a few who think it's a possibility. One of them suggested it to me in the first place. However, that it isn't a commonly held view is understandable. Though Jesus would've spoken in Aramaic—I've mentioned that before—from fairly early days Christians regarded what Jesus said, as recorded in the Greek language, as a command. We will need to look at these historical matters later on. However, the truth is that there is some grammatical evidence that suggests that understanding "ποιειτε" to be in the indicative mood rather than in the imperative mood is more appropriate. That is, that the complete sentence should be understood to be a statement and not a command, whether we find it once in Luke or twice in 1 Corinthians.

GB: Really? What's the evidence?

TS: It's a little complicated, but it mainly depends on the order of the words "τουτο" (*touto*) and "ποιειτε"—which comes first and which comes second. "Τουτο" is the Greek word, neuter in gender, singular in number and also nominative or accusative in case, meaning "this." The equivalent plural form is "ταυτα" (*tauta*), meaning "these." It's also neuter in gender and nominative or accusative in case. "Ποιειτε," which, as we've already discussed, is second person plural, meaning "do" is matched by "ποιεις" (*poieis*), which is second person singular. "Ποιεις," like "ποιειτε," can also be understood to be in either the indicative or imperative mood.

GB: And you're telling me all this for what reason?

TS: I think it's possible that no matter whether the demonstrative pronoun is singular or plural or whether the verb is second person singular or plural, the order in which the demonstrative pronoun and the second person verb appears in the Greek language might be relatively consistent. Indeed, I think it's possible that the order in which the demonstrative pronoun and the second person verb appears might largely depend on whether the imperative or indicative mood is involved.

GB: You think there might be a rule?

TS: It could be, though it may not be a strict rule. However, if we consider the overall content of a sentence we might be able to see a general rule and explain any exceptions. Of course we are only interested in those situations where "τουτο" or "ταυτα" is the object of the verb, that is, where they are recognized as being in the accusative case. This means we will be looking at "Do (singular or plural) this" or "Do (singular or plural) these (things)" or "You (singular or plural) are doing this," or "You (singular or plural) are doing these (things)." Of course the last two possibilities could occur in the form of questions.

GB: I think I follow, but go slowly. I suspect you've already investigated the matter.

TS: True. Let me report on my findings and you can be the judge of their worth.

GB: Okay.

TS: I was able to locate thirty five relevant instances, outside of the New Testament, and unrelated to the New Testament, dated between the sixth century BCE and a little beyond the end of the second century CE. I realize that's a fair spread of time and that the way words are used can vary considerably even over a few years. However it's all I've got to go on and I don't think it's helpful dividing the thirty five into smaller numbers for different time spans. Anyway, as I think you'll soon see, there does appear to be some consistency in usage over time.

GB: But we would need to exercise some caution, wouldn't we?

TS: Sure. Now to the findings! Thirty of the thirty five instances were where "τουτο" or "ταυτα" preceded "ποιεις" or "ποιειτε," and all but one, that is, twenty nine of the thirty instances were judged, by means of considering the context, to be in the indicative mood. The odd one out was fairly clearly in the imperative mood. There was one of those twenty nine instances where making the judgement that either the indicative or the imperative mood applied was difficult but in the end I decided that the indicative mood was involved. Of the five where "ποιεις" or "ποιειτε" preceded "τουτο" or "ταυτα," the remaining five, two were judged, again by consideration of the context, to be in the indicative mood, with the other three judged to be in the imperative mood.

GB: This is a little heavy going. However are you suggesting that as a general rule, if "τουτο" or "ταυτα" precede "ποιεις" or "ποιειτε" then the indicative mood applies and if it's the other way around, then the imperative mood applies?

TS: Yes. I think it all has to do with "stress," that is, "emphasis." Generally, if the mood is indicative there is little stress on the verb. The stress, even if only minimal, tends to be on the demonstrative pronoun. "You are doing *this*." Often a question is being asked about the "this" or "these." Why are you doing *these things*? If however the stress happens to be on the verb then the verb precedes the demonstrative pronoun. The assumption is that this is more likely to be the case, when the imperative mood applies. *Do* this! Make sure it happens.

GB: But what do you make of the exceptions?

TS: Well, in the one clear case where "ταυτα," as the demonstrative pronoun happens to be, immediately precedes "ποιεις" but the clause is in the imperative mood, the emphasis appears to be on what is signified by "these (things)." A suitable translation for the text is, "You have to attend to *these* matters." The requirement concerned a set of instructions that needed to be given to soldiers coping with fear, lined up ready for battle. The stress, being where it is, means that "these (things)" precedes the verb. Normally however one might expect the stress if any, to be on the verb itself.

GB: And what of the two instances where the "do" precedes the demonstrative pronoun but the indicative mood appears to be the case?

TS: I admit that the evidence for the second part of the general rule is not strong. That is, the idea that where "ποιεις" or "ποιειτε" precede "τουτο" or "ταυτα" then the imperative mood applies. There are, as I've said, only five instances anyway, that is, where "ποιεις" or "ποιειτε" precede "τουτο" or "ταυτα." However with respect to those two exceptions, the situation in both cases appears to be where the stress is on the doing. The translation of one, which involves "ποιειτε ταυτα," is, "You still act in an impious way and openly *do* these things." The translation of the other, involving "ποιεις ταυτα" reads, "Father, why are you *doing* these things?" The question occurs within a play where an ongoing dialogue revolves around the action being taken. In both of these cases, though the mood is indicative, what I will refer to as the "abnormal situation," the abnormal situation applies—the stress is on the verb rather than on the "these (things)." The stress being where it is, means that the verb precedes "these things," contrary to what one might expect in a situation where the indicative mood applies, where one might anticipate the emphasis, even if only minimal, to be on the "this" or the "these things."

GB: I think I follow. I'm glad we left this discussion for a new day. Now what about the situation in the New Testament itself and especially in those sentences where Jesus speaks of "do" and "this"?

TS: There are three texts where Jesus uses the "do" and "this" words together. Again, we're not looking at his actual words but only a Greek version of what he said. They occur in our passages that contain the remembrance words of Jesus at the Last Passover Meal. As we've already established, one is in Luke's Gospel, Luke chapter 22, the other two are found in 1 Corinthians, chapter 11. Omitting reference to these three for the moment, there are seven other relevant instances but they are not words spoken by Jesus. In similar fashion to what one finds in the Greek world external to the New Testament, the indicative mood rather than the imperative mood is by far the more common. All except one of the seven instances have "ταυτα" and in each of these cases "ταυτα" precedes "ποιεις" or "ποιειτε." The indicative mood applies in all of these instances. In the other instance, one involving "τουτο," "τουτο" follows "ποιειτε," it does not precede it. It is found in Mark 11. A question is being asked and so obviously, the indicative mood also applies in this case. The text reads, "If anyone asks why you are doing this, (untying a colt) tell him . . . ." This is obviously an exception to the general rule that we're applying but I hope you can see why it is an exception. The emphasis is on the activity of untying the colt. So, even though it's in the indicative mood, where one might ordinarily expect the emphasis, if any, to be on the "this" and so "τουτο" to precede "ποιειτε," because the emphasis is on the verb, the reverse applies.

GB: I've noticed that a couple of the indicative mood examples that you've given involve questions. Are questions very common in the samples we have access to, both in the New Testament and beyond?

TS: Excluding any reference to the three examples in Luke 22 and 1 Corinthians 11, of all of the thirty eight instances where the indicative mood applies—twenty nine plus two from without the New Testament and seven from within the New Testament—nineteen are in the form of questions. Incidentally, of the forty two usages of the demonstrative pronoun, whether in a sentence in the indicative or imperative mood, again excluding any reference to the three examples from Luke 22 and 1 Corinthians 11, "τουτο" and "ταυτα" occur in equal numbers, twenty one each.

GB: Okay but who cares? Sorry! I didn't mean that. Of course of paramount interest to me, is the question concerning the order of "ποιειτε" and "τουτο" in those three New Testament passages that we haven't dealt with so far, the passages usually translated, "Do this."

TS: The order is "τουτο" followed by "ποιειτε"!

GB: Of course my question was almost rhetorical. I could guess what your answer was going to be! What you're suggesting is that on the basis of the evidence presented, we would expected that what Jesus said was a statement—that what he said was in the indicative mood rather than a command in the imperative mood!

TS: Yes, though I know that the evidence is suggestive only. Whether, the indicative or imperative mood is involved in any of those cases outside of the three passages under discussion and where a question doesn't seem to be involved, can be debated. However, I've not understood the passages, outside of the New Testament any differently to those who have published translations. Whether my appeals to the notion of "stress" or "emphasis" are correct are also debatable. Suffice it to say that I think the evidence is *quite* suggestive. It appears to be a general rule, broken only by a few exceptions. The rule is that if the demonstrative pronoun precedes the verb, then the indicative mood applies. And we can appreciate why the exceptions are exceptions. This means that if we're to understand what Jesus said as a command then we're claiming that we have an exception to the rule. And why would it be an exception? Because the emphasis is on the "this"? Surely not!

GB: I see what you're saying. The "this," if the reference is either to the eating of the bread or the drinking of the wine, is a reference to a common feature of Passover meals in Jesus' day. Alternatively, if the "this" refers to the Passover meal as a whole, then the reference is to a meal that had been celebrated for hundreds of years. Either way, the "this" does not refer to something with which the disciples were not already familiar and so why would there need to be some special stress on the "this"? Besides, placing the stress on the "this" would have detracted from the command if the "do" was meant to be understood as a command!

TS: To be fair I suppose some people would argue that there needed to be emphasis on both the command and the "this" and that the order is irrelevant. The position they could adopt might be that the "this" that Jesus was referring to was in fact something novel, something that had to be thought about. That it involved, the bread and the wine seen in a new light.

GB: I suppose so.

"You are Doing This in Remembrance of Me"

TS: However, for me, it seems that if we had no bias towards translating what Jesus said at the Last Passover Meal, one way or another, we would translate it as a statement rather than as a command! Almost always, when the demonstrative pronoun precedes the verb, the verb is in the indicative mood. Besides, of the total of the ten instances in the New Testament where the verb and the demonstrative pronoun come together, the three instances in which we are interested would be the only ones, commonly regarded as being in the imperative mood! The indicative mood is the prevailing mood both outside of and inside of the New Testament. If there were any doubt about how to translate those words of Jesus I would have thought you would have used the indicative mood.

GB: For me, this suggestion that "τουτο ποιειτε"—I am getting more used to some of this Greek!—could be translated "You are doing this" has been illuminating. You could be right. Yet, I'm still not sure. Perhaps I'm biased!

TS: I understand your hesitancy. However, let me indicate how understanding "τουτο ποιειτε" in the 1 Corinthians text to be in the indicative mood can throw a different light on, different to the common understanding of, what Paul is trying to do in, that part of his letter. In 1 Corinthians chapter 11 Paul is concerned about something wrong in what the Corinthians were doing and were doing regularly, when they had their meals. He makes a reference to the Last Passover Meal to somehow or other deal with the issue. Of course if he referred to what Jesus said as though it were a command, then that would've had some force, without a doubt. A command of Jesus and any implications arising from the command are not to be ignored! However, let us concede, for the purpose of the argument, that he quotes Jesus as saying "You are doing this in remembrance of me" both with respect to the bread and the wine and then with reference to the latter, mentioning "whenever." The present tense indicative mood aspect of this quote, together with that "whenever" inserted just before he is to explain the implications of what Jesus said, could be regarded as being even more poignant than if Jesus had issued a command. He links the present indicative and the "whenever" with what he next says—"For whenever you eat this bread and drink the cup . . . " On this analysis he uses the *present* indicative and the "*whenever*" of what Jesus said to connect with their *present* and *ongoing* behavior. I am sorry if this is a little difficult to follow.

GB: No, I see the point. Are we going to look at that 1 Corinthians passage now?

TS: I think it would be more helpful if we still left that until later. Besides it has been a long day.

GB: Okay, but if what you're suggesting is correct, how come people have got it so wrong for so long?

TS: I think we should leave the general problem of people getting anything wrong and being wrong for long periods of time, for later as well. However, let me assure you that what we've discussed today is, in the end, not all that crucial when it comes to considering our main problem. At this point I am suggesting that either Jesus issued no command at all, or if he did, then it was with respect to the celebration of that Passover meal and Passover meals yet to come. If he didn't command it, it would still be natural for any disciple celebrating Passover in the future to view the meal as relating to his death. How could any disciple do otherwise? If Jesus did command it, then it would also be natural to see the command as applying to the Passover meal rather than any other meal. I realize however, that there are arguments against this view, that is, that the celebration of Passover meals is what is actually involved and we will probably need to consider some of those arguments in the future. What about getting together again, the day after tomorrow? Would that be okay with you?

GB: That would be good. See you again then, on Saturday. No matter how impatient I appear to be I want you to know how much I appreciate your efforts. I know that you're trying to be thorough. Though, in all honesty I will be glad when we finally get to work on that 1 Corinthians passage. Have we many more areas you think we should cover before then?

TS: A few, I think. Sorry. But let's stop for the day. It's getting late. See you Saturday.

"You are Doing This in Remembrance of Me"
EXPLANATORY NOTES: DAY 19

I am indebted to George May for suggesting to me that at the Last Passover Meal, Jesus might have said, "You are doing this . . . " rather than "Do this . . . ."

The reference to the "new covenant" in Jeremiah can be found in Jer 31:31–34 (NIV).

The *Thesaurus Linguae Graecae* search engine was used to examine the Greek literature external to the New Testament, within the times frames specified, for those instances where the pronouns—"this" or "these"—in the accusative case and the verb forms—"do" or "doing"—second person singular or plural, are associated with each other, and to note the order and context in which they appear.

In case the analysis by TS of the literature outside of the New Testament for the period sixth century BCE to about the end of the second century CE and separately, the literature inside of the New Testament, with the exclusion of three texts, for instances where τουτο or ταυτα preceded ποιεις or ποιειτε or vice versa, was confusing, the analysis is here presented in tabular form. See Table 7.

	τουτο or ταυτα preceding ποιεις or ποιειτε		ποιεις or ποιειτε preceding τουτο or ταυτα	
	Indicative Mood	Imperative Mood	Indicative Mood	Imperative Mood
Outside of the New Testament	29	1	2	3
The New Testament	6	–	1	–

Table 7
The incidence of "τουτο" or "ταυτα" preceding "ποιεις" or "ποιειτε" or vice versa in literature outside of the New Testament for the period sixth century BCE to about the end of the second century CE and the same for the New Testament (NAG) itself with the exclusion of three instances—those occurring in the texts—Luke 2:19; 1 Cor 11:24–25 (NAG).

Regarding the literature outside of the New Testament, the one case where "τουτο" or "ταυτα," in fact "ταυτα," precedes "ποιεις" or "ποιειτε," in fact "ποιεις," and where "ποιεις" is in the imperative mood but where the emphasis appears to be on what is signified by "these things" can be found in Xenophon, *Xenophon VI. Cyropaedia II.* Book 6, chapter iii, section 28, line 1, 186–87.

The two instances where "ποιεις" or "ποιειτε" precedes "τουτο" or "ταυτα," but where the indicative mood appears to be the case, can be found in *Diogeneis Sinopensis Epistulae* Epistle 28, section 4, 1ine 9,—the instance being "ποιειτε ταυτα"—and in Menander, *Samia*, line 452, 110–11—the instance being "ποιεις ταυτα."

The six New Testament examples of "τουτο" or "ταυτα," in fact "ταυτα," preceding either "ποιεις" or "ποιειτε," occur in Matt 21:23; Mark 11:28; Luke 20:2; John 2:18, 7:4;

Acts 14:15 (NAG). The one instance in the New Testament where "ποιεις" or "ποιειτε," in fact "ποιειτε," precedes "τουτο" or "ταυτα," in fact "τουτο," occurs in Mark 11:3 (NAG).

Day 20

The Last Passover Meal in John and the Lord's Supper in Hebrews

In spite of GB's desire to begin looking at certain chapters of 1 Corinthians, today, TS is of a mind to examine some passages to be found in John's Gospel and the letter to the Hebrews. Thankfully GB fairly quickly recognizes the significance of these passages, at least as others see them, and appreciates the value of the discussion that ensues.

GB: So it's not 1 Corinthians 11 today? Actually I have in mind both chapters 10 and 11.

TS: No. Again I apologize. I really do think we need to look at a number of passages before we get to those chapters. Today I wonder if we couldn't examine attempts some people have made to see references to the Lord's Supper and the Last Passover Meal in passages of the New Testament outside of the obvious ones. To simplify things I'd like to look at just one extensive passage in John's Gospel where some people think there is a reference to the Last Passover Meal and a couple of texts in Hebrews, where some think there are references to something like the Lord's Supper.

GB: Okay, if you wish. . . . You say "attempts"?

TS: I'm being frank. I am sure it's been with the noblest of intentions but I don't think these attempts have been all that successful, and that's all they've been—attempts.

GB: Why do you think there has been this drive to find such references?

TS: Well, both the Last Passover Meal, particularly what Jesus said at that meal about the bread and the wine, and the Lord's Supper, which is considered to be grounded in the Last Passover Meal, are, understandably, thought to be extremely important. I think it's believed that they are of such importance that you might expect to find

Part 3: The Lord's Supper

references to them in more places than the few in which they are traditionally found. For starters, the Last Passover Meal is reported in the Gospels—Matthew, Mark and Luke—why wouldn't there be a reference to it in John's Gospel as well? That there is no reference in John's Gospel to those statements about bread and wine that Jesus made at that meal and hence the meal itself, for some, is probably inconceivable. Anyway, no matter how they've come to this conclusion, some have the view that in John's Gospel there are in fact references to what Jesus said at the Last Passover Meal.

GB: Whereabouts?

TS: People point to chapter 6. It's here that John writes how on one occasion Jesus, using five barley loaves and two fish, fed about 5,000 men. You'll remember reading about it I'm sure. He then records how soon afterwards, while in the synagogue at Capernaum, Jesus spoke at some length about the subject of "bread." He spoke about himself as the true bread and declared that he was the bread of life that had come down from heaven. He also said that whoever came to him would never go hungry and that anyone who believed in him would never go thirsty.

GB: Ah. . . . I can see how some people might think that on that occasion he was saying something similar to what he said later during the Last Passover Meal as recorded in the other Gospels.

TS: Well, in a way I suspect he was. However, the setting for the Passover meal was quite different to that of the feeding of the 5,000 and Jesus speaking in the synagogue at Capernaum. I cannot see why what Jesus said after feeding the 5,000 cannot stand in its own right and not as an insertion of what he said somewhere else. . . . Let me continue with what Jesus said in the synagogue. Having referred to himself as the bread of life he went on to say, with a twist of expression, at least as it appears in the Greek, that he was the living bread, declaring that those who would eat of that bread would live forever. He then said that that bread was his flesh that he would give for the life of the world. John then records that when some of the crowd in anger asked one another how Jesus could give them his flesh to eat, Jesus told them that unless they ate the flesh of the Son of Man—a way he had of speaking about himself—and drank his blood, they would not have life, but that whoever did eat his flesh and drink his blood would have eternal life. John then went on to recount how Jesus said that his flesh was real food and his blood real drink and that whoever ate his flesh and drank his blood would remain in him and that he, Jesus would remain in the one who had so drunk and eaten.

GB: Wow. I've read that passage before, but it did not strike me at the time that it had so many reverberations of what Jesus said at the Last Passover Meal as recorded in the other Gospels. Oops. Of course, historically, it's the other way around. But again I can understand, even more so now how people might claim that what Jesus said as recorded in John was almost exactly what he said at the Last Passover Meal according to the other Gospels. However, they don't have to claim that what he said on this occasion was an insertion of what he said later—simply that he was saying the same sort of thing—without, interestingly, referring to any notion of remembrance. But, as you say, I guess the concerns of some is that John has to have reported the words of Jesus about the bread and the wine at the Last Passover Meal, somehow or other! They are so important. He can't have written his Gospel without mentioning what Jesus said about those things then and so consequently without mentioning, in a sense, the Last Passover Meal itself.

TS: Yes. I think that's the argument.

GB: Hang on. I've just had a thought. Could people argue that Jesus was dealing with the concept of remembrance by referring to that time when God gave bread to his people when they were wandering in the wilderness? I think Jesus was making some connection with that event, in what he was saying, as recorded in John chapter 6, if my memory serves me right.

TS: Yes, they could so argue and yes, you're correct. Jesus did make a connection between himself as the bread from heaven and the bread, the manna, that God gave the Israelites prior to their arriving in the land of Canaan. But it was a connection. He wasn't asking anybody to *do* something in remembrance "whenever" such and such, or stating that they were *doing* something in remembrance "whenever" such and such.

GB: No you're right.

TS: To continue. Besides the lack of reference to "remembrance," and putting that matter aside, there is another interesting difference between what is recorded here in John and the references to the Last Passover Meal in Matthew, Mark, Luke, and also 1 Corinthians. In John, Jesus, besides making no mention of wine, refers to his "flesh" rather than his "body." It may not be all that important but it's almost as though Jesus is purposefully being shocking when talking to the crowd. But, when later speaking to his disciples at the famous meal, rather than speaking to shock, he speaks in a somber as well as striking manner. Of course we need to remember again that Jesus on both occasions would've actually been speaking in Aramaic rather than in Greek.

GB: The John chapter 6 situation and the Last Passover Meal situation *were* very different weren't they!

TS: Yes. And I don't think we need to reflect too much on how in John's Gospel it's recorded that so many of the so-called disciples of Jesus were deeply offended at what Jesus said. I think we could say that from their point of view what he said *was* repugnant. . . . You know, I wonder if what Jesus said on that occasion wasn't meant to convey the idea that he was God's ultimate sacrifice in a way that is not so obvious in what he said at the Last Passover Meal. In Leviticus you read how the blood of a sacrifice was to be drained and then how some of it was to be sprinkled against the altar or on the horns of the altar or used in other ways and how in some cases the priests were given a part of the animal's flesh to eat. There were even situations where the person offering the sacrifice was allowed to eat part of the animal.

GB: I don't know much about any of that.

TS: It was just a thought. Anyway, we haven't finished with John chapter 6. After recording how some of the so-called disciples of Jesus were offended, John further relates how Jesus, in effect, asked would they be shocked if they were to see the Son of Man ascend to where he had come from. Presumably he was speaking about his resurrection and how extraordinary that event would prove to be. His words were "out of this world" just as the resurrection would be. But then, and this is important, just so that there would be no confusion, Jesus says to the "grumbling" disciples, "The Spirit gives life; the flesh counts for nothing. The words that I have spoken to you are spirit and they are life." To have spoken so directly about the value of his flesh and then to have said that the flesh was worth nothing, surely indicates that Jesus was speaking highly metaphorically when referring to the necessity of eating his flesh.

GB: I agree. And I notice that even though Jesus refers to his blood a couple of times he thinks it sufficient to simply refer to his flesh as counting for nothing. The emphasis has been upon bread, eating, and his flesh, hasn't it, not upon his blood and drinking!

TS: Yes. I think so! But he's taken what we all know to be the necessities for life—"food" and "drink"—and said that we need him as our food and drink for us to have that life which belongs to the end of the ages and to have that life now. You can see how that what John records *could* be considered to be John's way of handling the Last Passover Meal, but surely it's striking that what Jesus said in John chapter 6 contains no words of remembrance. I must admit however, that it's also true that neither Matthew nor Mark contain such words. But John chapter 6 couldn't contain words of remembrance because what is there relates to the feeding of the 5,000! What was said on that occasion has similarities to what was said at the Last Passover Meal but it was not the Last Passover Meal. We cannot forbid Jesus making similar statements from time to time, particularly in similar circumstances but in this case, the circumstances are very different.

GB: And we can't use what John records to fortify the idea of remembrance at all can we, even the idea that some ceremony needs to be performed on a regular basis?

TS: I don't think so.

GB: Have we finished with John chapter 6 now?

TS: Yes.

GB: What about the idea that there are references to the Lord's Supper in Hebrews?

TS: There are a couple of passages in Hebrews that some people think have the Lord's Supper in mind. They can be found in chapters 6 and 13. Just focusing on chapter 6 for the moment, in that chapter there is a reference to "those who have tasted the heavenly gift and have become partakers of the Holy Spirit and have tasted the goodness of the word of God and the powers of the age to come."

GB: And there are some who think that that's some sort of reference to people partaking of food in a type of Eucharistic ceremony?

TS: Yes.

GB: Surely that involves a stretch of the imagination. Just hang on a moment.—I'm looking at the text. . . . It's verses 4 and 5 isn't it? You can see how the writer elaborates upon his metaphor of "tasting" to extend what is tasted from "heavenly gift" to "the goodness of the word God." And it doesn't even stop there. The metaphor is further extended to include tasting "the powers of the age to come."

TS: I agree with you but if someone is anxious to see some aspect of something like the Lord's Supper in the text, then they can argue that what *you* see as extensions of the metaphor actually refer to the benefits of receiving the bread and wine of the Eucharist or Holy Communion. The argument could be that one benefit of partaking in the service is that of receiving the very goodness of the word of God—the word of God that is Christ himself. The second benefit, the argument could be, relates to the powerful aspect of the bread, which is the body of Christ. The recipient of that bread enjoys a special spiritual benefit here and now but it's also a benefit that belongs to the age to come.

GB: I see what you mean. You seem to have made a good case for what you don't believe to be the case! Though I still think that what you've said amounts to a considerable injection into a text that without that approach is relatively easy to understand. I've had a quick look at the context of the passage now and can see it clearly. It has to do with those who repented and became believers. The writer refers to them as having been enlightened and having received God's gift—perhaps the gift of forgiveness or even Christ himself, as the one who procured that forgiveness or perhaps even the Holy Spirit, spoken of in the next phrase. The reference to "the goodness of the word of God" could be a reference to Christ although it could relate to the gospel—the message from God. "The powers of the age to come" could be a reference to the powerful working of the Holy Spirit. I'm not sure. The next verse then speaks of what happens if such believers then commit apostasy. The last part of verse 4 together with verse 5, simply seem to be a description of God's blessings for those who become believers.

TS: I think you've actually indicated that the text is not a simple, easy to understand text, while at the same time pointing out that a more natural understanding of one sort or another is the way to go. The overall reference is to the situation that exists where believers repent, the enlightenment they receive and the blessings given to them by God. Not the partaking of a meal.

GB: And what about the passage we need to look at in Hebrews chapter 13?

TS: The passage of interest begins at about verse 9. The author is concerned that his readers not be led astray by false teaching and writes, "Do not be carried away by strange and various teachings." He follows this with, "It is well that the heart be strengthened by grace, not by foods, which have not benefited their adherents." It seems to me that the author, at this point in his letter, is probably concerned about a specific false teaching that has a focus on the eating of certain foods. The problem may have been that such foods were being prohibited under this teaching. I'm not sure. What he next says, I think, is to move away from the false teaching to something else, there being a link between the two subjects however, the link being the reference to food and eating. Anyway, he then says, "We have an altar from which those who serve the tent have no right to eat." At this point surely the reader would see a metaphorical reference to the tabernacle and the altar of that tabernacle.

GB: But saying, "We have an altar" also sounds like a reference to something that the recipients of the letter have, then and there, doesn't it, not just a reference to the *ancient* tabernacle and altar.

TS: You're right and yes it does seem as though there is a reference to the then and there. In fact I think that in making this statement the writer is referring to the sacrificial death of Jesus—something which, in a sense, by the kindness of God they have, then and there! Perhaps there is a link here also with that "grace" that he mentioned only a few words earlier.

GB: That makes sense.

TS: Well, having referred to the tabernacle and the altar of the tabernacle, the writer then goes on to say that in a certain case, the bodies of the sacrificial animals were not allowed to be eaten by the priests—that they were required to be burned outside, what he calls, the camp, the area outside of the tabernacle and its courtyard. This presumably is a reference to the sacrifice associated with what was called the Day of Atonement. He then says that similarly Jesus suffered outside the gate, I think by this he means outside of the city of Jerusalem, and that his readers should go outside with him and suffer abuse as he suffered. I think he has connected Jesus and his death with the animals and their being sacrificed on the Day of Atonement. Having done that he says that his readers should align themselves with Jesus and also suffer "outside the gate," as it were. I can't see that the passage has anything to do with a ceremony like the Lord's Supper.

GB: It's a very striking passage isn't it? It abounds in metaphor. I suppose that it's the reference to "altar" that suggests to some that "the table" of the Lord's Supper is in mind.

TS: I'm pretty sure that that's the case. But it's an *altar*—a reference to the altar of the tabernacle—not a table. Anyway we're going to have to look at that whole notion of "table," at some time in the future.

The Last Passover Meal in John and the Lord's Supper in Hebrews

GB: Are there other passages, apart from the 1 Corinthians texts in chapters 10 and 11 that we should look at because some people think they make reference in one way or another, to something like the Lord's Supper?

TS: Yes there are. We need to examine certain texts in the Acts of the Apostle about the breaking of bread and we will need to consider the so-called Agape meal seemingly referred to in the book of Jude. There may be others that it's thought we should reflect on but I think we will have had a look at the main ones before we've finished. Why don't we call it quits for today? We can begin afresh on Monday, if that suits you.

GB: No problem. See you then.

Part 3: The Lord's Supper

EXPLANATORY NOTES: DAY 20

For an example of the view that John chapter 6 contains a reference to the Last Passover Meal see Jeremias, *The Eucharistic Words of Jesus*, 107–08, where he states his belief that John 6: 51c is an independent version of Jesus saying at the Last Passover Meal, "This is my body which is for you."

TS in referring to John chapter 6, quotes directly or indirectly from verses 32–35, 51–56, and 60–63 (NIV).

The passages from Lev that TS had in mind were Lev 1:11,15, 3:2, 13, 4:6, 7, 16–18, 25, 30, 34, 5:9, 7:2, 14 (NIV), with reference to how the blood of a sacrificial animal was to be used and Lev 7:6, 7, 16, 31–36 (NIV), with reference to parts of an animal sacrifice being consumed by the priests or even the one who offered the sacrifice.

The verses in Heb chapters 6 and 13 that TS quotes from are 4–6 and 9–13 (NIV) respectively.

Day 21

Bread and the Breaking of Bread

TS prefers not to discuss references to the breaking of bread texts in the Acts of the Apostles at this juncture. Rather, he thinks that prior to that it would be more helpful to examine the place of bread in the world of God's people from ancient times up until the New Testament period. Though he believes that it is of limited relevance, TS also makes some reference to the Greek writer Athenaeus who wrote about bread in the Greek and Greco-Roman world. Furthermore, in addition to discussing "bread," TS reflects on the general practice of "breaking bread."

GB: Hi. I suppose that now it's on to the Acts of the Apostles.

TS: Well, actually, probably not. There are five passages in Acts that we need to look at and each of them refers to bread and the breaking of bread. So I think before we examine those five we should consider the place of bread and the practice of breaking bread in the world to which those early disciples belonged. Don't worry, we will look at those five passages the very next time we meet.

GB: Okay. And as usual, and I mean it, I'm happy to be guided by whatever you suggest.

TS: I know we briefly considered bread and its being broken when thinking about what Jesus said at the Last Passover Meal. The truth is I don't believe we really appreciate the extent to which bread formed part of the daily diet of Jewish people in New Testament times and even before the New Testament era. So I think it will help us if we now look at the part that bread played in people's lives as evident from the literature of the Old Testament and some literature from the inter-testamental period—the time between the two Testaments.

GB: Well, let's proceed to the Old Testament then.

TS: The Hebrew word often translated "bread" in the Old Testament is "*lechem*" (לֶחֶם). It's found almost 290 times in the Masoretic text of the Old Testament and in thirty of its books.

GB: What's the Masoretic text?

TS: It's regarded as an authoritative text of the Jewish scriptures. It didn't come into existence until fairly late. To what extent it agrees with the original Hebrew writings is debatable and of course basically unknowable. But it's the text scholars tend to appeal to when discussing the Hebrew of the Old Testament. I don't think we need to go into the ins and outs of its origins and reliability. Nor do I think we should be overly concerned about relying on it. It's the text I was referring to some time ago now, when I was talking about the word "name" in the Hebrew Scriptures.

GB: Okay.

TS: Back to "*lechem*." It's sometimes quite difficult to decide when translating the word, whether "food" or "bread" is the sense being conveyed. That it can be understood as either "bread" or "food" is an indication of how common bread was, as part of the diet of the ancient Israelites. As one example, 1 Samuel chapter 28 records how Saul had not eaten "food," "*lechem*," all day and night and how a woman, indicating to him that she would like him to have a piece of "bread," "*lechem*," then kneads and bakes flour to make unleavened bread. Actually there are special words for leavened bread and unleavened bread. "*Chāmētz*" (חָמֵץ) is leavened bread and "*matztzāh*" (מַצָּה) is unleavened bread.

GB: Can you give me some more examples from the Old Testament? I'm fascinated.

TS: Chapter 7 of Judges refers to a man who dreamt of a round loaf of barley bread tumbling into a Midianite camp. 1 Samuel 16 refers to a certain Jesse sending to a king Saul a donkey loaded with bread, a skin of wine and the kid of a goat. In 1 Kings 14 we read of Jeroboam instructing his wife to take ten "*lechem*" (often translated as "loaves" but they could've been more like rolls) to a prophet at Shiloh. A passage in Leviticus 26 is also worth quoting—"When I (God) break your staff (that is cut off your supply) of bread, ten women will bake your bread in one oven and they will bring back your bread in rationed amounts, so that you will eat and not be satisfied." Many times, "*lechem*" is mentioned in association with water. The idea being conveyed seems to be similar to what used to be regarded as "the bread and water" of English jails—the bare necessities for life. In chapter 4 of Ezekiel, God is reported as saying, "I am going to break the staff of bread in Jerusalem, and they will eat bread by weight and with anxiety, and drink water by measure and in sorrow because bread and water will be scarce." The point I'm trying to make, I hope it's obvious, is that bread, of some sort or another, was a common component of the diet of this Semitic people.

GB: The reference to barley bread suggests that there were different types of bread.

TS: Yes, I suspect that there would've been varieties based on different grains. For instance, in chapter 2 of Ruth, there's a reference to Ruth gleaning until both the barley and wheat harvests had finished. I guess the ancient Israelite used both barley and wheat to make different types of bread. Though, I'm not sure. Certainly "barley bread" gets a mention from time to time. But also I think that there were different types of grain-based cakes made from various ingredients in addition to the grain used.

GB: I suspect that their cakes weren't quite like ours!

TS: The evidence is tricky and I don't really know what their cakes were like but we can be fairly sure that as far as ingredients go, that they didn't have self-rising flour! Chapter 6 of 2 Samuel records that David, on a special occasion, to do with the arrival of the ark of the Lord in the city of Jerusalem—actually called the city of David—distributed a cake of bread "*challath lechem*" (חַלַּת לֶחֶם), a date cake "*eshpār*" (אֶשְׁפָּר) and a raisin cake "*ashīshāh*" (אֲשִׁישָׁה) I read somewhere that the Hebrew word, (חַלָּה) "*challāh*" (from which "*challath*" is derived) may have been a word for a cake with a hole through the middle, perhaps a bit like our doughnut! Chapter 8 of Leviticus also speaks of the "*challāh*"—one unleavened "*challāh*" and one "*challāh*" of bread mixed with oil, being involved in what was called a "wave offering." And Genesis chapter 18 refers to Sarah being instructed by Abraham to make cakes (עֻגוֹת) "*ugōth*" from fine flour. What type of cakes were these? What types of cakes were any of these? The date and raisin cakes may not have been grain-based cakes at all and indeed none of the references to "cakes" may have been to cakes as we think of as cakes. Perhaps as an indication of how varied a recipe for "bread" could be it's worth considering what's recorded in chapter 4 of Ezekiel. Although made to be food for a stringent vegetarian diet and not as a delicacy, Ezekiel is instructed to take "wheat, barley, beans, lentils, millet and spelt, put them in one vessel and make them into bread." He is then told to eat it as though it were "barley bread." Perhaps the variety that was used was also meant to suggest that grains and other foods were in short supply. It presumably wasn't the nicest of breads!

GB: So, even though we can't be sure what different "cakes" were really like, it's fairly obvious that a variety of "cakes" were available.

TS: Well, some of my examples may be a little misleading. What David did was for a special occasion and the wave offering was a special offering. And Abraham's family was not the average family either. However, with the earlier passages that I've mentioned in mind, I think that what we have is a fairly clear indication that bread, made simply from one grain or another, was an important component of the regular diet of ordinary people.

GB: You mentioned the inter-testamental period. What do we learn about bread and its use in that era? Do we see the same sort of picture?

TS: I think so. Again, "bread" seems to be part of a basic and common diet. In a work called *The Book of Tobit*, Tobit is told not to give any of his bread to sinners. Sirach in his *Book of Wisdom* forbids the same sort of thing—presumably putting limits to charity. In another writing called *Joseph and Aseneth,* there is a reference to "the bread of life." There's also a reference to what is called the Messianic Banquet, the banquet for the Messiah at the end of the age, in the Qumran community's *Rule of the Congregation* in which it is said that no one should take "the first fruit of the bread" before the priest, because he has to bless it. He also has to bless the wine. Afterwards it is said that the Messiah will stretch out his hands towards the bread. I'm not sure what that was supposed to mean. Philo Judaeus in one of his works makes reference to a common meal comprising only of bread and salt.

GB: That last reference is interesting. It seems to imply that an entire meal might consist of basically just bread. I was sort of getting that picture anyway.

TS: Well yes, I think that that's the implication that you would draw from some of the Old Testament references that I've mentioned. But now let's have a look at the New Testament literature! The Greek word, "ἄρτος" (*artos*), occurs ninety five times in the New Testament, the most common translation being, "bread" or "loaves." The four Gospels contain most of the references, with twenty four instances occurring in John's Gospel, twenty one of these being in chapter 6 alone—the chapter that deals with the feeding of the 5,000. While "ἄρτος" might sometimes refer to "food" the prime reference seems to be to "bread" in some form or another.

GB: I suddenly realize that what the 4,000 and 5,000 were given as food, on those two different occasions, was fish and bread. Bread was obviously a substantial part of the meal that those people had that day. And I remember how that for the feeding of the 5,000 Jesus took five loaves and two small fishes that belonged to a boy. Obviously the boy had those loaves for his own meal. The bread was to be the main part of his meal.

TS: And that probably suggests to us, that in his case, the loaves were indeed small. I have come across one translation that says that they *were* small, just as you said, but there is no word for small in the Greek text. We simply guess that they were small.

GB: I wonder what ordinary larger loaves looked like and where his loaves, if they were small, more like buns?

TS: My guess is yes. And as for larger loaves I would have thought they were either round in shape or long and rounded. But I don't really know. I don't think they would've looked like our angular oblong-shaped loaves! But back to Jesus and the feeding of the 5,000. Remember how with that extraordinary event in the background Jesus referred to himself as "the bread of life." We spent a fair bit of time on the account in John chapter 6 on Saturday. That statement, alone, highlights the importance of "bread" as food. Perhaps the people of Jesus' day could refer to bread as being necessary for life in an idiomatic sort of way, much the same way as many of the world today could do so. But I suspect it would have been much closer to reality for them than for us.

GB: And some other examples from the New Testament? Oh, the obvious—"Give us today our daily bread" in the so-called "Lord's Prayer."

TS: A better translation might be something like, "Give us today the bread of tomorrow" or "Give us our needed bread today." Other references? In Luke chapter 4 we are told how Jesus who had not eaten for forty days and being hungry was tempted by the devil who said, "If you are the Son of God command this stone to become bread." Eating bread would have broken his fast. John the Immerser is described as a person, eating no bread and drinking no wine in chapter 7 of Luke. Even though Jesus had fed the 4,000 the disciples later mistakenly believed that Jesus was "having a go at them" when he said "Beware of the leaven of the Pharisees and the leaven of Herod," because on that occasion they had forgotten to bring sufficient bread. The incident is recorded in Mark chapter 8. In 2 Corinthians 9 we find Paul referring to God, who supplies seed to the sower and bread for food.

GB: You suggested a moment ago that sometimes the Greek word might actually refer to "food," rather than just "bread."

TS: I think that sometimes that is a real possibility. In 2 Thessalonians 3 Paul writes that he did not eat anyone's bread without paying for it and later in that chapter that certain people, whom he is concerned about, should work, without any fuss being created, in order to be able to eat their own bread. Here, he may have used "ἄρτος" as a general way of referring to "food" or "meals" rather than simply "bread" itself. In Mark's Gospel, chapter 3 there is an account of Jesus and his disciples not being able "to eat bread" as a consequence of being surrounded by a large crowd. The word "ἄρτος" appears in plural form and so perhaps should be thought of as a reference to a "meal" or even "meals," the text to read something like, "There was such a large crowd that Jesus and his disciples could not even eat a meal, any meal." That "ἄρτος," the normal word for bread, should be used to refer to "food" or "a meal" in itself suggests how important bread was as part of many diets. I said the same sort of thing when referring to the Hebrew word, "*lechem*."

GB: Yes and what you say makes sense. But what did ordinary people eat besides bread and let's include fish?

TS: I don't really know. I guess they ate various vegetables and fruit. I'd be fairly sure they ate grapes from time to time. The fruit dishes served at the Passover meal also come to mind and then you've probably read how Jesus, ostensibly, I think, went to find figs on a fig tree.

GB: Yes. I found that passage slightly puzzling.

TS: As others do! Back to the Old Testament, for a moment, if you don't mind. In 2 Samuel there is an interesting account of an occasion when David and some of his supporters—all tired and hungry—were being pursued by his son Absalom. At a place called Mahanaim, some people, sympathetic towards David and concerned for his well-being and that of his men, offered them "wheat and barley, flour and roasted grain, beans and lentils, honey and curds and sheep and cheese from cow's milk." Of course this was not an ordinary occasion—a king needed help—but I guess it's indicative of what could be available at different times for different people.

GB: And as far as meat dishes are concerned people must have eaten lamb from time to time. They ate lamb at Passover meals of course, as I recall.

TS: Yes they did. Well, I guess many did. But Passover was a special occasion. I suspect that the poor didn't eat lamb very often at all. There is a passage in the Old Testament book Leviticus that stipulates that for a sin offering a person is required to offer a goat or a lamb. However if he cannot afford these he is to bring two doves or two young pigeons. Furthermore, if he cannot afford these, he is to offer some flour. There are other passages that refer to what the poor could do as an alternative to the normal expectation. Perhaps the very poor ate very little meat of any kind. And anyway, there were restrictions, detailed in Leviticus, on what meat could be eaten by anyone. Only certain animals could be eaten and there was a list of those birds that were forbidden.

GB: I guess for the very poor such restrictions were probably irrelevant. One can understand how bread, where the poor were concerned, might have been the main part of most meals. However, I suppose one would expect, even with respect to the poorer people, at special meals, if they ever had them, and certainly where wealthy people were involved, at a banquet say, that delicacies and a variety of foods would be provided that were not normally "on the table."

TS: I think so. It might be significant that at those meals to which Jesus was invited, some of them probably being special meals, even being considered as "banquets," there is no mention of bread as one of the items of food. However, the truth is, that no food of any type is mentioned in connection with any of those meals! I take it that what was served on those occasions was of little interest to the Gospel writers. Whatever the case with those meals, and many of them might have been formal or semi-formal in character, it still seems apparent that, for most ordinary Jewish folk, bread was a common component of most meals—though it's possible that an evening meal consisted of better fare than any earlier meal of the day. Yet still, it's interesting that, at a village called Emmaus where two disciples were sitting having an evening meal with Jesus, though to begin with they didn't know it was Jesus, bread was still part of that meal.

GB: I get the picture. As unusual as it might appear to us, it seems that "bread" was part of the staple diet for many people, for perhaps most of their meals, at least in the Jewish world. Was it the same in the Greco-Roman world?

TS: I would have thought so. I can't imagine why it would have been any different but I haven't looked into that, particularly with respect to how the poor fared. However, we do know a little about what the *well-to-do* ate, particularly at their formal or semi-formal meals. There is a lengthy discussion on various types of bread available at these meals in a work by Athenaeus. He was a Greek of the second and third centuries CE, and wrote what were originally fifteen books, entitled *The Deipnosophists*, meaning something like, "The Banquets of the Learned" or The Learned Banqueters." The books cover eating and drinking habits across many centuries mainly in the Greek world and mainly in association with formal meals. In one section, where he writes about different types of bread available, his discussion centers around which ones were easily digested and which ones weren't! He also records in one of these books that at a wedding, given by a certain Caranus, there were many different types of fancy bread and that in the course of the meal two different servings of bread as big as a platter were provided. In the same work he makes a further reference to big loaves being served at an Attic dinner party. In another place he refers to a certain Arcesilaus who, having some people to dinner and being informed by a slave that the bread had run out, "burst into laughter, clapped his hands, and said, 'What a party we are having, my friends—we forgot to buy enough bread! Run slave!'"

GB: Arcesilaus seems either to have had a good sense of humor or that he simply knew how to deal with a tricky situation that might have been potentially embarrassing.

TS: Either alternative is a good suggestion! Anyway from these few snippets it seems fairly clear that in the Greco-Roman world, well particularly the Greek world, bread, fancy or not, was an important component of their formal meals.

GB: And perhaps for the ordinary meals of most people as well.

TS: I would think so.

GB: Can we now have a look at the matter of "breaking bread"? I remember the other day, your making reference to the idea that bread, if it were in the form of a loaf, had to be broken in order for it to be distributed.

TS: True. I said something like that. And yes, I was just about to get to that matter. Outside of the New Testament we can't find many references to bread being broken, either in the Jewish world before the time of Jesus or in the ancient Greco-Roman world generally.

GB: Why do you think that's so?

TS: I can't be sure. I would have thought that Athenaeus would have made some comment about bread being broken but I can only recall one occasion when he mentioned something to that effect. Actually, on the whole, I think he's more interested in the drinking of wine than the eating of food, bread or otherwise! Anyway, the text I'm thinking of is a reference by Athenaeus to a certain Phylarchus, an historian, who wrote in the third century BCE, and who recorded that, "Among the Galatians, many loaves are broken into pieces (literally "much broken bread"—"ἄρτους πολλυς κατακεκλασμενους" [*artous pollus katakeklasmenous*]) and placed in heaps on the tables." But to return to your question as to why there might be so little reference to the breaking of bread, outside of the New Testament, it could be that in the case of the Greco-Roman world, we need to look in literature which is less focused on formal meals than the books of Athenaeus. And I haven't done that. I'm not sure that there's much literature available of that nature anyway. Alternatively or additionally, it could be that "breaking bread," together with the giving of thanks or having a blessing, however one words it, was a more common feature of meals eaten by Jewish communities than elsewhere.

GB: Are there any references in the Jewish world to bread being broken apart from what we find in the New Testament?

TS: Yes, at least a couple. In the *LXX*, the famous Greek version of the Old Testament but also containing other Jewish literature, in Jeremiah chapter 16, there's a statement, "There shall be no bread broken "κλασει ἄρτος" (*klasei artos*) in mourning." The idea being conveyed in that part of the chapter seems to be that there would be so many dead, that people wouldn't even try to have a meal at a gathering where the dead would be mourned. "Bread broken" could be an idiomatic expression for having a meal. The Masoretic Hebrew text says something similar. It refers to people not breaking (bread is understood) for (the comfort of) those who mourn. The relevant Hebrew word underlying what could be translated, "shall be broken" is "*pāras*" (פָּרַס)—"to break." There is another reference to bread being broken in the *LXX* in chapter 13 of Ezekiel. Here the text speaks of "a handful of barley and 'pieces of bread'"—"pieces of bread" being "κλασματων ἄρτων," (*klasmatōn artōn*)—literally "broken breads." The equivalent Hebrew text refers similarly to "handfuls of barley and bits of bread." The Hebrew word underlying "bits" is "*path*" (פַּת), a piece."

GB: You've mentioned the two Hebrew texts. Are there other references in the Old Testament Hebrew to the notion of "breaking" in connection with "bread," or even just the idea of "pieces of bread"?

TS: Yes, just a few. The word "*path*" also appears in Proverbs, chapter 28 where it's stated that a man will do wrong (even) for a piece of bread. Then there's the word, "*kikkār*" (כִּכָּר), also meaning "a piece." It's found in Proverbs chapter 6 where the reference is to a man, who because of his involvement with prostitutes, will be left with only a piece of bread. The same word is also found in Jeremiah, chapter 37, where it's said that a certain king, Zedekiah, ordered that Jeremiah the prophet be given a piece of bread every day from what was called, "the street of the bakers." There may be more examples.

GB: So, is that about it from the Old Testament?

TS: That'll do.

GB: Which means, I hope, that we can now look at the New Testament, and in particular the Acts of the Apostles.

TS: Yes. But it's been important to consider "bread" and the "breaking of bread" outside of the New Testament, beforehand, because there is a belief that in the New Testament, especially in the Acts of the Apostles, some references to the breaking of bread are in fact references to an early Christian ceremony somewhat similar to what today we call the "Lord's Supper."

GB: But, as I think you're implying, not all such references in the New Testament should be so understood.

TS: Yes. You're quite right. For instance in the feeding of the 4,000 and the feeding of the 5,000 Jesus broke the loaves and although we rightly think that there was something special in his doing that, it wasn't an activity involved in a remembrance ceremony. The point I've been trying to make today is that bread was often used in meals, that it was sometimes broken and that it certainly existed in pieces. That seems to me to be fairly obvious. Where the bread was baked in the form of what we might consider to be loaves or in the form of smaller sized items such as buns or rolls, one would expect that the bread would often need to be broken into smaller pieces before eating. It may be that here and there, bread being such a common part of people's diet, a reference to the breaking of bread is used as an idiomatic way of referring to a meal. However, that would not belie the fact, but indeed would support it, that bread was very much part of a staple diet for many people and that often, it was broken before being consumed.

GB: I'm convinced. I didn't need convincing in the first place! Is it the Acts passages now?

TS: Well, yes, but say tomorrow. Would tomorrow be okay?

GB: Make it Wednesday.

TS: Okay. Wednesday it is. See you then.

Part 3: The Lord's Supper

EXPLANATORY NOTES: DAY 21

The five references to the "breaking of bread" in the Acts of the Apostles can be found in Acts 2:4, 46, 20:7, 11, 27:35 (NIV).

The account of Saul not having eaten food all day and night and how a woman baked him some bread, is recounted in 1 Samuel 28:20–25 (IHG).

The additional examples that TS gave of the usage of "*lechem*" (לֶחֶם) in the Old Testament can be located in Judg 7:13; 1 Sam 16:20; 1 Kgs 14:3; Lev 26:26; Ezek 4:16–17a (IHG).

For additional information on the usage of "*lechem*" in the Old Testament see Explanatory Notes: Day 18.

The matter of Ruth gleaning until the barley and wheat harvests had finished is recorded in Ruth 2:23 (IHG).

The episode of David distributing bread to celebrate the arrival of the ark of the Lord in the City of David can be found in 2 Sam 6:17–19 (IHG). The reference to the one unleavened "*challāh*" (חַלָּךְ) and a "*challāh*" of bread mixed with oil, involved in a wave offering, can be found in Lev 8:26 (IHG) and the matter of Abraham instructing Sarah to make "cakes" is recorded in Gen 18:6 (IHG).

The recipe for the bread that Ezekiel is instructed to make can be found in Ezek 4:9 (IHG). That he is to eat it as though it were barley bread is recorded in 4:12 (IHG).

For the reference to "bread" in *The Book of Tobit* see Tobit in Blomberg, *Contagious Holiness*, 68 and http://st-takla.org/pub_Deuterocanon/Deuterocanon-Apocrypha_El-Asfar_El-Kanoneya_El-Tanya__1-Tobit.html—*The Book of Tobit*, chapter 4, 17.

For the reference to "bread" in Sirach's *Book of Wisdom* see Sirach in Blomberg, *Contagious Holiness*, 60 and http://st-takla.org/pub_Deuterocanon/Deuterocanon-Apocrypha_El-Asfar_El-Kanoneya_El-Tanya__5-Wisdon-of-Joshua-Son-of-Sirach.html—*The Book of Sirach*, chapter 12, 6.

For the reference to "bread" in *Joseph and Aseneth* see Blomberg, *Contagious Holiness*, 73. See also http://archive.org/stream/josephasenathconoobroo/josephasenathconoobroo_djvu.txt, chapter XVI.

For the reference to "bread" in *The Rule of the Congregation* see Blomberg, *Contagious Holiness*, 83. See also https://www.bc.edu/dam/files/research_sites/cjl/sites/partners/cbaa_seminar/qumran.htm—*The Rule of the Congregation*, Col. 2, 17–21.

For the reference to "bread" in Philo Judaeus see Blomberg, *Contagious Holiness*, 85. See also http://humweb.ucsc.edu/gweltaz/courses/history/hist_5B/Lectures/therapeutae.pdf—Philo, *De Vita Contemplativa*, 37.

The feeding of the 5,000 is recorded in Matt 14:13–21; Mark 6:32–44; Luke 9:10–17; John 6:1–13 (NIV). The feeding of the 4,000 is recorded in Matt 15:29–39; Mark 8:1–10 (NIV).

That a boy had the five loaves and the two small fish with which Jesus fed the 5,000 is recorded in John 6:9 (NIV).

The reference to Jesus speaking of himself as "the bread of life," is found in John 6:35 (NIV).

What is often referred to as the Lord's Prayer is found in two different forms—Matt 6:9–13 and Luke 11:2–4 (NIV). The account of Jesus being tempted by the devil to command that a stone become bread is recorded in Luke 4:3 (NIV). The reference to John the Immerser eating no bread and drinking no wine can be found in Luke 7:33 (NIV). The mistaken belief of the disciples that Jesus was making a reference to their not having brought sufficient bread is recorded in Mark 8:14 (NIV). Paul's reference to the one who supplies seed to the sower and bread for food is located in 2 Cor 9:10 (NIV). Paul writes of his not eating anyone's bread without paying for it in 2 Thess 3:8 (NIV). In 2 Thess 3:12 (NIV) he says that people of the Thessalonian church should work so that they can eat their own bread.

The text that refers to Jesus and his disciples being unable to eat a meal because of the greatness of a crowd is located in Mark 3:20 (NIV).

The episode of Jesus looking to have figs from a fig tree is recorded in Mark 11:12–14 (NIV).

The occasion when, out of concern for their welfare, a range of food was offered to David and his men, can be found in 2 Sam 17:28–29 (NIV).

The Old Testament regulations applicable when a person was unable to offer a lamb or a goat or even two birds, for a sin offering, are recorded in Lev 5:5–13 (NIV). Another passage which refers to what a poor person could offer as an alternative to the normal requirement is Lev 12:6–8 (NIV). It relates to the purification of a woman after she has born a child.

Restrictions stipulated in the Old Testament concerning which animals could be eaten and which birds could not be eaten are detailed in Lev 11 (NIV).

The account of Jesus having a meal involving bread with two disciples in the village called Emmaus is recorded in Luke 24:30 (NIV).

The references by Athenaeus to various types of bread and their qualities can be found in *II Athenaeus* Book III, 115c–116a, 46–51. The references to bread being served at a wedding and large loaves being served at an Attic dinner party can be found in *II Athenaeus*, Book IV, 128d, 112–13 and Book IV, 134e, 144–45, respectively.

Part 3: The Lord's Supper

The reference to the work by Phylarchus concerning Galatians having "much broken bread" is located in *II Athenaeus,* Book IV, 150d, 220–21.

The reference to Arcesilaus can be found in *IV Athenaeus,* Book X, 420c, 472–73.

The *LXX* Jeremiah and Ezekiel texts referred to by TS are *LXX*, Jer 16:7, *LXX*, Ezek 13:19.

The quotations by TS referring to pieces or a piece of bread are located in Prov 28:21, 6:26; Jer 37:21 (IHG).

Day 22

The Lord's Supper in the Acts of the Apostles

At long last TS decides that it is time to examine certain passages in the book of Acts where reference is made to the "breaking of bread." However, in attempting to prepare the ground for his position he first of all examines the New Testament as a whole to see if there exists a technical expression for that activity. Later, as the discussion develops, TS focuses on two texts in the second chapter of Acts, at least one of which is regarded by some as an expression for something akin to the Lord's Supper.

GB: So finally, the Acts of the Apostles. You mentioned five passages we should especially look at. Where in Acts are they, though I've a rough idea for some of them?

TS: Chapter 2, verses 42 and 46, chapter 20, verses 7 and 11 and chapter 27, verse 35.

GB: I guess you're going to suggest that these references aren't at all unusual. If ordinary folk often ate bread and needed to break it before eating it, then finding such references in the Acts of the Apostles should not be a surprise.

TS: Yes. You've got it in one. However, that position proves to be a difficult pill for some people to swallow. We *are* going to examine those passages today, but to prepare the way we will first need to look more generally both at the book of Acts and other parts of the New Testament.

GB: As if I should be surprised at your approach! Let's go!

TS: We came across the verb "κλαω" (*klaō*), "I break," although not in that form, the other day, and also the noun "ἀρτος," "bread." In the New Testament, these two words, in various grammatical forms, occur in conjunction with one another sixteen times. In addition to the five occurrences in Acts, there are four texts which speak of Jesus breaking bread during the Last Passover Meal—one in each of the Synoptic Gospels and one in 1 Corinthians chapter 11. There's another occurrence in 1 Corinthians chapter 10, which we can translate, "Is not the bread that we break a participation in the body of Christ?" The two words are also in conjunction with one another where Luke records Jesus, after his resurrection, having a meal with two of his followers in the village of Emmaus. We came across that incident the other day. The other five occurrences are found in the Synoptic Gospels where they record the feeding of the 4,000 or the 5,000. Luke records only one of these events.

GB: As you said the other day, I wouldn't think that anyone would suggest that the feeding of the 4,000 or 5,000 was a reference to something akin to the Lord's Supper.

TS: No. I think we can put those five references aside. And we also don't need to look at the four examples that relate to the Last Passover Meal. That *was* the Last Passover Meal! Nonetheless, perhaps we should note that in each of these four cases, the same expression is used—"ἄρτον . . . ἔκλασεν," (*arton . . . eklasen*). However, we should also note that the texts differ as to what words lie between "ἄρτον" and "ἔκλασεν." Though each of the actual sets of words is similar, they differ in detail. None of them is the same. Never the less, essentially, the record in each is that Jesus took bread, gave thanks or gave a blessing and broke it.

GB: Is that same expression—"ἄρτον . . . ἔκλασεν,"—used in the other, hmm, seven instances, or in any of those instances?

TS: Interestingly, no. Not even in one of them. Sure, these other references still contain "ἄρτος" and "κλάω" in some grammatical form or other but the grammatical form and sentence structure is not, "ἄρτον . . . ἔκλασεν." In fact, except for two instances, they each differ one from the other in terms of their grammatical form and the structure of the sentence in which they are imbedded. With respect to those two exceptions, the form and structure is "ἄρτον . . . ἔκλασας," but in one case there are six words intervening and in the other, only two. One of the instances is recorded in Acts 27:35. In the lead up to this verse there is an account of a ship in danger of founding. Paul is onboard under guard. He advises the soldiers and the sailors of the ship to eat some food because they have not eaten for fourteen days. In verse 35 we read that having given such advice, by way of example, he then takes some bread, and having given thanks to God, breaks it and begins to eat. In the second case, which can be found in Luke chapter 24, it's the resurrected Jesus who, about to have a meal with those two of his followers in the village of Emmaus, takes bread, blesses it, breaks it and gives it to them.

GB: I wouldn't have thought that the first instance had anything to do with a Lord's Supper type of ceremony. I wouldn't even think that of the second, although I suppose some people might argue to the contrary, though I can't really see how. I remember, because I looked it up just recently, that the text in that instance says something about the eyes of the disciples being "opened," their recognizing Jesus at this point and then it records him disappearing. One could suggest that perhaps they recognized who he was when they observed the nail prints in his hands or by the way he gave the blessing at the meal but I don't recall Luke giving any such information. Anyway, it just seems like an account, though extraordinary, of a meal and one in which these two disciples recognized who Jesus was.

TS: I think that's correct. We can hypothesize as much as we like but the text simply says that their eyes were opened and they recognized him. Getting back to those seven texts, taken as a whole, it's probably fairly obvious that I am trying to make a general point. If we look at their grammatical form and the sentence structure involved, apart from the two instances just mentioned, in which there are still differences even if only with respect to sentence composition, there is no set grammatical form and sentence structure that applies across all instances.

GB: And the relevance of that?

TS: Well, it means that there is no evidence that there is a *technical* expression in the Greek of the New Testament for "breaking bread." So whether we're looking at the five examples in the Acts of the Apostles, one of which, in Acts chapter 27, we've just referred to, or the one in 1 Corinthians chapter 10, which we will look at again, down the track, or the one case in Luke chapter 24 to which reference has also just been made, we cannot point to a technical expression that refers to a specific practice. We cannot approach any of these texts arguing that a set practice is in mind because there is a set expression. There isn't such an expression.

GB: What are the actual expressions we have in those seven instances?

TS: Besides the one already referred to, "ἄρτον . . . κλάσας," which we've mentioned occurs twice, the others are, "κλάσει τοῦ ἄρτου" (*klasei tou artou*), "κλῶντες . . . ἄρτον" (*klōntes . . . arton*) (there are three words intervening), "κλάσαι ἄρτον" (*klasai arton*), "κλάσας τὸν ἄρτον" (*klasas ton arton*), and "ἄρτον ὃν κλῶμεν" (*arton hon klōmen*).

GB: I see what you mean. . . . So can we *now* look at the five references to the "breaking of bread" in the book of Acts?

TS: I think so. But we've already dealt with one—the one in Acts 27, verse 35. I don't think we need to visit that verse again.

GB: Sure.

TS: Of the four that remain why don't we start with the two references to the breaking of bread in Acts chapter 20? In Troas on the first day of the week, believers were gathered together to break bread. That reference is found in verse 7. They were all together in a third story room where Paul had been speaking to them for a long time. Probably around about midnight, a young fellow named Eutychus, having fallen asleep, fell out of a window. Paul went down to where he was, embraced him and pronounced that he was still alive. He then went back upstairs, broke bread—that reference is found in verse 11—ate it and continued speaking until daybreak.

GB: It's almost comical. Eutychus couldn't keep his eyes open during a long sermon and dozed off! Paul investigates, deals with the problem, and then continues talking!

TS: Yes it does sound somewhat comical. And it's odd the way the record simply says that Paul bent over him, embraced him and then said to the others, who would've been quite alarmed, having assumed he was dead, "Don't worry he's alive!" But back to our texts! Let's consider the second reference first. Verse 11, in part, reads, "When Paul had gone up (presumably from being downstairs) and had broken bread and eaten, he conversed with them (the believers)" The mention of "eating" after breaking the bread suggests that the reference was all about having a meal, whether it was a meal of bread or whatever. I know that some might suggest that, yes, from one point of view, it was an ordinary meal but that additionally there were some special elements added to it that made it a special meal. But there is no indication that such was the case. Verse 11 seems simply to refer to an ordinary meal.

GB: The text refers only to Paul breaking bread and eating it. Does this mean that he ate alone at that point in time?

TS: I'm not sure. It could've been the case that everyone was having a meal at this juncture and perhaps that Paul was presiding over the meal or that Paul alone was having a bite to eat before he continued talking. Whatever the case, if verse 11 is referring to an ordinary, if somewhat simple meal, then it's difficult to argue that verse 7 is referring to a special Christian ceremonial meal.

GB: Why is that exactly?

TS: Well, because a very similar expression is being used in both verses, though as we've pointed out, they are not the same expressions. In verse 11 the Greek is "κλασας τον άρτον" and in verse 7 it's "κλάσαι άρτον," with no words intervening in either case. The idea that one expression should be understood to refer to the breaking of bread as part of an ordinary meal and that the other expression should be understood as a reference to a special ceremonial meal, expects too much of our imagination. And these verses relate to the same general occasion and occur in close proximity to one another.

GB: What do you think the relationship is between verses 7 and 11 given that both mention the breaking of bread?

TS: One can't be absolutely sure, but I think in verse 7 we're being informed that the believers came together to have a meal. Having met together but before they participated in their meal, Paul spoke to them at great length. At around midnight, after the Eutychus episode, they finally got down to the meal, as recorded in verse 11, a meal over which Paul presided. Well, that's my reconstruction, my guess, as to what happened.

The Lord's Supper in the Acts of the Apostles

GB: Okay. What about the two remaining verses? Both are in Acts chapter 2, if I remember correctly.

TS: Yes. They are verses 42 and 47. Why don't we look at verse 42 to begin with and then lead into verse 47?

GB: Okay, of course. You really do things slowly don't you? Verse by verse, bit by bit!

TS: I can't help it. The issues we're dealing with are contentious. They can't be dealt with quickly as though there were no complexities. However, I'll try to be as brief as possible. I don't want you falling out of a third story window. I wouldn't trust me to handle the situation as Paul did and come up with a similar result! Verse 42 reads something like this—"They (the early disciples) devoted themselves to the apostles' teaching, and to the fellowship and to the breaking of bread and to the prayers."

GB: Hmm. "Devoted themselves . . . to the breaking of bread." I can see how the matter of "devoting themselves to the breaking of bread," if that's a correct reading of the text, could be seen as an indication that some type of ceremony was involved. It's the use of the word "devoted" that could lead a person to suggest that.

TS: I think you're right. The verb "προσκαρτερω" (*proskarterō*), the first person singular, indicative mood of the word translated, "devoted themselves," carries with it a strong sense of purpose. In this context the form used means something like "they focused their attention on." That doesn't mean however that automatically we should believe that a ceremony was involved. In fact, as the text makes clear, those early disciples were devoted to a *number* of things—the teaching of the apostles and the fellowship and the prayers, in addition to the breaking of bread. And I don't think that the order in which these matters are placed, is all that relevant, except perhaps for the first one mentioned—the teaching of the apostles. One can see how it might have had some sort of priority. And I suppose "the fellowship" and "the breaking of bread" might well go together. But I think we will see that more clearly in a moment.

GB: I've now located the verse. Hmm. The next few verses record how the apostles were doing extraordinary things, like performing "miracles" and how other people—I take it the writer means, those who were not disciples, but I could be wrong—became quite fearful. It would be very disturbing, worrying, unnerving, being on the outside, as it were, but seeing "signs and wonders" performed by those on the inside. And then the writer, you told me it was Luke, tells how the believers were all together and shared what they owned with one another—I hope I understand the text correctly—and sold what they owned. I suppose that meant that some of them sold some of the things that they owned, to give to those who were poorly off. What an extraordinary time it must have been.

TS: Yes, quite extraordinary and I think your understanding of the verses is probably pretty close to the mark. And then if you read on you'll see how every day those early disciples went to the temple. They steadfastly attended—it's that word, "προσκαρτερω" again—the temple, and with one accord. At this point in Luke's account—it's just an extension of his Gospel—he refers again to the breaking of bread. That's in our verse 46. He writes that they did this in their homes, eating food with glad and generous hearts. It was a great time. By the way, the word that we translate "eating" comes from the verb, "μεταλαμβανω" (*metalambanō*). In this type of context, "λαμβανω" (*lambanō*), the root word behind "μεταλαμβανω," has the sense of "taking." "Μεταλαμβανω" may well carry the additional sense of "sharing." The idea being conveyed may be that they took food—they ate food—sharing the food. Sharing was a dominant characteristic of the life of those believers at that time.

GB: Yes, how extraordinary! However, what do you think the connection is between the first mention of the breaking bread, in verse 42 and the second mention of breaking bread, in verse 46, if any?

TS: Well, that's what I was getting at. With respect to the first mention of "the breaking of bread," "τη κλασει του αρτπου" (*tē klasei tou artou*), the text makes no mention of where they did so. It was irrelevant. Luke was describing four things that occupied much of their time. It may be that the second mention of the breaking bread "κλωντες . . . αρτον" (*klōntes . . . arton*), which he describes as occurring "in their homes" or, perhaps closer to the sense, "from house to house," was simply another reference to the same thing but with an indication of where they did this. Notice how that the second reference is associated with their eating—even sharing—food with glad and generous hearts and also with their attending the temple together. What we might be seeing here is that whereas many of them, most likely at the same times, attended the temple as a group, they certainly couldn't have had a meal together there. Though the outer courts of the temple were extensive they were not a place for ordinary people to have an ordinary meal no matter how great or small the number involved. And there wasn't anywhere else in the city that was large enough for a substantial number of them to have a meal with each other. However, in smaller numbers they could break bread together in some of their own homes either inside or outside of the city. "From house to house"—there are just two Greek words involved—"κατ' οἰκον" (*kat' oikon*)—"κατ'" is an abbreviation for "κατα" (*kata*), a preposition, and "οἰκον" refers to "house" or "home"—could imply that they visited one another and consequently shared their meals in various houses. With this understanding of the situation the first reference to the breaking of bread could've been a more general description of what in fact is spelt out more specifically later on.

GB: What you're suggesting is that the second reference could've been a type of explication of the first.

TS: Yes. But of course Luke also wants to indicate that when they did come together in their private homes, to have this meal together, they did so with great joy. One of the clinchers for me, that having an ordinary meal is in mind, is that in that verse 46 the phrase, "breaking bread in their homes," is followed by the statement, "they partook of food"—"τροφης" (*trophēs*). The Greek word, "τροφη" (*trophē*) means "food." My take on the text is that the "breaking of bread" was a general way, perhaps an idiomatic way of referring to having a meal—in this part of the text, having a meal in various people's homes. However, the "partaking of food" probably indicates that it wasn't only bread that was consumed, although bread may still have been the main component of those meals. And note that the text does not say, "They partook of the Lord's Supper," or used some other expression, that indicated that they took part in a special ceremonial meal.

GB: But still, those who disagree with you could say that "breaking bread" and "they partook of food" refer to different activities, even if they're related.

TS: I guess so. However, the more I think about it, the more likely, it seems to me that the expression "breaking bread" was being used idiomatically in both verses 42 and 46 for having a meal, albeit a meal probably mainly consisting of bread. Verse 46 indicated that those early followers did so in their private homes, with the expression "partaking of food" probably indicating that the meal was not of bread alone.

GB: Playing "Devil's advocate," does the use of the definite article in the first instance not imply that some special ceremony was involved? You referred to "του ἀρτου." I take it that "του" is a particular form of the definite article.

TS: Yes, it is. The definite article is in the genitive case. And its appearance here, I suppose, could indicate that something formal was involved, but not necessarily. Determining the significance of the presence or absence of a definite article in the Greek language is notoriously difficult. I think I've said that before. And unfortunately, we have nothing similar with which to compare it. We don't have an example somewhere else of the same construction but *without* the definite article. Remember how rare it is to find any mention of "breaking" in conjunction with "bread" outside of the New Testament in the first place and remember also how dissimilar are the various phrases available to us in the New Testament, phrases involving those same words. However, what should be noticed is that what we do have in the text is the presence of the definite article in all four matters—the teaching, the fellowship, the breaking of bread and the prayers. Perhaps the idea being conveying to the reader is how important, how significant all these things were.

GB: I follow what you're saying. But, if you're correct, why is it that some people believe that there *is* a reference to a special ceremonial meal in either or both of verses 42 and 46?

TS: I can't really answer that. Who knows what influences come to bear upon the views that individuals take in this matter! Suffice it to say, that if you are used to seeing a reference to something like the Lord's Supper, even if only in an elementary form, in these texts, and I think that's the situation with some, or if you want to see it there, you will probably assume that it is there. But we should ponder a little on what else is referred to in verse 42. There are three other activities mentioned in addition to the breaking of bread. There was the teaching of the apostles. This would've entailed many matters. The fellowship is not precisely defined but their "κοινωνια" (*koinōnia*), their fellowship, would presumably have involved their meeting together, being well disposed towards one another, since they shared a common bond, and shared their experiences and ideas with one another. The prayers, whatever they were, would presumably have varied, though some, if not many, might have had a set character. Many might have been drawn from the Old Testament. Presumably many of their prayers would've had a focus on Jesus. Again, we're guessing. However, that the breaking of bread involved a specific celebratory act, something akin to what it was like to participate in the Last Passover Meal, would seem to me to be a little out of character compared with the nature of the other three activities. That one of the activities was a ceremony but that each of the other three was characterized by a variety of matters, seems a little odd to me. Though, my simply saying that, doesn't rule out that a ceremony was being referred to.

GB: But doesn't the phrase, "the breaking of bread" sound odd? Why not simply say that they ate bread or ate food? Or is this your point about the possibility of the phrase being idiomatic?

TS: Yes. I know it's only a guess but I do think that "breaking bread" could've been a popular idiomatic way of referring to having a meal of bread or mainly bread or where bread was involved to some extent or maybe, sometimes even when there was no bread involved. However I would have to say that given the variety of ways in which the phrase, "breaking of bread" could be expressed, the idiomatic expression, if that's what we have, did not have the one consistent form.

GB: I understand. . . . But for comparison, are there other expressions in the New Testament that mean something like, "having a meal" whether bread is involved or not?

TS: Well, we've already come across one such expression. It involves the use of that verb, "μεταλαμβανω." That verb is used three times in the book of Acts in connection with the word for food, "τροφη." As we mentioned just a moment ago, in Acts 2:46, it's recorded that the early believers took/ate/shared food. The same expression is used twice in Acts chapter 27, where Paul is urging those people who have been with him on a ship to, "take food." We mentioned that occasion earlier. Just a couple of verses or so later, Luke uses a related verb, "προσλαμβανω" (*proslambanō*)—perhaps we could translate the word as it occurs at that point as, "partook"—to describe how in the end they did take some food. And in the ninth chapter of Acts the simple verb, "λαμβανω," from which both, "μεταλαμβανω" and "προσλαμβανω" are derived, is used when Luke describes how Paul, after the trauma of losing his sight and then recovering it, took food. However it is probable that it is only in the first instance, the one occurring in Acts chapter 2, that the meals being described are meals being taken at normal times.

Strictly speaking, the combination of any of the verbs together with "τροφη" simply means, "taking," in one sense or another, "food."

GB: And are they the only instances in the New Testament where that verb, "μεταλαμβανω" or its relatives appear in conjunction with "τροφη"?

TS: I think so.

GB: But what about the word, "eating"? In Greek, can that simply refer to "having a meal"?

TS: Yes of course. The Greek word for "I eat" is "ἐσθιω" (*esthiō*). For instance, when Jesus is referred to as "eating with tax collectors and sinners," the comment surely relates to his having a meal with certain people. We can use our word, "eating" in much the same way—in, for instance, the sentence—"I'm eating out tonight." . . . As a matter of fact, I seem to recall that some time ago I suggested that the phrase "ate bread," found in Mark chapter 7, I think it was verse 2, might mean "ate a meal." And that probably isn't the only place in the New Testament where that phrase or similar occurs, with perhaps that meaning. So eating bread could be another way of conveying the idea of having a meal. By the way, if this is true—the use of the word "bread" to stand for "a meal"—this is another indication of how common the eating of bread was.

GB: Okay. Thanks for all that. . . . If you're right, "breaking bread" might have been a general way of referring to "having a meal," especially where bread had some part to play in the meal, whereas "taking food" could have been a general way of referring to having something to eat and, I guess, maybe something to drink, whatever food was involved. And "eating" or "eating bread" could have been used, at least sometimes, to refer to doing the same sort of thing. Anyway, whatever the case, I think of considerable significance, at least for me, is that in Acts chapter 2, those early believers are described as having many of their meals together. . . . Having a meal together was considered to be a fairly binding affair wasn't it?

TS: Normally. Sharing in a meal meant that you shared a common purpose. You were family. You were well disposed towards the others—things like that. And these believers shared that one belief that Jesus was the Christ who had died for them and the one whom God had raised from the dead. They were now bonded together in a way in which they had never been bonded before. Some of them might have been enemies beforehand. Some might have been now sharing a meal with others that beforehand were complete strangers. Having a meal together, perhaps a very common and simple meal, was not only a way of expressing their common belief and the significant relationship that they now had with each other but also an expression of the kind regard in which they now held each other.

GB: Would it have been a simple meal because that was a more normal meal for most, but also an appropriate meal given that their attention was now directed towards the Christ and not inward looking and focusing on having a good feed?

TS: My guess is that both of those matters probably applied. Perhaps it was also a way of making sure that the poorest among them would in no way be embarrassed by some of the wealthier ones having more elaborate fare. They were caring for one another, as the text about selling property makes clear.

GB: So having a meal mainly of bread might have served a number of purposes and for many, if not most, it might have been fairly normal fare.

TS: Yes. I think the picture is as follows—They broke bread in homes, presumably as families or extended families, perhaps also with friends and neighbors who had also become believers, choosing houses that could accommodate them. And as I suggested a moment ago, perhaps some came simply as visitors. Their meals were simple, consisting mainly of bread. And the bread was broken and distributed to all those present. Though they could come together and did so in large numbers in the temple, so extensive was its precincts, having a meal together could only occur in "their houses" and with smaller numbers. That they *ate* together indicated that they *were* together, each being conscious of the close connection they had with each other. This was not a mob phenomenon where individuals do not count. They ate simply, not in any way pretentiously or with self-interest at heart. What they had discovered about Jesus was what had brought them together in a way nothing else could. That's my take on it.

GB: That does fit with their extraordinary community spirit, selling things they owned and giving to those who were in need. Their "togetherness" went way beyond ordinary family ties didn't it? And maybe that reference to "generous hearts" was just another way of describing the assistance they gave to each other particularly to those who were less well off. And perhaps "breaking bread" *was* a short hand way of saying, having simple meals, maybe often, of bread.

TS: I think so. . . . Wait a minute! That question you asked a moment ago—"Why not just say, 'They ate bread?'" One could ask the same question of why it is that in chapter 16 of Jeremiah, according to the *Septuagint*, I mentioned this text the other day, the statement goes something like, "There will be no bread broken in mourning the dead." Why didn't the text simply say, for example, "There will be no eating of bread in mourning the dead"? There, it seems to me, is a fairly clear case of "breaking bread" standing for "eating bread," or maybe, even, "having a meal."

GB: Good point! . . . Now, I don't like raising the following but it's been on my mind, so I'd better mention it. Whatever *we* think, what did early Christians think about those texts in Acts chapter 2? Did they think that at least one or both of them *did* refer to something like the Lord's Supper?

TS: I suspect so. *The Didache*, probably written somewhere between the end of the first century and sometime in the third century, I've mentioned that work before, has the following instruction—"Now concerning the Thanksgiving, (to be understood as the Eucharist?) thus give thanks. . . . And concerning the broken bread: We thank You, our Father, for the life and knowledge which You made known to us through Jesus Your Servant." A further instruction was—"But every Lord's day gather yourselves together, and break bread, and give thanksgiving after having confessed your transgressions." My guess is that the writer, in referring to "broken bread" and "break bread," recognizes the existence of a ceremonial practice based on what Jesus did at the Last Passover Meal. Of course he makes no statement that explicitly connects the activities that he refers to with the second chapter of the book of Acts. It would not surprise me, however, if the writer had have been asked if there was such a connection, that he would've replied, "Yes."

GB: And other early Christian writers?

TS: In a letter written sometime in the second century by a man called, Ignatius, I've mentioned him before as well, to Christians in Ephesus, there is an instruction to obey "the bishop and the presbytery, with an undivided mind, breaking one and the same bread which is the medicine of immortality and the antidote to prevent us from dying but which causes that we should live forever in Jesus Christ." Again, though there is no direct connection being made between "breaking . . . bread" and the verses of Acts, chapter 2, it's likely that he's referring to a practice where bread was broken, which bread was viewed as being Jesus himself, a practice presumed to be in line with what Jesus did and said at the Last Passover Meal. And, as with *The Didache*, I'd not be surprised if Ignatius did see such a connection.

GB: So you think that some early Christians probably did understand our verses in Acts, chapter 2 to refer to some type of a ceremony, even if simply a ceremonial meal?

TS: I'm pretty certain that some did. However, something written in the second century or even in the first, should not be used to dictate to us how a text written, say in the sixties or seventies should be understood. The textual material has to stand in its own right and we must endeavor to understand it, by and large, on its own. From time to time, we may need to look at background material, as we've attempted to do, but in the end it's the text itself that determines what was said or done. I am not saying that we shouldn't consider what some of the early Christians thought about this text or that and we will need to do that from time to time as we continue our discussions. It's just that the Biblical text has priority, certainly because it is the Biblical text, but also for historical reasons. It is, as it were, first cab off the rank.

GB: We really didn't look again at those two texts in Acts chapter 20, did we? But it seems to me that that would be unnecessary. As you've pointed out, there doesn't appear to be any set expression associated with the breaking of bread in the Acts of the Apostles or anywhere in the New Testament. Furthermore, it's obvious to me that bread was a common feature of Jewish meals and that breaking it was what was required when distributing parts of a loaf of bread to others. Consequently, I think I'm with you. I can't see that there really is a strong case that can be made from the textual material itself, that "breaking bread" in the Acts of the Apostles is a reference to celebrating something even a little like the Lord's Supper. That's the way you would put it and I think I'm agreeing with you.

TS: I try to be realistic however. I am sure that others will not see things that way. . . . I think we deserve a break. This has been a very long session. Longer than any we've had so far, I think! But we will probably fare better with our evening meal than those ancients who might have had only pieces of bread to eat. Actually, why don't we share a meal with each other tonight? Here, at my house. Is that possible?

GB: That would be great. I've got nothing on.

TS: And could we meet again, after tonight, say, on Friday? Would that be okay?

GB: No problem. What will we be looking at then?

TS: I think it's about time we examined what is commonly called "Agape meals."

EXPLANATORY NOTES: DAY 22

The three references in the Synoptic Gospels and the one in 1 Cor that speak of Jesus breaking bread at the Last Passover Meal can be found in Matt 26:26; Mark 14:22; Luke 22:19; 1 Cor 11:23–24 (NIV).

The "breaking bread" phrase in 1 Cor 10 is found in verse 16 (NIV).

The account of Jesus breaking bread with the two disciples whom he met with on the road to Emmaus is located in Luke 24:30 (NIV).

The references to "breaking bread" in association with the feeding of the 4,000 or the 5,000 in the Synoptic Gospels can be found in Matt 14:19, 15:36; Mark 6:41, 8:6; Luke 9:16 (NIV).

The two similar instances of "ἄρτον . . . κλασας" referred to by TS are to be found in Luke 24:30; Acts 27:35 (NAG).

The expression "κλασει του ἄρτου" is found in Acts 2:42, "κλωντες . . . ἄρτον" in Acts 2:46, "κλασει ἄρτον" in Acts 20:7, "κλασας τον ἄρτον" in Acts 20:11, and "ἄρτον ὀν κλωμεν" in 1 Cor 10:16 (NAG).

For an example of understanding Acts 2:42 and 46 as referring to something like the Lord's Supper, see, Bruce, *The Book of the Acts*, 74. Uncharacteristically, compared to many others, Peterson in *The Acts of the Apostles*, 61, believes that neither of these verses refers to a Christian rite. He is of the view that the breaking of bread "describes the initiation of an ordinary meal in the Jewish fashion of breaking a loaf with the hands and giving thanks to God."

TS discusses the meaning of the Greek phrase, "κατ' οἰκον" found in Acts 2:46 (NAG), suggesting that it has the sense of, "from house to house." The same expression is used in Acts 20:20 but there the plural form for "house" is used, the words being—"κατ' οἰκους" (*kat' oikous*) (NAG). In Acts 20 Paul recounts to the Ephesian elders how when he had been with the believers in Ephesus he had taught them publicly and in their homes. There may not be any great significance in the use of the plural as opposed to the singular.

With reference to the significance of "having a meal together" in the ancient world, at least with respect to formal meals, Fotopoulos, in *Food Offered to Idols*, 160, makes the following comment—"Fellowship" (κοινωνια) was an important concept within the formal meal entailing a relationship among the host, guests and deities involved. Greeks, Romans, Jews and Christians followed the same basic structure for the formal evening meal, regardless of location, occasion or meaning."

The verb "μεταλαμβανω" in association with "τροφη" occurs in Acts 2:46, 27:33–34 (NAG), the verb, "προσλαμβανω" in similar association occurs in Acts 27:36 (NAG),

Part 3: The Lord's Supper

and the verb "λαμβανω" also in association with "τροφη" can be found in Acts 9:19 (NAG).

For one understanding of the dimensions of the precincts of Herod's Temple see www.jewishvirtuallibrary.org/jsource/History/secondtemple.html.

References to Jesus "eating with tax collectors and sinners" can be found in Matt 9:10–11; Mark 2:15–16; Luke 5:30 (NIV).

For a lengthy article on the nature of Herod's Temple, its construction and design, see http://www.mycrandall.ca/courses/ntintro/jerusaltempl4.htm.

Other places in the New Testament, in addition to Mark 7:2, where "ate bread" perhaps meaning "ate a meal," or where there is some similar connection between "bread" and "a meal," include Mark 3:20, 7:5; Luke 14:1, 15 (NIV).

The reference to there being "no bread broken in mourning" can be located in Jeremiah 16:7 (NIV).

TS quotes from *The Didache,* sections 9, 14.

The reference to what Ignatius wrote can be found in his *To the Ephesians*, 20.2. See also www.newadvent.org/fathers/0104.htm (chapter 20).

Day 23

Agape Meals

TS does not believe that a discussion on "love feasts," also known as "agape meals," is all that important, given GB's interests. However, in trying to cover an area, that some of GB's friends might think is relevant, TS works through some textual material external to the New Testament that relates to or could relate to these feasts. Finally he focuses on the well-known verse in Jude—verse 12. Interestingly, he prefers an alternative to the word "blemishes"—a common translation of one of the words in that verse.

TS: Hi. I know we've been taking a long and circuitous route to get there but one day we *will* look at your concerns with the Lord's Supper.

GB: I don't have concerns about the Lord's Supper really. I just want to be clear about what it's supposed to mean, my part in participating in such a practice, what its origins are and why people believe that it's necessary. It obviously has its roots in the Last Passover Meal but I appreciate how you've tried to point out that the Gospels are limited in their reporting of that meal and limited in recounting what Jesus said about it. I am still struggling with your suggestion that maybe there never was a command. I appreciate that it was a remembrance meal. I also understand that in the New Testament, references outside of the Gospels to something like the Lord's Supper, 1 Corinthians being an exception, which we're still to examine, are at least suspect, if they exist at all. But now you want to consider "agape meals"? I've come across the term somewhere but I can't quite remember in what connection. But I guess, because they're meals, "agape meals" must have something to do with the Lord's Supper.

TS: Well most people believe there is some relationship. Just so that we don't think we're dealing with something very odd, the word "agape" is simply a transliteration of the Greek word for love—"ἀγαπη" (*agapē*).

GB: Of course! I'd forgotten. "Αγαπη" is one of those significant words indicating how believers are to treat one other. We are to love each other—genuinely seeking each other's good. And now I recall that an "agape meal" was that sort of meal in which believers expressed that love for each other or that it was a meal that by its very nature was an *expression* of their love for one another.

TS: Well, that is what it was supposed to be like—both those ideas I think—at least in theory. I suspect that rather than look at the Biblical side of things first, it might be a little more helpful if we consider a few relevant writings of some early believers.... There is an interesting reference to an agape meal, in a letter written early in the second century, a letter that Ignatius wrote to a people called the Smyrnaeans. We've come across him a couple of times now. In this letter he instructs the believers to follow their bishop pointing out that it is he, the bishop, who is the one who can hold a valid Eucharist, or alternatively, that it could be any person to whom he delegates that responsibility. Ignatius then goes on to declare that without the bishop it is not permissible to baptize or celebrate an "ἀγαπην" (*agapēn*), which I think he understood as a "love-feast" or an "agape meal." It's not clear that he's equating having an agape meal with participating in the Eucharistic celebration but he may be. Alternatively he could see them as related in some other way.

GB: I didn't realize that an agape meal and the Eucharistic celebration or something like the Lord's Supper, as I prefer to call it, may have been the same thing.

TS: Well, that may never have been the case. However, I think it's not unlikely that to begin with, the Eucharistic celebration took place within or perhaps at the end of such a meal. Tertullian, you mentioned him to me when we were discussing baptism, writing towards the end of the second century or at the beginning of the third, appears to refer to them as separate practices in his work, *On the Soldier's Crown*. In this he refers to the Lord commanding that the sacrament of the Eucharist be eaten at meal times.

GB: Does he use the word, "ἀγαπη"?

TS: No. He wrote in Latin and the words he used for "at meal times" were, "*in tempore victus.*"

GB: I'm not much wiser. Did he say anything else about this matter?

TS: Well, in another work, his *Apologies*, he writes about the believers and their dinner, using the Latin word "*coena.*" He also refers to their meal as a banquet, a "*convivium.*" He describes the Christians having prayers, eating a modest meal, not drinking too much and then singing some songs. Perhaps these songs had their origins in Scripture. Interestingly, he says that such a dinner is called by the Greek name for love but the word he uses is the Latin word "*dilectio.*"

GB: So he used three different Latin words to refer to the same thing!

TS: It looks that way.

GB: The reference to "not drinking too much"— was he concerned with people becoming inebriated?

TS: I think so. I guess he would've thought that people should be sober enough to know what they were doing and be genuine in their prayers and in their references to Scripture and so on. But to continue. There is another reference to what looks like "agape meals" in an apocryphal work, entitled, *The Epistle of the Apostles* possibly written sometime in the second century. By "apocryphal" I mean, that it's not as its title implies and that it's to be considered as largely fictional. In the text, Jesus supposedly speaks about an apostle who had been released from a prison. Jesus is supposed to have said that before something, which he calls "the memorial to him," has been completed and before the "Agape" has been finished, the same apostle would be thrown back into prison. My guess is that "the memorial to him" was a ceremony in remembrance of the Lord Jesus. If this is correct, then what he wrote suggests that the meal and the remembrance ceremony were to some extent separate, although one may have followed closely upon the other or was intimately associated with the other.

GB: A remembrance ceremony! I wonder if the writer thought that Jesus had commanded his followers to regularly remember him and his death in the form of some sort of ceremonial meal—the Lord's Supper!

TS: Probably. I'm pretty sure that the idea that Jesus had issued a type of "command" was an early one.

GB: Anyway I can see how a Eucharistic type celebration and an agape meal might have gone hand in hand. Perhaps these practices developed over the years, maybe differently in different places, and as a consequence of how people perceived their relationship.

TS: I would have thought so. In fact in some places, in the course of time, some of these agape meals seem to have degenerated into very unseemly affairs, if they weren't like that in the first place. A certain Clement of Alexandria, I think I've mentioned him before, but I may not have, writing about the same time as Tertullian, was scathing in his attacks on some who were applying the word, "agape" to their special meals. For one thing, he was highly critical of the lavish nature of these meals. He also wrote of the practices of those whom he described as the Carpocratians and their "love feasts" which he said should not be so termed, given what he perceived to be the grossly immoral behavior at such meals. On the other hand, Origen, a very influential Christian, writing in the first half of the third century, rose to the defense of the agape meal in a dispute he had with a person called Celsus. Later a Canon of what is called the Council of Gangra, held between 325 and 381, condemned anyone who despised those who "out of faith" held love feasts in honor of the Lord and who themselves refused to accept invitations to attend these meals.

GB: Obviously the meals and those who took part in them came in for some severe criticism. Otherwise there wouldn't have been a need for such a Canon.

TS: True, but I think that some of this criticism must have been thoroughly justified. Some of these meals seem to have become highly secular in character and, in fact, having meals of any sort in church buildings was outlawed in the Synod of Hippo held towards the end of the fourth century. This position was reinforced by what is called the Trullian Council, which was held late in the seventh century. In the end it's quite clear that whatever the relationship was between "agape meals" and Eucharistic celebrations in the early days, in time, the two became quite separate practices even if they weren't originally.

GB: I notice that you regularly refer to "agape meals," "agape feasts" or "love feasts." I take it that in Greek, for example, a word for "meal" or "feast" is also used alongside of "agape." What word is that?

TS: How interesting that you should ask the question! Well, no. The actual word "ἀγαπη" seems to have become a somewhat technical word in the particular context of meals. "Αγαπη" is simply the word for "love" as I said. However, when translating it, in the texts to which we've referred, the sense to be conveyed is that of a "love meal."

GB: I thought that when you were referring to Ignatius and his use of the word "ἀγαπη" and what he meant by that, that you were being short-handed in the way you spoke. But now I realize, no. You meant what you said! The word "ἀγαπη" itself is being used to mean, "love meal"!

TS: That's it! In fact, what we should soon do is to look at that one text, actually one verse, in the Scriptures, from which this usage seems to have arisen—Jude 12. But just before we do so, a couple of brief comments about a few references outside of the New Testament that simply refer to believers having meals together, which meals are not termed "agape" meals. Well, at least not explicitly.

GB: One text, one verse? I'm interested.

TS: But as I said, firstly let's make some reference to what we might see as simply meals shared by believers, mentioned in texts external to the New Testament. There's an interesting letter written by a man called Pliny, the then governor of a Roman province called Bithynia,—present-day northern Turkey—written around the year 112 to the emperor Trajan. In it he reports on the behavior of some early believers.

GB: I've heard of Pliny and that letter.

TS: Well, as you might know, in that letter he mentions how these early believers, customarily, on a fixed day of the week, met early in the morning before dawn, said certain things to a Christ as though he were a god and bound themselves by an oath (he used the Latin word, "*sacramentum*"—I think I've mentioned that word before) not to act improperly. With reference to this last matter he mentions such behavior as stealing, committing adultery, and not keeping promises. He goes on to report how the group would then break up but meet again later to have an ordinary meal. In his letter there is no indication of what they might have called such meetings, either the meeting early in the day or the one later when they had a meal together. Maybe those early believers to whom he's referring didn't call either of those meetings by a special name. Then there's a Minucius Felix, writing somewhere between the second to the middle of the third century who in one of his works refers to the banquets of the Christians, using the Latin word, "*convivium*." Writing in defense of them he describes them as being temperate in character and free from sexual immorality and so unlike some of the Gentile meals that were well known for the sexual liberties taken on those occasions.

GB: Presumably those Christians could have termed their meals, "agape meals" but you're saying that we don't know whether they did or not.

TS: True. Finally, I mean I've come to the end of my examples, there's an interesting piece by a certain Cyprian of Carthage, written around the middle of the third century in which he invites an acquaintance to sing some psalms during a meal—something spiritual to listen to. The meal he refers to is probably a main meal, it being held towards the end of the daylight hours. He describes the day as one of "holiday rest" and perhaps the time of day or the day itself as "a time of leisure." He speaks of the meal as being temperate in character and looks forward to it being a time of "gladness" and "heavenly grace."

GB: By "holiday rest" and "a time of leisure" did he consider the day to be a type of Sabbath?

TS: I'm not sure. Again however, there is no reference to an "agape meal," though, if asked, he might have described the meal he referred to as such. Nevertheless, whether meals were described as "agape meals" or not, the point I am trying to make now is that not only in the Acts of the Apostles, but elsewhere and external to the New Testament there is evidence that the early believers often met together and probably on a regular basis, to have a meal. Having such a meal indicated that there was a bond of fellowship between them. They had something of significance in common. It was the Lord, the one who had died for them, that united them. It was not their occupations, their family ties, their intellectual interests, their social status or what they shared culturally that brought them together regularly to have these meals. It was Jesus the Christ, the one whom God had raised from the dead and had appointed judge over all men.

GB: I detect a preacher's tone! I'm not in any way put off. To the contrary! It's good to hear that sort of stuff! But, what of that one text, that one verse, Jude 12, from which the "agape meals" seem to have gotten their name? I've looked it up. It reads, in part, "These people are blemishes on your love feasts."

Part 3: The Lord's Supper

TS: Let me make a suggestion as to a possible alternative translation.

GB: Sure.

TS: The Greek word "σπιλαδες," (*spilades*), rendered "blemishes" could come from the noun "σπιλος" (*spilos*), meaning blemish or "σπιλας" (*spilas*), meaning something like a reef—rocks beneath the surface of the sea or a river. Verse 12 and the one following are highly metaphorical in character and certainly a reference to a "reef" would be consistent with other terms that Jude employs, as I hope you'll see. If we accept that the idea of "reef" is in mind then verse 12 would read something like, "These are the ones, in your "ἀγαπιας" (*agapais*)—I won't translate that for the moment—sunken rocks, feasting together fearlessly, pasturing themselves. They are clouds without rain, blown along by the wind, autumn trees without fruit and uprooted—twice dead." Verse 13 continues in a similar vein—"wild waves of the sea, casting up the foam of their own shame, wandering stars for whom the nether gloom of darkness has been reserved for ever." I don't think it's all that important but I thought I'd raise the matter of these two ways of reading "σπιλαδες."

GB: But if there is a reference to "reefs" or "sunken rocks," that would suggest that such people can cause others to "founder" in their faith. Wouldn't that be the case?

TS: Yes. You're quite right. On the other hand, a "blemish" is also something of significance but it would constitute a description of how these people detract from what should be the true character of the meals, rather than focus on them as posing a danger to those who took part in them. Whichever way we look at it, Jude is warning against a group of people and the way they behave. The letter as a whole has these people in its sights.

GB: The word, "ἀγαπαις"—I take it that that's the plural of "ἀγαπη"—means "love feasts"?

TS: Well, it's plural in number but dative in case. It's governed by the Greek word "ἐν" (*en*) meaning "in." The preposition takes the dative case. The nominative plural is "ἀγαπαι" (*agapai*).

GB: Okay. But you mentioned that you think that the word, "ἀγαπη," normally translated, "love" developed a technical sense, the sense of "love feast." That's what I was getting at.

TS: Well, that's what's interesting. Except for how later Christian writers did in fact use the word in the context of meals, one wouldn't automatically mention the word "feast" or any word for "meal" in any translation involving simply "ἀγαπη." One wouldn't normally do that anywhere in the New Testament. I admit that Jude uses the word, "συνευωχουμενοι," (*suneuōchoumenoi*) which we translate "feasting together," three words later, in the Greek text, and I guess that's one reason why we might refer to a meal, when translating the word "ἀγαπαις" used earlier. But why not translate "ἀγαπαις" without any reference to "feasts"? There's also that preposition "ἐν" and a definite article before the word and a sort of pronoun, which some people refer to as a possessive determiner, meaning "your," after the word, that we probably need to keep in mind. The phrase of interest is "ἐν ταις ἀγαπαις ὑμων" (*en tais agapais humōn*). Actually the definite article is of no consequence to us. It's just part of the construction involving the possessive determiner.

GB: How would you read that phrase, well the text as a whole?

TS: I think something like this—"These people are reefs 'in your lovings,' boldly carousing together, feeding and looking after themselves" *et cetera*. I admit that "lovings" is not a normal word to use in such a sentence. Perhaps "love things" or "love events" would be more appropriate, keeping in mind however, that "ἀγαπη" is not an adjective. "Αγαπητος" (*agapētos*) is the relevant adjective. Perhaps the simple word "loves" would be suitable. A translation, using any of these suggestions, taking regard to the context as a whole, would, I think, amount to an example of *sarcasm*.

GB: Ah. So you're suggesting that Jude is referring to something like, "your so-called love occasions"?

TS: Yes.

GB: Does the phrase "ἐν ταις ἀγαπαις ὑμων," I think I've got the phrase right, occur anywhere else in the New Testament?

TS: Unfortunately no, although there is some minor manuscript evidence for something like it occurring in the second chapter of 2 Peter, but it's poorly attested. However, if that manuscript evidence were to be trusted it could be that the writer there was alluding to the text in Jude but by way of a pun.

GB: Okay. Interesting. I won't go there. Back to Jude. So is Jude saying something like "What you or others might refer to as expressions of your love for one another, those occasions when you come together to have a feast, they are in fact, nothing of the sort"?

TS: Yes, I think so. And when you think about it, it's clear that overall Jude is absolutely scathing towards those whom he's warning against and paints their behavior in the worst possible light. I think in total, Jude's words amount to something like this— *"At these so-called love events, in which you join them, these people carouse together with extreme bravado, thinking of nothing but themselves, as they munch away. They are people of no substance, though they might have an outward appearance to the contrary. They have no self-control, being driven this way or that way according to their delights. They have nothing to offer anyone. Dead beyond dead! Completely out of control! The furious froth they generate characterizes their shamefulness. They wander here and there, aimlessly, back and forth, the darkness in the end, being their only destiny."* I haven't got Jude's imagery here completely right I'm sure, but I think he's saying this sort of thing.

Part 3: The Lord's Supper

GB: Wow! There's nothing lovely about these people he's referring to, is there! And once you take in the big picture of what Jude says, the "so-called love events" of these believers are what they are because of the behavior and character of certain appalling people—people with whom they should not be mixing. They're dangerous.

TS: I think "dangerous" is the right word. And Jude wants to make it clear that they could make shipwreck of any unwary soul. Their community meals may have been spoken about as though they were expressions of love but they were nothing of the sort. His readers are being warned about such people in the starkest possible manner.

GB: If your understanding is correct it would appear that the idea that early Christian community meals should be called "ἀγαπαις" was based on a misunderstanding of what Jude was trying to convey.

TS: That certainly could be the case. Even if it isn't, the setting of "ἀγαπη" in Jude, the only such setting in the New Testament, is a very negative one.

GB: But of course, the word "ἀγαπη" occurs many times in the New Testament doesn't it?

TS: Indeed. I was only referring to the use of "love" in the context of "meals." Interestingly, Jude himself uses the word "ἀγαπη" or a related word, in one form or another, several times.

GB: Where?

TS: Well, the recipients are described as loved "ἠγαπημενοις" (ēgapēmenois) by or in God in verse 1. In each of verses 3, 17, and 20, Jude uses the adjective "ἀγαπητος" either referring to his love towards them or God's love towards them or both. Three times the noun "ἀγαπη" is used—once in verse 2, another in our verse 12 of course, and a third time in verse 21. The "ἀγαπη" of verses 2 and 21, verses that surround our verse 12, relate to the love that comes from God. With so much emphasis on God's love for them one might expect that in verse 12, the reference there would also be in terms of that same love. However, if what I am suggesting is correct, that is, that Jude is using sarcasm in that verse, then the reference to the meals in which the "beloved" are participating, being situated between the two references to the absolutely pure, unspoiled love of God, perhaps highlights the depravity exhibited at those meals. These meals show little or no indication of an understanding of the great love of God. If we don't grasp something of what it means for God to love us we will not be able, genuinely, to love each other.

GB: I knew that Jude's letter was pretty full on but I didn't appreciate the colorful and, as you put it, scathing language, that he uses. I think I'm sold on "reefs" by the way. I think "blemishes" is a little too mild for Jude.

TS: I reckon so.... I don't think our excursion into "love-feasts" has been all that important but people do refer to them from time to time and make some sort of

Agape Meals

connection between them and the "Lord's Supper." I've just been trying to deal with that sort of perspective. Anyway I think we're now ready to examine some sections of the 1 Corinthians letter.

GB: Actually I do need to go pretty soon. I'm meeting up with a colleague in about an hour's time. Sorry. Could we look at 1 Corinthians tomorrow?

TS: Sure, though in the one day we'll only be able to bite off a small piece of all that's relevant there. The letter is likely to occupy us for several days. But we'll get a start tomorrow. See you then.

Part 3: The Lord's Supper
EXPLANATORY NOTES: DAY 23

References to the Greek text of Jude come from NAG.

The quotes from Ignatius can be found in Ignatius, *To the Smyrnaeans* 8.1–2, 238 and the quotes from Tertullian can be located in Tertullian, *On the soldier's crown*, 3.3 and 4 in *A New Eusebius,* 183, and Tertullian, *Apologeticus*, XXXIX. 16–18, 180–81.

Other quotes came from—*The Epistle of the Apostles,* section 15; Clement of Alexandria, *Paedagogus*, Book II, chapters 1–2; Clement of Alexandria, *Miscellanies*, Book III, chapter 2; Origen, *Against Celsus*, Book I, chapter 1; Council of Gangra, Canon XI; Synod of Hippo, Canon XXIX; Trullian Council, Canon LXXIV; Pliny, *Epistolae*, X. 96.7 in *A New Eusebius*, 14. See also http://ancienthistory.about.com/library/bl/bl_text_plinyltrstrajan.htm. letter XCVII; Minucius Felix, *Octavius*, chapter XXXI; Cyprian, *Epistle 1, To Donatius*, 16.

The verse in 2 Pet chapter 2 that could involve some reference to Jude 12 is verse 13. Bauckham, argues for such a connection and that a pun is involved, in *Jude, 2 Peter*, 77.

Day 24

Corinthian Meals—The Cup of Blessing which we Bless

Today's discussion is quite long. TS points out the significant link that existed in the Greco-Roman world between idolatry and food particularly where formal meals were involved. He also spends considerable time dealing with the place of wine in such meals. The origin of the phrase, "the cup of blessing which we bless" then becomes the focus of their discussion. Finally, TS makes an attempt to paraphrase the rhetorical question in which it is imbedded, the rhetorical question that follows and the concluding statement.

GB: Hi! I've been thinking. Some days we've dealt with some fairly complicated matters. However, yesterday's subject was relatively easy going and interesting to boot. But I agree with you, I don't think it was all that relevant given my questions.

TS: I think you'll find today's chat much more to the point. We've come a long way and there is still some way to go yet but we're on the downhill run.

GB: So we're now going to look at 1 Corinthians. I suppose we'll focus on chapters 10 and 11.

TS: We won't be looking at chapter 11 today or for a few days. We'll need to work our way through the second half of chapter 10 first. However, to begin with, we probably should look at the background to that part of Paul's letter and make a few brief comments about what he says in the previous two chapters.

GB: Let's go!

TS: In his 1 Corinthians letter, Paul deals with a number of issues. He seems to have learnt a lot about how the believers in Corinth were faring just prior to the time of writing and is quite concerned about various matters. Chapter eight begins with a new area of concern. It has to do with believers eating food that has knowingly been offered to idols. To begin with, he may have had in mind meals served in the precincts of a temple. The situation he considers is one where a believer, whom he refers to as a weaker brother, has qualms about eating such food but influenced by other believers, who seemingly have no such concerns, eats that type of food. Paul points out that that brother has caused himself serious harm and has in fact sinned. So too, he argues, has the brother who caused that brother to stumble, as it were. It's obvious that Paul considers that the matter of believers having a meal consisting of food that has knowingly been offered to idols is a very serious one. It seems to me that, in summary, that's what chapter 8 is all about.

GB: And chapter 9?

TS: Well, chapter 9 is somewhat of a problem. It seems to center on Paul and his rights as an apostle. And this would appear to be odd given that chapter 10 again takes up the matter of food. I think that a good case can be made for seeing that what Paul writes about in chapter 9 still relates to the question of food and idolatry, as did chapter 8. It's true he *does* have a great deal to say about his rights as an apostle—the Greek for what we might translate as a "right" is "ἐξουσια" (*exousia*). But it's in terms of his not *availing* himself of those rights. I think that what he's saying to the Corinthians is that they *too* should consider giving up what they see as their rights, their freedom, with respect to what they choose to eat, for the sake of others. Also, if you look carefully at what he wrote in that chapter, you can still see how he explicitly mentions food, a number of times, in one way or another.

GB: I think I need to see it for myself. . . . Well, yes. There's a reference to, "Do we not have our right to eat food and drink?" verse 4. . . . And then another to, "Who plants a vineyard without eating its fruit? Who tends a flock without getting some of the milk?" verse 7. . . . And then he writes about the ploughman and the harvester hoping for a share of a crop, verse 10. . . . And the people serving in the temple obtaining their food from the temple, verse 13. . . . Oh and then I see that it's in this chapter that he makes that famous statement, "To the Jews I became like a Jew to win the Jews . . . to those outside the law I became like one outside the law that I might win those outside of the law . . . to the weak I became weak that I might win the weak, I have become all things to all men so that by all means I might save some." I've skipped a few bits, I know.

TS: You've done well, in spite of being in a hurry. That last quote is a very inspiring statement. And those hearing the letter read would've been Jews—a people under the Law of Moses, Gentiles—a people outside of that law and, whether Jews or Gentiles, the weak—those who were troubled by eating meat or food that had once been offered to idols. At the very end of the chapter, you can see how he writes about running to obtain the prize and training and beating his body to make it his slave—very athletic

Corinthian Meals—The Cup of Blessing which we Bless

imagery. I think his point is that the Corinthians too have to consider disciplining themselves over what they choose to eat.

GB: Well then, how does the first part of chapter 10 follow on from all of that? I'll let you do the talking!

TS: At the beginning of chapter 10 he returns directly to the subject of idolatry but in terms of how, in the past, Israel had been idolatrous and how as a consequence, God had severely dealt with them. Twice he explicitly refers to what happened to Israel as a way of warning the Corinthians—*they* must strenuously avoid temptations to idolatry. He has a famous line—"If anyone thinks he stands, be careful lest he fall!" He has now moved away from considering how a brother with no concerns about eating food previously offered to idols should take into account the weaker brother with the sensitive conscience. Now, his point is how every believer should avoid idolatry but his focus is still on food and its potential connection with idolatry.

GB: What intrigues me is that although many of the Corinthian believers would've been Gentiles, Paul seems free to refer to what happened to ancient Israel as though even the Gentiles would've been familiar with those parts of the Jewish Scriptures.

TS: Didn't one of us raise this matter in one of our earlier discussions?

GB: Yes, perhaps. I'm not sure.

TS: Well, anyway, I think the explanation for the situation is at least twofold. Firstly, some of these Gentiles would've been people who had attached themselves to the Jewish Synagogue in Corinth and had acquired knowledge of the Old Testament as a consequence. Secondly, we know that Paul had previously been in Corinth for about a year and a half and that would've given him ample time to instruct many of the new Gentile believers, who previously had little if any knowledge of Jewish history, about God's dealings with his ancient people in the past.

GB: That makes sense. Another matter! I suppose the answer is obvious, but how strong was the connection between idolatry and food in the world of the Corinthians?

TS: An important question. There was a very close and tight connection, at least in the Gentile world. And the differences between how Jews and Gentiles conducted their meals were stark. For the Jew and consequently, in principle, for the believer, whether Jew or Gentile, food was to be viewed as a gift from the one and only God for whom there could be no physical idolatrous representation. It was customary, at least for the godly Jew, before partaking of a meal to acknowledge who God is and to give thanks to him for the food he supplied. Such a prayer could take the form of, for example, "Blessed are you, O Lord our God, King of the Universe, who produces bread from the earth." Probably for most, once the blessing had been given, there was then little recognition of anything specifically spiritual being associated with the meal, other than that it was God's gift. Things were very different in the ordinary

Greco-Roman Gentile world. First of all, for the Gentiles, much of the meat consumed in their world would initially have been sacrificially offered to one god or another. It might be that they ate such meat in the temple where the sacrifice had been made or in a dining room attached to the temple, the temple having provided the meat served in the dining room. But food other than meat could also be offered to the gods and such food could be shared between the gods and the diner. In such circumstances, the connection between the food, whatever it consisted of, and idol worship, was absolutely unavoidable, deeply rooted and very obvious.

GB: Do we know much about these temples?

TS: There is some debate about what temples with such dining rooms existed in Corinth in Paul's time. However it seems certain that one of them was the Asklepieion—a temple associated with a god physician—to whom many came looking for healing. And yes we do know a bit about what these temples were like architecturally but I don't think that that's all that relevant. To continue. An alternative to eating in the precincts of a temple was to call in at a type of fast-food outlet and there to eat food prepared for you that had also previously been part of a temple sacrifice or offering. Another possibility was to buy such food at a market place and to consume it later at home. Even if the meat, for example, had not been sacrificed to one of the gods, you might perform a private sacrifice in the grounds where you lived, before preparing the meat for your meal.

GB: Okay. . . . I can understand that if you ate such meat in a temple where it had been sacrificed you would consider the meat having some religious value. I guess the same would also apply where you had conducted some sacrificial rite with an animal being prepared for a meal to have at your home. However, would the same thing really be the case where you had a meal in a temple dining room or when you simply bought your meat in the market place?

TS: If you knew that it had been sacrificed, and you would normally assume this to be the case at least when eating in a temple dining room, then the answer is "Yes." And the sacrificial character of the meat, indeed of any food that had been treated in any way religiously, was envisaged as belonging to that food, as it were, even as it was consumed.

GB: I think I understand. By the way, you and I are mentioning "meat" a lot. I would have thought that perhaps many people couldn't have afforded to have had much meat.

TS: Well, maybe amongst the Greeks of Corinth that wasn't such a problem. Besides, it may have been that the Corinthian believers, well, especially the heads of the households that were believers, were relatively well-to-do people.

GB: Fair enough.

TS: Anyway, back to the nature of Corinthian meals in general! There was another aspect of their meals that made their meals, if I can put it this way, very religious. We believers sometimes talk about having "fellowship" with one another. The Greek word for "fellowship" is "κοινωνια." I mentioned that word, in passing, the other day. We tend to think that in itself it's a very Christian concept. However, you wouldn't have thought so if you had lived in the Greco-Roman world. In that world, the concept behind "κοινωνια" was a common one, associated, for example, with people simply having meals together. The *word* was not an uncommon one. When having a meal, the participants saw themselves as having fellowship with one another by eating the same meal. Additionally, because it had been, from their point of view, hallowed by one or more of the gods, people saw themselves as also being in fellowship with that god or those gods. So, for example, at a meal to which one had been invited by a host, both the host and the guests were understood to be in fellowship with one another and also with the gods associated with that meal.

GB: Surely this wasn't characteristic of all their meals.

TS: You may be right. The evidence external to the New Testament, that we have, relates mainly to formal meals. And, interestingly, I think, much of the latter part of chapter 10 of 1 Corinthians also relates to formal meals. However, this is not to claim that for Paul, what is written there did not have widespread application. But to return to your point. It may well have been the case that in many instances, where ordinary people were having meals, little attention was given to things of a religious nature. It's not easy to tell. Presumably it would depend upon how religious you were. Perhaps the truth is that most people were very religious. In those days, in the Greco-Roman world, it was generally considered to be very important to have a good connection with the gods if at all possible. That was because your health, your business dealings, your relationships with others and your general happiness could be affected by the gods, though the gods could do whatever they wanted to do at their whim and leisure.

GB: How terrible to be so vulnerable.

TS: Yes. We Christians, too lightly, accept the fact that our God, the one and only God, the one who created and runs the universe, cares for his people, loves his people. How often do we give him thanks for his abundant goodness towards us and praise him for his faithfulness, his righteousness and his justice?

GB: Possibly, hardly ever, to our shame!

TS: What we're doing right now seems a bit lame doesn't it. . . . But, it's what we're working on. Back to the Corinthians. Given the way their gods could behave but the desirability of having them on side, it's understandable how meals that had religious undergirdings could be considered to provide very good opportunities for establishing good "fellowship" with them. And formal meals were generally quite religious and they were possibly more common in their society than ours. From their point of view there were good social, economic and political reasons for having such meals, wherever and whenever they were held. And of course, we mustn't think that Jewish people didn't have their ideas about fellowship. I'm sure that most if not all pious Jews saw their meals as ones in which they enjoyed fellowship with each other and also with God, particularly if they rightly saw him as their supreme benefactor—not only as the benefactor who supplied them with their food.

GB: I think you indicated some time ago that *wine drinking* was also a feature of Greco-Roman meals, especially formal meals. Did that have any part to play in the Gentiles making connections with the gods?

TS: Very much so. Oh, by the way, when I refer to the gods, I am really making reference to what might be termed "the immortals." These include those who were regarded as divine beings but also those viewed as "the heroes." The heroes were human beings who had superhuman qualities by virtue of the fact that they had descended, in part, from one god or another. But, as to wine drinking, a formal meal could begin with a cup of wine mixed with honey. Then, throughout what we would see as the main part of the meal where most of the food was consumed, there could be a little more wine drinking. Perhaps for some occasions, "little" would not be the right word. However, generally, it was after the main meal when most of the wine was drunk. Indeed some descriptions of these meals are such that you could be excused for thinking that their meals mainly consisted of drinking wine!

GB: But in what way was the drinking of wine involved in making connections, as you put it, with the immortals—your term?

TS: Well, although customs varied over time and different practices were held in different places, it was apparently not uncommon between the main part of the meal and the dessert and drinking session that followed—yes, desserts of one sort or another were generally served—to pour out libations to three or so gods or immortals. A libation involved taking a cup of wine and pouring it out on the ground or floor or into a fire, at the same time as calling out the name of the god. It acknowledged the god's presence and the god's right to participate in the meal. Then, at other times, or indeed immediately following a libation, it seems you would toast the gods. The making of libations and perhaps particularly the giving of toasts could also occur during the second part of the meal, the part characterized by the drinking of large quantities of wine. I'm not sure that "toasting" is the right word. But I think something like toasting was the case. You might drink a toast to a fellow guest but perhaps it was more commonly for the gods that you "raised your cup" or "lowered your cup." I'm not really sure and I must confess that I don't always find it easy to differentiate between a libation and what I've called a "toast." That second part of the meal could last for a long time, hours in fact, and many toasts could be made. During the meal you might also sing a hymn or two to one or more of the deities.

Corinthian Meals—The Cup of Blessing which we Bless

GB: Besides drinking wine, toasting, making libations and eating a dessert, what else did people do, if anything, during that second part of the meal?

TS: You might enjoy music provided by a flute girl, engage in philosophical discourse, deal with business matters, speak of family affairs, play games or engage in certain sexual activities, of which I will not speak any further. But all this meant it was important to be both convivial and reasonably sober throughout most of the activities or discussions. Consequently, the wine consumed during the second part of the meal was normally diluted with water seemingly within only approved ratios of water to wine, so that one would be able to remain somewhat sober for much, if not most, of that time. It was drunkenness among other things that seems to have been responsible for bringing some of those "love feasts" that Christians held, into disrepute. My guess is that these "love feasts" followed a similar pattern to those formal meals held in Gentile society. Oh, and by the way, wine consumed during the first part of a formal meal, might not be so diluted, and consequently, generally, only small quantities were taken of this wine if one wanted to be sober for most of the extended meal.

GB: I wonder if we could now move onto the latter section of chapter 10 of 1 Corinthians.

TS: Sorry. Yes. Though what formal Greco-Roman meals could be like might help us better understand some of what Paul says there.

GB: Fair enough.

TS: I think a helpful place to start is at verse 14 where Paul writes, "Shun the worship of idols." or putting it another way, "Have nothing to do with idolatry." If you read through the rest of the chapter, it's fairly obvious that what follows is, in general terms, related to that injunction. I think that that's important to keep in mind. What then are we to make of verses 16 and 17, which read, "The cup of blessing which we bless, is it not a fellowship—κοινωνια—in the blood of Christ? The bread which we break, is it not a fellowship –κοινωνια—in the body of Christ? Because there is one bread, we who are many are one body, for we all partake of the one bread"?

GB: I can see now how these words might have some connection with what you said about the Greco-Roman formal meals and the notion of "fellowship," though I would have thought that they relate more directly to our celebration of Holy Communion or the Lord's Supper. In fact I know that those words or similar are often recited when people participate in Holy Communion or the Lord's Supper.

TS: Well, one of the problems we have in understanding the text is the temptation to write back into it what we traditionally have derived from the text in the first place. The language used by Paul is language we've incorporated into our theology of Holy Communion or the Lord's Supper and indeed in some cases, as you've mentioned, into the very liturgy associated with the rite itself, if I am permitted to use the word, "rite." So when we come to this passage, it *automatically* speaks to us of the rite.

Part 3: The Lord's Supper

GB: So, you're suggesting that originally, when Paul had these words penned, it was not a reference to something like the Lord's Supper?

TS: I don't believe that we should quickly jump to that conclusion, though I think that what Paul says here may well echo what Jesus said at that Last Passover Meal. After all, Paul connected "the blood of Christ" with a cup, "the cup of blessing," and "the body of Christ" with bread, "the bread we break." At the Last Passover Meal, Jesus made very similar connections. But one interesting difference between what was said at that meal and what is said here by Paul, is the order in which reference is made to the cup and the blood of Christ on the one hand and the bread and the body of Christ on the other. The order in one meal is the reverse of the order in the other. People generally ignore this difference or consider it to be of no account.

GB: And do you have an explanation?

TS: To begin with, stating the obvious, if this passage really does relate to something like a Lord's Supper celebration then we don't have a highly formalized liturgical statement that correctly mirrors the order in which Jesus made his remarks about the bread and the wine at the Last Passover Meal. I don't want to appear to be offensive, but if what Paul wrote *is* meant to reflect what Jesus said at that Last Passover Meal, then it would seem as though he was a little careless. He got the order of things wrong! However, in reality, I don't think Paul was careless at all. My suggestion, for what it's worth, is that firstly, he was writing about meals that these Christians shared with each other, that secondly, these meals would have been formal to some extent, and thirdly that they would've had certain features similar to those of the typical Greco-Roman formal meal. They came from the Greco-Roman world why wouldn't the meals they now had share certain characteristics with the meals they used to have?

GB: I've never thought about what their meals were really like. But your suggestion makes sense.

TS: Well, I think that his first reference being to wine rather than bread was because of the dominance of wine at Greco-Roman formal meals. These meals were characterized by the drinking of wine and could begin with a cup of wine. He mentions bread probably because he wants to say something about Jesus as bread. But in his use of the word "bread" he could also be understood to be referring to the meal as a whole because "bread" might have been considered to be a common way of referring to a meal, even in the Gentile world. Remember how significant the place of bread could be in a meal. We dealt with this a few days ago. By the way, I don't think I mentioned earlier that bread was often used as a spoon with which to obtain other morsels from a watery base. But I may have. . . . I'm not denying the possibility that Paul had the Last Passover Meal in the back of his mind. As I think I said a moment ago, I suspect he did. What I'm suggesting is that he was in fact writing about meals that these Corinthians shared with each other because they were followers of Christ, but that these same meals shared some characteristics with other meals of those times and culture. However, the significant difference between their meals and the normal formal meals of Greco-Roman society was that theirs lacked the idolatrous elements of the pagan world. Those elements had given way to what I would think would have been grand references to the Lord Jesus Christ and presumably also to God the Father.

GB: But doesn't the very phrase "The cup of blessing which we bless" suggest that a liturgical setting is in mind?

TS: I once thought so, but there's little evidence, if any, that that's the case. The shorter phrase "the cup of blessing," "το ποτηριον της ευλογιας" (*to potērion tēs eulogias*), does have some resemblance to what the synoptic Gospels record for the Last Passover Meal, but the differences are obvious. Mark and Luke refer to "ποτηριον ευχαριστησας" (*potērion eucharistēsas*) within a statement which in effect says, "Having taken the cup he gave thanks," while Matthew interposes the little word, "και" (kai), meaning "and," between those two words. Something that should be noted is that though in Mark and Matthew the reference is to the cup taken after the meal, in Luke the reference is to a cup taken before the main meal. I suspect that some may argue that the order of "wine" first and "bread" second in the passage in chapter 10 that we're discussing is simply a reflection of the order in which Luke has things, although Luke does refer to a second cup taken after the main meal. We did talk about what Luke wrote, some time ago now. As a rejoinder to this, I would say that in Chapter 11, where Paul is clearly reporting what was said by Jesus at the Last Passover Meal, Paul has the correct order of "bread" first, followed by "wine" second. No, Paul hasn't been careless in what he wrote earlier, in any way.

GB: I wouldn't have thought so. He might write with flare and flourish but surely as you say, if he meant to mirror the Last Passover Meal, he would get the order right.

TS: Let me continue. I've used the *Thesaurus Linguae Graecae* program in order to locate when and by whom the phrase "το ποτηριον της ευλογιας" was used in ancient times. The phrase is not found in any of the Greek literature before the time of Christ and is only found once before the fourth century CE. Irenaeus, we've mentioned him before, writing in the late second century says "For we offer to God the bread and the cup of blessing." It would appear that he's referring to a Christian rite in which the phrase, "the cup of blessing" might have formed part of some accompanying liturgy. And presumably this usage has its origin in the Corinthian text. But it's the only early evidence for such a liturgical usage that I could find.

GB: Is it possible that the phrase was in use in Aramaic in the Jewish world around about or before the time of the writing of the Corinthian epistle?

TS: I've looked into that and I don't think we have any evidence to support that suggestion either. If the phrase were part of a liturgy used around the time of Christ it probably would've been in a form of Hebrew know as Mishnaic Hebrew. The phrase we would be looking for is "כּוֹס שֶׁל הַבְּרָכָה" (*kōs shel habberākāh*). The Aramaic equivalent is somewhat similar—I think it's something like "כּוֹס דִּי בְּרָכָה" (*kōs dī barākāh*)—I could be wrong. However, whether in Hebrew or in Aramaic, use of the phrase in those early days is unknown. That's not to say that the Greek phrase couldn't have had, for example, a Jewish origin. We just don't know about such an origin. It could have been that "the cup of blessing" was a phrase used casually by people but not in a highly technical sense. Again, we just don't know.

GB: Do we have any evidence for a phrase a little like but not the same as "το ποτηριον της ευλογιας" being used—I think I've got the Greek right?

TS: You're spot on. Yes, a shorter version, namely, "ποτηριον ευλογιας," can be found in a couple of documents dated second century or thereabouts but the truth is we're really struggling to conclude that Paul was using a well-known liturgical phrase. In fact the longer phrase—"the cup of blessing which we bless" (το ποτηριον της ευλογιας ὁ εὐλογουμεν [*to potērion tēs eulogias ho eulogoumen*])—cannot be found at all until the fourth century.

GB: I wonder how many people know all this.

TS: I wouldn't think many. The paucity of the occurrence of the Greek phrase "το ποτηριον της ευλογιας" or even "το ποτηριον της εὐχαριστιας," (*to potērion tēs eucharistias*)—the cup of thanksgiving—I won't go into any details, but the situation with that phrase is no better with respect to early Christian literature—should act as a caution against assuming that its occurrence in 1 Corinthians is a reference to a Christian rite. Look, I think the best evidence that we have suggests that either Paul used a phrase that was around, used from time to time but not in a technical sense, or that it originated with him.

GB: But still—I feel as though I'm now acting again as the Devil's advocate—the reference to the blood and the body of Christ alongside of the reference to the cup and bread, does remind us of the words uttered by Jesus at the Last Passover Meal, doesn't it?

TS: I agree. I've already said that what Paul wrote may well have had those Last Passover words of Jesus in mind. But we should not forget the type of meal that the Corinthian believers, particularly the Gentile ones, had been used to, at least when they formally met together. Something I think I should mention is Paul's use of the first person plural in these couple of verses that we've been discussing. I think it's at least four times. My guess is that Paul is referring to meals that in the past he had shared with them. They may not have been formal meals, at least not all of them, but some of them could've been.

GB: But, I'm still playing Devil's advocate, any formal meal could've been a Eucharistic type of meal, or associated with a special Eucharistic ceremony, couldn't it?

TS: True, though I've already pointed out, the cup is mentioned prior to the bread in contrast with the order in which the words of remembrance are uttered at the Last Passover Meal. And I'm saying that I don't think this order should be ignored or lightly glossed over. Besides I've also suggested that if what Jesus said were a command then a once a year ceremony would've been in mind. Paul could've been referring to a once a year ceremony in this passage but the feel I think you get from it is that this was a formal meal but one held more often than that.

GB: What about the use of the definite article—"*the* cup of blessing"? Does this not suggest that a special cup was involved, a cup used in a special ceremony?

TS: I'd like to leave discussion on special cups to sometime later. Suffice it to say here, that there could've been a special time during the meal when such a blessing was given or just that a special feature of the meal was the giving of that blessing, whenever that was. The use of the definite article could be an indication of something like one or the other of these possibilities. To say the obvious, there was a tendency in formal meals to do things formally! But that doesn't mean that there was a designated cup for use only in a special ceremony.

GB: Whatever the actual situation, it's absolutely obvious that you're trying to make the case that what is being referred to in the text is not a celebration of the Lord's Supper or similar!

TS: Again I want to say that I strongly suspect that Paul had in mind some of those words that Jesus uttered at the Last Passover Meal. However, if we acknowledge that the context for the passage under consideration is one where the concern is that believers should have nothing to do with idolatry, if we consider what formal pagan meals with their idolatrous character were like, if we recognize the importance of the notion of fellowship as an aspect of meals shared with others and if we make some guesses as to how these Corinthian believers might have transformed such meals into believers' formal meals, I think one could understand the text we've been discussing as follows—"*When together we drink our wine to bless our God, it is not offered as a shared toast to the gods. Is not our cup, the one over which we bless our God, drunk with thanks by us who share in Christ who shed his blood for us? When we share our meal it is not because we share an allegiance to the gods. Is not our breaking of bread, our sharing, a oneness in Christ? Though many, we are one because we share in the one who is our bread, our sustenance.*"

GB: When you put it like that, what you've been arguing for makes considerable sense. Paul could've been referring to a christianly transformed formal meal in which believers of all sorts took part—culturally, similar in many ways to the meals they'd been used to, but radically changed. The gods are out but God and Christ are in!

TS: Nicely put. . . . I think that's more than enough for today. Look at the time.

Part 3: The Lord's Supper

GB: Just a couple of other things. Sorry. I notice that sometimes there is a reference to "blessing" and sometimes to "giving thanks" and that two different Greek words are involved and that you also made a reference to "God" in your paraphrase. Why did you do that and what is the difference between "blessing" and "giving thanks"?

TS: I'll try and answer those two questions together. I think the idea of a "cup of blessing which we bless" may *well* have been Jewish in origin, while not necessarily being a set piece of liturgy. I think that it's somewhat a strange phrase, at least strange to our ears. Did people really bless a cup? Of course not! I suggest that what we have is an idiomatic expression, the phrase as a whole meaning something like "a cup of wine from which we drink in honor of God, blessing him—a cup used to bless him." Upon drinking from that cup, you were expressing how wonderful, majestic, praise worthy God is. And inherent in so blessing God was a note of thanks. You were thanking him for the relationship that he had established with you and that enabled you to see how wonderful he is. Blessing and thanksgiving go hand in hand, almost interchangeably. Because blessing is what Paul refers to in the text we are considering I thought it proper to refer to blessing God. But I also included the notion of giving thanks. But to be sure, I don't know whether in what he said here that Paul actually had in mind some reference to God as distinct from Christ. . . . I think it's interesting that with respect to the accounts of the Last Passover Meal, Matthew and Mark refer to a blessing given by Jesus in association with the breaking of bread but Luke and Paul, referring to the same event, write of Jesus giving thanks. With respect to the wine, Matthew and Mark record Jesus giving thanks, as does also Luke, although his reference is to a cup taken before the breaking of bread. In Paul's account he mentions neither blessing nor giving thanks when speaking of the wine.

GB: And what you've made me aware of is that while Paul, later in his letter, when referring to the Last Passover Meal uses the word for "giving thanks" and I know it's only in association with the bread, he uses the word for "blessing" in the passage we've looked at today. In that passage he may not have had the Last Passover Meal in mind as much as you suspect.

TS: You might have a point. Look, it really has been another marathon today—perhaps the longest day so far. We must finish up. Is Monday okay for meeting again?

GB: Can we make it Tuesday? I've got a couple of pressing appointments on Monday.

TS: Come to think of it, I've got some things to do then as well. Tuesday it is.

EXPLANATORY NOTES: DAY 24

For a somewhat more traditional, though independently creative view of what Paul refers to when he writes, "the cup of blessing which we bless" and other phrases and statements in 1 Cor 10, 11, understood to be references to the Lord's Supper, or elements of the same, see Wright, "The Breaking of Bread," in *Paul and the Faithfulness of God*, 1344–48. See also 427–29 of the same work.

The Greek words of 1 Cor 10:16 referred to by TS are taken from NAG.

At the beginning of 1 Corinthians 10 (NIV), the references that Paul makes to aspects of Israel's history are numerous. He refers to their passing through the Sea of Reeds, under the leadership of Moses and the presence of the cloud created by God—Exod 14 (NIV). He mentions the supply of manna and the water from the rock that God provided for his people—Exod 16, 17 (NIV). He refers to the fact that most of them perished in the desert—Num 14 (NIV). He recalls the episode of Israel worshipping the golden calf and engaging in revelry and the occasion when Israel engaged in sexual immorality with Moabite women and the worshipping of Moabite gods and the many that died on both occasions—Exod 32; Num 25 (NIV).

A reference to Paul's stay in Corinth and who became believers there can be found in Acts 18 (NIV).

References to the cited Jewish blessing, to be said at the beginning of a meal, can be found in Carson, *Matthew*, 342 and Blomberg, *Contagious Holiness*, 105.

Fotopoulos, in chapters 2–5 of *Food Offered to Idols*, 49–157, discusses several possible sites where the Corinthians might have eaten food offered to idols. He concludes that the Asklepieion with its dining room is the most likely and perhaps the only candidate.

References to idolatry and its connection with food in the Gentile world can be found in Fotopoulos, *Food Offered to Idols*, especially chapter 6—"Food, Wine, and Sexual Relations—Greco-Roman Dining as More than Just a Meal," 158–78. See also Cheung, *Idol Food in Corinth*, Phua, *Idolatry and Authority*, and Tomson, *Paul and the Jewish Law*.

The works of Fotopoulos, Cheung and Tomson as well as that of Phua, cited above, also deal with 1 Cor 8:1—11:1 or sections thereof in some detail. The most relevant chapter in Tomson's work is chapter 5, "1 Corinthians 8–10: 'On Idol Offerings,'" 187–220. For Fotopoulos it is chapter 8, "Exegetical Study of 1 Corinthians 8:1–11:1," 208–50 and for Cheung it is chapter 3, "Exegetical Investigation of 1 Corinthians 8:1–11:1," 82–164. Phua's concluding chapter, chapter 7—"Conclusions," 201–08—provides a summary of his understanding of 1 Corinthians chapters 8–10.

For the view that some of the Corinthian believers were well-to-do, see Judge, *The First Christians*, 464–525.

Fotopoulos in *Food Offered to Idols*, 164, 176, 187 comments on the nature of "κοινωνια" in the Greco-Roman world and refers to Burkert, *Greek Religion*, 57, in which this matter is also discussed, 164.

Much of what TS said concerning the importance of food, sacrificed or otherwise offered to the gods, for one's relationship with the gods, the importance of formal meals for social, political and economic reasons and the nature of formal meals is reflected in what Fotopoulos wrote in his chapter 6.

Smith, *From Symposium to Eucharist*, chapter 2, "The Greco-Roman Banquet," 13–46, writes at length about the nature of formal Greco-Roman meals. There are a number of references to libations in his work but 28–32 provide a general background.

The phrase "το ποτηριον της εὐλογιας," used by Irenaeus is found in Irenaeus, *Fragmenta deperditorum*, Fragment 36, lines 16–17.

I am indebted to George Athas, who informed me of the likelihood of the Mishnaic Hebrew "כּוֹס שֶׁל הַבְּרָכָה" (kōs shel habberākāh) being used rather than the Hebrew "כּוֹס־הַבְּרָכָה" (kōs-habberākāh) and who gave me a hint of what its Aramaic equivalent would be. I am also indebted to him for contacting Maurice Casey who via Stephanie Fisher informed him, Athas, that he knew of no examples of the Hebrew expression or its Aramaic equivalent as old as the time under consideration. He, Casey, also pointed out, referring to Bokser, *The Origins of the Seder*, that at the time of Jesus there was debate as to some elements of the Passover meal with Jewish people rewriting the Passover rite after 70 CE. My thanks to both Maurice and George.

Jeremias believes that "כּוֹס שֶׁל בְּרָכָה" (kōs shel berākāh) is an established technical term for the cup of wine over which grace after the meal was said"—see Jeremias, *The Eucharistic words of Jesus*, 87, note 8. He indicates that the evidence for this can be found in Strack and Billerbeck, *Kommentar zum Neuen Testament aus Talmud und MIdrasch*, 628, 630f. This conclusion, though obviously based on material written later than Paul's 1 Cor text may suggest, and did suggest to Jeremias, that such a term was also in use in Paul's time. If, as it is alleged, the term was used in association with a grace said after the meal, and, according to Jeremias, 87 that Paul was making use of that technical expression, then, that Paul should begin this part of his text with wine and then refer to bread, is still an oddity.

The two references to "ποτηριον εὐλογιας" mentioned by TS can be located in Origen's, *Homilae in Jeremiam*, Homily 12, section 2, line 22 and in *Josephus et Aseneth*, chapter 8, section 11, line 5.

The longer phrase, "το ποτηριον της εὐλογιας ὁ εὐλογουμεν," first found in Chrysostom, writing in the second half of the fourth century, can be found in *epistulum i ad Corinthos*, homilae 24, section 3, lines 43, 63.

Day 25

Corinthian Meals—The Table of the Lord

The discussion begins with a focus on the matter of idolatry and Paul's concern that the Corinthians disassociate themselves from the idolatry of their world. Then TS examines the use of the Hebrew word for "table" in the Old Testament and how the equivalent Greek word was used both inside and outside of the New Testament. TS also comments on the absence of the definite article in a Greek phrase of interest and while considering possibilities of what that phrase might mean declines to come to a firm conclusion at this time.

TS: Hi there. Is it okay today if we do a little recapping and then I'll take it from where we left off in chapter 10 of 1 Corinthians?

GB: A good idea.

TS: About one third of the way through chapter 10, Paul, without tempering his expression in any way, simply says that they must have nothing to do with idolatry. Then, from my point of view, he in effect, says, "When we meet together as believers and share in a meal, we don't have idolatrous practices at that meal do we? To the contrary our meals are all about Christ." In my mind there is no question about it—he is concerned with idolatry. He's certainly not focused on some early Christian ceremony or rite. And now, in verse 18 he proceeds by referring to the sacrificial practices of the people of Israel and points out that in eating what is sacrificed upon an altar they associate themselves with that altar and all that that altar represents. He is reinforcing the point that in their world eating food that has been sacrificed to, or in any way offered to, a god is, in practice, associating oneself with the pagan, idolatrous ideas involved in that food being offered to that god. Next he raises the question about whether a sacrifice or an idol amounts to anything.

GB: Ah, now I remember. I find what Paul says at this point a little confusing. He seems to be saying that they don't amount to anything but in the next breath indicates that they do, or at least that the idols do—that when the offerings are made, they are actually made to demons and not to God.

TS: I know what you mean about being confused. Something I haven't mentioned previously is that there is a thought that throughout chapters 8 to 10 Paul is using a literary device that technically can be called "deliberative rhetoric." In this case, it would mean that what we see as an expression of Paul's point of view actually consists of two points of view—the Corinthians' and his. He writes what he imagines the Corinthians, or at least what *some* of them, might think and then follows this with his response and he does this a number of times throughout these three chapters. I don't think it's been all that necessary to consider that idea up until now but at this point it might be helpful to do so. Let's propose that Paul first of all says what he thinks the so-called knowledgeable and indeed yes, somewhat informed, Corinthian believers might say—"But meat is just meat and idols are just idols. They are nothing." The idea would then be that Paul responds with—"Well, when the pagans (literally "the nations") make their offerings they actually do make them to demons, to real entities, and not to God." On this analysis, he isn't replying by referring to idols as structures made of wood or stone but rather to what he considers genuine beings, demons—realities that exist in association with the idols.

GB: I can't remember if it was you or someone else who said that when we think of demons we think of "evil spirits" but that for a Greek or a Roman the reference to demons was a reference to spiritual entities that could be considered as either good or bad or neither. The word "demons" is a way of referring to what you termed, the immortals—the divine beings and the heroes.

TS: I may have said something like that but whether I did or not, what you've said is correct. In Acts chapter 17 Paul is recorded as saying to the members of what was called the Areopagite Council that he perceived that they were "very religious." The words "very religious" are a translation of the Greek term "διεσιδαιμονεστερους" (*deisidaimonesterous*). However, if we translated the word literally we would probably say something like—"very reverent towards demons." Anyway, back to chapter 10 of 1 Corinthians. Having stated that the demons are a reality, he then says, "I do not want you to have fellowship ("κοινωνους" [*koinōnous*]) with demons." There's that word "κοινωνια" again.

GB: I've now got the passage in front of me. Paul follows this with "You cannot drink the cup of the Lord and the cup of demons. You cannot partake of the table of the Lord and the table of demons. Shall we provoke the Lord to jealousy? Are we stronger than he?" I notice, by the way, that, except for the last two questions, Paul uses the second person "you." Perhaps he doesn't include himself in these declarations because he certainly doesn't see himself as involved with the demonic world. His remarks are directed pointedly towards *them*! *They* must not have anything to do with that world. But, regardless of all of that, in mentioning "the table of the Lord" and "the cup of the

Lord," don't we now have a clear reference to something like "Holy Communion"? And by the way, is there another reference here to "κοινωνια" in what the English translation has as "partake"?

TS: To answer your second question first, no, but the verb that's used, the infinitive of which is "μετεχειν" (*metechein*), and that's the actual word in the text, means much the same. And I think your remarks about Paul's use of the second person, it's actually second person plural, are perceptive. But now regarding your first question, almost everybody seems to jump to the same conclusion that what we have here is a clear reference to the "Lord's Supper" or similar. However, there are some difficulties associated with that understanding.

GB: Oh? . . . Well I guess the first thing you might point out is that "the cup," the reference being to wine, is mentioned before "the table," with its connection being to "bread." The Last Passover Meal has the cup and the bread, where they are associated with the remembrance statements, the other way around.

TS: Correct. And secondly, although perhaps one might not consider it to be all that significant, the actual reference is to "table," as you've been careful to say and not simply to "bread." Whereas using the word "cup" can be appropriate when making a reference to wine, in whatever context, the word "table," in the Greco-Roman world does not automatically suggest that "bread" is in mind. However, what is of more importance is that in that ancient world there is no such thing, as far as I can tell, as "*the* cup of demons" or "*the* table of demons." These two concepts, as far as I am able to ascertain, are unknown in Paul's world. I suppose one could say that that isn't a problem. Paul with his unique understanding of spiritual realities may have coined the phrases. The truth is, however, that in the Greek text there is no definite article before "Lord," "table," "cup" or "demons." Now that's not an abnormal situation where a proper noun like, "Lord" is involved, and we often need to supply the definite article in those sentences where the word "κυριος" (*kurios*), the Greek word for "lord," occurs. However, that the definite article is absent in the case of "table," "cup" and demons" needs to be seriously thought about. Perhaps the definite article should not appear in an English translation.

GB: So you could retranslate the text as follows, "You cannot drink a cup of the Lord and a cup of demons. You cannot partake of a table of the Lord and a table of demons"?

TS: Exactly. It's not that we shouldn't translate the text with definite articles throughout. It's just that we don't have to and we shouldn't automatically do so. You can see how, if one does insert the definite article before "cup of the Lord" and "table of the Lord," out of consistency, one has to insert it before, "cup of demons" and "table of demons." And that's where the problem arises. We would then have two novel concepts—"*the* cup of demons" and "*the* table of demons." And I don't know what *the* cup

Part 3: The Lord's Supper

of demons and *the* table of demons means. Why not try and see what the sentences might mean with the definite article appearing only before "Lord"?

GB: Well, even without the definite article, don't the phrases, "a cup of the Lord" and "a table of the Lord" suggest that something quite formal is being referred to?

TS: That's a possibility. However, in that case, I suspect that most people would actually prefer the definite article to appear before "cup" and "table." Its presence, it would be argued, makes it so much more obvious that the backdrop to the phrases is a formal celebration, such as the Lord's Supper. But before we assume that such a backdrop is indeed the case, we need to have a look at the idea of "cup of the Lord" and "table of the Lord" in a little more detail.

GB: "Cup of the Lord" first!

TS: Could do. However I think I'd prefer to look at "table of the Lord" first. I think "cup of the Lord," while possibly a little more interesting, is perhaps more complex and so I'd like to leave that till later.

GB: Okay. "Table of the Lord"!

TS: Firstly some brief comments about how "table" is used in the Old Testament. I know we're looking at the New Testament but Paul was steeped in the Old and looking at those scriptures might just give us a bit of a feel for how Paul might have been using the Greek word for table—"τραπεζα" (*trapeza*) in the text we're examining. Anyway, I would not have thought that examining the Old Testament usage would hurt. Indeed such an examination might be helpful in other ways. The Hebrew word for "table," "שֻׁלְחָן" (*shūlcān*), occurs there about sixty six times and at heart it's a reference to an elevated structure of some sort. More than half the time it refers to "the table of the presence," a special table that was placed in the tabernacle and later in the temple. Interestingly, that was a table on which bread was placed. I might refer to that table again later. About twenty five times it's used to refer to a table or tables in other settings. Just one example—it comes from 2 Kings. From time to time, the prophet Elisha passed through a village called Shunem. A wealthy woman there persuaded her husband to provide a small room for the use of the prophet whenever he should pass by. In the room was placed "a bed, a table, a chair and a lamp."

GB: Very homely!

TS: True. Though not every table that's mentioned in the Old Testament was used for food, generally the table was a structure upon which food was or was to be placed and sometimes the fundamental reference is to what was on the table—the food, the meal—rather than the table itself. Indeed sometimes it's not clear, or indeed important, if the reference is to a meal or a table on which a meal has been set. For instance a reference in 1 Samuel 20 to Jonathan getting up from a table in fierce anger might have been a reference to the meal he was having, the table at which he was sitting, or both. In Isaiah chapter 21 the text reads, "They set the tables, they spread the rugs" and while the prime reference might be to a physical structure, it's really the meal to be had at that table that is the ultimate focus. On some occasions, the dominant focus is not so much the table or the food upon the table but the social aspects of people having a meal together—"Your sons will be olive shoots around your table," a text from Psalm 128, and "Two kings will sit at the same table and lie to each other," a text from chapter 11 of Daniel.

GB: And I remember the words from Psalm 23—"You, Lord, prepare a table before me in the presence of my enemies." And I guess that there the focus is on God and his great kindness towards David.

TS: Yes, I think so. As is obvious, "*shūlcān*" occurs in a variety of contexts. There is a text in Proverbs, "She, wisdom, has also set her table" where the reference is clearly to a metaphorical table of good things. You can also see here an example where the word is really used to refer to what's on the table rather than the table itself. The same is true of your quote from Psalm 23.

GB: Are there any references to "the Lord's table"?

TS: A table is sometimes identified as one belonging to a specific person—for example, there is an instance of "my table" where the reference is to David's table and another to "his table," where the reference is to King Solomon's table. And yes, there are also a few references to "the Lord's table"—two in the first chapter of Malachi. In Ezekiel chapter 44 there is also a reference to "my table"—the table being God's table. In each of these last three instances the table being referred to is, "the table of the presence." That same table is also referred to in chapter 41 of Ezekiel but as "the table before the Lord." To complete the picture, in Ezekiel chapter 39, God is recorded as speaking of a type of eschatological table of judgment as "my table."

GB: Putting that last reference and the ones to David and Solomon aside, do the others you've just mentioned suggest that the table of the Lord in the 1 Corinthians passage might have something like, "the table of the presence" as part of its background? You mentioned that "the table of the presence" had bread placed upon it. Maybe simply mentioning "table," if "the table of the presence" was in mind, was Paul's way of referring to "bread"!

TS: Perhaps. It's difficult to tell but it's worth thinking about. If you are *right*, then I think it's not the bread that's the focal point but rather that idea of the presence of the Lord. You've just reminded me of an ancient Jewish saying that goes something like this, "Where, at a communal meal, words from the Torah are quoted, it is as though the people present have eaten from the table of God." Maybe the idea in this saying was that by speaking the very words of God, it was as though you were present at God's table, hearing him speak, though in fact you were at your own table. From what

I've read, Jewish people not only had the concept of "the table of God" but also the concept "table of demons."

GB: These two concepts, taken together, do seem to be similar to what we're looking at in 1 Corinthians don't they?

TS: Yes. But to get back to the possibility of "the table of the presence" of the Old Testament being behind "table of the Lord" in our Corinthians text, I certainly don't think we should see in what Paul said some reference to Old Testament practices associated with the tabernacle or temple although I can see how others might differ with me on that. "The table of the presence" was, as I've mentioned, for the placement of bread, the bread being eaten by Aaron and his descendants and was almost certainly an indication of such priests sharing, as it were, a meal with God. Some incense was also set alongside the bread and it was to be thought of as an offering to the Lord by fire. There is a reference to the table of the presence, though it is not directly called "the table of the presence" in the book of Hebrews in the New Testament. It simply forms part of the description the writer gives of the ancient tabernacle. I wouldn't want to suggest that among the early believers there was meant to be some priestly caste and some ongoing sacrifice to God made possible only by such a special group. Again, I know others would disagree with me. For the time being, however, let's return to just considering "table," but now, how "table" is used in the New Testament.

GB: Fire away. I didn't think an examination of "table" in the Old Testament could have been so interesting.

TS: The Greek word translated "table" in the New Testament is "τραπεζα," as I mentioned earlier. It occurs there about fourteen times and, like the Old Testament "*shūlcān*," refers to an elevated structure on which things are placed. Almost all references are associated with food. One exception is where Jesus is described as overturning the tables of the money-changers. There is also just that one reference to the "table," mentioned in fact in connection with what we might translate, "the bread of the presence," in Hebrews, as I've just said. Another example of its use is found in that parable that Jesus told—it may not have been a parable in its entirety—where reference is made to the rich man's table from which the poor man Lazarus longed to eat. Then there's the table that the Canaanite woman referred to, when she said to Jesus that even the dogs under the table eat the children's crumbs. Other examples? The table that Jesus spoke of as his table from which some would eat and drink when his kingdom came, and then there's the table that Paul referred to, quoting from one of the Psalms, when he said "May their table become a trap and a snare."

GB: It seems that, like the Old Testament references, while the primary reference is to the object, the table, sometimes it's the food or meal on the table or even the social setting of the table that's the real focus.

TS: Yes. It was probably much the same in the Greco-Roman world, though it's a little difficult to tell. Athenaeus, whom I've mentioned before and who wrote a lot about formal meals, has a number of references to tables being used for the conveying of wine and food. He refers to a certain Nicostratus who told a servant girl about his having had enough to eat, though he could still enjoy a "Good Daemon"—a reference to wine, the "Good Daemon" being a way of speaking of Dionysus, the God of wine. Speaking rather rudely to her, from our point of view, he then ordered her to pour out the wine and to do it quickly and then to pick up the table and get it out of his way. My guess is that that was the table on which the vessel or vessels of wine had been placed but I suppose it could have been the table on which the food had been set. He also has a quote from a Theophrastus, writing on drunkenness, who referred to what happened at the ending of a particular meal. A small quantity of unmixed wine was taken, a toast was made in honor of "the Good Daemon" and having made some sort of obeisance, the wine was taken from the tables.

GB: But these examples seem to center on the use of tables for food and wine.

TS: Yes, you're right. However, Athenaeus makes an interesting comment in one place, about how the word "τραπεζα" was used in ancient times. He says that the word was employed in a general sense and he then illustrated what he meant by this, by saying how the word "tables" was used to refer to "courses," that is, various courses served at a meal. To what extent this practice was carried over into, say first century CE times, I'm not really sure. I suspect that separate courses were however, served on separate tables, or if on the same table, at different times.

GB: Is there any evidence that the Greeks considered that, somehow or other, a table could be associated with a god?

TS: I suspect that the table that Athenaeus mentioned in connection with Nicostratus and at least one of the tables that were mentioned in his reference to Theophrastus were associated with "the Good Daemon." However I could be wrong. Certainly Athenaeus mentions a Philochorus who refers to a gold table dedicated to Asclepius, and also a Diodorus Siculus, though speaking of an Egyptian setting, mentions a table of a god which table stood next to a couch. Athenaeus, this time quoting from Pyrgion writing on Cretan customs, also refers to a table at the right of certain entrance halls that was called "the table of Zeus, god of strangers." I think the idea was that guests, invited or uninvited, could use that table for the purpose of having a meal and drinking some wine. It could also be that when they sat at such a table they considered themselves to be sharing a meal with Zeus. I don't know.

GB: Any other examples?

TS: I don't think I have any more that would throw further light on the use of the word "τραπεζα" in association with the gods. But before I forget I think I should draw your attention to one usage of the word found in the Greek *Septuagint,* the *LXX.* In two places in chapter 1 of Malachi "τραπεζα" is used in connection with the word "Lord," with the table referred to being, "the table of the presence." I've already mentioned those two verses. But now I'm focusing on the use of the Greek language there, not the Hebrew. There are no definite articles involved but because a particular table is involved, "the table of the presence," the translation should refer to, "the table of the Lord."

GB: So does this indicate that perhaps we should translate "table of the Lord" in 1 Corinthians chapter 10 as, "the table of the Lord"?

TS: If we were only looking at this one phrase in 1 Corinthians, chapter 10, there being only two words involved, "table" and "Lord," I think the response would be that we couldn't be sure how to translate it. Nonetheless, whatever we suggest, the "table" of 1 Corinthians chapter 10 definitely has something to do with the Lord. I think there are two main possibilities. It could be that there the word "table" is primarily a reference to a physical table, with some sort of meal being associated with it. Alternatively it's possible that the reference is actually to a meal and what happens at that meal and its social setting. The word "μετεχειν," the infinitive of the verb "μετεχω" (*metechō*), the word used in connection with the table and cup in our verse and translated "partake" has the sense of "to share with." So Paul is saying something like "You cannot share a table of the Lord with a table of demons." There are just two verbs involved—"to be able"—with "not" it is "cannot" in our text—and "to share with" and they each occur just once. Now he could be meaning that you cannot have a table dedicated to the Lord and also a table dedicated to any demon—presumably a demon such as Asclepius, Dionysus or Zeus—using the plural "demons" to allow for the reference to be to any demon. Alternatively he might be saying something like, "You cannot have a meal that is associated with the Lord and at the same time a meal that is associated at any time with any of the demons, in terms of anything you do or say at such a meal."

GB: The first alternative relates to having dedicated tables. And having both, one dedicated to the Lord and another dedicated to some demon, would have been a very serious matter. However, I would have thought the second alternative to be just as disturbing and perhaps the more likely. It relates to what happens at a table. However, I suppose Paul could have had both of your alternatives in mind.

TS: That's certainly possible, though I think, along with you, that the second alternative is the more likely. If he is making any reference to "a table dedicated to the Lord," I suggest that it's his recognition of the fact that they had changed or should've changed the custom of having tables dedicated to this demon or that, to one where there was just one table associated with the one and only Lord. And, if he is making such a reference, I don't think we are entitled automatically to say that what he's referring to is a special table used in a ceremony like Holy Communion. If there were special ceremonies, I suspect that they were ones transformed from having pagan perspectives to Christian ones. But we'll probably return to that idea later. I repeat, there are no definite articles involved in the phrase. I still think we should keep that in mind. And furthermore, I think we obtain a better feel for what is going on if we now consider the phrase, "a cup of the Lord." So I don't want to be too dogmatic at this point.

GB: Okay. But I'd think it's probably too late to start on that now.

TS: Absolutely. I really didn't think that we would spend this much time on "tables" but we have! See you tomorrow then, if that's okay?

GB: No problem. See you tomorrow.

Part 3: The Lord's Supper

EXPLANATORY NOTES: DAY 25

Fotopoulos, in *Food Offered to Idols,* bases his analysis of 1 Cor 10:1–11:1 on the idea that deliberative rhetoric permeates that part of the text. See especially his chapter 7, "Social-Rhetorical Issues," 179–207.

Paul's remark to members of the Areopagite Council, "I perceive you are very religious" can be found in Acts 17:22 (NIV) and the Greek word translated "very religious" that TS discusses has been taken from NAG.

The reference, to a room prepared for Elisha can be found in 2 Kgs 4:10 (IHG), to Jonathan arising from a table in anger, in 1 Sam 20:30 (IHG), to setting the tables and spreading the rugs, in Isa 21:5 (IHG), to sons being olive shoots around the table, in Ps 128:3 (IHG), and to two kings sitting at the same table, in Dan 11:27 (IHG).

The text, "You prepare a table before me" is located in Ps 23:5 (IHG).

The text concerning wisdom and her table can be found in Prov 9:2 (IHG).

The reference to "my table" being King David's table can be found in 2 Sam 9:7 (IHG) and the reference to "his table" being King Solomon's table can be found in 2 Chr 9:4 (IHG).

The references to a table associated with the Lord, designated, "the Lord's table," are located in Mal 1:7, 12 (IHG) and to a table associated with the Lord, designated, "my table" are found in Ezek 44:16, 39:20 (IHG). The phrase "the table before the Lord" is mentioned in Ezek 41: 22 (IHG).

There is a reference to a saying by a Rabbi Shimon ben Yohai—"If three have eaten at one table and not spoken words of Torah on it, it is as though they had eaten of the sacrifices of the dead. But if three have eaten at one table and have spoken words of Torah on it, it is as if they had eaten from the table of God" in Cheung, *Idol Food in Corinth,* 106–07. In that same work Cheung also writes, "any first-century Jew could easily have referred—and did refer—to εἰδωλόθυτα (*eidōlothuta*) with appellations like 'table of demons,' even apart from temple settings," 104. "Εἰδωλόθυτος" (*eidōlothutos*) from which εἰδωλόθυτα is derived, means something like, "that which is offered to idols."

Exod 25:23–30 (IHG) provides details on the construction of the table of the presence and Lev 24:5–9 (IHG) refers to the bread to be placed on that table.

The phrase "the table of the presence," found in the New Testament, can be located in Heb 9:2 (NIV).

The reference to Jesus overturning the money changers can be found in Matt 21:12 (NIV), to Lazarus longing to eat from the rich man's table, in Luke 16:21 (NIV), to the Canaanite woman who spoke of the dogs under the table eating the children's crumbs, in Mark 7:28 (NIV), to Jesus speaking of those who would eat at his table in his kingdom, in Luke 22:30 (NIV) and to Paul's quote from one of the Pss concerning a table becoming a trap and a snare, in Rom 11:9 (NIV), the Ps being Ps 69:22 (NIV).

The quote by Athenaeus from Nicostratus concerning the servant girl and the table she had to remove can be found in *VIII Athenaeus*, Book XV, 693b, 152–53 and the quote from Theophrastus, writing on drunkenness, occurs in the same work, Book XV, 693c and d, 154–55.

The reference by Athenaeus as to how the word, "τραπεζα" was used by some in the past can be found in *VII Athenaeus*, Book XIV, 641d, 248–49.

The quote by Athenaeus from Philochorus concerning the table dedicated to Asclepius can be found in *VIII Athenaeus*, Book XV, 693e, 156–57 and his reference to Pyrgion concerning the table of Zeus can be located in *II Athenaeus*, Book IV, 143f, 186–87.

The reference by Diodorus Siculus to a table of a god situated next to a couch can be found in *Diodorus Siculus, Library of History, III,* Book V, 46.7, 226–27.

The Greek text in 1 Cor 10:20 has been taken from NAG.

Day 26

Corinthian Meals—The Cup of the Lord

Today, TS painstakingly works through Greek texts outside of the New Testament that refer to cups in association with drinking and the gods. He focuses on the different verbs used and the grammatical way that the gods are addressed. After considerable discussion he invites GB to offer his understanding of "You cannot drink a cup of the Lord and a cup of demons."

TS: Hi There. I hope our session today will not be too long but I fear otherwise. Things often seem to be simpler to begin with than they turn out to be!

GB: No worries. I find some of the stuff we talk about to be quite fascinating.

TS: I'm glad. I know I do repeat myself here and there but that's because I think it'll help.

GB: You don't repeat yourself all that much. Actually, every day we cover such a lot of ground, and I think it's helpful from time to time to be reminded of some of the things that we've previously talked about.

TS: Well, today we're going to be looking at the phrase "You cannot drink the cup of the Lord and the cup of demons," "οὐ (*ou*—not) δυνασθε (*dunasthe*—you are able) ποτηριον (*potērion*—cup) κυριου (*kuriou*—of the Lord) πινειν (*pinein*—to drink) και (*kai*—and) ποτηριον (*potērion*—cup) δαιμονιων (*daimoniōn*—of demons). I should point out again, that there are no definite articles in the Greek. A more cautious translation of the phrase would be "You cannot drink a cup of the Lord and a cup of demons." And as I said before, I don't think that the concept "*the* cup of demons" exists in the Greek literature. There were individual cups for individual demons or deities but not a single cup for a number of deities.

GB: But why then, is the reference to "a cup of demons" rather than "a cup of a demon" in the sense of "a cup of any demon"? I think you were sort of dealing with this issue when you were referring to the phrase "a table of demons."

TS: Yes I was. At least I was trying to. I think it's because at their meals, I mean the meals of the Greco-Roman world, perhaps particularly their formal meals, any number of gods might be referred to. It was a world of many gods.

GB: But then, why wouldn't Paul say "cups of demons"? I'm being stubborn aren't I!

TS: No. Well, maybe. Perhaps he didn't because he wanted to place in opposition to "*a* cup of the Lord" the phrase, "*a* cup of demons," in the sense of "any cup of demons," a situation involving both to be absolutely avoided, of course. And the phrase "a cup of demons" matches with what Paul almost immediately next says—"a table of demons." And I didn't think Paul's use of that phrase was of any great concern.

GB: Fair enough. And I was ignoring the importance of style!

TS: Possibly. Anyway we do need to keep in mind that chapter 10, our chapter here, is essentially about idol worship. Even if it's thought that there are some references to something like the Lord's Supper, that's not Paul's main concern here. Note again that he said earlier, "Shun the worship of idols."

GB: I get the point. It's fairly obvious that idolatrous behavior is Paul's fundamental concern, at least up until this mention of tables and cups.

TS: And I think it goes beyond this point. Again, I think I should mention that, as with the earlier text—"the cup of blessing which we bless ... the bread which we break," wine, referred to by means of the word "cup," precedes "bread," though in this case, it's actually "table." I've already mentioned the important part wine played in the formal Greco-Roman meal and again I'm suggesting that Paul had such meals in mind except that I don't think he restricted what he says here to formal meals. But now let's consider the phrase, "a cup of the Lord." Some time ago, I decided to examine references to "cup," of any type, textually associated with a god, gods, "the heroes" or a human being, in the Greek literature dated anywhere between the sixth century BCE and around the end of the second century CE. I was interested in the grammatical case assigned to a god or gods and the like, the context involved, and where relevant, any verb used in close association with the cup.

GB: Why all this need for detail?

TS: I used to assume that understanding these texts in the Greek literature was a fairly simple matter but I had a few nagging doubts and wanted to investigate further. It turned out that the texts are much more complex than I had originally believed. We, today, are of course, simply trying to come to an appropriate understanding of "a cup of the Lord" and "a cup of demons." But I think my research might help. And,

I think if we work ultimately on the first phrase, an understanding of the second will automatically follow.

GB: How many references did you come across?

TS: It's difficult to be precise about the number and not be misleading. In terms of references to a god, hero, or human being, having some association with a cup or cups and toasts or libations, I had a list of fifty one. However some of these references occurred in the same sentence or in otherwise close association with each other. I'm sure there's more but it seemed to me that it was a good enough sample to work with. I came across one where a libation was made to some snakes but where no relevant grammatical case was actually involved. I ignored that example. But it was pretty well the exception. I can't remember ignoring any others that I found. Almost all of the references came from the one work, *The Deipnosophists,* also referred to as "The Learned Banqueters." I've mentioned that work and its author Athenaeus before. I mentioned him a lot yesterday!

GB: You've mentioned him a few times now.

TS: True. Well, what he wrote is helpful. And even though he wrote late in the second century or early in the third century CE, in *The Deipnosophists* he cites over 700 Greek authors of earlier times and in doing so refers to over 2,000 Greek writings. The work is written as though there is this one extraordinary banquet with a large number of guests interacting with each other about a number of matters relating to food and to drink and other subjects regarded as fit for conversation around the dining table.

GB: And I guess that you're going to "take me on a trip" that will reflect on your research.

TS: If that's okay with you.

GB: No problem. And I suspect that you're suggesting that while we will be looking at what he wrote at one point in time, we will in fact be seeing what banquets were like in very different eras.

TS: Yes. In fact, more often than not, he refers to an earlier writer. And sometimes, this earlier writer, from whom he quotes, refers to eating and drinking habits of even earlier times. His vast number of quotes and other references are, however, almost certainly biased. They tend to relate to formal meals often partaken of by the important and wealthy. But his collection of materials is never the less really quite informative. *The Learned Banqueters* is a complex work and, as I've said, has the overall appearance of being a record of the conversations of numerous learned people taking part in a marvelous dinner. It's made up of fifteen books. Of particular significance for us today are Books 10 and 11. The first deals with "drunkenness" and Book 11 with "cups."

GB: I guess Book 11 was probably your main source of information, given our text.

TS: Yes. And the Book actually does focus on cups and in particular, different types of cups, rather than on drinking, making libations or toasting. Amazingly, he mentions about one hundred different cups, each with its own name although as he admits, in some cases, the same cup may have gone by different names at different times or in different places. I also ought to mention Book 15. Though that Book focuses on perfumes there were some sections there that were also of some help. Now, as I was saying, his sample is somewhat restrictive. Yet quite often his reference is to a custom that's reported as being widespread among a particular group of people. The problem is however, that the description of the custom, even if correct, is a custom associated with a group of people at a particular point in time. Customs change over time and, of course, vary from place to place.

GB: So in using any of his information to assist us in understanding "a cup of the Lord" or "a cup of demons" we are somewhat limited.

TS: True. Nonetheless I believe it's worth the effort to see what he says. I think *The Deipnosophists* together with the odd couple of other sources that I found, are pretty well all we have of relevance, to work on, outside of the New Testament. To have his material has to be better than nothing.

GB: Well, what do we learn from his Books?

TS: Before going into details, I think I ought to prepare you, as it were, for how we'll travel before we arrive at our destination. Firstly, I want us to consider the phenomenon of "lettered cups." Then we could look at what we call "libations." Next it might be helpful to examine those texts where "toasts" or "pledges" are made to human beings. Then I think we could examine those examples where a reference to a god is idiomatic in character. I'll explain what I mean by that later. Finally I suspect it will help, as we think on these things, if we consider the notion of "honoring" a god, whether by way of a libation or by some other means.

GB: This sounds complicated.

TS: It is. It's a bit of a maze but in the end I think we can come to a reasonable understanding of what is meant by "to drink a cup of the Lord and a cup of demons."

GB: Well then, "lettered cups" first, right?

TS: Yes. I don't think what can be referred to as "lettered cups" were all that common. As their name suggests, the cups had letters on them. On some, the letters were made of gold. I suspect that such cups were more commonly found in the households of the very wealthy. The letters on these cups spelt out the name of a god or a title for that god. What is interesting is that the god's name or the title appears in the genitive case. "Διος Σωτηρος" (*Dios Sōtēros*) is one example. Another is "Διονυσο" (*Dionuso*) with Athenaeus arguing that in that case the second "o" represented "ou," well, the Greek equivalent. Literally one could translate the first as, "Of Zeus, Savior." He was the head of the gods, and the second, as "Of Dionysus." He was the god who supposedly introduced wine to the Greeks. He is also often referred to as "The Good Demon." Both of these gods are mentioned a number of times in *The Deipnosophists*. There is another reference to a lettered cup—one dedicated to Artemis—although we don't have what letters actually appeared on that cup. The problem needing to be faced is the significance of the genitive case. Does it mean, for example, that the cup was the cup that belonged to Zeus? Was it the cup that was reserved for a libation to him or for a type of toast to him? Does it mean that the cup was to be used "in honor of" Zeus? It could be that all of these possibilities are correct.

GB: I take it that the existence of these lettered cups raises the question of whether or not "a cup of the Lord" in 1 Corinthians chapter 10 is a reference to a lettered cup.

TS: Yes, it does, but my response is, "Almost certainly not." The section in *The Deipnosophists* where Athenaeus refers to the lettered cups, mentions three ancient authors. Two lived in the fifth century BCE and one in the fourth and third centuries BCE. I think lettered cups were a phenomenon of relatively distant times. Besides, I believe there is a more defensible understanding of "a cup of the Lord."

GB: You mentioned a few days ago and then again yesterday, the matter of "toasting." Could you indicate again what might have been the difference between toasting and making a libation and again exactly what was a libation?

TS: By "toasting" I mean something very similar to what we mean when *we* offer a toast. But let's focus on libations and the making of libations. As I've mentioned before, it was very important to have the gods on your side at all times, if possible. Inviting a god to be part of a meal was one way of trying to achieve this. Pouring out some wine on the ground or floor, while uttering the name of a god, was giving that wine to the god and so having him share in the meal. And the gods had to be honored and making a libation was one way of honoring a god. However, when reading the texts that I've looked at, it's not always obvious whether a libation to a god was being performed or whether some sort of "toast" to a god was being made or whether both were occurring. Any toast, whatever its form, would certainly have been an honoring of the god. Some verbs used in association with wine and a god, are more suggestive of a libation or an honoring of some sort being made than others. Ones of this nature that come to mind are—"ἀνακειμαι" (*anakeimai*) meaning something like, "I dedicate," "σπενδω" (*spendō*) meaning, "I pour," "ἀποσπενδω" (*apospendō*) meaning, "I pour out," and "σπονδοποιεομαι" (*spondopoieomai*), meaning probably, "I pour a libation." The verb "προσδιδωμι" (*prosdidōmi*), meaning, "I pour out" or "I give besides" is another possibility and "ἀποδιδωμι" (*apodidōmi*), meaning, "I render what is owed," another.

GB: Can you give me some examples of where some of these words are employed?

TS: Sure. Athenaeus refers to a text that says "having poured out the wine, (the verb here is, 'οἰνοχεω' [*oinocheō*]), they would pour out wine (the verb being 'ἀποσπενδω') to the gods from a phial." In another place, he quotes an author saying that a certain Lysimachus gave each of 300 guests a silver cup, then "made a libation" ("σπονδοποιησανενον" [*spondopoiēsanenon*] from "σπονδοποιεομαι"), "pledging to them all." The Greek word used here for "pledging" is "προπιειν" (*propiein*)—the infinitive of the verb "προπινω" (*propinō*). I think that in the Greek dialect that Paul used, the word "προπιειν" would have been "προπινειν." In this text one would be forgiven for assuming that Lysimachus made a libation to his guests. However, I think it more likely that Lysimachus made a libation to a god first as a precursor to toasting the 300—perhaps both from the same cup of wine. Athenaeus also quotes from a physician, Philonides, who wrote that "when the undiluted wine is poured out ("προσδιδομενων" [*prosdidomenōn*] from "προσδιδωμι") during dinner ... the Greeks call upon the Good Demon—that was, as I've said, another common way of referring to Dionysus—doing honor ("τιμωντες" [*timōntes*] from the verb, "τιμαω" [*timaō*], I honor) to the deity." A certain Theophrastus, a philosopher of the third and fourth century mentions a cup called the rhyton, which he says was rendered ("ἀποδιδοσθαι" [*apodidosthai*] from "ἀποδιδωμι") to the heroes alone.

GB: I guess the context itself could indicate that a libation was being made, even if those sorts of verbs weren't present.

TS: Yes, that's possible, but one can jump to conclusions that might not be justifiable. Recognizing that the god or gods is in the dative case, where that's the situation, I think can help in this regard. The first of the examples I've just given has "the gods" in the dative case and the last of the examples has "the heroes" in the dative case. The dative case can imply that something is offered "to" the god or gods. But deciding whether or not a libation is involved does depend, as you rightly suggest, on context, particularly if one of those key verbs is absent. Consider the following example. Athenaeus quotes from a report on a certain Dionysius—not to be confused with the god, whose name sounds so similar. Dionysius had in a room a gold table dedicated to the Greek god of medicine, Asclepius. When he had drunk (the word is "προπιων" [*propiōn*] again derived from the verb "προπινω," and again the "n" is absent) undiluted wine, to him, that is, to Asclepius, he had the table removed. The Greek, translated "to him," is in the dative case. Dionysius may well have made a libation but alternatively he may have offered what we might call, a toast. The problem is that, "προπινω" is a verb that's more commonly associated with human beings making pledges or giving toasts to one another. When I mentioned that verb earlier, a pledge or a toast was being made to 300 guests of Lysimachus. But back to Dionysius. Whatever he did, it was certainly a way of honoring the god.

GB: Could we now have a look at the matter of people toasting people? Obviously Lysimachus is one example.

TS: Yes. Now to some others. Athenaeus refers to a certain Anacrean, a Greek poet of the sixth and fifth centuries BCE, who wrote how with a skypphos full of wine he toasted (the word is "ἐξεπινον" [exepinon] literally meaning to "he drank out" or "drained" [that is the cup]) to the white-crested Erxion. "Ἐξεπινον" comes from the verb "ἐκπινω" (ekpinō). Athenaeus then explains how that although Anacrean used "ἐξεπινον" instead of the word "προεπινον" (proepinon) from the verb "προπινω," what occurred was really pledging "προπινειν" (propinein) (here the "n" is present), meaning to offer to another to drink ("πιειν" [piein]) before ("προ" [pro]) oneself. I find what he says here a little complicated but I think the general gist of what Athenaeus reports is clear. Though Anacrean uses the word for "toasting" he really had "pledging" in mind. Note how that both "ἐξεπινον" and "προεπινον" have as their root the word, "πινω" (pinō), I drink, "πιειν" being the infinitive of "πινω." Paul uses "πινειν" rather than "πιειν." And of further interest is that the words. "Ερξιωνι τω λευκολοφω" (Erxiōni tō leukolophō) appear in the dative case. That's what makes it clear that a toast is being offered. Erxion is probably a reference to the king, Darius.

GB: It seems from what you've just said, and I found it to be *quite* complicated, that as part of what certainly looks like a toast, the person being toasted drank first.

TS: Yes. But don't forget that this is Athenaeus referring to what Anacrean wrote many centuries earlier. To what extent such a custom existed or persisted through the centuries, I think, is unknown. It might have persisted but became a more complicated affair. In another place Athenaeus mentions a reference to Alexander the Great, whom he also describes as "the king," and a certain Proteas, a person who spent a lot of his time drinking ("πιειν"), a drinking buddy of his, toasting each other. Alexander filled a cup and after drinking ("πιων" [piōn]—derived from "πινω") from it he toasted ("προυπιε" [proupie]—derived from "προπινω") Proteas, who took the cup and in turn drank ("ἐπιειν" [epiein]—again derived from "πινω") from it to the applause of everybody present. Shortly afterwards, Proteas asked for the same cup and after drinking ("πιων") from it, he toasted ("προυπιε") the king. Alexander took the cup but could not finish it off and collapsed. Sorry that I've read it out in such a disjointed fashion. Anyway, "προπινω" is again the verb used for toasting and the Greek words for "the king" appear in the dative case. In this situation it looks like the custom was for the person proposing the toast to drink first, make the toast and then for the other person to drink. But perhaps I'm reading it wrongly.

GB: I wouldn't know! Anyway they drank from the same cup!

TS: Yes, that's another interesting feature. Sometimes people seemed to have drunk from the same cup but others had individual cups. Remember Lysimachus who supplied each of his 300 guests with their own cup. I'll give you another example of a toast being made to a person. In this particular text there is no verb involved but clearly a toast is being made. Athenaeus refers to a person having four chutridia—the chutridion was another one of those many special cups—of strong wine to King

Ptolemy and the same again to the king's sister. The words, "King Ptolemy" and "the sister" in the Greek, are in the *genitive* case. Perhaps, "in honor of" is understood. One last example. Athenaeus cites a certain Critias who reported that while the Chian and the Thasian drink out of large cups from left to right and the Athenian does the same but using small cups, the Thessalian use large cups but to whomever they wish. The customs being referred to are in terms of the size of cups used and the order or lack thereof in which toasts are made to each other. Again no verb is involved but in this instance the dative case applies with respect to the word for "whomever." We translate the text, "to whomever."

GB: Interesting. It's fairly obvious that you don't even have to have a verb to indicate that a toast or maybe even a libation is the case. It's the context and the presence of dative or genitive cases that indicates that some honoring has gone on.

TS: Yes, I think so. But deciding whether it's a libation or a toast to a god can be the tricky part—at least if my suspicion is correct and toasts could be made to the gods.

GB: I understand. Do we have any examples of where a libation, that is, the pouring out of wine on the floor or ground, is made to a person?

TS: I came across one instance that seems to indicate that this did indeed take place. Athenaeus quotes a certain Ion of Chios who after referring to one who was obviously Zeus, the people's King, Savior and Father, spoke of pouring libations—using the Greek verb, "σπενδω"—firstly to Zeus, then to Heracles—a son born to Zeus and a human called Alcmene—next to Alcmene herself, then to Procles, king of Sparta, and finally to the descendants of Perseus, a Greek hero. Though I am not sure, perhaps we should see this occurrence as an exception recognizing that the humans mentioned have strong connections with the gods! Even Procles was considered to have come from the lineage of Perseus.

GB: We have some descriptions of what people *did* when making libations or when making toasts. Do we have any examples of what people *said*?

TS: Yes. I'm pretty sure that I mentioned some time ago that, at their formal meals, the wine the Greeks drank was mainly undiluted wine. They wanted to remain sober for as long as possible in order to enjoy most of the occasion. They might have some undiluted wine during the main course, but only a small amount. Commonly, after that main course, they would drink considerable quantities of diluted wine. I'm mentioning all of this again just as a backdrop to what I now want to say. Diodorus Siculus, I referred to him in connection with "tables," a Greek historian of the first century BCE, in a history written by him concerned with part of that period, said that when the undiluted wine was served during a meal—it could be served during the main meal— they greeted it, saying, "The Good Demon," but when the cup containing the diluted wine was passed around after the meal, they cried out, "Zeus Savior." The verb that we can translate "I greet" is, "προσεπιλεγω" (*prosepilegō*), and "ἐπιφωνεω" (*epiphōneō*) is the verb that we can translate, "I cry out" or "I call out." The physician Philonides, whom we've also already come across, though writing with other matters mainly in mind, said much the same sort of thing. I also think he fairly clearly indicates that libations were involved, when both the undiluted wine and diluted wine were served.

GB: How do you know?

TS: I've already mentioned how Athenaeus reported Philonides using the word "προσδίδωμι," meaning "poured out," during the main meal in connection with calling upon the "the Good Demon."

GB: Sorry. I'd forgotten.

TS: No problem. And Philonides is also reported saying, "But with the first cup, of diluted wine given after the main meal, they choose "Zeus Savior." That it was the first cup probably indicates that the wine was first poured out as a libation to Zeus. Thereafter the people would drink.

GB: And what is the grammatical case in which "the Good Demon" and "Zeus Savior" appear?

TS: Interesting! In the Diodorus Siculus quote, they are in the genitive case but in the Philonides quote, they are both in the accusative! While the verb "ἐπιφωνεω" occurs in both texts—in Philonides with respect to the Good Demon, and in Diodorus Siculus with respect to Zeus—"προσεπιλεγω" occurs only in the Diodorus Siculus text and that's with respect to the Good Demon and "ἐπιλεγω" (*epilegō*) meaning "chose" occurs only in the Philonides text and that's with respect to Zeus. It's a bit complicated. Look I think the main difference between Diodorus Siculus and Philonides, in this matter, is that Philonides in one instance indicates that the god's name was called out at the same time as a libation was involved and in the other that the god Zeus was chosen for the making of the libation whereas Diodorus Siculus in both instances refers to how the god was addressed, this address itself indicating, by the use of the genitive, that what was happening was in honor of the god and at least consistent with a libation.

GB: Complicated for sure. But I think I get it. . . . You mentioned *idiomatic* expressions.

TS: Thanks for keeping me on track. I mentioned earlier that in trying to locate in the Greek literature references to a "cup," of any type, textually associated with a god, gods, "the heroes" or a human and in connection with toasts or libations, I came across fifty one instances. In two of these instances, the god or whatever is in the accusative case, fourteen are in the dative and thirty five are in the genitive. For us, it's the genitive ones we're most interested in because "the Lord" and "demons" in our 1 Corinthians chapter 10 text are in the genitive case. Of the thirty five genitive cases, about twelve or so seem to involve short hand ways of simply referring to the wine involved rather than the god. And eleven of these are located in the same section in one of Athenaeus's Books.

GB: Sorry, are you saying that in these twelve or so cases, a god in the genitive case was somewhat idiomatic for the drink itself?

TS: Yes. Let me give you a few examples. Athenaeus is quoting others and the following seem to me to be reasonable translations of what Athenaeus reports—"Fill a Zeus Savior for him," "Take a Hygieia (the goddess of health) for yourself," "Quickly pour out a Good Demon thatton (a special cup)," "I could accept a Good Demon," "You jumped up and left before taking first a Good Demon or a Zeus Savior."

GB: I guess if the reference is to "a Good Demon" then undiluted wine is being referred to, whereas "a Zeus Savior" probably indicates that diluted wine is involved and I think it's the verbs used which really convey the idea that the drink itself is the focus—"fill for him," "you didn't take" *et cetera*.

TS: I think so, but that's not to rule out that a libation to this god or that god had not been made previously.

GB: Well, that leaves more than twenty instances where the genitive is the grammatical case used but where an idiomatic expression is not involved.

TS: Well, I don't think that an idiomatic expression is involved in these instances but in some cases it could be. It's difficult to tell. Anyway I've already mentioned a few where my guess is that they're idiom free. Here are some others—"After these things, most of them called for a cup to the Good Demon, some to Zeus, the Savior, others to Hygieia, one selecting one deity, another, another," "There came the therikleios of Zeus, the Savior," "From a very large lepaste she drinks undiluted wine to the Good Demon," "Gulping down a metaniptris to the Good Demon," "Accept this metaniptris to Hygieia," "Pour out for him a metaniptris to Hygieia"—the therikleios, lepaste and metaniptris were special cups. I really don't think the last two examples could have been idiomatic expressions given that "Hygieia," the goddess for health, as far as I know, didn't represent a particular type of wine. Anyway, none of the verbs that we've thought would probably indicate that a libation was involved appear in any of these instances, but that's not to say that a libation was not being made. And notice that although the genitive case is involved in all cases just cited, in the English translations we seem obliged to use the word "to," as though the dative case applies.

GB: Yes. Perhaps the usage of the genitive is itself a type of idiomatic way of portraying that honor is being paid to the god.

TS: You could be right. The use of the genitive is somewhat odd! Idiomatic or not, in the sense that you're suggesting, what I've tried to point out, by using these examples, is that the instances cited could've been, in effect "toasts" to one god or another. All in all, there would've been some sort of honoring of the god or goddess, whether or not

Part 3: The Lord's Supper

a libation was involved and even where the honoring was superficial. You were honoring the god or goddess one way or another. That's what we do. We honor people, when we toast them. And remember what Philonides wrote—"When the undiluted wine is poured out during dinner . . . the Greeks call upon the Good Demon doing honor to the deity." Though he was referring to a libation he certainly connects the making of that libation with the notion of honoring.

GB: I think we must be just about ready to consider our text—"You cannot drink a cup of the Lord and a cup of demons." Or am I mistaken?

TS: No. It's time! It's been a long day and a complicated process, as I suspected it might be. Would you be happy with my asking *you* the question "What do you think our text means?"

GB: No problem, but I'll need to take it easy. Why don't I begin by saying what I think it doesn't mean? Firstly, I doubt that a reference is being made to lettered cups. You indicated that you thought they were rare and belonged to an earlier historical period. Secondly, there is neither a verb nor the presence of a dative case that would give any indication of a libation being made, though as you said, nonetheless, a libation could be involved in such circumstances. But I certainly can't imagine that as believers, the Corinthians would've been making a libation to the Lord. If they had have been I'd have expected Paul to have argued against that practice.

TS: And the verb used by Paul is about as simple as you can get—"πινω"—"I drink." It's the same verb that was used by Athenaeus when commenting on Anacrean's use of "ἐξεπινον" and also used of Proteas who was said to drink a lot. The word was "πιειν" a different form of the same word "πινειν," the actual word that Paul used. It doesn't give anything away. It's just simply, "to drink" or "drinking." But please continue.

GB: And I really don't think that there's an idiomatic expression involved—there's no indication that the nature of the wine is an issue. The genitive case is used however and I realize that that's important. However, I don't think the use of the genitive implies that there was a cup that was considered to be the Lord's cup. As you pointed out, the reference is not to "*the* cup of the Lord."

TS: And so?

GB: Well, not contradicting what I've just said, I guess the phrase "a cup of the Lord" could be a reference to "his cup" in the sense that it might be a reference to a cup, any cup, used to honor the Lord. You've indicated that the genitive case could be a way of referring to giving honor to a god. I think you're right. And of course, Paul says, "You cannot drink a cup of the Lord and a cup of demons." So I think I am left with an understanding that in effect is "You cannot drink a cup of wine in honor of the Lord and at the same time drink a cup, any cup, in honor of a demon, any demon."—the honoring of a demon being conveyed by way of a libation or a "toast." And I suppose Paul used that rather neutral word, "drink" in order to cover both what the Corinthian believers do and what the idolaters do, though what they actually do, one offering a libation, the other not doing that—at least I can't believe that they did do that—is very different. I guess the Corinthians might have taken a drink at some stage or another of their meal and said, "To the Lord, Our Savior." I think that that's a real possibility. I am not sure that I want to call this "a toast" though I guess that my way of putting it makes it sound like a toast. It's just that I don't think that Paul has in mind some casual off the cuff exclamation made during a meal.

TS: I agree. But, well done! I know I'm biased, but I think you've got it! You know, my belief is that if you come to the text, without any pre-conceived notions about what it means, but with an understanding of Greek practices, you would say, this is a reference to "giving honor to." You could argue, somewhat backwardly, that this was what was meant, by looking at what "drinking a cup of demons" might mean. That expression wasn't an idiomatic expression for a type of drink. And there is no indication that a lettered cup is being referred to. Almost certainly making libations to the gods or in any way honoring them in the drinking of wine is what is in mind. In opposition to that, Paul makes reference to "drinking a cup of the Lord." If that didn't involve a libation, and one could hardly think so, then surely honoring him in some other way, like making a toast—I know you're reluctant to call what they did, "a toast"—would be the most obvious thing to think of when deciding what Paul had in mind.

GB: Yes, I think you're right.

TS: I know that it might be considered helpful if we had in any of our texts outside of the New Testament, something similar to what Paul wrote—"ποτηριον κυριου" but with the name of some god or goddess instead of "the Lord." But I don't think we do. There are a couple of texts similar to our "cup of the Lord" but they're not all that helpful. "Μεγαλην Διος Ζωτηρος ἀκατον" (*Megalēn Dios Zōtēros akaton*) is one. It's a reference to "a large akatos of Zeus Savior" in a sentence that could be translated either as, "Everyone, with a large akatos, said, 'To Zeus Savior,'" or alternatively as, "Everyone, had a large akatos of Zeus Savior, that is, of diluted wine." The first possibility is that Zeus was being honored, perhaps by way of a libation or, if not, by way of a simple toast. The second recognizes that an expression is being used idiomatically. Even if the latter is the case, it could've been that a libation was performed prior to everyone having a drink! Again, note the difficulties we have in understanding exactly what's being conveyed!

GB: In trying to understand our text you've given a lot of attention to Greek customs associated with drinking and the gods!

TS: That's an understatement!

GB: I take it that one of your points is that there is no way we should rush to this text and say it has to do with a Christian ceremony, something like the Lord's Supper.

Part 3: The Lord's Supper

TS: Yes. Absolutely! It could've been a custom but one that was somewhat similar to a custom that the Corinthians were used to. The use of the genitive makes one pause to think. It could well have been a gesture made some time during the whole meal, when they purposefully honored the Lord in opposition to honoring any of the gods. In fact Paul is saying that they couldn't do both, no drinking to demons alongside of drinking to the Lord.

GB: So perhaps the Corinthian believers, during their meals together, were saying, with upraised cup or whatever, "To the Lord" or even "To Jesus, Savior" as opposed to "To Zeus Savior"—each expression in the genitive case!

TS: Quite possibly.

GB: You concluded yesterday's discussions by raising two possibilities for understanding the phrases "a table of the Lord" and "a table of demons." Either they referred to a table dedicated to the Lord and a table dedicated to demons or a meal associated with the Lord and a meal associated with demons. Given that "a cup of the Lord" and "a cup of demons" relate to drinking, I would have thought that the tables related to eating, that is, having a meal.

TS: Yes. Pretty obvious isn't it. When you put both sets of phrases together and include what Paul says about them you have him making a statement something like—"*You cannot have, you must not drink, a cup of wine in honor of the Lord and at the same time drink a cup of wine in honor of any of the deities. Make sure there is no such idolatrous drinking associated with drinking to the Lord. And you cannot have, you must not have, any of your meals under the auspices of the Lord, and at the same time consider that these meals also need to have the demons present.*"

GB: I think it all makes sense. And if you're correct, this verse has nothing to do with the Lord's Supper. . . . Whew. It's been a very long session hasn't it? Could we have a break for a couple of days?

TS: Would meeting again this Saturday be okay?

GB: That would be fine. See you then.

EXPLANATORY NOTES: DAY 26

The Greek text from 1 Cor 10:21 that TS discusses is taken from NAG.

The references to "lettered cups" that TS mentions, can be found in *V Athenaeus*, Book XI, 466e, 262–63 (the Zeus Savior cup), *V Athenaeus*, Book XI, 466e–f and 467a, 262–65 (the Dionysus cup), and *V Athenaeus*, Book XI, 466e, 262–63 (the cup associated with Artemis).

For some general comments on libations see Smith, *From Symposium to Eucharist*, 28–30, 114–17.

The reference to pouring out wine from a phial can be found in *V Athenaeus*, Book XI, 482b, 340–41, the reference to Lysimachus can be found in *V Athenaeus*, Book XI, 466c, 236–37, the reference to Philonides can be found in *VIII Athenaeus*, Book XV, 675a–c, 52–55, and the reference to Theophrastus can be found in *Fragment* 122, section 1, line 1. This reference to Theophrastus is also mentioned in *V Athenaeus*, Book XI, 497e, 422–23. The cup translated "rhyton" is "ῥυτον" (*ruton*) in the Greek.

The reference to Dionysius can be located in *VIII Athenaeus*, Book XV, 693e, 156–57.

The reference to Anacrean and the cup skypphos ("σκυπφος"—sometimes appearing as "σκυφος" elsewhere) can be found in *V Athenaeus*, Book XI, 498c, 426–27 and the reference to Alexander the Great and his drinking companion Proteas can be located in the same volume, Book X, 434a–b, 72–75.

The matter of the toast being made to King Ptolemy and to his sister can be located in *V Athenaeus*, Book XI, 502b, 452–53.

The citing by Athenaeus of Critias can be found in *V Athenaeus*, Book XI, 463f, 224–25.

The reference to Ion of Chios can be located in *V Athenaeus*, Book XI, 463b–c, 220–23.

The quote from Diodorus Siculus can be found in *Diodorus Siculus, Library of History II*, Book 4, 3.4, 348–49.

The quotations referred to by Athenaeus that contain references to a god, the noun being in the genitive case, and a cup appearing to operate as an idiomatic expression for the wine itself, can be found in *VIII Athenaeus*, Book XV, 692f–693c, 150–55.

The list of six quotes illustrating the contexts in which more of the instances involving the genitive case could be found are located in *VIII Athenaeus*, Book XV, 693f, 150–51, *V Athenaeus*, Book XI, 471c, 284–85, *V Athenaeus*, Book XI, 485e–f, 360–61, *V Athenaeus*, Book XI, 486f, 366–67, *V Athenaeus*, Book XI, 487a, 366–67, and *V Athenaeus*, Book XI, 487b, 368–69, in that order.

The reference to "a large akatos of Zeus Savior" can be found in *VIII Athenaeus*, Book XV, 692f, 150–51.

Day 27

Corinthian Meals—the Markets and being a Guest at a Meal

In winding up his discussion on 1 Corinthians chapter 10, TS looks at Paul's views on buying food at the market place and how to respond to a tricky situation that could occur when invited to the dinner of an unbeliever. On the previous Tuesday he had mentioned the possibility of Paul's use of "deliberative rhetoric" in 1 Corinthians chapters 8 to 10 and appeals to that idea again.

GB: What's on the menu for today? Excuse the pun. I think that it will have something to do with meals, if we're still looking at 1 Corinthians chapter 10.

TS: We are, and you're right. We're still on the subject of meals. To recap! At the beginning of chapter 10 Paul refers to some occasions when Israel was guilty of idolatry and God's judgement upon them at the time. He writes that this acts as a warning to the Corinthians. Then, having said, "So shun the worship of idols" he refers to those meals—I suspect formal meals that they have together as believers—meals that they had together with Paul in the past—verses 15 to 17. After making his statement about the connection that exists between a sacrifice and its altar—the Israelite altar or the pagan alter in verses 18 to 20—he then deals with what I think would apply to any of their meals—meals when celebrating something special, meals with family, meals with friends and the like. It was with such meals in mind that he said "You cannot drink a cup . . . you cannot partake of a table . . . " in verse 21.

GB: Which we spent a lot of time on last Wednesday!

TS: Yes! Next, in verses 23 and 24 he makes a few comments about not seeking your own good but indeed the good of your neighbor. I think he's counteracting any possible suggestion that might be made by the Corinthians to the effect that his instructions

Corinthian Meals—the Markets and being a Guest at a Meal

demand more than is really necessary. He responds to what he considers they might say by stating that they need to be concerned about what leads to the healthy growth of others. Perhaps you can see here, that deliberative rhetoric that I mentioned earlier. Given this type of perspective, I'm suggesting that firstly Paul records a comment that he envisages the Corinthians could make in response to what he's been saying or indeed a comment that they had already made in the past. *Their* comment, actual or possible, is, "(Surely), all things are lawful!" to which *his* response is "But not everything is helpful." He then repeats the statement "All things are lawful!" and by doing so he might actually be recording his agreement with it. But then he makes the further response, very similar to his first, "But not all things build."

GB: Yes, I can see how deliberative rhetoric might be what we have here.

TS: Anyway, we're now at the point that we're primarily interested in today. Paul makes a brief statement about buying food at the market where meat was sold. His advice is that for the sake of their consciences and maybe also for the sake of other people's consciences, they should not ask questions about the origin of the food that they're buying. He gives as a reason for this advice that the earth and everything in it belongs to the Lord. Yes, there really isn't anything wrong with the meat, the food, and no matter what its origin. However, if, when they're buying, they ask where it comes from, they're creating a problem for themselves and maybe for anyone else who happens to become involved. I suspect that he has in mind the following scenario—You ask, because the origin of the food worries you. Then when you are told, yes, it came from a temple sacrifice, you automatically create for yourself a problem of conscience. If you *now* buy the food you will have twangs of conscience. Otherwise you wouldn't have asked the question in the first place. You then might also create a problem for any other believer who understands what has happened and who might be sensitive to your way of thinking. What is the solution to the problem—your problem or anyone else's? Just don't ask!

GB: From what you said earlier it might have been difficult to find food, meat in particular, that hadn't been offered in sacrifice to an idol. When buying meat at these markets, Paul is saying that they should just simply accept what is offered. Viewing it correctly as coming from the Lord's world anyway, there can't be anything wrong with it. Is that the way they were meant to see things?

TS: Yes, I think that's the picture. Anyway, next, in verses 27 to 30, he deals with circumstances that could arise upon being invited to a meal by an unbeliever. He again refers to the strategy of not asking about the origin of any of the food. However, he then considers the situation where someone at the meal—it could be the host, but not necessarily so—points out that a particular item of food has been offered in sacrifice. When this situation arises his instruction then is that they should not eat it. He says that they should adopt this approach out of consideration for the conscience of the man who asked it. Here, it seems that he's not so much concerned with how the believer's conscience might fare. In fact their conscience won't be troubled if they simply don't eat that particular item. No, he's concerned with how the person asking the question would or might think about a believer, who, having been informed of the origins of that item of food, then eats it. The unbeliever would see the food as associated with the gods and would probably get the wrong message if a believer then ate it. Paul may be using the notion of conscience in a way that's slightly foreign to our way of thinking about conscience. I think that we can better understand what is next said, beginning part way through verse 29, if we again use a deliberative rhetoric approach. Such an approach however, will suggest that the usual translations are a little misleading.

GB: So how do you think that part of the text and what follows it should read? How do you think it should be understood?

TS: Something like this—Paul firstly gives expression to a response that he anticipates some of the Corinthians might make to what he's just said— *"But why should my liberty be determined by another person's conscience? If I take part in the meal with thankfulness, why am I denounced because of something I thank God for?"* Then, in reply to this supposed response, Paul, keeping in mind his imagined reference to their thankfulness towards God, says *"Well, then, (claiming that you want to be thankful towards God), whatever you eat or drink or whatever you do, indeed, do it all for the glory of God. Don't cause anyone to stumble, whether Jews, Greeks or the church of God."* Paul's concern for the welfare of others is a concern for the welfare of all—non-believing Jews, non-believing Gentiles and fellow believers. He then reinforces this position by saying how he, himself, tries to please everybody in everything he does. I am sure he's not trying to parade himself in any way as a noble fellow. He simply wants others to follow his example. In case however, that there is some question about his motive, he explains—"not seeking my own profit, but that of many, that they may be saved." His final words at this point in the letter are "Be imitators of me, as I am of Christ." These are his concluding words to what he has to say about eating meat or food generally, that has been offered to idols.

GB: So in dealing with how one should behave at meals held in a variety of circumstances and how to buy meat at the markets, he gives, as reasons, ones that relate to the benefit of oneself, the welfare of others and the promotion of the glory of God. Paul is right on top of things isn't he?

TS: Yes, indeed he is!

GB: But what he says here, as important as it is, does not directly bear on the matter of the Lord's Supper does it?

TS: No. But I now hope that it's fairly obvious that chapter 10 as a whole, hangs together. Its overarching concern is idolatry and the proper behavior of believers in an idolatrous world. I don't think the chapter says anything about the Lord's Supper.

Corinthian Meals—the Markets and being a Guest at a Meal

GB: I'm inclined to agree.

TS: Well, I think that's enough for today. I know it's been a short session but this partly makes up for that long session we had a few days ago. What about meeting up again on Monday? Would that be okay? Next time we could begin to look at that important section of Chapter 11—the one that mentions the Lord's Supper.

GB: At last! Can't wait, but will! Monday is fine but it would need to be early evening. School is back on and I suspect that I'll only be able to manage meeting up with you every two or three days, from now on. If this would be okay with you, would you be able to come to my place, say, for an early dinner and we could take things from there? Of course, normally Saturdays wouldn't be a problem or even a Sunday afternoon.

TS: I understand. I was forgetting about your circumstances. Dinner at your place would be fine. Thanks very much but please don't go to any trouble whatsoever. Yes, Saturdays and Sunday afternoons would obviously be okay. On Monday then, if I turned up around five pm would that be alright?

GB: No problem. See you at 5, Monday.

Part 3: The Lord's Supper
EXPLANATORY NOTES: DAY 27

For the notion that Paul is using deliberative rhetoric in this section of 1 Cor, see Fotopoulos in *Food Offered to Idols*, 237–39, 246–47.

Day 28

Corinthian Meals—Corinthian Behavior

In today's discussion TS outlines more on how he thinks formal meals were conducted in the Greco-Roman world—the nature of dining rooms, reclining, seating or standing arrangements and who supplied what food. In looking at some of the verses of the latter half of chapter 11 of 1 Corinthians, TS suggests that Paul is somewhat sarcastic in the way he addresses a problem while also showing his severe displeasure at the existence of the problem. The significant question that TS poses for GB is however, the explicit nature of the problem itself.

TS: That was a great meal. But please make any future meals as simple as you like.... Today's session will be somewhat longer than Saturday's but fortunately we have the whole evening in front of us. I hope you didn't mind that Saturday's discussion was as short as it was.

GB: Of course not! Wednesday's "drinking a cup of the Lord and a cup of demons" was massive. Saturday sort of balanced it out!

TS: Fair enough. We've travelled a long way before arriving at this point. I've tried to indicate that chapters 8, 9, and 10 of 1 Corinthians essentially deal with problems arising from believers eating food that has been sacrificed or in some way offered to idols. In doing so I've hoped that it would have become obvious that elements of these chapters do not have to be understood as references to a Christian rite or ceremony like the Lord's Supper. Rather, I've tried to show how those sections in chapter 10 that are popularly assumed to speak of the Lord's Supper, instead relate to ordinary features of Corinthian meals, though for believers, meals that were Christian in character. Paul's concern is that when they get together to have a meal as believers or indeed when they have meals under any circumstances they are to avoid any association with idolatrous practices or beliefs.

Part 3: The Lord's Supper

GB: And you've pointed out how Paul in that chapter also discusses the matter of buying meat at a market place and how to behave as a guest at someone else's dinner if a question arises concerning the idolatrous origins of any food served.

TS: Well, Paul wanted to be comprehensive in dealing with food and idolatry. He covered a range of possibilities. But now in chapter 11 it's clear that he is concerned with different matters. At the beginning of the chapter he refers to the subject of head coverings. I suspect that what he says here has as a backdrop a custom in the idolatrous world of people approaching an idol with their heads covered, but I could be wrong. Anyway, it's obvious that he's now left behind the business of eating food offered to idols. After raising the subject of head coverings he then refers to matters associated with what is commonly called the Lord's Supper. It's quite clear, no matter how we interpret the various elements of what he says here, that at heart they relate to the believers having a meal together, a meal of one sort or another.

GB: If it isn't to do with idolatry, what's the actual problem that he's now addressing? From my reading, it's clear that there was a problem!

TS: Your question is making me put the cart before the horse, in terms of what I was planning to do. But it's a good one and perhaps it deserves a response even at this stage. I think one way to come up with the answer is to look at what Paul gives as the *solution* to their problem. See the solution and from that work out what the problem was that required that solution! It comes almost at the end of the chapter. He says there, "So then my brothers, when you come together to eat, wait for each other." Well, that's a fairly popular way of translating it. The Greek words behind, "wait for each other"—"ἀλλήλους ἐκδέχεσθε" (*allēlous ekdechesthe*) seem to have the sense, "show proper respect for one another." Now that *could* mean, "wait for each another," but I think it more likely means, "share with each other." Either way, in answer to your question, the problem seems to be that in their meals they have not been treating one another, from Paul's perspective, in a proper manner.

GB: Could you elaborate? *Why* weren't they waiting for each other or sharing with each other?

TS: Let me give you some idea of what their meals were probably like. Although some of the believers were undoubtedly Jewish, the picture I think we get from this letter of Paul's is that most of the believers were Gentiles. And probably their cultural background would have been predominantly Greek, though we would expect their customs to have been influenced by their Roman world as well.

GB: This sounds interesting.

TS: Something that might be thought to be of importance is the size of their dining rooms—that is, if the house—it would have to have been a reasonably sized house—had a dining room. The older styled Roman dining room, called a *"triclinium,"* could only fit up to nine people but there might have been more than one of these in a particular house. Other types of dining rooms, both Roman and Greek, could accommodate more. The Roman "*convivium*" could cope with six to twelve guests while a traditional Greek "ἀνδρων" (*andrōn*) could accommodate from fourteen to twenty two or thirty six or even more. If the number of people present exceeded the size of the dining room, then some would have to eat somewhere else—perhaps in an area called the "*atrium*." The "*atrium*," found in many of the houses of the wealthy, was generally a large open space with perhaps a fountain set somewhere within it. For those having their meal in the dining room itself, be it a "*triclinium*" or whatever, the preferred posture for eating was generally that of reclining. Elsewhere, people would probably have to sit or stand. If the numbers present exceeded those that could be accommodated in the normal dining room or rooms, then the host would most likely serve the less important guests their meals in the "*atrium*" or somewhere else.

GB: I can see how this could lead to some guests being discriminated against. And the basis on which the discrimination might have occurred would probably not have been a Christian one.

TS: True. However, nowhere is there a hint in what Paul says that this was the actual problem he was addressing.

GB: So you raise this issue and it's probably irrelevant!

TS: Yes, I think so, though I could be wrong. But I've mentioned it because I believe that some think that it might have been the cause of the problem. Another possibility—the translation I gave a moment ago reflects this view—is that some people, those considered to be of lower status than others, may have had to wait until those considered to be of higher status were served first. This was certainly true in the normal course of events where slaves were part of the household, a not uncommon situation. Slaves were invariably involved in the delivery of dishes and wine. And most likely in any large house where Christians met there still would have been slaves carrying out such duties and many others. And normally they would've been required to eat their meal at a different time to that for the guests or family—probably at a later time.

GB: But would this have been the case where some of the guests were slaves but slaves in another household? I take it that some of the believers in Corinth could've been slaves and hopefully they were invited to those meals in which believers took part.

TS: I'm pretty sure they would've been invited but how they would've been treated as guests is an interesting question. Whatever the situation in that case, you can see how an understanding that what Paul was saying was, "Wait for one another," would be appropriate if the general picture I've just painted—people of higher status being served before those of lower status—were true.

GB: But you obviously think there was something else going on?

TS: Yes. There's evidence that for many formal meals the host supplied only certain basics such as bread and wine. The guests were expected to bring their own special fare. That might include special bread delicacies and more expensive wine. However, essentially it meant that if you liked your rare duck, fresh oysters, special herbal dishes or whatever, you brought those dishes and feasted on them yourself. Imagine that you were a slave or a free person from one of the poorer classes and not used to attending formal meals as a guest on a regular basis, if at all. But you have now become a member of a group that did not previously exist in the Greco-Roman world—a group made up of believers, believing that Jesus Christ is Lord. The members of this group, being bound together in this extraordinary way, like any group of significance, decide to meet regularly in a formal setting, perhaps as often as the Corinthian letter elsewhere might suggest, once a week. You, like everybody else, have to bring along your own main dish or dishes. If you came from the poorer echelons of society the food you would bring for your needs would be of the most basic nature. The disparity between your meal and the meals of the well-to-do would be enormous. The situation could be, as it were, so much in your face. It could be ever so humiliating.

GB: But wouldn't that sort of thing have happened to some extent in Greco-Roman meals, anyway?

TS: Well yes, but to a limited extent. I think it was Plato (TS is in error—see the *Explanatory Notes*) who spoke, with some sarcasm, of a meal where the host had dishes of delicacies but the guest did not, much to his chagrin. Yet the truth is that the composition of those who attended formal meals in that society was generally reasonably homogeneous, as I think I tried to point out earlier. It would be members of the one family, a group of friends or a set of people with common interests that met together to discuss political, social, philosophical or economic matters or just to have fun. These formal meals were for one's enjoyment or benefit generally, and that meant getting together with people who generally came from a similar cultural, educational, and social background. One would not expect the differences among meals brought by such guests to be as marked as those would be where the guests were made up of the poor and the rich.

GB: And the believers in Corinth came together because they were believers not because they shared similar backgrounds or enjoyed the same economic privileges.

TS: Absolutely. But I may have been misleading you just a little. In the case of the Corinthians many may have come from the wealthier and more "well-to-do" sections of their society. I mentioned something like this the other day. There may have been a measure of homogeneity. Yet, the extremes of that society could have been represented as well. Its nature was such that many from a lower stratum were often dependent socially and economically upon others of greater standing, and thus influenced by them. They may have become believers through their "betters," as it were, and came along as well. At these Corinthian dinners there could have been present, rich and

Corinthian Meals—Corinthian Behavior

poor, free and yes perhaps slave, the educated and the poorly educated, the culturally sophisticated and the "Barbarian" and the high-born and the low. And of course, Jew and Gentile and also women and men!

GB: By that last remark are you suggesting that women and men didn't normally eat together at such meals?

TS: The evidence is unclear. A century or two earlier, these meals were mainly just for men. At about the time in question however, it seems that women featured somewhat more at these meals than previously. I suspect, from what Paul says later in his letter, that at the Corinthian believers' meals, both women and men were present. Of course, understandably, in the Greco-Roman world, women would've accompanied men where the meal was a family gathering, with members coming together to celebrate a birthday or a wedding, for example. And women, particularly upper class women, may have met together for a meal, in the absence of men, from time to time, for whatever reason.

GB: Anyway, back to the main matter. You're suggesting that the solution to the problem that Paul addressed was, "share with each other." Right?

TS: Yes. I think so. Part of the evidence for this is what Paul says immediately upon having stated the solution to the problem. He writes, "If anyone is hungry, he should eat at home." Was he implying that some, when they came to the meal, were greedy and that consequently others remained hungry? Possibly so but only if he were saying that those who were greedy should eat at home first and so not be tempted to be greedy when they came to the dinner. Alternatively, and I think more likely, Paul is speaking somewhat sarcastically. I suspect he's saying something like, *"If upon sharing your dishes with others, you people who bring your rich dishes have to forgo some of your preferred and more exotic food, well, eat at home so that you won't feel those supposed hunger pangs of yours!"*

GB: I guess another possibility is that Paul's advice was to the poorer of those present, if they are being described as the hungry ones—to go and eat at home before coming to the dinner.

TS: Maybe, but I find it difficult to believe that "eat at home" was an injunction applicable to those from the poorer classes. My understanding is that in Corinth, as seems to be the case elsewhere, the poorer people lived in what we might call high-rise units with no facilities for cooking. They cooked outside using portable grills or got their food from a fast-food outlet, already cooked. I think I mentioned the fast-food outlets the other day. Though I suppose that "eating at home" could be understood to be "eating in your house," no matter where the food had been cooked—the Greek word involved can mean "house" or "home," my understanding is that the poor didn't do that, at least not when a main meal was involved. Besides can you really imagine Paul saying "If you end up being hungry because you didn't bring enough to eat, because you're poor, well, then you had better just eat at home beforehand"?

GB: You're right. That wouldn't be Paul at all! . . . Doesn't Paul say something about people being hungry, earlier in the passage? . . . Yes, I've got it here—verse 21.

TS: He does but I suspect that in that verse he *is* referring to the poorer people rather than the wealthier. I'd like to say something more about what Paul says there later on, if that's okay?

GB: Sure.

TS: I think it's now about time that we went back to where Paul begins his comments on the whole subject and take it from the beginning. You might find it helpful to follow the text now that you've got your Bible open at the spot.

GB: Right.

TS: What we're interested in starts at verse 17. This is where Paul begins to deal with this new issue. And he doesn't begin politely. He uses some very strong words. "In the following instructions I have nothing good to say about you. When you come together it is not for the better but for the worse." He then says "In the first place" without ever later referring to "the second place"—his concern with their behavior is so great that his agitation simply carries him along without his actually itemizing matters—"In the first place, when you come together as a church I hear that there are divisions among you and I partly believe it."

GB: You say he doesn't refer to a second place but—I'm looking at the text—when he uses the word, "for," a few times further on, isn't he giving other reasons as to why he is so concerned?

TS: I suppose you could be right. Perhaps I shouldn't place too much emphasis on their being no "second place." Let's just stop for a moment and see how the word "for" is used. I think it comes from the Greek word, "γαρ" (gar) often meaning something like "as" or "since." Actually, I see now that it's used in our verse 17—"For in the first place . . . and so on." He is giving his "first place" reason for why he doesn't commend them when they come together. Then he uses it in verse 19—"For there must be divisions." He's giving some sort of explanation here as to why there must be divisions—we'll get to that in a moment. But I wouldn't think that this was a "second place," a type of "secondly" to his first point. . . . Then in verse 21 he refers to "For in eating" *et cetera*—we'll get to that as well. Here I think it's offered as an explanation to what he says in verse 20. No I don't think you'd call that a "secondly" or a "thirdly." It looks like he uses "γαρ" as a word that links various parts of what he wants to say, by way of explanation for what he has just said, and as a means by which he can say something else, at least as far as these verses go.

GB: Sorry.... Just a thought. Interesting that he says, "as a church." What did he mean exactly by that?

TS: I think in using the Greek word that we translate church—"ἐκκλησια" (*ekklēsia*)—he's referring to their coming together as a formal gathering, an assembly. I'm not sure that he means much more than that. In their case, however, it was an assembly or a meeting of believers that had a meal as one of its main components.

GB: Thanks. You mentioned earlier that you thought this could've been on a weekly basis. What makes you think so?

TS: Well, towards the end of the letter, Paul talks about setting aside moneys to be used as a gift to assist the Jerusalem believers, who were undergoing some severe difficulties at the time, and he suggests that they should do this on the first day of every week. His suggestion would make sense if they did indeed meet on a weekly basis, although admittedly that would not mean that they had a meal together every week. But now, to return to what Paul said in our chapter 11—"I hear that there are divisions among you." That there might have been divisions—"σχισματα" (*schismata*), the singular, "σχισμα" (*schisma*) is the word from which the word, schism is derived—would've been of serious concern to Paul. The existence of a split or splits within their gatherings, which should've been characterized by a common bond, would've been no small matter for him, nor should it have been. His saying "And I partly believe it" or "I can hardly believe it" might sound a little odd, but perhaps Paul is also being sarcastic here or perhaps somewhat dramatic or even both! It could be that he's indicating that he really doesn't want to believe it, but that he actually does.

GB: You suggest that something Paul says might have been uttered in a sarcastic vein. How can you be sure?

TS: We can't be sure. When we're engaged in face-to-face conversations, we recognize sarcasm and the like by inflections in speech or odd facial expressions *et cetera*. You can't reproduce that in a written script unless you use accents or marks of various kinds to convey something of that nature. The original Greek doesn't contain such in its script. One has to guess about things like sarcasm on the basis of what one perceives is the sense being conveyed, given a wider context. To continue!

GB: Sorry. I should let you get on with it.

TS: No problem. Your remarks are always appreciated.... I think the next thing that Paul says is also somewhat sarcastic and consistent with what he's just said. He goes on—"For there must be differences among you." Here he uses the word, "αἱρεσεις" (*hīreseis*)—the singular of which is "αἱρεσις" (*hīresis*) from which the English word "heresy" is derived—not "σχισματα." One wonders if Paul doesn't have in mind something like "heresies"! In, as I've suggested, a somewhat a sarcastic vein, he in effect says, "There have to be differences among you so that one can tell which ones of you are genuine or acting properly and which ones aren't!" My suggestion here is that he's raising the matter of "acting properly" or "being genuine" without saying at this point what is proper or genuine and what isn't. He's making people very much aware of the idea that when they meet together something very improper is occurring. And then we have our highly important statement, "When you come together it is not the Lord's Supper you eat." At least that's how many translations put it, even if not in those exact words. The Greek text reads, "Συνερχομενων οὖν ὑμων ἐπι το αὐτο οὐκ ἐστιν κυριακον δειπνον φαγειν." (*Sunerchomenōn oun humōn epi to auto ouk estin kuriakon deipnon fagein*).

GB: That doesn't help me much.

TS: The first word, "συνερχομενων" relates to coming together, "οὖν" is "when," "ὑμων" is "you," "ἐπι το αὐτο" means something like, "for the same purpose" or "for the same event," "οὐκ" is "not," "κυριακον" relates to "lord," "δειπνον" is the common word for "meal" and "φαγειν" is "to eat."

GB: The translation you gave didn't refer to, "for the same purpose."

TS: No. Some translators omit that part of the text. I'm not sure why. It may be that they think it's superfluous. I think otherwise. I think Paul wants to refer to something like "for the same 'thing'" because they don't behave as though it is "for the same 'thing.'" But moving on! Well actually skipping that verse—I want to return to that very important text later, but not today. Let me continue with what Paul says, pointing out his ongoing strong language. He continues—"For in eating each one goes ahead with his own meal. "Προλαμβανει" (*prolambanei*) is the word that can be translated, "goes ahead," and it could suggest that the problem was people not waiting for each other, but not necessarily so. It could mean that they were going ahead with their meals, oblivious to the meals of other people.

GB: That is, "oblivious of other people and what they ate."

TS: Exactly. And I think what he then says confirms this idea. He continues. "One is hungry and another is drunk." I suppose that you could take what he says here literally, but I think, almost certainly that Paul is writing hyperbolically. He's exaggerating, but by doing so he's driving home the point that some have next to nothing to eat or drink, whereas others have oodles. Notice how there is no suggestion here of "And I can almost believe it"! As I've already mentioned, when he said that earlier, I think he was either being sarcastic or being dramatic or both.

GB: In fact he doesn't seem to have any doubt about what he's reporting, except perhaps when he makes that initial comment.

TS: True. Anyway, he then follows up with a rhetorical question, "Don't you have houses to eat and drink in?" Actually, the word, translated, "houses" ("οἰκιας" [*oikias*] from "οἰκια" [*oikia*]) is the not same as that which is translated "home" ("οἰκῳ" [*oikō*] from "οἰκος" [*oikos*]) in Paul saying, "If anyone is hungry let him eat at home."

I've referred to that noun "οἶκος" before but it was in a different grammatical form "Οἶκος" can refer to home or house but "οἰκία" tends to refer more to a house as a structure. However, what I suggested earlier I think applies in this case also. As with his mention of "home" so to with his reference to "houses" here, his words are directed to the wealthy. Again, I think there's a touch of sarcasm—"*If you want to eat up big and drink to the full, do so in your houses.*" He then continues, but with no lack of severity and with another rhetorical question—"Do you despise the church of God and humiliate those who have nothing?" The words, "the church of God," highlight the fact that their coming together to share in a meal constitutes a gathering, an assembly under God. It is God's gathering. There is a note of solemnity in his choice of words here. But furthermore, as it seems to me, the question in its context is confirmatory of the idea that the problem he's addressing is the rich believers ignoring the reality of the poorer bringing, by comparison, very little to the dinner table. I think he's also making it clear that those who, in his words, "have nothing" very much feel the situation—they are humiliated. In the normal course of events the poorer folk would've enjoyed a formal dinner only very occasionally and then it would've been with others from similar circumstances. The meal that they were now attending, I think, fairly often, was a meal at which they are being made acutely aware of their relative poverty.

GB: I think I really do see the picture now.

TS: Unable to contain what looks like his anger—if not anger, then severe displeasure—he then says, "What shall I say to you? Shall I commend you in this? No, I will not." . . . I should now stop at this point in the text and return to the verse we're really interested in, verse 20, the one that refers to the Lord's Supper. But I think that it would be a good idea if we left our discussion of that until, say, Wednesday evening or whenever it suits. We would then have more time to spend on the matter and we could do so with fresh minds.

GB: As anxious as I am for us to look at that verse, would Thursday evening be okay, again around five pm, at my place and for a meal?

TS: That would be great. See you then.

Part 3: The Lord's Supper

EXPLANATORY NOTES: DAY 28

Paul deals with the issues relating to head coverings in 1 Cor 11:2–16 (NIV). The Lord's Supper material is found in 1 Cor 11:17–34 (NIV).

For a discussion on why the Greek phrase commonly translated "wait for each other" might be better understood to mean, "share with each other" see Garland, *1 Corinthians*, 554–55. Garland cites a number of other authors and their views regarding how to understand the phrase.

For comments on the possible dining rooms, their nature, how many they could accommodate and whether or not reclining or otherwise might be the situation in various settings, in the Greco-Roman world, see Murphy-O'Connor, *St Paul's Corinth*, 158–59 cited in Garland, *1 Corinthians*, 536, and 153–58 of Murphy-O'Connor's same work cited in Cheung, *Idol Food in Corinth*, 37, note 41. See also Fotopoulos in *Food Offered to Idols*, 161–62. Fotopoulos mistakenly refers to "δειπνον" rather than "ἀνδρων."

TS refers to a number of Greek words as he discusses verses 18, 19, 21 and 22. The Greek text can be found in NAG.

Regarding social and economic inequality in the Corinthians' world and how this might have influenced how the Corinthian Christians behaved at their community meals, see Garland, *1 Corinthians*, 542–43.

I am indebted to Edwin Judge for the idea that, in accordance with the situation elsewhere in Greece, it was unlikely that the poorer people of Corinth ate at home not having cooking facilities in their houses, eating instead at fast-food outlets as one alternative.

Perspectives on what might be provided by the host of a Corinthian formal meal, what guests might be expected to bring to such a meal and disparities that might exist between what the well-to-do and what the poorer people might bring to such a meal can be found in Garland, *1 Corinthians*, 539–44.

The idea that the Corinthian believers gathered for a formal meal on a weekly basis is based on the request by Paul for the Corinthians to make contributions for the poor in Jerusalem, on the first day of every week. TS mentions this later in the conversation. The request that Paul makes can be located in 1 Cor 16:2 (NIV).

The reference to Plato by TS is in error. The account of a meal where the host had dishes of delicacies but the guest did not, much to his chagrin, is a somewhat comical one but described by Marcus Martialis in his *Epigrams*, Book 3, LX. It can be found in *Martial Epigrams*, I, 244–45. It reads, "Since I am no longer asked to dinner, at a price as formerly, why don't I get the same dinner as you? You take oysters fattened in the Lucrine pool. I cut my mouth sucking a mussel. You have mushrooms, I take pig fungi. You set to with turbot, I with bream. A golden turtle dove fills you up with its outsize rump. I am served with a magpie that died in its cage. Why do I dine without you, Ponticus, when I'm dining with you? Let the disappearance of the dole count for something; let's eat the same meal."

For a comparison between the likely composition of the Christian community at Corinthian and other formal associations in the Corinthian world, see Judge, *The Social Pattern of Christian Groups*, 60 where he writes "If the Corinthians are at all typical, the Christians [at that time in the Graeco-Roman world] were dominated by a socially pretentious section of the population of the big cities. Beyond that they seem to have drawn on a broad constituency, probably representing the household dependents of the leading members . . . The interests brought together in this way probably marked the Christians off from other unofficial associations which were generally socially and economically as homogenous as possible." See also his *The First Christians in the Roman World*, 465, in which he writes, "the Pauline churches . . . were not (in modern terms) lower-class. But the gospel was promoted by well-to-do patrons to their social dependents . . . The novelty of the first churches then was that they brought people of different social status into a new kind of structure, building up a new community."

Fotopoulos in *Food Offered to Idols*, 167, is of the view that traditionally formal meals were the domain of males. However Corley in *Private Women Public Meals*, 31–33, 181 believes that women were beginning to attend public meals with men around about the first century CE. That Paul later writes in 1 Cor 14:34–35 (NIV) on the issue of women speaking at Corinthian formal gatherings may suggest that they were present at the formal meals which may well have been part of those formal gatherings.

For a reference to the poorer classes not eating at home, using portable grills and living in apartments, see Garland, *1 Corinthians*, 542.

Day 29

Corinthian Meals—the Lord's Supper

In today's session, verse 20 of 1 Corinthians 11 is dissected in detail. TS points to a number of features of the verse that often appear to be ignored by translators. Understandably, GB questions why this would be so, and is a little amazed at the understanding of verse 20 reached by TS.

TS: Are we ready for "the Lord's Supper"?

GB: Absolutely. 1 Corinthians chapter 11, verse 20. I've got it here in front of me. "When you come together it is not the Lord's Supper you eat"

TS: Well, just before we look at the text in some detail, could I make the following point? Did you notice that when we went through what Paul said both before and immediately after that verse, there was nothing in anything he said there, that we looked at, that related to a Christian rite? I hope you don't mind my using that word "rite." What he said, all had to do with their meals and Paul's considerable disquiet at their behavior at those meals.

GB: There's no question about that, unless I've been unduly influenced by the way you've explained things to me. But I don't think so. In fact, now that I reflect on it, what does seem odd is the appearance of that one verse, verse 20, in the midst of what seems to be references to poor behavior at their meals. Except for that verse you wouldn't think there was any reference to any special custom like Holy Communion. No I don't mind the use of the word "rite." I understand what you mean. Of course I know that later on Paul talks about the Last Passover Meal and I guess that what he says there makes us think that verse 20 does indeed relate to a Christian custom or rite.

TS: We'll get to Paul's reference to the Last Passover Meal in due course. But for now, let's look at what he says regarding "the Lord's Supper." To begin with, I need to point out several things. Firstly, in the Greek there's no definite article, that is, there is no, "the," before "supper." Next, the word "δειπνον," translated "supper," could just as easily be translated "meal." That's what "δειπνον" basically means, though it would seem from its usage in the New Testament that it's almost always used where a formal meal, a banquet, a special meal, a meal to which guests could be invited, is in mind. Thirdly, the statement is a negative one. It speaks of what is not, not of what is. Finally, the word translated "Lord's" is derived from the adjective "κυριακος" (*kuriakos*), not the noun "κυριος" which we often translate "Lord."

GB: Is there any great significance to that last point?

TS: I think so. This is the only place in those writings of Paul's that we possess, where that word can be found. Indeed it's only found once elsewhere in the New Testament. It occurs in chapter one of Revelation. English translations of its use in 1 Corinthians make it look as though it's a noun in the genitive case. But it's an adjective that takes its grammatical case from the noun it qualifies which in this text is in the nominative case. The noun is "δειπνον." Now Paul uses the noun, "κυριος"—Lord—regularly. It's used four times in the previous chapter, three of these being in the genitive case. We spent some time considering "a cup of the Lord" and "a table of the Lord." "Κυριος" is the word used in these instances and it occurs in the genitive case. In the present chapter it occurs once before our verse—in the dative case—and six times after it—four of these being in the genitive case, although one of them is where the case is determined by a preposition.

GB: The use by Paul of the adjective "κυριακος" in our verse 20 certainly looks out of place then. It exists in the midst of usages of the noun "κυριος." From what you've said—five times that noun occurs before it and six times after it—all within just two chapters!

TS: Correct. But it's not so much "out of place" but rather "chosen on purpose for a good reason." But I know what you mean. Outside of the New Testament the adjective is reasonably well known but not much before New Testament times. Using that search engine, the *Thesaurus Linguae Graecae* I was only able to locate three instances where the word occurs prior to Paul's usage in 1 Corinthians. Two are found in a fourth century BCE document and the other in a second to first century BCE text. It would appear that the concept of something being "lordly," that's the sense behind "κυριακος," was not a common one, at least not up until the time of imperial Rome.

GB: Is there some significance in that? Why would it become more common when the Caesars began to rule?

TS: My guess is that it was *because* of their rule that the concept became more significant and therefore more common. There's a work entitled "Vocabulary of the Greek

Testament," written by a James Moulton and a George Milligan which under the heading of our word "κυριακος" lists several instances where the word is used but the earliest occurrence given is for the year 68 CE. And they almost all relate to the idea of "imperial ownership," that is, something that relates to the Emperor. There's one reference that speaks of that very idea, where a Greek word "κτησις" (*ktēsis*), meaning something like "ownership," is the noun used, the noun that the adjective qualifies. The adjective, together with the noun, speaks of "imperial ownership." Another reference concerns a camel provided for imperial service. There's another that deals with imperial revenue and another with the imperial treasury. The word basically indicates that something or other has to do with the Emperor. It comes "under his umbrella" as it were, or to put it another way, if it's "lordly" it has the "Emperor's stamp" upon it.

GB: How extraordinary. You mentioned that it's found in the first chapter of the book of Revelation. What's the context there?

TS: John says that he was "in the Spirit on the Lord's Day." We're tempted to think that this was a reference to the first day of the week, the first day of the week being the same day of the week as the day of the resurrection of the Lord Jesus. If we're correct in this surmise and if his use of "κυριακος" was such that the word was meant to convey something akin to the sense of imperial ownership then it would seem that he was conveying the idea that the day had been given a special significance to it by God. The day had, as it were, the "Lord's stamp" on it. So presumably John wasn't saying that the day came from the Lord or that it had the character of the Lord. If he wished to make this sort of claim, the noun "κυριος" would have sufficed.

GB: So are you suggesting that somehow or other we should see in the translation of the text in 1 Corinthians the idea of "special significance being given to the meal," a meal having the Lord's "stamp upon it"—using your phrase?

TS: Yes. But it isn't easy to convey that sense in a simple translation. A word for word translation of our verse would read something like, "When you come together to eat, it is not a Lordly meal." I know I've used the word "Lordly" a number of times already but it's not a very common word and sounds as though we are using old-fashion English. I think that a reasonable translation would go something like "When you come together to eat, it is not a meal that the Lord would own as his" or "a meal with which the Lord would associate himself." That Paul is saying, "The Lord doesn't approve of their meal," is implied but that statement in itself does not convey any sense of ownership. Notice, by the way, that I've avoided using a definite article before "meal" and that I've used the word "meal" rather than "supper." More importantly, note how we actually don't have a title to anything.

GB: What do you mean?

TS: The statement being made by Paul is that the sort of meals the Corinthians have when they assemble together cannot be said to be ones that are Lordly. A description

Corinthian Meals—the Lord's Supper

is being given of what their meals are not like. Their meals are being characterized in terms of what they are not. Their meals are not in any sense being given a formal title. There isn't a reference to a meal that they don't have or that they did have, that has a title. Paul is stating that their meals are such that they cannot be described as "Lordly." For three verses before our text, and for at least two verses after our text, the focus is on the behavior of the Christian believers at their formal meals and what Paul thinks of that behavior. The text itself is of the same ilk. Their meals are not ones that the Lord would own.

GB: This is astonishing! It's now quite obvious what Paul is actually saying. But how come it's been understood so differently by so many?

TS: Well, the early Christian writer, Clement of Alexandria may have had a similar understanding to the one I've just been promoting. It's difficult to tell. In a text written around the end of the second century CE he wrote about women who upon becoming intoxicated might remove part of their clothing so bringing moral harm to both themselves and men. With this situation in mind he then said how careful those to whom he wrote should be when in the presence of the Lord, otherwise what the apostle Paul wrote to the Corinthians would apply to them. At this point he wrote "Ζυνερχομενων ὑμων οὐκ ἐστι κυριακον δειπνον φαγειν" (*sunerchomenōn humōn ouk esti kuriakon deipnon fagein*). Compare this with what we have in 1 Corinthians 11:20: "Ζυνερχομενων οὖν ὑμων ἐπι το αὐτο οὐκ ἐστιν κυριακον δειπνον φαγειν." Except for the omission of "ἐπι το αὐτο" by Clement, we mentioned that little phrase before, what he and Paul wrote is almost identical. Like Paul, Clement was certainly concerned about inappropriate behavior. He could have been claiming—as I believe Paul was so doing—that a meal where improper behavior was present was not a meal that the Lord would own. It's not as though Clement doesn't also make comments about a Eucharistic ceremony. He does, but in doing so he does not seem to equate the Eucharist with "κυριακον δειπνον."

GB: Fascinating. But still, today, people understand the text differently and so my question still is "Why?"

TS: And an interesting question. We've already discussed a very similar one when we looked at that verse in Matthew chapter 28 to do with baptism. Whatever explanation applies to an individual, who knows? But, in general, when people decide upon a certain understanding and that understanding becomes widespread, it becomes difficult to accept that the understanding is incorrect. The reformers faced such situations. It was never easy for them to convince others that some of the theological beliefs that were commonly held were false. I'm sorry to say it but sometimes pride also comes into the equation. However, we can be as innocent and as humble as anybody and still get things wrong. I'm sure that that was the situation with Wycliffe, for example.

GB: I've heard of Wycliffe. He was one of the early reformers wasn't he?

TS: Yes. And he was quite a scholar. He is often remembered for his translation into English of the Bible. I really don't know but he may have been one of the first people, in anything like the modern era, to think that the text in 1 Corinthians 11:20 was a reference to a Christian rite. He based his translation of the Scriptures, a translation he made sometime in the fourteenth century, on an ancient translation called the Latin Vulgate—I've mentioned it before—made about ten centuries earlier. And interestingly, the Latin Vulgate uses the Latin adjective "*dominicus*" for "Lordly" and not the noun "*dominus*." The adjective together with the noun "*cena*," meaning "meal"—normally a three-course dinner held in the afternoon—are in the accusative case and appear as "*dominicam cenam*."

GB: What did Wycliffe's translation actually say?

TS: In old English he wrote for our text "*Therfor whanne ye comen togifere in to oon, now it is not ete the Lordis soper.*" In his work "*On the Eucharist*" he referred to "how the Corinthians agreed to the partaking of the Lord's Supper and each one took with him his own bread and wine . . . He [the apostle] chided them gently in this matter and added instruction as to this sacrament." A consideration of what he wrote here makes it fairly clear that he considered that the "*Lordis soper*" was a reference to a Christian rite or perhaps the bread and wine associated with that rite. Later, Tyndale, in the sixteenth century, working from Hebrew and Greek texts for his translation of the Bible, rendered the verse and the first half of the next verse "*When ye come to gedder a man cannot eate the lordes supper. For every man begynneth a fore to eate his awne supper.*" Notice by the way, how it appears that Wycliffe, and perhaps also Tyndale, thought that the problem that Paul was addressing was that people were eating their own food, that is, they were not sharing.

GB: You say that Wycliffe may have been the first person to consider that the text spoke of a Christian rite? Surely not!

TS: I was referring to something like the modern era but even then I said that I really didn't know. Someone else with far more knowledge than I have may think otherwise. At least one doesn't come across the term "the Lord's Supper" in early Christian writings all that much. If we ignore what Clement of Alexandria wrote, except for one other document of uncertain date, there is no evidence that anyone before the fourth century called a ceremony or rite, that some might claim was akin to the Lord's Supper, by that title—"the Lord's Supper." The term "the Eucharist," referring to something like "a thanksgiving," I think I've said that before, was used instead, with the first known use of that term occurring around 110 CE. The term sometimes referred to the elements, that is, the bread and the wine of the ceremony but at other times to the ceremony or the rite itself. It's interesting that in notes accompanying each of the Catholic translations—The Douay-Rheims Bible, The Knox Translation of the Bible and the Jerusalem Bible—the reader is informed that the text in question is making a reference to a genuine meal. In the New Jerusalem Bible, the editors are more cautious, simply

Corinthian Meals — the Lord's Supper

referring, in a note, to the Lord's Supper as something with which the Corinthian meal is compared. In that note, the Lord's Supper is not identified as the Eucharist, the term "Eucharist" being used later in notes that relate to verse 26 and following.

GB: I see. Of course, as you mentioned briefly earlier, what was considered "the Eucharist," if thought of as the rite itself, might have been known by the term "Agape" though "the Eucharist" and "the Agape Meal" were certainly regarded as distinct practices later. By the way, what is that document of uncertain date you mentioned?

TS: The document, purportedly written by a certain Hippolytus of Rome, with a possible date of about 215 CE—I'm sure I mentioned him and the document in one or more of our earlier discussions —has been difficult to reconstruct and the authorship and date are in dispute. The relevant sentence could be translated "The catechumen may not take part in the Lord's Supper." The catechumen was a person undergoing instruction about things like the Lord's Supper. What is quite commonly called "the Eucharist" may have been known as "the Lord's Supper" from time to time and it may have been considered that the term had its origin in the Corinthians text well before Wycliffe. There simply isn't any evidence that I know of that the term was widely used before Wycliffe. What is interesting is that if you were looking for a title to a practice, a custom, a rite, from either of chapters 10 or 11 of 1 Corinthians, I think the only one that would suggest itself from the textual material itself would be "the Lord's Supper." But as I've tried to demonstrate "κυριακον δειπνον" (*kuriakon deipnon*) is not a title to anything. By the way, "δειπνον" is a neuter noun and "κυριακον," paired with the noun, is the neuter form of the adjective "κυριακος." The same words appear whether they are in the accusative or nominative case.

GB: Thanks. . . . However, though I know I'm simply being persistent, might not the term, "the Eucharist," having, as you say, a basic meaning of "thanksgiving," have a connection with the reference in chapter 10 to "the cup of thanksgiving"?

TS: Not really. The actual reference is to "the cup of blessing" not "the cup of thanksgiving." We dealt with that matter a number of days ago. In chapter 10 the Greek word "εὐλογιας" is used, not the word "εὐχαριστιας." True, as we said before, Luke refers to Jesus during the Last Passover Meal giving thanks, "εὐχαριστησας," over a cup before the main meal and then over the bread at the beginning of the main meal. And Mark refers to Jesus giving thanks over the cup after the bread had been blessed, as does Matthew. Paul in his account also refers to the giving of thanks over the bread. And I guess that probably it's those texts or the Last Passover Meal as a whole that in some way led to the term "the Eucharist" arising. But in 1 Corinthians chapter 10 it's "the cup of blessing" not "the cup of thanksgiving." Anyway, we ought now to finish up for the day.

GB: We've still got to tackle Paul's reference to the Last Passover Meal in the last part of chapter 11 haven't we?

TS: Yes we do. But let's leave that till, say, Saturday. Would Saturday be okay?

GB: Saturday would be great. I feel that we're getting closer to the end of our discussions.

TS: It's been a long haul hasn't it? But we are getting there. I only hope that what we've talked about, sometimes at some length, has been helpful. Our chats have certainly been helpful to me. You've made me work more than I really wanted to but it's been good! Enough of that! See you Saturday.

GB: Okay. See you then.

Corinthian Meals—the Lord's Supper

EXPLANATORY NOTES: DAY 29

The word "δειπνον" occurs sixteen times in the New Testament (NAG). Almost all instances refer to a meal or meals of some significance. The only possible exception is a meal given for Jesus and his disciples at the home of Martha—John 12:2 (NAG), though such a meal was hardly likely to have been ordinary. Three occurrences relate to the Last Passover Meal itself—John 13:2, 4, 21:20 (NAG), three to the description of meals where the scribes endeavor to occupy places of honor—Matt 23:6; Mark 12:39; Luke 20:46 (NAG), one is a reference to Jesus giving instructions on whom to invite to a special meal—Luke 14:12 (NAG), three refer to the parable that Jesus told of the great supper—Luke 14:16, 17, 24 (NAG), two to an eschatological banquet—Rev 19:9, 17 (NAG), and one refers to a banquet for Herod—Mark 6:21 (NAG). Additionally there are the two references in 1 Cor 11: 20–21 (NAG).

In referring to the Greek text for 1 Cor 11:20 and when referring to the Greek for "thanksgiving" and "blessing" TS uses NAG.

The word "κυριακος" is used in Rev 1:10 and 1 Cor 11:20 (NAG).

The word "κυριος" occurs in 1 Cor 10 in verses 21 (twice) and 26 in the genitive case, and in verse 22 in the accusative case. In 1 Cor 11 it occurs in verse 11 in the dative case, verses 23, 26 and 27 (twice) in the genitive case, in verse 23 that case being determined by a preposition, in verse 23 in the nominative case and in verse 32 in the dative case. See NAG.

The texts, written before New Testament times, where the word "κυριακος" can be found are *Astrampsychus Oracula*, chapter epuist, section 1, lines. 54, 56—written fourth century BCE and *Liber Jubilaearum* Fragment c, line 44—written first or second century BCE.

The references to usages of "κυριακος" cited by James Moulton and George Milligan can be found in, Moulton and Milligan, *The Vocabulary of the Greek Testament*, 364.

The Greek text in which Clement of Alexandria writes of what Paul wrote to the Corinthians can be located in Clement of Alexandria, *Paedagogus,* Book 2, chapter 2, subchapter 33, section 5, line 3. For an English translation see http://www.newadvent.org/fathers/0209.htm The Paedagogus, Book 2, chapter 2. Clement's reference to the Eucharist can be found in that same chapter.

For Wycliffe's translation of 1 Corinthians 11:20 see Wycliffe, 1 Corinthians. For his association of the Eucharist with the "Lord's Supper" see Wyclif, "On the Eucharist," 2, (14), in *Advocates of Reform*, 72.

For Tyndale's rendering of 1 Corinthians 11:20 see his 1 Corinthians.

The document of uncertain date and composition that TS considered used the term, "the Lord's Supper" to refer to a rite that we would consider akin to the "Lord's Supper" is that often considered to be written by Hippolytus—*The Apostolic Tradition*. See *The Apostolic Tradition*, 27.1 for the reference to "the Lord's Supper." Ignatius is possibly the first person we know of to use the term "Eucharist" to refer to a ceremony or rite that we might regard as similar to the "Lord's Supper." The reference can be found in Ignatius, *To the Smyrnaeans*, 238. The text there reads, "They remain aloof from Eucharist . . . because they do not confess that the Eucharist is the flesh of our saviour Jesus Christ which suffered for our sins."

For the notes in The Douay-Rheims Bible, The Knox Translation of the Bible, The Jerusalem Bible and The New Jerusalem Bible, that relate to 1 Corinthians 11: 20 see Moore, *The Complete Notes of the Doway Bible*, 305, Knox, *The Knox Translation of the Bible*, 174 (N. T.), note 5, *The Jerusalem Bible*, 303 (N. T.), note 11h, and *The New Jerusalem Bible*, 1903, note 11c.

Day 30

Corinthian meals—the Last Passover Meal

Does Paul in 1 Corinthians 11 refer to a "remembrance rite" just after he relates what the Lord Jesus did and said at the Last Passover Meal? This is the question that TS poses for GB. GB, although he appreciates much that TS says about that meal and its significance for the Corinthian believers and their meals, is inclined to answer maybe yes or maybe no. He isn't sure.

TS: Hi there. Good to see you. . . . Let's get down to business. I think the most persuasive argument for the idea that the Corinthians practiced a Christian ceremony or rite rests on that part of chapter 11 where Paul refers to what the Lord Jesus did and said at the Last Passover Meal and the subsequent statements that Paul then makes. And he leads into that matter with a statement that's meant to make the reader "sit up and take notice." He writes, "I received from the Lord what I delivered to you." We don't know how he received from the Lord what he is about to say. It could've been directly by way of a vision. Alternatively, some indirect process could have been involved, such as the information being passed on to him by one or more of the Apostles. Whatever the means, the reader is meant to take solemn notice of what follows. But it's still important to remind ourselves that up to this point he's been writing about the behavior of the Corinthians at their communal meals, and that he will conclude this part of his letter with how they *should* behave at those meals.

GB: I notice that in the text, that word, "for" appears again. Any comment?

TS: I think Paul, having again referred to his not commending them, in verse 22 is about to lead into another matter that they should recognize as having bearing on their behavior. Before I go on however, I should say something about the word translated, "delivered." It comes from the verb, "παραδίδωμι" (paradidōmi), "I deliver." Paul really wants to convey the idea, "You know exactly what I am about to refer to. You have this information. I handed it over to you. I delivered it to you." It may also be true that in this context, there is the idea, that what Paul delivered to them was part of his official and set teaching. It's interesting that at the beginning of chapter 11, Paul says, that he commends the Corinthians partly because they have kept the *traditions* that he had *delivered* to them and then proceeds to talk about head coverings. The word translated, "traditions" comes from the noun "παραδοσις" (paradosis) and you can see how it is related to "παραδωμι," the "delivered" word, which word comes up in this verse.

GB: So what Paul says to them in verse 23 should come as no surprise and should be understood to be a matter of some significance.

TS: Exactly.

GB: We did go through, two or three weeks ago now, what Paul reports that Jesus did and said at that Last Passover meal. However, should we, could we, go through that again?

TS: I think we need to. Paul's account has slightly more to it than Luke's and differs from that account here and there. However, Paul first of all establishes the historical setting by saying "On the night that he was betrayed." He then refers to Jesus taking the bread, giving thanks and breaking it, saying, "This is my body which is for you. Do this in remembrance of me." Luke records, "This is my body which is *given* for you. Do this in remembrance of me."

GB: You're going to leave it as a type of command?

TS: Yes, by and large, even though I think the weight of textual evidence indicates that what Jesus said is in the indicative mood. . . . Then Paul writes, "And likewise the cup, after supper, saying, 'This cup is the new covenant in my blood.'" Luke includes the phrase, "which is poured out for you." The words that we translate "after supper," in Greek, are "μετα το δειπνησαι" (*meta to deipnēsai*). "Δειπνον," the word for meal, and "δειπνησαι" are obviously related. "Δειπνησαι," an infinitive in form, comes from the verb "δειπνεω" (*deipneō*), meaning, "I make a meal." Paul continues with Jesus saying, "Do this as often as you drink it in remembrance of me." Luke omits these last words. You might remember that there is even some question mark over what Luke originally recorded—that it's even less than what the translators tend to give us. But I've chosen to refer to, what is called "the longer reading."

GB: I remember. Is there much *significance* in the differences between what Luke records—let's accept the longer reading—and what Paul records?

TS: Overall, I don't think so. However differences in *detail* may have *some* significance. Paul records "as often as" and Luke doesn't. Luke, in the longer reading, records how Jesus refers to remembrance, only with respect to the bread, but Paul records remembrance words being uttered with respect to both the bread and the cup. Because Paul records two remembrance statements and Luke only one in the reporting of what

Corinthian meals—the Last Passover Meal

Jesus said, Paul uses the Greek word for "this" four times whereas Luke only uses it three times.

GB: And you think that there could be some significance in *these* differences, what I'd have thought were only very slight differences?

TS: Well it looks as though Paul is concerned to stress something or other while not being concerned to include the words "which is poured out for you." As I said, overall I don't think the differences are all that significant but it's interesting, isn't it, that he would omit such a phrase as "poured out for you"? I'm not suggesting that the differences are important for our understanding of what was said at the Last Passover Meal. However, I *am* suggesting that Paul has purposefully stressed some elements of what Jesus had said, which he considers important for what he is about to say. At the same time he has been prepared to omit another matter that I think, under different circumstances, he would've regarded as very important.

GB: Sorry for interrupting but Paul does record Jesus saying, "which is for you" with respect to his body. Omitting "which is poured out for you" with respect to his blood really doesn't seem to be all *that* important.

TS: Maybe you're right. Perhaps we shouldn't see much, if any significance in that omission. Paul, if he had decided to check on what he had said at this point, may or may not have decided to include the phrase "which is poured out for you." We'll never know. Anyway, let me explain why I think Paul refers to the Last Passover Meal at all in this 1 Corinthians letter. I think that Paul is so concerned about the behavior of the Corinthians at their meals that he decides to use the most famous meal of all, at least from the believers' point of view, the Last Passover Meal, to contrast that meal with their meals. He wants to indicate how their behavior is out of kilter with what one would expect when one considers the Last Passover Meal. And now for the most important point I am trying to make at this stage. He does this, in what he is about to say, by treating, after a fashion, their meal as though it *were*, in effect, the Last Passover Meal.

GB: But what happened at the Last Passover Meal had nothing to do with disciples not sharing their meal with one another or even their not waiting for one another so that they could all eat at the same time.

TS: I see what you're saying but let me explain. The focus that Jesus brought to bear on the Last Passover Meal was with respect to his death and it being for the benefit of the disciples and for those who would become disciples. And he either said that the Passover meal was all about him—they were partaking of the meal in remembrance of him, indeed all Passover meals had been about him—or he was *asking them*, then and there, *to see* that their Passover meal *was* all about him and probably, to view future Passover meals in the same light. Paul, whatever he omits, does report, as you've deftly pointed out, that Jesus said, "This is my body which is for you." And with such words,

Paul is highlighting the death of Jesus for others. Yet the problem that Paul is addressing is the behavior of Corinthian believers at their communal meals. I recognize that the death of Jesus on the one hand and the behavior of these Corinthians at their meals on the other, might seem to be relatively unrelated. But such a perspective arises because of a failure to take into account an extremely important matter.

GB: I'm listening.

TS: That Jesus died to save sinners placed every believing Corinthian on the same footing. They were all equally in debt to God for his mercy. Where was this equality being portrayed in their meals? It was divisions and differences that characterized their meals, as Paul rightly exclaimed. The death of Jesus, so much the focus of the Last Passover Meal, was *for the Corinthians*, as well as, of course, for others. At their meals their behavior suggested that in a particular way the death of Jesus was *not* for them!

GB: I understand . . . and if I could add, the death of Jesus was the great loving act of God. Using partly your words, where was this love being portrayed in their meals? Where was this love poured out upon them being reflected in the way they treated one another?

TS: It wasn't. Well, it was certainly limited.

GB: This idea that Paul decided to treat their meal as though it were, in some fashion, the Last Passover Meal, is pretty novel though isn't it?

TS: It's not completely novel. There are a few other people who've held a somewhat similar view. I must tell you about some of them sometime. And the idea is not completely without precedence of some sort. I think it was Plutarch who appealed to what he saw as ideal meals, as examples for how meals in general should be conducted. For the Corinthians, the Passover meal was certainly the standout meal. It wasn't so much a model for meals however, as the meal that made all future Christian meals so special. . . . I know I'm asking a lot of your patience but please hang in there.

GB: Of course.

TS: I now need to further develop my argument. Having referred to "this" four times, in his reporting of what Jesus said at the Last Passover Meal, Paul then says, "For." It's that word again. He is about to explain how that remembrance has a part to play in their meals. He says, "For as often as you eat *this* bread and drink the cup, you proclaim the Lord's death until he comes." I think Paul's use of "this" in his statement is his way, at this point, of linking the Last Passover Meal with the Corinthians' meal. Jesus spoke of "this" four times, according to Paul, and now, says Paul, I'm speaking of "this"—your meal, not just the Last Passover Meal.

GB: But it could still mean that the Corinthian meal as a whole or in part was actually an early Christian rite or custom, couldn't it? If it wasn't something like what we call "the Lord's Supper," "Holy Communion" or "the Eucharist," maybe it was some simple ceremony on which these ceremonies are based.

TS: Why don't we call what you are supposing might have existed, "a remembrance rite"? I don't think that it's a term in popular use but perhaps it will do for us, while recognizing respectfully that some would vehemently want to say that it was *more* than a remembrance rite. However *we* will know what *we* mean. Yes, I understand that that's a traditional way that the text is understood. I hope to show otherwise, though it can be difficult. Once we've made up our minds on certain issues and have maintained those views over a long period of time, to change them, no matter what the arguments against those views might be, can be almost impossible. I used to think something along the lines you've suggested but now I think that there really isn't any strong evidence that such a rite is being referred to in this text. I certainly don't think there is any clear evidence that in the passage we are discussing, there was a *problem* with some remembrance rite, no matter what its form. What Paul says both at the beginning and at the end of this section of his letter is, "when you come together to eat," not "when you come together to take part in a rite."

GB: But I suppose he might be appealing to a rite or custom that the Corinthians engaged in, as part of their meal or in some way connected to their meal, *in order to show*, somehow or other, how their behavior was appalling when they came together to eat.

TS: That's possible but I don't think that's evident from the text. Let me now elaborate on why Paul said exactly what he said. For starters, I think almost everybody would agree that when Paul refers to "the eating of this bread and the drinking of the cup," he's making some reference to—he's making some link with—the Last Passover Meal. He has just *referred* to that meal. By the way, I think that in this phrase, the word "this" could be understood to apply to both the bread and the cup but Paul is not concerned to make that clear. Notice that here the order for "bread" and "cup" does indeed conform to the order for "bread" and "cup" as just reported by Paul when speaking of the Last Passover Meal. And I should also point out that Paul refers to "*the* cup," rather than "*a* cup" both here, and again, when referring to the Last Passover Meal. The definite article *does* appear in the Greek in these instances. Undoubtedly at this point, when he says, "For often as you eat this bread and drink the cup," he is still making some connection with the Last Passover Meal. There was the *one* cup, *the* cup, when Jesus made reference to his blood.

GB: I see what you're saying. However the word, "this" seems to suggest that Paul is connecting the Last Passover Meal with a present practice.

TS: Yes, but he is not necessarily making a connection with a remembrance rite! In addition to having the Last Passover Meal in his mind, I think he's also making a reference to the community meals shared by the believers. Remember our discussion the other day about how the word "bread" could stand for a meal and how the phrase "drinking a cup of the Lord" was most likely a reference to a way of honoring the Lord at a meal. They had meals, and from what Paul said in chapter 10, presumably they honored the Lord during their meals by "drinking a cup" to him.

GB: I understand what you're saying, that is, that Paul is trying to link the Last Passover Meal with their meals, their ordinary though formal meals, and not a "remembrance rite," but I still don't think the point you're trying to make is all that obvious from the text.

TS: Let me persevere. I think that it's Paul's use of the word "this" that is one of the keys. Let me elaborate. He could just as easily have said, "For as often as you eat the bread and drink the cup, you proclaim the Lord's death until he comes," that is, without using the word "this." And I suppose one could then say, that now Paul was referring to a remembrance rite. But he did use the word, "this." I think, by using the word "this," Paul is moving, as it were, through the reference to the Last Passover Meal to his ultimate concern—their believer community meals. Though he has undoubtedly been referring to the Last Passover Meal, the "this" could be a pointed way of referring to their meal—the meal the Corinthian believers share or are supposed to share with each other.

GB: Yes, but you're simply stating your position. The "this" could have been a reference to a remembrance rite rather than their ordinary though formal meal!

TS: You're right, but in doing so, one has to introduce a "remembrance rite" out of the blue! There is no earlier reference to such a rite or custom! Instead, Paul has been talking about the *meal* they often have. I know that some will argue that from what Paul writes in a moment it's clear that a remembrance rite is in view, but I will get to that matter later.

GB: Okay.

TS: Let me proceed with my argument. So far, I haven't considered the possible significance of Paul, unlike Luke, referring to the *two* remembrance statements. Nor have I referred to the possible significance of the word, actually one word in the Greek—"ὁσάκις" [*hosakis*]), meaning "as often as"—used once by Jesus, as reported by Paul, although Jesus wouldn't have spoken in Greek, and then once again used by Paul in his own statement. Regarding the first matter—the use of the two remembrance statements by Paul, I think Paul has quite consciously quoted those two remembrance statements to apply more forcefully the relevance of the Last Passover Meal to their meal, a meal being celebrated some years later. The remembrance notion is not lost on him. It had a binding future aspect. It had relevance for their community meals. It has relevance for all meals that bring believers together, no matter when. Jesus said, "Remember" or "You are remembering."

GB: And the significance of Paul's mention of "as often as" twice? I think I can guess. Jesus said "as often as" to the disciples at the Last Passover Meal. And now all disciples, including these Corinthian believers, are to celebrate their meals in such a way that displays certain things made obvious in that Last Passover Meal, "as often as" they have those meals.

TS: Yes. You've got it! And notice the close connection that Paul makes between the two "as often as" phrases. I suppose I could use the one English word "whenever." That simplifies things. Paul doesn't report Jesus using the word "whenever" with respect to the bread. He introduces the word "whenever" when reporting on Jesus speaking about the cup. Mention of the cup comes after mention of the bread. "*This* cup is the new covenant in my blood. Do this *whenever* you drink it in remembrance of me." At the beginning of the next statement, the one made by Paul, Paul refers to "whenever" again. "For, *whenever* you eat *this* bread and drink the cup you proclaim the Lord's death until he comes." In the Greek, the word "ὁσάκις" actually occurs at the head of the sentence and before the Greek word for "for," "γαρ." "Γαρ" normally comes second or later in sentences. Paul, in his placement of "ὁσάκις," links, as closely as he can, the "this cup" words uttered by Jesus to the "this bread" words made in his own statement. I think this is his way of "sliding," as it were, from the Last Passover Meal to the Corinthians' community meals.

GB: You're really looking at what Paul said by using a literary microscope!

TS: I've had to. As you said, the viewpoint I am advocating is by and large "novel." But let me now try to summarize what I've been trying to say. By using the double remembrance statements, compared to Luke's reference to one such statement, by having that extra "this" in that extra remembrance statement, by including another "this" in connection with their bread, their meal, by using the two "whenever" words and by having the "whenever" words in relatively close proximity to one another, Paul is tightly tying the Last Passover Meal to their meal thereby indicating that that first meal has *ramifications* for their meal. And I still think their meal was an ordinary, though formal meal, a meal partaken of by believers.

GB: Let me think about it for the moment.... The two remembrance statements, the extra "this" and another one added by Paul, the two "whenever" words and the way they're aligned—okay. Okay. Your argument has some substance. Could you explain how the Corinthians, meeting together as a community of believers for a meal, would constitute proclaiming the Lord's death?

TS: Sure. An important question! We need to remember how unusual their gatherings were. They lacked the homogeneity one would expect in typical Corinthian formal meals. They had one thing that united them. That which brought together, Jew and Gentile, free and slave, male and female, wealthy and poor, high born and low born, cultured and, from many a Corinthian's point of view, uncultured, that which brought them together, was the Lord himself and his death for each one of them. That was the death that gave them the same status before God, the death that made them one! Every time this heterogeneous group met together for this richly personal and intimate sharing of a meal, this special "κοινωνια," this "fellowship," it was the gathering itself that proclaimed his death, at least in principle.

GB: You use the words "in principle." What are you getting at?

TS: Of course *Paul* doesn't say "in principle." And perhaps I shouldn't have said "in principle." They are proclaiming the Lord's death simply by their coming together. It's the Lord's death that *brings* them together. But to *some* extent, they *aren't* proclaiming the Lord's death, by the way they behave, but they should be!

GB: I think I understand. Just as the Last Passover Meal proclaimed the Lord's death, so their meals did the same but not as pointedly as they should have.

TS: So, can you see why Paul might treat their meal as though it were the Last Passover Meal? Tying in the Last Passover Meal with their meal is part of Paul's way, a very powerful way, of making the Corinthians reflect on how they behave at their meals, making them feel ashamed of how they are currently behaving and bringing them to the realization that they need to change their ways. Their meals should proclaim the Lord's death and powerfully. The community meals of all believers, throughout all time, should proclaim the Lord's death, powerfully, until he comes.

GB: I get what you're saying but I have to confess that what Paul says next, I have the words here, right in front of me, verses 27 and 28—those words seem to suggest to me that some kind of rite or custom *is* being referred to. He writes of, "the bread," "the cup of the Lord," "the body and the blood of the Lord," then "eating the bread" and "drinking of the cup." I know you said you would look at this part of the text later. Could we do that now? Are the definite articles there in the Greek?

TS: Yes and yes. We should look at those verses now, at least in a preliminary sort of way, and yes, definite articles do accompany every noun. I also ought to point out that "the Lord" in both instances is a translation of the Greek noun "κυριος" not the adjective "κυριακος."

GB: I understand. And you did mention how often "κυριος" appears around the one usage of "κυριακος" in verse 20. And I realize that the Greek for "the cup of the Lord" here isn't the same as the Greek for "a cup of the Lord" in chapter 10.

TS: True. And that does suggest, that whatever we make of what Paul is saying here, the reference in chapter 10 is to something different. There, as I've argued, "drinking a cup of the Lord" was placed in opposition to "drinking a cup of demons," at their meals. Here, "the cup of the Lord" harks back to the Last Passover Meal. But let's return to verses 27 and 28! I think that primarily what Paul is doing here is still treating their meal as though it were the Passover meal. It's his way of shocking the Corinthians, making them appreciate how abominable their behavior at their meals is. "The bread" is a reference to "the bread" that Jesus broke and passed around, saying about it, "This is my body." "The cup of the Lord" is a reference to "the cup" that Jesus passed around, saying about it, "This is the new covenant in my blood." Understandably, Paul's next reference is to "the body and the blood of the Lord."

GB: But Paul says, "Whoever eats the bread or drinks the cup." Surely that's a reference to something that the Corinthians are doing or could do, not a reference to the Last Passover Meal.

TS: I think it's *both*. That's my point. And when you read on in verse 28 "Let a man examine himself and so eat of the bread and drink of the cup," he is still treating their meal and the Last Passover Meal as one, although by now he's beginning to slip back into speaking of their meal alone.

GB: You could be right. I think I'm caught in a balancing act. In my view, there could be a reference to a rite or custom based on the Last Passover Meal. Alternatively, it could be that Paul is involved in a type of "double play" —their meal and the Last Passover Meal brought together as though one. I'm not really sure.

TS: I think at this point we probably should call it quits for today. Perhaps you could just let those two possibilities roll around in your mind. Don't worry, we will return to this whole question again. When we do I think it will be helpful if we examine verses 27 and 28 in more detail, particularly verse 27 and also we will need to examine the verses that follow on from verse 28. Would meeting again tomorrow in the afternoon be too soon? Would another day be better?

GB: No, tomorrow afternoon would be fine. Say around 2.00?

TS: 2.00 it is!

PART 3: THE LORD'S SUPPER

EXPLANATORY NOTES: DAY 30

The relevant section of what Luke recorded that Jesus said at the Last Passover Meal is found in Luke 22:19–20 (NIV) and the Greek text that TS refers to has been taken from NAG.

The view that Paul is treating the Corinthians' meal as though it were the Last Passover Meal is not completely novel. For instance see Woodhouse, "What is this meal?" and "The Body of the Lord," and May, "The Lord's Supper: Part 1" and "The Lord's Supper: Part 2." Barrett also has an understanding of the Corinthians' "Lord's Supper" that is somewhat similar to the viewpoint expressed by TS—see Barrett, *The First Epistle to the Corinthians*, 264 and his *Church, ministry and sacraments*, 67–70.

The idea that one meal can be used as a contrast to, or a comparison for, other meals was apparently not without precedence in the ancient world. Plutarch in his *Quaestiones convivales* ("Table Talk") describes a number of dialogues that he uses as examples for what he regards as "proper" dinner conversations. To what extent the conversations corresponded to real dialogues is not easy to determine. They can be found in *Plutarch's Moralia VIII*, Books I–III and IV–VI, 4–281 and 290–515 respectively and *Plutarch's Moralia IX*, Books VII, VIII and IX, 4–103, 108–211, and 218–99 respectively.

In another work, *Septem Sapientium Convivium* ("A Banquet of the Seven Sages"), Plutarch describes a banquet that is clearly an invention and highly idealized. That Paul might have used the Last Passover Meal as a means by which an appraisal could be made on what the Corinthians were doing at their meals, is not inconsistent with what Plutarch did, although done differently and created for different reasons. *Septem Sapientium Convivium* can be located in *Plutarch's Moralia II, The Dinner of the Seven Wise Men (Septem Sapientum Convivium)*, section 146B–164D, 348–49.

It is common for protestant commentators to readily assume that 1 Cor 11:17–34 has as its backdrop a rite referred to as, "the Lord's Supper." For a relatively modern example see Garland, *1 Corinthians*, 533–57. For an earlier example see Grosheide, *First Epistle to the Corinthians*, 263–77.

Day 31

Corinthian Meals—the Last Passover Meal—Consequences for the Corinthians

Is TS building a good case for his position or is it that he's just very persuasive? Do the 1 Corinthians texts that they've been discussing really mean what TS argues that they mean? These are the questions that GB tries to answer.

GB: Hi. I've been doing some thinking overnight. You could be right about Paul treating the Corinthians' meal as though it were the Last Passover Meal, but I can understand how people really think that Paul is referring to a rite or custom when he writes about "eating the bread" and "drinking the cup of the Lord." I suppose part of the problem is that these sorts of phrases are so much part of many of the liturgies involved in the celebration of "the Lord's Super." Oh, don't worry. I am convinced that that title can't legitimately come from 1 Corinthians 11:20. But it's a title that many Christians now commonly use.

TS: I think your surmise about the influence of our liturgies could be correct but people would still argue that it's the text of Scripture that has influenced the liturgies not that the liturgies influence our current understanding of the text. But let's get back to the passage. I suggested yesterday that we should look at verses 27 and 28 in more detail as well as the following verses. I'm going to try and do that now. We must be prepared to concede that we do have a reference here to an early Christian rite or custom if the evidence points that way or otherwise if the evidence is to the contrary.

GB: Go for it. Although I suspect you've already made up your mind.

TS: Maybe! Verse 27 reads as follows, my translation—"Therefore whoever eats the bread or drinks the cup of the Lord in a contradictory manner will be guilty of the body and the blood of the Lord." I think the "therefore" is important. It certainly links what he writes here with what he's just written, which concludes with those words—"For whenever you eat *this* bread and drink the cup, you proclaim the Lord's death until he comes." Let's work with the possibility, as I've been trying to argue, that what Paul says here could be understood as his treating their meal as though it were the Last Passover Meal. He's quoted Jesus as saying, "This cup is the new covenant in my blood, do *this whenever* you drink it in remembrance of me" and followed that with "For *whenever* you eat *this* bread ... you proclaim the Lord's death until he comes." Well then, the "therefore" of verse 27 would indicate that we've not left that perspective behind. I think one of the things he's implying is that given that the proclamation of the Lord's death is so important, the Corinthians should be very careful that how they behave, does indeed bring about just that.

GB: I get the point. I notice that your translation has some unusual features, if I can call them that. My translation has "in an unworthy manner" but you said "in a contradictory manner." Furthermore, you said, "guilty of the body and the blood of the Lord" whereas my translation has "guilty of profaning the body and the blood of the Lord."

TS: Yes. Let me explain. Firstly, I think that the Greek word often translated "in an unworthy manner," "ἀναξίως" (*anaxiōs*), actually does carries with it the notion of "contradictory" and I am suggesting that "in a contradictory manner" is not an inappropriate translation in this instance. I admit, however, I may be stretching its meaning somewhat. None the less, the Corinthian believers, by their behavior at their meals, are acting in contradiction to what the Lord's death implies. Secondly, for the English words "guilty of profaning" there is just the one Greek word "ἔνοχος" (*enochos*), which simply means "guilty." Our translations generally tend to soften what Paul is saying here. I think what he's getting at is that anyone who behaves in a manner that's contradictory to what the death of the Lord means for believers—among other things, that all are equally indebted to God for his loving mercy and all stand in the same relationship to God by virtue of that death—is opposed to the Lord. And, anyone who acts contrary to what that death brings about—among other things, his people brought into fellowship with him and with one another—is opposed to the Lord. And historically, those who were opposed to the Lord were the ones who brought about his actual death! I am sure that the phrase, "the body and the blood of the Lord" is a reference to his death. Such a person is guilty of just that, his death. These are terribly severe words and he's going to utter more severe words before he's finished.

GB: Do you think that the belief that a rite or custom is being referred to, has influenced the way people translate the text?

TS: I do! The phrase "in an unworthy manner" is used in our liturgies to have people reflect upon the quality of their moral life, which is all to the good, but it misses the notion of "contradiction." The phrase "the body and the blood of the Lord," as used in our liturgies, is probably meant to focus on the bread and the wine pointing to the body and the blood of the Lord, but why shouldn't we simply focus on the death of the

Corinthian Meals—the Last Passover Meal—Consequences for the Corinthians

Lord itself? And I know that the extended phrase "guilty of profaning the body and the blood of the Lord" is used in our liturgies to indicate that "shameful treatment" of the Lord's body and the blood and hence also, in some way, the bread and the wine, is involved, if we come to Holy Communion with sin in our lives that has not been dealt with. But "guilty of profaning" fails to recognize that the offence that Paul is referring to should be treated more seriously than a "profanity"!

GB: The behavior of the Corinthians at their community meals was *contradictory* to what the death of the Lord had brought about and so they were in a frame of mind that said that they were guilty of his death, not just guilty of profaning his death! I get it! They *are* severe words.

TS: Let's continue. In verse 28 we read, "Let a man examine himself and so eat of the bread and drink of the cup." While I think that Last Passover Meal language is still being employed, Paul is more and more slipping back into just talking about their meal. For the English word "examine" we have the Greek word, "δοκιμαζετω" (*dokimazetō*)—the third person singular imperative of the verb "δοκιμαζω" (*dokimazō*). It does have the sense of "examine" but also carries with it the idea of "approval." The examination should have a positive outcome. That's the hope. I know that traditionally this verse is interpreted to mean that people should reflect upon the spiritual side of their life before taking part in "the remembrance rite" but let's consider an alternative. We should notice that "a man" is indefinite. It points to no one in particular, just as the "whoever" of the previous verse is indefinite. I think it's indeed true that here Paul is calling upon the believers as individuals to examine something. What they have to examine is how they conduct themselves at their believer community meals. The "a man" could've been an oblique way of referring to the host—he certainly could alter the way things happened at the dinner—but it could be a reference to anyone, particularly the well-to-do.

GB: That doesn't mean, however, that believers shouldn't examine themselves before they partake of a "remembrance rite."

TS: Of course not. But, in the case of the Corinthians, I think that the behavior that they were to examine was what they did at their ordinary, though formal, meals.

GB: I understand what you're saying.

TS: Notice that if one thinks that a Christian rite or custom is what the text is referring to, both in verse 27 and verse 28, then it's the Christian rite—I think I'll continue by referring to it simply as a "rite"—that is, in principle, the problem. It's the Christian rite in which they've participated and have done so in a way contradictory to the Lord's death. It's the Christian rite in which they have been involved and have been so involved in a manner that makes them guilty of the body and the blood of the Lord. It's the Christian rite that should be preceded by self-examination. But clearly the problem is simply but profoundly in terms of whether or not they wait for one another or whether they share with one another, as we've discussed previously! In verse 28 Paul, using the Last Passover Meal imagery, but also referring to what they eat and drink at their community meals, is urging these Corinthians to reflect on what they've been doing and then conduct their meals in a manner worthy of approval—of God's approval!

GB: I think what you've now said pretty well clinches the matter. I think maybe you're right.

TS: But we haven't finished. In verse 29 Paul writes, "For anyone who eats and drinks, not discerning the body, eats and drinks judgement upon himself." I realize that the word "body" could be understood as a reference to the Lord himself and that "discerning the body" might mean something like, truly understanding what it means to eat the bread, of which Jesus said, "This is my body." And for sure, there is a reference in verse 27 to "the body and the blood of the Lord." Note however, Paul does not say, "discerning the body *and the blood*" in verse 29. He makes reference only to the body. The word translated "discerning" is "διακρινων" (*diakrinōn*), coming from the verb "διακρινω" (*diakrinō*) and "discerning" is not a bad translation. However, at heart it has the sense of "making distinctions." I wonder if Paul isn't being clever here, using a word that could also be understood as "making distinctions," when the making of improper distinctions has been their problem. But back to a consideration of "the body." I think Paul's reference here is to "the body of the Lord," meaning, "the Lord's people." He works with that idea in the very next chapter, using that same Greek word for body "σωμα" (*sōma*) as here, over a dozen times. And in that chapter he makes the classic statement "For by one Spirit we were all immersed into one body—Jews or Greeks, slaves or free." I think that "discerning the body" means "recognizing what being the body of the Lord, his people, really involves." They are all one in the Lord and there is to be no discrimination! There are to be no distinctions! They are to be equally honored. And if a person does not discern the body of the Lord appropriately he falls under the judgement of God.

GB: And that's severity for you. I doubt that *we* would see that what the Corinthian believers were doing was so serious. However, I guess it's worth thinking about how the social, economic and other distinctions might have, for some, led to, even unconsciously, snobbery, and this snobbery might have gone hand in hand with the well-to-do not sharing food with the less well off. Anyway, I think I understand Paul's perspective. For Paul, the death of the Lord himself, was in question.

TS: Yes. I'm sure you're right. Let me now put together the four verses—verses 26, 27, 28, and 29—in terms of what he actually said but also in terms of the thinking behind what he said—"*So you see, whenever you eat this bread—I am reflecting on the bread of the Last Passover Meal but I have in mind your actual meals—and drink the cup—I am reflecting on the cup of the Last Passover Meal but I have in mind your drinking at your believer community meals—the death of the Lord is proclaimed. It is proclaimed*

Corinthian Meals—the Last Passover Meal—Consequences for the Corinthians

by what brings you together for your meals—the death of the Lord—just as that death was proclaimed by our Lord at the Last Passover Meal—a death to be proclaimed until he comes again. Therefore, whoever eats the bread—your meal—or drinks the cup of the Lord—I am still reflecting on the Last Passover Meal but I have in mind your meals and your drinking at these meals—in a way that is contradictory to what the death of the Lord means for your meals—that everyone should be treated with equal honor—is guilty of the death—the body and the blood—of the Lord because he is in effect opposed to him. Every individual should look closely at what he is doing at these meals and so eat the bread and drink of the cup in an appropriate manner—that is, you should share your meals. Anyone, who eats and drinks without recognizing the nature of the body of the Lord, his people, brings the Lord's judgement upon himself." Of course, the actual straightforward statement made by Paul isn't at all stilted in style like this rendition! And I don't think the Corinthians would have had any problem in understanding what he was saying in his simpler statement and particularly if there had been no special ceremony involved.

GB: In fact if a special ceremony had been involved, what he wrote doesn't make it all that clear.

TS: I agree.

GB: . . . I've just realized again how often the word "Lord" has been used in the passage we've been discussing. I wonder if that's significant.

TS: Hmm. Let me check again. . . . It's there in verse 21, as the adjective of course. Then twice in verse 23, once as "Lord Jesus." It's there again in verse 26 . . . verse 27 twice . . . and finally in verse 32, although we haven't got to that verse yet. Anyway that makes seven times. And is its usage significant? It could be. If Paul is really looking at the behavior of believers at their formal meals, as I've been trying to indicate, then the use of "Lord" could simply be Paul's acknowledgement that there is only one Lord at their meals as opposed to the many lords—the gods and heroes, who are no lords at all—for whom libations were performed and toasts offered, at pagan meals.

GB: That makes sense. And I can see now how what he wrote hangs together. I can *also* see how a particular translation can be, to some extent, the product of a belief that Paul had in mind an elementary rite, as well as, of course, the Last Passover Meal.

TS: Anyway, let's continue. Paul has more to say about judgment. He goes on, "That is why many of you are weak and ill, and some have died." We cannot be exactly sure of what Paul is referring to here, but he maintains that the consequences of their poor behavior are of momentous proportions. He then issues another call for them to make an assessment of their behavior. If they judge themselves correctly and of course do something appropriate about their fault, then they won't come under God's judgement. Although, he continues, when God judges them it is for their benefit so that they will not be condemned along with the rest of the world, the unbelievers.

Part 3: The Lord's Supper

GB: I really do have much more confidence in your point of view, now. Either there is one problem—the way they're conducting themselves at their community meals or there are two problems one to do with their meals and the other to do with some "remembrance rite," and the two problems would seem to be tangled together in a confusing sort of way.

TS: Too confusing for that possibility to be acceptable, I'd suggest. Of course Paul doesn't finish at this point, as we're already aware. It's now that he gives the solution to the problem, the very practical solution—*"So then, my brothers, when you come together to eat, share with one another. But if anyone objects and considers himself hungry because he has had to share, then let him eat at his own house before he comes. Otherwise you will come under judgement."* This is the first time he's used the term "brothers" since the beginning of chapter 10. I think that by using the word "brothers" he's drawing back just a little from his stern approach.

GB: He may have used the term "brothers" to be more conciliatory or maybe not, but he still ends with what you think was a piece of sarcasm and again a stern note of judgement.

TS: True. He regards the matter he's been addressing as a very serious one and wants to conclude with a warning. . . . Where do you think we're at now? I mean, with respect to the "Lord's Supper," "Holy Communion," "The Eucharist" or what we've been calling lately a "remembrance rite"? I mean, as far as references being made to such in the New Testament?

GB: You mean, in terms of what we've been discussing from way back?

TS: Yes.

GB: You want me to summarize?

TS: Yes, just briefly. Only on what you see as the crucial issues!

GB: Okay. Here goes. There was a Passover meal at which Jesus referred to his death as being the great salvation remembrance event. He either commanded his followers to now see Passover Meals in this new light whenever they celebrated Passover or if he didn't command that, he explained to them that all Passover meals were really related to that great salvation event, his death. Believers in the days to come did meet with one another to share meals, but they were ordinary meals, though probably simple in nature. There was a meal that Jude refers to which he may have spoken of with some sarcasm as a love type of meal though it was anything but. Later, at least some Christians adopted the term, "agape" for their community meals, though in the course of time these meals fell into disrepute. Paul, in a letter to Corinthian believers, gives considerable attention to the problem of their eating food that had been sacrificed to or in any way offered to idols. Though many think that he makes two references to the Lord's Supper in chapter 10, before having supposedly used such a title, those

Corinthian Meals—the Last Passover Meal—Consequences for the Corinthians

references don't seem to be associated with a Christian rite nor is there such a title as "the Lord's Supper." Finally, when Paul deals with believers coming together to have community meals, recognizing that they're treating one another improperly at these meals, he superimposes the Last Passover Meal on their meals, as though they were Last Passover Meals, in order to condemn their behavior. . . . I could say a lot more but you said I should be brief!

TS: Well done! And if you think that what you've just said is true, what conclusion would you come to regarding the evidence in the New Testament for a ceremony or rite, involving bread and wine, that believers took part in after the death of Jesus, any ongoing celebration of the Passover by believers, aside?

GB: I would conclude that there isn't much evidence, if any. And that would mean that there isn't much, if any evidence that the New Testament believers thought that Jesus had issued a command that such a ceremony, somewhat like our Lord's Supper, be celebrated on a regular basis. Though I can understand that those believers who celebrated Passover in the past would probably continue to do so in the future even if they now thought about Passover somewhat differently. Of course, celebrating Passover is not really the same thing as celebrating something like our Lord's Supper, I know. . . . But to be strictly honest with you, I still have doubts—lingering doubts. You're fairly persuasive and I feel some pressure to agree with you. Nonetheless, I recognize, as you've now said a couple of times, that if you're used to a particular point of view, or I might add, very attracted to a particular point of view, it's difficult to change to another. In my church we have the Lord's Supper every week and I can see, for all my reservations about ceremonies, how importantly it's regarded by others and how helpful it can be.

TS: But the issue is not whether the Lord's Supper is a very helpful custom, nor how such a custom might have arisen, but whether participating in it is mandatory.

GB: Yes. I realize that. . . . I need to think on things for a few days. Could we meet again, briefly, on Wednesday night? Say after dinner, about 7 o'clock. My place will do.

TS: Sure.

Part 3: The Lord's Supper
EXPLANATORY NOTES: DAY 31

The Greek words in verses 27, 28 that TS examines come from NAG.

In chapter 12 of 1 Cor Paul refers to the noun, "σωμα" (body), a total of eighteen times. The word in one grammatical form or another is found in verses 12 (three times), 13, 14, 15 (twice), 16 (twice), 17, 18, 19, 20, 22, 23, 24, 25, and 27 (NAG).

In determining where and how many times the word "Lord," as noun or adjective, occurs in the section of 1 Cor 11 that he and GB have been examining, TS used the NAG.

Day 32

The Lord's Supper—Final Considerations

GB is mainly concerned with what the early Christians, on the one hand, and what the Reformers, on the other, thought of the Lord's Supper or the Eucharist. And why is it that such people thought differently to what TS seems to believe? Was TS simply trying to be different? What does GB himself really believe? What will he do about the Lord's Supper?

GB: Hi. I wish I could be absolutely certain that you're on the right track. My disillusionment with ceremonies as being the be-all and end-all encourages me to think that you might be. The fact that so many believers today hold a different view, however, pushes me a little in a different direction. It might help me if you could briefly outline for me the sort of things that early Christians said concerning the "Lord's Supper" or the "Eucharist," you know what I mean—remembrance occasions. I know you've already done a little of this.

TS: Sure. I've already mentioned the letter that Pliny, the Roman Governor of Bithynia, sent to the Emperor Trajan about the Christians getting together to have a meal. Pliny of course wasn't a Christian. And I've also referred to a document purportedly written by a Hippolytus of Rome where reference is made to the Lord's Supper. I've also cited a number of works that deal with "agape" meals.

GB: Yes. I was hoping you could add to this list.

TS: No problem. There's a piece written by Clement of Rome, about 80 CE, on the subject of what we could call "church order" and the roles of apostles, bishops and deacons. In it he refers to the Lord having ordered that "offerings and service . . . be performed . . . at the appointed times and hours." The context for this statement seems to be that of the sacrifices that the Lord God commanded be performed under the Mosaic Law. However some might believe that the reference is to Jesus commanding that a ceremony relating to his death should be observed on a regular basis. Then there's Ignatius of Antioch who, around 110 CE wrote about both the Eucharist and an agape meal. But, if I remember, I've also made some reference to what he said earlier as well.

GB: Yes, you did.

TS: What he wrote was very graphic—"I want the bread of God which is the flesh of Jesus Christ . . . and for drink I want his blood." Although we can't be certain, it could be that he thought that at the Eucharist or as the Eucharist, the actual flesh and blood of Christ was present in some sense. Around 155 CE a certain Justin of Caesarea wrote of the Eucharist that it was food but not "common" food and that this food, being blessed by prayer, enabling those who receive it to be nourished, was the flesh and blood of Jesus who was made flesh. This sounds even more like the idea that the bread and the wine had become the real flesh and blood of Jesus. He also stated that the apostles had passed on what Jesus had said to them, that is, that they had to do this in remembrance of him. I think I've already mentioned some of what Justin said before also.

GB: Yes, I'm pretty sure you did. I realize now that you've already made several references to what early Christians believed about these things.

TS: I'll try not to repeat myself too much. I'll also try to be brief.

GB: You're doing okay.

TS: Then there's Irenaeus of Lyons, who wrote around about 180. He held the view that the bread took on two realities, one heavenly and one earthly and that the person who partook of the Eucharist, the body of Christ, was nourished in his own body. He also wrote about the necessity of the Holy Spirit's presence in the Eucharist in order for forgiveness of sins and eternal life to be made available to those taking part. In *The Didache*—we don't really know when it was written, perhaps somewhere between the first and third centuries, as I think I've mentioned previously—there's a reference to the believer in the Eucharist receiving spiritual food and drink and this is connected with the receiving of eternal life. I think that in that work there are also indications that it was believed that in the Eucharist a sacrifice was being performed. And Tertullian of Carthage writing around 200 seems to have had such a view. It also seems, perhaps consistent with that notion that he believed that the actual body of Christ was present in the Eucharist but in what sense is difficult to tell.

GB: I'm getting the picture. Not one that I warm towards.

TS: Perhaps I'll only mention a few more. Clement of Alexandria, who wrote about the same time as Tertullian, while believing that the terms "flesh" and "blood" in John chapter 6 were metaphorical in character, seems to write rather mystically, in my mind, of the Word, by which I think he meant Jesus, being mixed with water in the

Eucharist, as the wine is mixed with water. He also made statements like, "drinking the blood of Jesus is partaking of the Lord's immortality." I could mention Cyprian of Carthage, writing around the middle of the third century and Minucius Felix, not sure when the work under his name should be dated—maybe somewhere between 160 and 300—and a few others. But I think I'll wind up with a brief reference to Augustine of Hippo writing late in the fourth century. Of course, there are relevant statements that were made in various councils beginning with the Council of Gangra spanning the years 325 and 381. But I won't go into those.

GB: I don't think you need to. But what of Augustine? I guess that what he said was probably fairly weighty.

TS: Well, the reformers seemed to think so. I'll just mention a few things. For starters, in one work of his he argued that in John chapter 6 the reference to the flesh and blood of Jesus was undoubtedly metaphorical. In another work he made a related statement in two different places, but with some variation, to the effect that when Jesus had the bread at the Last Passover Meal, he held in his own hand, himself. However, when he first mentioned this he qualified the statement by adding "after a manner." Then in another place he dealt with the problem of how the body of Christ can be present in the Eucharist when Christ is in heaven. He resolved the problem by explaining that the body of Christ is also the body of Christ understood as his people and that the bread that is made from many grains, and the wine that is made from many grapes, "represent"—my word—the many who are the members of Christ's body. Consequently he said that what people see when looking at the bread and the wine, is their "own mystery."

GB: How interesting! Do you think that some of those you've mentioned really believed that Jesus was *physically* present in the bread and the wine?

TS: I think it's very difficult to tell, though I'd like to say "No." or at least "Not many." It seems to me that people wanted to say that he was there but often they seem to have meant by that, that he was spiritually there. Some of them claimed that it was the Spirit who brought about that spiritual feature, if I can put it like that. However the truth is that people tended to write as though the bread was actually his body while being bread, and that the wine was actually his blood while being wine. I think that what was happening was that they were trying to repeat exactly what Jesus said, while still wrestling with the reality of the existence of the bread and the wine. And because it was a "wrestle" it meant it was a mystery. I think that some of the thought–forms they appealed to are foreign to our way of thinking and this in itself can make it difficult for us to understand exactly what they were saying. Sometimes I think that what they were saying wasn't too clear to them!

GB: Well, it hasn't been all that clear to me!

TS: Another thing. In some instances, when writing about the Eucharist, the emphasis by the author seems to be on the giving of thanks to God for the bread and wine as gifts rather than for the death of Jesus for the forgiveness of sins. Finally, though the rite or ceremony was almost certainly different and conducted differently in different places and at different times, it seems to have been quite formal in character. For example, generally, only those in leadership roles were allowed to preside over the Eucharistic ceremony.

GB: Were there any of those early Christians who thought that Jesus *hadn't* commanded that his followers partake in something like the Lord's Supper, reservations that we might have about what they practiced and believed, aside?

TS: I don't know that you could say that about any of them. Perhaps the earliest reference we have to the belief that Jesus did make such a command is that made by Clement of Rome, as I pointed out earlier. It may have been that from at least that time on early Christians thought that Jesus did issue such a command. You have to decide whether that sort of evidence should outweigh what you think the New Testament says or doesn't say.

GB: I understand. If the early Christians were muddled and certainly they seemed to get a number of things wrong, how come they got things so muddled? And how come the reformers didn't see the truth, as you've portrayed it? I suppose your answers might be much along the lines of what you said earlier in the context of baptism.

TS: Well, to put things very simply, I think that the early Christians did what we all like to do. We want to simplify the matter of righteousness and if we can latch onto something relatively simple, a ceremony or ceremonies, participation in which grants us spiritual benefits, we will do so. Having the ceremony mysterious and only able to be conducted by authorities also seems to help. I'm sorry if I'm speaking so forthrightly. And to make the matter one of necessity is all to the good. Necessity means obligation, and conformity to that obligation results in people feeling that they've achieved something.

GB: Don't worry. I know what it means to find satisfaction in performing ceremonies, provided that you perform them *correctly*!

TS: And as far as the reformers are concerned, we expect far too much from them. The battles they fought were extremely difficult. And they fought amongst themselves. And that didn't help their overall cause. The clarity with which they wished to see things was not easily gained and for various reasons. They appealed too much to what early Christians wrote. True, they did believe that the Scriptures had final authority. However, if they could find an early Christian writer that seemed to have similar views to theirs, that added support to their claims. If in addition they could refer to something that such a writer wrote that seemed to be in opposition to an opponent's view, then that was all to the good.

GB: Why did they resort to the writings of these people so much?

TS: As I've already indicated, finding any support always helped. But it was a bit more complex than that. Being in dispute with the established church, it could be argued, meant that they were coming up with something *entirely* new, something for which there was no precedence, that their interpretations of Scripture were *completely* novel. Appealing to what had been written by Christians earlier, people we refer to sometimes as the Early Fathers or the Church Fathers, could counteract such a charge. The same could be said for when they were in dispute with one another.

GB: What were the disagreements that they had with each other about, I mean in connection with what we've been discussing?

TS: Look, I'm no expert. I think there were a number of things. However, I gather that their disputes were mainly around what Jesus meant when he said, "This is my body" and "This is my blood." Consequently they disagreed over what the Eucharist or Lord's Supper was or should be about and what really happened when a person ate the bread and drank the wine. There were three main views. Broadly put, a Lutheran view was that although the bread and wine were not changed into the body and blood of Jesus they were still, in some real sense, the body and blood of Jesus. A view from people like the reformer Calvin was that Jesus was really there but not bodily, only spiritually. Another reformer, Zwingli—I mentioned him some time ago—and his followers considered that the bread and wine were purely symbolic. All that I've just said has been put too simplistically. However it was these sorts of differences that dominated the arguments they had with each other.

GB: And they found appealing to these Early Fathers was helpful?

TS: It was admitted that a text of Scripture like "This is my body," could be understood one way or another and if an appeal to an ancient authority could resolve the matter, why not try that approach. Unfortunately for the reformers while one of the Early Fathers might be seen to support a particular view or a particular interpretation of Scripture, another could be appealed to who didn't. Sometimes in defense of a position, different reformers at loggerheads with one another, appealed to the same writings, understanding them differently. One can imagine, as happened, one reformer referring to what Augustine had written, saying something like, "Augustine said, 'Christ held himself in his own hands'" with another saying, "No. Augustine said, 'Christ held himself in his own hands, after a manner.'" And in the end, for all the attempts by some reformers to present a united front, sharp divisions amongst them remained, particularly about the nature and significance of the Eucharist.

GB: Yet they did hold some things in common.

TS: Yes they did—some very important things such as the authority of Scripture. And we shouldn't be hard on them. Indeed we owe them a great deal. And would we have argued or behaved very differently given their circumstances? I think not.

GB: Did any of *them* think that Jesus had not issued a command that his followers partake in something like the Lord's Supper and on a regular basis?

TS: I don't think so. I don't know of anyone who expressed even a doubt. There might have been someone or other but I don't recall ever coming across such a person, though I only know a little, and I stress a *little*, about the ones who are well known. Again the issue for us is not what the reformers believed but what you think the New Testament says or doesn't say. Historically, we know that people get things wrong. The Galatians got things wrong and that was only a very short time after they had first heard the gospel. I think I've mentioned that before. It must have been near to impossible for the reformers to look dispassionately at the New Testament documents and consider them apart from the pressures of the debates in which they were engaged and apart from some of the influences of the cultural, philosophical and religious world into which they had been born.

GB: I understand. . . . Thanks for being patient with me and in effect going over some of those things you mentioned earlier. I appreciate that. In asking my questions about the early Christians and the reformers I pretty well knew the sort of things you were likely to say. I just wanted the reassurance that we were not coming up with something new for the sake of it being "new"—that they really did get things wrong and that we need to try and get them right.

TS: The hankering after something new is always a temptation. I hope I haven't fallen into it.

GB: I wondered about that but I don't think so. . . . Where to now? I mean in our "discussions" as you call them. In all honesty, I listen and make some occasional comments or raise the odd question. But you do most of the talking and rightly so.

TS: I know, but you prod me this way and that and I've always valued your remarks. . . . Well, over quite some time now we've looked at the subjects of baptism and the Lord's Supper. I think it might now be helpful to consider them in the light of the gospel, that is, as the New Testament understands the gospel.

GB: That sounds interesting, but we're not going to do that right now, are we? It's getting late.

TS: Of course not. What I've got in mind would take another couple of sessions, I think. In fact there might be some advantage in just reflecting with leisure on what we've covered up to this point. Actually, I don't know about you but I have a number of commitments over the next few weeks and I'm wondering if meeting again in a month's time would be too far away?

GB: No. The truth is I'd also appreciate a reasonable break. I have quite a bit of study to do before some exams and this term's teaching has become more demanding than I thought it would be. A month or so in the future would be fine.

The Lord's Supper—Final Considerations

TS: Right. I'll contact you in a few weeks' time and we can settle on a convenient date. All the best for your exams.

GB: Thanks.

PART 3: THE LORD'S SUPPER

EXPLANATORY NOTES: DAY 32

For a few writings and authors that give or are thought by some to give early perspectives on Christian meals, Agape meals or the Eucharist see—Pliny, *Epistolae*, X. 96.7 in *A New Eusebius*, 14—see also http://ancienthistory.about.com/library/bl/bl_text_plinyltrstrajan.htm, letter XCVII; *The Apostolic Tradition*, 22:1–3, 25:1–15, 26:1–3, 27:1–2, 28:1–6; Clement of Rome, *The First Epistle to the Corinthians*, 36.1, 40.1–5 in Richardson, *Early Christian Fathers*, 60, 62—see also http://www.newadvent.org/fathers/1010.htm, chapters 36, 40; Ignatius, *To the Smyrnaeans*, 7.1, 8.1–2—see http://www.newadvent.org/fathers/0109.htm, *To the Romans*, 7.3—see http://www.newadvent.org/fathers/0107.htm, *To the Philadelphians* 4.1—see http://www.newadvent.org/fathers/0108.htm, and *To the Ephesians*, 20.2—see http://www.newadvent.org/fathers/0104.htm, each in *Ignatius of Antioch* 238, 181, 197, and 95, respectively; Justin, *Apology 1*—see http://www.newadvet.org/fathers/01265.htm, chapters 65–67—see also Stevenson, *A New Eusebius*, 66–67 and Richardson, *Early Christian Fathers*, 287; Irenaeus, *Against Heresies*, Book IV, 17.5, 18.2, 18.4, 18.5, Book V. 2—see also Richardson, *Early Christian Fathers*, 387–88; Irenaeus, *Fragmenta deperditorum*, Fragment 36—see http://www.newadvent.org/fathers/0134.htm, 37; *The Didache*. http://www.newadvent.org/fathers/0714.htm—see also Stevenson, *A New Eusebius*, 127, 129, sections 9, 10, 14; Tertullian, *On the soldier's crown*, 3.3–4 in *A New Eusebius*, 183—see also http://www.newadvent.org/fathers/0304.htm, chapter 3; Tertullian, *Apologeticus*, XXXIX. 16–8 in *Tertullian Apology de Spectaculis*, 180–1—see also http://www.newadvent.org/fathers/0301.htm, chapter. 39; Tertullian, *De Resurrectione Mortuorum*, 8 in Evans, *Tertullian's Treatise on the Resurrection*, 27 see also http://www.newadvent.org/fathers/0316.htm; Tertullian, *De Oratione*, 6, 19 in Evans, *Tertullian's Tract on the Prayer*, 11, 25—see also http://www.newadvent.org/fathers/0322.htm, chapters. 6, 19; Clement of Alexandria, *Paedagogus*, Book I, chapter 6, Book II, chapters 1–2; Clement of Alexandria, *Miscellanies*, III. II. 10 in *Alexandrian Christianity*, 45; Origen, *Against Celsus*—see http://www.newadvent.org/fathers/0416.htm, Book I, chapter 1, Book VIII, chapter 33; Cyprian, Epistle 1, *To Donatius*, 16—see http://www.newadvent.org/fathers/050601.htm, 16; Cyprian, Epistle 62, *To Caecilius*, 14, 17—see http://www.newadvent.org/fathers/050662.htm, 14, 17; Minucius Felix, *Octavius*, chapter XXXI—see http://www.newadvent.org/fathers/0410.htm, chapter 31; Augustine, *Epistulae XXII*, *St Augustine Select Letters*, 45–6—see also http://www.newadvent.org/fathers/1102022.htm, chapter 1. 3; Augustine, *Confessions*, VI, II in, *St Augustine Confessions*, 269, 71—see also http://www.newadvent.org/fathers/110106.htm, Book 6, chapter 2; Augustine, *On Christian Doctrine* 3: 16: 24—see http://www.newadvent.org/fathers/12023.htm, Book 3, chapter 16; Augustine, *Exposition on Psalm 34*—see http://www.newadventure.org/fathers/1801034.htm; Augustine, *Sermon 272*—see http://www.earlychurchtexts.com/public/augustine_sermon_272_eucharist.htm;

Council of Gangra, Canon XI—see http://www.newadvent.org/fathers/3804.htm, Canon XI.

Chung-Kim in *Inventing Authority*, in reviewing debates among Luther, Zwingli, Calvin, Westphal, Hesshusen and others, finds references by them to numerous Church Fathers with Augustine being the main one. Others, whom she mentions as being referred to in the debates, and not referred to by TS, include, Ambrose, Athanasius, Basil, Chrysostom, Cyril, Hilary, Jerome and Theodoret. She argues that in their debates the reformers appealed to the Church Fathers for a variety of reasons but mainly either to support the position they espoused or to undermine an opponent's. She also argues that the reformers sometimes appealed to a Church Father with the idea in mind that his interpretation of a difficult text was likely to be correct, unless that interpretation was contrary to their view! A brief perusal of her work readily informs the reader of the main issues that engaged the reformers in their disputes with one another.

Reference to the contention over what Augustine said concerning Christ carrying himself in his own hands can be found in Chung-Kim, *Inventing Authority*, chapter 4, "Calvin and Westphal, Continued *Second Phase of the Debate* (1557–1558)," 75–98.

Author's Comments

A week after they had last met to discuss the "Lord's Supper" GB, in a phone call to TS, indicated that he had been a little worried that TS might not approve but that he had already decided to attend a service of the Lord's Supper. He had decided to do this even before the end of their discussions. In fact he had been to several such services. TS was a little embarrassed that GB was at all concerned. GB explained that he thought that the Lord's Supper services that he attended were thoroughly uplifting. The people at the services seemed to be very sincere but most importantly he thought that it was helpful for him to consciously consider afresh the significance of the death of Jesus for him and for all those who believed in him. He didn't see it as obeying a command that Jesus might have given and he did appreciate that perhaps Jesus had never issued such a command. Rather, he saw his taking part as being involved in a very meaningful ceremony. He explained to TS that of course he realized it was a ceremony symbolic of a meal and symbolic of the fellowship one had with other believers in the Lord Jesus.

TS was delighted that GB had made up his own mind during the course of their discussions and told GB that he had no problems with the decision GB had made. TS nonetheless indicated that he felt awkward that GB had been reluctant to tell him but glad that GB seemed to see things the way he did. However, he couldn't stop himself, towards the end of their conversation, saying something like—"As long as the ceremony is helpful, as long as it isn't misleading, as long as it doesn't claim for itself some historical precedence that's not warranted and as long as it isn't considered mandatory, then take part in the ceremony to the full." I could imagine a smile slowly appearing on GB's face!

TS concluded their conversation by asking if it was still okay for him and GB to continue their chats for just two or three sessions longer. He again explained that he thought it would be helpful to consider Baptism and the Lord's Supper in the light of the gospel as presented in the New Testament. GB said that he had every intention of meeting up with TS again and that he looked forward to the next meeting, very much so. They then agreed upon a date for their next meeting—about three weeks later.

PART 4

The Gospel and the Sacraments

Day 33

The Gospel in the New Testament

How are the Greek words "εὐαγγελιον" (euangelion) and "εὐαγγελιζομαι" (euangelizomai) used in the New Testament? Are the words used differently outside of the New Testament? These questions constitute the main component of the journey that TS travels today. From time to time GB wonders if where TS seems to be taking him relates to the subjects of baptism and the Lord's Supper. In the end he sees the connection, though in a way that recognizes that there isn't one.

TS: Good to see you again. And thanks for your phone call. How were the exams?

GB: They were okay.

TS: I suspect you've done better than you let on.

GB: I was happy enough with the results. Regarding that phone call, I felt I needed to tell you what I'd already decided to do before we met again. Perhaps I should've told you earlier. Anyway, today if you're adhering to your plan I take it we're going to be looking at the gospel as it's portrayed in the New Testament.

TS: Yes, that's the idea. We need to see how the gospel relates in any way to the practice of baptism and the celebration of the Lord's Supper. It's some time ago now but you'll probably remember how, when we first began chatting, we looked at Galatians and I made a comment that in that book there is a greater relative frequency of the noun "gospel" and the verb, often translated, "proclaiming the gospel," when considered together, than in any other book of the New Testament.

GB: I remember your saying something like that. I also recall how you said I should try and keep that letter in mind throughout our conversations. I must confess that I hardly gave it much thought once we really got into the subject of baptism and then the Lord's Supper. I think I'll still refer to that ceremony by that title, if you don't mind.

Part 4: The Gospel and the Sacraments

What we did required a fair bit of concentration on my behalf and after a while the Galatian letter just faded from my thinking.

TS: I must admit that the same happened to me as well. And yet I think that its message has always been relevant to our discussions. Remember how in one way or another, in that letter, Paul touched on observing special days, undergoing the rite of circumcision, and conforming to certain restrictive food laws. Remember how he indicated that the gospel meant that none of these restrictions or special observances were necessary. I know he didn't mention baptism or something like the Lord's Supper but one would've thought that the principle he was arguing for would've implied that they weren't absolutely necessary as well.

GB: Perhaps he didn't make any mention of the Lord's Supper because, if your view is correct, no such ceremony really existed at the time. Although for believing Jews, if they were to continue to celebrate *Passover*, even if they were now to celebrate it in a new way, the *Passover* would still be a ceremony in which they participated. He could've mentioned celebrating Passover I suppose. But baptism was around. Why wouldn't he have mentioned that, if what he said applied to baptism as well?

TS: I'm not sure. It might've been that it had become such a highly valued ceremony for believers, Jew and Gentile, that Paul didn't want to undermine its value or deny its significance by associating it with those other matters. Perhaps it never entered his head to mention it since the issues he was dealing with, in the main, had Old Testament roots—they came from the past—whereas baptism belonged to the new world of the proclamation of the gospel of the Lord Jesus Christ. At the same time however, he and others may never have seen it as a compulsory ceremony.

GB: Of course some might argue that he didn't make reference to it because it *was* a compulsory ceremony!

TS: Yes, undoubtedly. However I still think that to insist on it being mandatory goes against the main arguments that Paul used in that letter. Simply put, I think that the demand that any ceremony is obligatory is a demand contrary to the gospel. . . . Now I remember! We had a conversation just like the one we're having now, earlier, when we were looking at the Galatian letter some months ago!

GB: True. And I remember saying something about what my friends at church might or might not say!

TS: Yes. Well anyway, I think it would now help us in our thinking if we looked at the nature of the gospel as it's recorded in the pages of the New Testament. However, I think it would be too easy to get bogged down by referring to one passage or another and claiming that this or that was the gospel unless we restricted ourselves to those passages where the actual words used for the gospel and proclaiming the gospel occurred. Of course the gospel is referred to in various ways in the New Testament

The Gospel in the New Testament

without those actual words being used but examining passages where they do in fact occur will keep us on the straight and narrow. Besides, the words are used numerous times.

GB: I understand.

TS: Let's look at the noun "εὐαγγελιον" (*euangelion*)—gospel—to start with. First, a few statistics! The noun is found seventy five times in the New Testament with its greatest concentration being in Philippians and Galatians. It occurs in those letters nine and seven times respectively. In Philippians the bulk of the instances relate to the fellowship that Paul had with the believers in promoting the gospel. It also occurs nine times in Romans, eight times in each of the Corinthian letters, seven times in Mark and six times in 1 Thessalonians.

GB: I take it that it can also be found in the Greek literature external to the New Testament?

TS: Yes indeed! Using the *Thesaurus Linguae Graecae*, for the period sixth century BCE to the early part of the second century CE we can locate, in various forms, about forty five instances of either the neuter noun, "εὐαγγελιον" or its female equivalent, "εὐαγγελια" (*euangelia*). Sometimes it's difficult to know whether the plural neuter form of "εὐαγγελιον" which is "εὐαγγελια"—nominative or accusative case—or the singular female form, also "εὐαγγελια"—nominative case—is being used. We don't need to worry about that except to say that I think the ratio is about 3 to 1 plural neuter nouns to singular female nouns and one can normally tell the difference, with most of the female forms being found in the *Septuagint*. Oh, and I suppose I ought to point out that all instances where a plural form in any grammatical case is used, a single item seems to be in view. And it may be worthwhile knowing that about one half of the total references are found in works by Plutarch who lived during the first and second centuries CE.

GB: Does "εὐαγγελιον" or "εὐαγγελια," where either noun occurs in the literature external to the New Testament, mean something like "good news"?

TS: Yes, they both seem to have that sense. Often the good news is with respect to a battle being won, or an enemy having died. Understandably the good news is generally of a fairly specific nature. For example, and to cite a case were warfare and death is not involved, there's a reference to the good news being received that a brother of a certain Antiochus had been found safe and well.

GB: So translating "εὐαγγελιον" in the New Testament as "good news" is okay? Oh, and are there any examples of the female noun in the New Testament?

TS: No, the female noun is not found in the New Testament, nor are there any examples of "εὐαγγελιον" in a plural form. And yes, generally, I think that something like "good news" as a translation for "εὐαγγελιον" or one of its forms, where it occurs

323

in the New Testament, is appropriate. However, in a couple of instances—in chapter 2 of Romans and in chapter 14 of Revelation where the context is one of judgement—something like, "solemn news" may better portray the sense of what is intended.

GB: Okay, that's given me a general picture of things. . . . I suppose that the gospel in the New Testament is essentially about Jesus isn't it? It's got to be!

TS: Well yes you're right. But we need to keep in mind that in the New Testament there are various, what I might call "formulations" of the "εὐαγγελιον." True it has a primary focus on Jesus—especially his death and resurrection. That focus cannot be overestimated. The Gospels—big "G"—are all about Jesus. And there is that wonderful statement by Paul in 1 Corinthians chapter 15 where he reminds the Corinthians about the gospel he preached to them—that Christ died for our sins, that he was buried and that he was raised on the third day. However, the gospel has a breadth and depth not to be captured by any simple definition that we might like to produce. It is found in a variety of contexts and linked to a variety of issues. For example, it comes from God and is about him. It is proclaimed, it is announced. It is true and glorious. It relates to the great judgement day. When lived by, it results in both suffering and blessing. It is the substance of Paul's preaching.

GB: I see what you mean. Are there any references in the New Testament where "εὐαγγελιον" is not about Jesus?

TS: I think there are three such. There is one instance where "εὐαγγελιον" refers to a particular announcement made by an angel on a specific occasion. You can find it in Revelation. There are also a couple of references to what might be termed aberrations of the true gospel.

GB: So, unlike the instances we can find in the Greek literature external to the New Testament, where all sorts of situations are being referred to over an extensive time period, in the New Testament it almost always refers to something to do with Jesus, in one way or another. It has an almost singular focus. I wouldn't have thought otherwise.

TS: Yes. However, there is also another interesting difference between what we find in the New Testament and what can be gleaned from the Greek literature external to the New Testament. In the New Testament all but four of the seventy five instances are accompanied by the definite article. In two of the seventy five instances the definite article is also accompanied by the Greek word "τουτο"—the words together conveying the meaning of "this." In the Greek literature outside of the New Testament there are only three instances from the sample of forty five where the definite article appears. From the perspective of the New Testament, of all the "good news" events, ideas, situations and pronouncements in the world, there is this one and only supremely "good news" announcement from God.

GB: What about those four exceptions in the New Testament? Is there anything special to be learnt from them?

TS: In two of the examples, the actual reference is to "a different gospel"—aberrations of *the* gospel. One instance occurs in 2 Corinthians, chapter 11 and the other in Galatians chapter 1. In a third example the reference is to "an eternal gospel," one that could be understood as a particular gospel for a specific occasion other than the one that centers on Jesus Christ. I made reference to that text a few moments ago. It can be found in chapter fourteen of Revelation, as I said, and it's a gospel, proclaimed by an angel to all who live on the earth, declaring that the hour of God's judgement has come. The remaining example is found in verse 1 of Romans, chapter 1. I'm not sure in this case why there is no definite article. Perhaps it's for reasons of solemnity or maybe it's a consequence of the grammatical construction involved. The text has Paul identifying himself, in part, as an apostle set apart for, "εἰς" (*eis*), the gospel of God. One assumes that the definite article has to be part of the English translation, though it is absent in the Greek.

GB: Thanks for all that. . . . The fact that the definite article is almost always present in the New Testament but hardly ever there in the literature external to the New Testament has got to be significant. However, what exactly is the relevance of all that we've just been discussing, I call it, "discussing," for the issue of the sacraments, or if not considered as sacraments, the ordinances?

TS: My apology. I do get carried away and sometimes can't stop myself going into details that I realize are not particularly pertinent. What's significant is this—in all of the seventy five occurrences of the word "εὐαγγελιον," there is not a single reference to either baptism or, as we're calling it, the Lord's Supper. Of the seventy one instances where the reference is to *the* gospel one might have expected an indication, in at least one or two, that those ceremonies constituted *part* of that glorious gospel, if indeed they do amount to an aspect of that gospel.

GB: People say that one can't argue from what is not there. That is, it could be said that, in this case, baptism and the Lord's Supper might have been so obviously part of the gospel that they didn't need to be mentioned.

TS: As a counter to this idea, one is entitled to point out that here and there many of the features of the gospel could've been assumed, but the writers couldn't stop themselves from mentioning those aspects. The gospel relates to the truth of things. The gospel is wonderful. It's glorious. The gospel can bring suffering. And so on. How could they not spell out this and that about the gospel? Are we to believe then that these sacraments or ordinances *were* assumed by the writers of the New Testament but that they didn't rate high enough in their minds for even one explicit mention of either one of them to be made in connection with any of their references to the "εὐαγγελιον"? Maybe there were no such assumptions! Anyway, we haven't finished yet. There's the verb "εὐαγγελιζομαι" (*euangelizomai*), obviously related to the noun "εὐαγγελιον," a verb that is often translated, "proclaiming the gospel" or similar. We should now look at its usage both in and outside of the New Testament to complete the picture.

GB: In the New Testament is the verb really just a reference to "preaching" or "proclaiming the gospel"? From what you've said, that's the way the translators tend to handle it.

TS: Well, deciding how to translate "εὐαγγελίζομαι" in whatever grammatical form it's in, is not a simple matter. Sometimes the translation needs to contain the word, "gospel" or similar, but not always. The idea behind the verb is that of making an important announcement or even a great or grand announcement. And sometimes the context makes it abundantly clear that the gospel is in mind. The noun, "εὐαγγέλιον" itself might be present. One wouldn't need to have the word "gospel" twice in the translation! I might refer to this matter again later. Furthermore, as one might expect, there are Greek verbs other than "εὐαγγελίζομαι" that simply mean "proclaiming" or "announcing" or the like. So, one of the problems for the person reading an English translation, which might say something like "he preached the gospel" is knowing what the Greek was that gave rise to that translation. Was the noun "εὐαγγέλιον" there alongside of a verb, not "εὐαγγελίζομαι," but a verb meaning "proclaiming" or "announcing"? Was the verb "εὐαγγελίζομαι" there but unaccompanied by "εὐαγγέλιον"? Did the text contain both "εὐαγγέλιον" and "εὐαγγελίζομαι"?

GB: I get it. Anyway, what about some examples indicating how the verb is used in the New Testament and what it mainly refers to there, compared with how is it used in the Greek literature outside of the New Testament?

TS: You read my mind! And that's not difficult to do. An examination of the Greek literature apart from the New Testament, dated from the sixth century BCE up until the early part of the second century CE provides us with fifty five instances of "εὐαγγελίζομαι" and two instances of the verb "εὐαγγελίζω" (*euangelizō*). The latter is categorized as being in the active voice and the former as either passive or what is called middle voice. I made mention of "middle voice" some time back. Although some forms of the verb can be either middle or passive I think it's pretty easy to decide whether middle or passive voice is the case and middle voice predominates. Most of the instances can be located in either the *Septuagint*, the writings of Flavius Josephus, a Jewish historian, or the writings of Philo Judaeus, a Jewish philosopher.

GB: I still don't know much about "middle voice."

TS: Don't worry about that. As I said before, often a suitable translation treats the verb as though from our point of view it is active. Sometimes however, the translation needs to be in the passive voice.

GB: Okay. . . . Josephus and Philo wrote around the time of the New Testament didn't they?

TS: Yes. Josephus lived around the last two thirds of the first century CE and Philo lived from about 20 BCE to about 50 CE. But to continue! My own view is that when looking at the instances in the literature external to the New Testament, as a very general rule, "εὐαγγελίζομαι," in whatever grammatical form it's found, can simply be translated in terms of "making the announcement" or similar, where two conditions are met. Firstly there needs to be an explicit reference to what the announcement is about and secondly what is announced needs to be directly connected to the verb in that part of the text. As another very general rule, if an explicit reference to what is being announced is not mentioned, or if what is announced is not directly connected to the verb in that part of the text, then the translation needs to contain a reference to something like "good news." The fact is that in all of the fifty five examples found, the announcement is about something that was actually "good news," to some extent or another, from some person's point of view, whether or not a suitable translation contains words like "good news." But I must confess that these rules are indeed very general. I don't think it's an easy task for the translator to decide whether or not a reference to "good news" or similar is required.

GB: I think I know what you're saying but I'm not sure.

TS: Let me give you some examples. In the following, it's clear what is being announced. It's made explicit in the various situations—"They announced that it was the time to reap," "The blossoming of an almond tree indicates that there will be a plentiful supply of fruit," "The women declared to the men that they had seduced some Hebrews turning them from their God." In other texts, it seems appropriate to explicitly mention that it's actual "good news" that's being conveyed. Examples—"Are husbands (returning home from being away) eager to send good news about themselves to their wives (who are waiting for them to return)?" "I do not walk around the market place brightly rejoicing in the good luck of the others, holding out my right hand, and telling the glad tidings to anyone I think would announce what they hear yonder." "Good news should be announced quickly but bad slowly." "The Philistines sent Saul's armor to the land of the Philistines, sending glad tidings to their idols and to the people." In this latter set of examples, there is no mention, in direct association with the verb, of what is explicitly being said or intending to be said, but it's obviously "good news."

GB: The examples are helpful. Thanks. You say however that your rules are only very general rules. There are exceptions?

TS: Well, sometimes it's not clear whether reference should be made to "good news" or not. In the following, "good news" is part of the translation but I don't think such an inclusion is really necessary—"The good news that Gaius had made a complete recovery was announced by travellers," "Joshua announced the good news of the impending capture of the city," "You shall meet someone who will bring you good news that your asses are safe" and "A deserter brought good news to Vespasian concerning the disposition of the general's troops." "Announced good news" or "brought good news," for example, could be replaced simply by "announced," "declared" or "revealed." It's tricky!

GB: I notice that you have no examples where the word "preaching" or similar occurs.

TS: I didn't come across any instances where that would've been appropriate. Sometimes the news is of such a nature that one must be careful not to give too grand a sense to the announcement or whatever, by using a word such as "proclaiming" or even the word "announcing." In some cases the reference is probably to something as simple as "conveying the information." As originally used, say, centuries before the New Testament era, the verb may have conveyed the sense of a messenger delivering his news with considerable flourish or gravitas. I remember coming across the idea of this possibility somewhere or other.

GB: And in the New Testament? What's the situation there?

TS: "Εὐαγγελίζομαι" is found fifty two times in the New Testament and the active form, "εὐαγγελίζω" twice. The active form can be found in the chapters 10 and 14 of Revelation. "Εὐαγγελίζομαι" occurs fifteen times in the book of Acts, ten times in Luke, seven times in Galatians, six times in 1 Corinthians and three times or less in other books of the New Testament. And note, the greatest relative frequency, the greatest concentration, occurs in the letter of Paul to the Galatians! Perhaps of no great significance, but I'll mention it—when you compare the usage of "εὐαγγελίζομαι" in the New Testament with its usage in the Greek literature outside of the New Testament, the distribution of voices, moods and the number of instances of the verb forms occurring as infinitives or participles, is quite similar.

GB: However, this would make one think that the sort of comments you've made about the way "εὐαγγελίζομαι" could be translated in the Greek literature external to the New Testament could also apply to the way it could be translated in the New Testament itself.

TS: Yes, although remembering how the usage of the noun differed in those two sets of literature, one should be cautious.

GB: You're right. Are there any obvious differences?

TS: Well, for starters, in the New Testament there are four instances where "εὐαγγελίζομαι" is mentioned in close association with "εὐαγγέλιον" and on each of these occasions "εὐαγγέλιον" is delivered by "εὐαγγελίζομαι" Given that what is being announced is "good news," the verb itself doesn't need to be translated in such a way as to refer again to "good news." I mentioned that sort of phenomenon a moment ago. In each case, the verb is commonly translated simply by such as "preach," "proclaim," or "announce." The words "preach," "proclaim," "announce" and even "declare" tend to convey the idea of something "sober" or "grand" being brought to notice. There are another four instances where the verb is in relatively close association with the noun "εὐαγγέλιον." There are no examples in the Greek literature external to the New Testament where both noun and verb are found in close or reasonably close proximity.

GB: Does the difficulty of knowing whether or not one should include any reference to "good news" in the translation, arise in the New Testament?

TS: I think so and those very general rules that I mentioned earlier, in my mind, do come into play from time to time. In cases such as the following excerpts from the New Testament—"I was sent to announce these things to you," "They did not cease teaching and proclaiming Jesus the Christ," "We declare to you the promise made to the fathers," "the message I proclaimed to you," "I should proclaim him among the nations," "Timothy having declared to us your faith and love" and "the mystery of God announced to his servants the prophets," what is announced or proclaimed is made explicit. One doesn't need to refer to, "good news." In other cases, although there is no explicit reference to what is announced or proclaimed, again, the introduction of "good news" may be judged to be unnecessary depending upon what English verb is used. For example, when Jesus referred to the requirement for him to preach in other towns beyond Capernaum and when Paul wrote of his preaching to the Galatians in the weakness of the flesh, using the word, "preach" or "preaching" in these cases allows the translator to omit any reference to "good news."

GB: But are there instances where we *could* mention "good news"?

TS: Oh yes and particularly when it's very obvious that what is being proclaimed, announced or declared, *et cetera*, is indeed "good news." My impression is that the majority of cases fall into this category. Of the many examples one could give, the following are just a few—Jesus preaches good news to the poor, Jesus preaches the good news of the kingdom of God, Peter and John preach the good news to many Samaritan villages, Philip proclaims the good news about Jesus to the Ethiopian Eunuch and preaches the good news in many towns, Paul proclaims the good news to the Jews at Antioch concerning what God had promised, he declares he is ready to preach the good news where Christ has not already been named, his reward is that in preaching the good news he makes it free of charge, the writer of Hebrews refers to those who formerly had the good news announced to them but failed to enter because of disobedience and the writer of 1 Peter speaks of the prophets of times past and their involvement in the things which have now in their time been announced ("ἀναγγελω" [*anangelō*] is the verb used) to his readers by those who preached the good news to them through the Holy Spirit.

GB: But in some of those examples it would seem that the translator wouldn't *have* to use the words "good news" or similar.

TS: You're quite right. Perhaps translators should use more caution in introducing "good news." Using verbs such as "proclaiming," "preaching," "announcing," "declaring" or "revealing" could be sufficient. In certain contexts, using such words can also convey the sense of providing information in a grand or sober manner. You would've noticed that.

GB: I *notice* how you consistently use "good news." You wouldn't use the word, "gospel"?

TS: I was hoping to get to that point, or rather the possibility of using various words as alternatives to "good news." I've just tried to be consistent without raising that possibility until now.

GB: But "gospel" would be one possibility?

TS: Well, yes. Of course!

GB: I take it that the problem of what word to use applies to both the noun "εὐαγγελιον" and the verb "εὐαγγελιζομαι." And it's obvious that in the case of the verb the problem could be whether to introduce a noun alongside of the verb or not and what noun to choose.

TS: You're quite right. Perhaps I should've raised that issue when discussing the noun.

GB: No problem. You're trying to cover so much it's a wonder you keep track of where you're actually going!

TS: Sometimes I think I actually do lose my way! . . . Regarding alternative words to "good news," I think "great news" or "sober news" might sometimes be better. Additionally, as you've suggested, "gospel" might be okay as well. The thing about "gospel" is that in its origins it's simply a particular rendition of "good news" but used in a technical sense. Given that in the New Testament the noun "εὐαγγελιον" is almost always accompanied by the definite article, turning it into a pseudo–technical word, the English word, "gospel," is not at all inappropriate. It stands for "*the* good news" or "*the* great news" or "*the* sober news."

GB: Could you give me some examples where you think that "great news" or "sober news" would not be out of place when translating the verb?

TS: Sure—Jesus saying "I must proclaim the great news of the kingdom of God," Jesus "preaching (the verb "κηρυσσω" [*kērussō*] is used) and announcing the great news of the kingdom of God," and the angel Gabriel saying to Zechariah "I was sent to you to bring you this sober news"—the birth of his son, John. Using the words, "great," "sober" or similar, conveys something of the "*gravitas*" that seems to be associated with the situation. You can find each of these examples in Luke's Gospel. Another example in that Gospel, a very interesting one, relates to the preaching of John the Immerser. Having written that John spoke of the coming of the Messiah and his judgement, Luke then says "With many other exhortations he preached 'sobering news' to the people." To say he preached, "good news" seems quite inappropriate. Perhaps a reference to his simply preaching would have been adequate. All four texts have the verb "εὐαγγελιζομαι" in the absence of the noun "εὐαγγελιον."

GB: I noticed that one of the examples you gave of the use of "εὐαγγελιζομαι" was of Paul writing about Timothy "declaring" to him, Paul, certain people's faith and love.

This is obviously not a reference to declaring *the* gospel or even an aberration of the gospel. Are there many such examples?

TS: That's probably the only one, at least where only the verb is involved. The example I gave of the noun, "εὐαγγελιον" being used in a special sense—a "gospel" being announced as an "eternal gospel"—is one of those examples where both the noun and verb are in close association with one another. It's probably another example where proclaiming *the* gospel that centers on Jesus is not in view.

GB: Overall, however, I take it that the verb, like the noun, has Jesus as the main reference. Someone proclaims the gospel concerning Jesus.

TS: Yes, that's correct. What's clear, both within the New Testament and in the Greek literature external to the New Testament, is that a messenger, an "ἀγγελος" (*angelos*)—you can detect the relationship between a messenger, a message, and announcing a message—proclaims, announces or declares something of moment, something of importance. And, in the Greek literature outside of the New Testament it appears that the message of the messenger is always "good news," to some extent or another. The same is nearly always true in the New Testament. However, in the case of the New Testament it is fundamentally God's message concerning his Son that's being proclaimed and those who announce it, declare it, or proclaim it, do so simply as his messengers.

GB: A good reminder. . . . Again you've gone into considerable detail and again it's been an interesting trip. But what significance does it have for our consideration of the sacraments, or what some would only refer to as the ordinances? I think I can guess now, what you're going to say.

TS: If your guess is that of all the occasions when "εὐαγγελιζομαι" or "εὐαγγελιζω" are used in the New Testament, there is not a single statement that connects either of the verbs with either one of the sacraments or, if preferred, "ordinances," then your guess is close to being correct! There is however, one such statement. It occurs in that chapter 1 of 1 Corinthians where Paul says that God did not send him to baptize but to proclaim the gospel. In the New Testament there is that one connection between "εὐαγγελιζομαι" and baptism but the statement, in effect, disconnects them! The gospel is here. Baptism is way over there! And remember the book of the New Testament with the greatest relative frequency of the noun and verb taken together?

GB: Yes. Galatians! Galatians! And yes, I had forgotten about that particular text, though you did mention it. But it was some time ago now.

TS: And Galatians is the letter that speaks against any mandatory notion being attached to circumcision, special days and dietary regulations. And now, given what Galatians says and remember, it wasn't only Galatians, and how "the gospel" and "proclaiming the gospel" are used in the New Testament and that they are never associated in any positive way with the sacraments or if one prefers to call them, ordinances, does it really seem possible that for believers certain ceremonies are obligatory? That their observance is a necessary addition to confessing that Jesus Christ is Lord, to being a believer, to being led by the Spirit and to walking in the Spirit? That this is so because there were supposed commands given by Jesus to that effect? I know it sounds biased, but I think "supposed" is the right word!

GB: It doesn't really seem at all right does it? I was thinking the other night that it would be as though God said, "You are free from the Law but you now have to abide by two new laws. You must be baptized and you must celebrate the Lord's Supper. Being baptized replaces circumcision and celebrating the Lord's Supper replaces celebrating Passover." Some might also envisage God saying, "You must observe a special day, the first day of the week. That day replaces the seventh day of the week." For God to make such statements would seem to me to be very strange. However, I can imagine that even if some people had been privy to all our conversations throughout these months, many at this point would simply protest "But that there are no obligatory ceremonies or special days, *can't* be right." One thing they might say is, "The Israelites had to live under many regulations. There were special sacrifices to be made and special ceremonies, days and feasts to be observed. Why is it that we shouldn't have to abide by some regulations ourselves? Some regulations are good for us!"

TS: The life of a person taken captive in battle or the life of a prisoner in a jail is circumscribed by regulations. It can be no other way. As Paul put it in his letter to the Galatians "Before faith came, we were guarded under the Law, having been restrained until the faith that was planned beforehand should be revealed." But for those who are released from captivity, from imprisonment, there is freedom, wonderful freedom. The Law enforced by God upon the Israelites, if they were to be his people and he was to be their God, explicitly told them what they must do and what they must not do. And it wasn't only in terms of the observance of special feast days and the like. They were commanded to tell the truth in a court of law and not to commit adultery. They were commanded to leave some of their gleanings in their fields for the poor. Under the gospel of the kingdom, Jesus who came to fulfill the Law taught those of us who would be his disciples the absolute necessity of being trustworthy in *all* our dealings with each other, of not committing adultery even in our *thinking* and of assisting the poor in *all manner* of circumstances. Believers have been freed from a precise Law with its highly specific constraints, to live by the Spirit, under the unbounded law of loving God with everything we have and loving our neighbor as we love ourselves. In a very proper sense, there are regulations but they are bigger, bigger by far than the observance of ceremonies, even helpful ones.

GB: I must not forget Galatians. And I remember reading in the book of the prophet Hosea that God desires mercy and not sacrifice. Even in the Old Testament one can see what really counts coming to the surface.

TS: And those words from Hosea were quoted by Jesus at least a couple of times. And it wasn't just the prophet Hosea. The prophet Samuel made a similar statement. And other similar words are found in the Psalms, Proverbs and the book of the prophet Micah.

GB: I knew about Jesus quoting Hosea but not about those other references.... I admit that from time to time, as we've chatted, I've oscillated a little in my thinking but if what you've been saying is correct, and I think you really have persuaded me, the implications are enormous.

TS: From some points of view yes but for some individuals I don't think that what I've been arguing for would make much difference to the way they live or even think. But look at the time! It's been one of those very long sessions again.

GB: Don't worry I've been really interested, although occasionally I've wondered whether you've needed to go into as much detail as you did. But, as I've said before, I guess you are just trying to be thorough.

TS: Not all that thorough really. Well, maybe, though someone might say that I haven't been thorough enough! Could we leave our next session until after the weekend? Say, until Monday? Would Monday be okay? It shouldn't be a very long one. I just want us to consider what follows from what we've looked at today and the sort of conclusions I've been trying to drive towards.

GB: No problem. Monday would be fine. And as always, I'm looking forward to it. Please come for a meal at my place. Any time after 6 o'clock would be okay.

TS: Monday at 6.00 or thereabouts, it is!

Part 4: The Gospel and the Sacraments

EXPLANATORY NOTES: DAY 33

For examples of "εὐαγγελιον" in the literature outside of the New Testament see Plutarch, *Plutarch's Lives V*, Agesilaus, chapter 33, section 5, line 1, 92–93—the passage relates to the good news of an Arcadian victory, Plutarch, *Plutarch's Lives VII*, Demosthenes, chapter 22, section 2, line 2, 52–53—the Athenians proceeded to make thank offerings for the good news of Philip's death, and Plutarch, *Plutarch's Moralia III*, "Sayings of Kings and Commanders," section 184, line 5, 82–83—Antiochus offered sacrifices to the gods to celebrate the good news that his brother was safe.

"Εὐαγγελιον" in the context of judgement is found in Rom 2:16; Rev 14:6 (NAG).

The statement about the gospel that Paul said he preached to the Corinthians can be found in 1 Cor 15:1–8 (NIV).

To cite a few examples of the various aspects of the gospel referred to by TS see—Mark 1:1; Rom 15:19; 1 Cor 9:12, 15:1–4 (NIV)—it concerns Jesus; Mark 1:15; Acts 20:24; 2 Cor 11:7 (NIV)—it comes from God and is about God; Matt 4:23; 1 Thess 2:9 (NIV)—it is proclaimed and announced; 2 Thess 2:1; Gal 2:14 (NIV)—it is true; 2 Cor 4:4; 2 Tim 1:10 (NIV)—it is glorious; Rom 11:8 (NIV)—it relates to the great judgement day; Mark 10:29; Phlm 13 (NIV)—when lived by it results in both suffering and blessing; Gal 2:2; 2 Tim 2:8 (NIV)—it is the substance of Paul's preaching.

The one instance where "εὐαγγελιον" probably refers to a particular gospel for the one occasion can be found in Rev 14:6 (NAG) and the two instances where "εὐαγγελιον" refers to an aberration of the gospel are located in 2 Cor 11:4; Gal 1:6 (NAG).

The four instances in the New Testament where "εὐαγγελιον" appears without the definite article are found in Rom 1:1; 2 Cor 11:4; Gal 1:6; Rev 14:6 (NAG).

The three instances in the literature external to the New Testament where "εὐαγγελιον" appears with the definite article can be found in Plutarch, *Plutarch's Lives IX*, Demetrius, chapter 17, section 5, 1ine 8, 40–41, in Appian, *Appian's Roman History IV*, Book 3, chapter 13, section 93, line 12, 126–27, and in Appian, *Appian's Roman History IV*, Book 4, chapter 4, section 20, line 9, 172–73.

"Εὐαγγελιον" in one form or another can be located in the *LXX*, twenty times, in the writings of Flavius Josephus, thirteen times and in those of Philo Judaeus, twelve times.

The two instances in the literature external to the New Testament where "εὐαγγελιζω" occurs can be found in the *LXX*, 1 Kgs 31:9 and 3 Kgs 1:42.

"They announced that it was the time to reap." can be found in Philo Judaeus, *Philo I*, section 115, line 5, 92–93, "The blossoming of the almond tree indicates that there will be a plentiful supply of fruit." in Philo Judaeus, *Philo VI*, Book 2, section 186, line 3, 540–41, "The women declared to the men that they had seduced some Hebrews turning them from their God." in Philo Judaeus, *Philo VIII*, section 41, line 1, 188–89, "Are husbands (returning home from being away) eager to send good news about themselves to their wives (who are waiting for them to return)?" in Plutarch, *Plutarch's Moralia IV*, section B, line 6, 20–21, "I do not walk around the market place brightly rejoicing in the good luck of the others, holding out my right hand, and telling the glad tidings to anyone I think would announce what they hear yonder." in Demosthenes, *Demosthenes Orations, II*, section 323, line 3, 226–29, "Good news should be announced quickly but bad slowly." in Philo Judaeus, *Philo X*, section 99, line 6, 48–49, and "Philistines sending good news to their idols and to their people" in the *LXX*, 1 Kgs 31:9.

"The good news that Gaius had made a complete recovery was announced by travellers." can be found in Philo Judaeus, *Philo X*, section 18, line 4, 12–13, "Joshua announced the good news of the impending capture of the city." in Josephus, *Josephus V*, section 24, line 3, 12–13, "You shall meet someone who will bring you good news that your asses are safe." in Josephus, *Josephus V*, section 56, line 3, 194–95, "A deserter brought good news to Vespasian concerning the disposition of a general's troops." in Josephus, *Josephus II,* 143, line 1, 618–19.

Robinson in an unpublished paper considered that "εὐαγγελίζομαι" had its origins in the two words, "εὖ" (eu), an adverb meaning "well," and "ἀγγέλλω" (angelō) meaning "I report," "I bring news of" and the like. Hence the idea that originally "εὐαγγελίζομαι" was used of a herald or similar making an announcement with flourish.

Even though the number of New Testament instances of "εὐαγγελίζομαι" and "εὐαγγελίζω" and the number of those external to the New Testament that were examined were relatively small, the distribution of voices, moods and the number of instances of the verb forms occurring as infinitives or participles were quite similar. See Tables 8 and 9.

Voice/Source	Passive	Middle	Active	Total
New Testament	5	47	2	54
External to the New Testament	5	50	2	57

Table 8
Distribution of the passive, middle and active voice for the verb forms "εὐαγγελίζομαι" and "εὐαγγελίζω" in the New Testament (NAG) and external to the New Testament

PART 4: THE GOSPEL AND THE SACRAMENTS

Mood, Infinitive, Participle/ Source	Indicative	Imperative	Subjunctive	Optative	Infinitive	Participle	Total
New Testament	20	–	4	–	10	20	54
External to the New Testament	17	3	–	1	12	24	57

Table 9
Distribution of the indicative, imperative, subjunctive and optative moods, and occurrences as an infinitive or as a participle for the verb forms "εὐαγγελίζομαι" and "εὐαγγελίζω" in the New Testament (NAG) and external to the New Testament

The two instances of "εὐαγγελίζω" occurring in the New Testament are located in Rev 10:7, 14:6. In Rev 10:7 the verb is in the indicative mood and in Rev 14:6 it occurs as an infinitive (NAG). Outside of the New Testament this active form is found in *LXX*, 1 Kgs 31:9; 3 Kgs 1:42. It occurs as a participle in 1 Kgs and as an infinitive in 3 Kgs.

The four instances where "εὐαγγελίζομαι" is mentioned in close association with "εὐαγγέλιον" and where "εὐαγγέλιον" is delivered by "εὐαγγελίζομαι" are found in 1 Cor 15:1–2; 2 Cor 11:7; Gal 1:11; Rev 14:6 (NAG).

The four instances where the verb is in relatively close association with the noun "εὐαγγέλιον" are found in Rom 10:15–16; 1 Cor 9:18; Gal 1:6–8 (twice) (NAG).

The sentences or phrases, "I was sent to announce these things to you," "They did not cease teaching and proclaiming Jesus the Christ," "We declare to you the promise made to the fathers," "the message I proclaimed to you," "I should proclaim him among the nations," "Timothy having declared to us your faith and love" and "the mystery of God announced to his servants the prophets" are located in Luke 1:19; Acts 5:42, 13:32; 1 Cor 15:2; Gal 1:16; 1 Thess 3:6; Rev 10:7 (NIV) respectively.

Mention of Jesus referring to the requirement for him to preach in other towns beyond Capernaum is made in Luke 4:43 and the statement by Paul speaking of his preaching to the Galatians in the weakness of the flesh is made in Gal 4:13 (NIV).

The references to Jesus preaching good news to the poor can be found in Matt 11:5; Luke 4:18, 7:2 (NIV), his preaching the good news of the kingdom of God in Luke 16:16 (NIV), Peter and John preaching the good news to many Samaritan villages in Acts 8:25 (NIV), Philip proclaiming the good news about Jesus to the Ethiopian Eunuch and preaching the good news in many town in Acts 8:35, 40 (NIV), Paul proclaiming the good news to the Jews at Antioch concerning what God had promised in Acts 13:32 (NIV), Paul declaring he is ready to preach the good news where Christ has not already been named in Rom 15:29 (NIV), Paul's reward being that in preaching the good news he makes it free of charge in 1 Cor 9:18 (NIV), the writer of Hebrews referring to those who formerly had the good news announced to them failing to enter because of disobedience in Heb 4:2 (NIV), the writer of 1 Peter speaking of the prophets in times past and their involvement in the things which have now been announced (ἀναγγελω) (NAG) to his readers by those who preached the good news to them through the Holy Spirit in 1 Pet 1:12 (NIV).

The texts that TS suggests could have the words, "great news" or "sober news" rather than "good news" can be found in Luke 4:43, 8:1 (NIV)—great news—and Luke 1:19 (NIV)—sober news.

The passage in Luke's Gospel where he writes of John the Immerser preaching "good news" or rather "sober news" is located in Luke 3:18 (NIV).

The reference by GB to Timothy declaring to Paul the faith and love of others can be found in 1 Thess 3:6 (NIV).

The 1 Cor 1 text where Paul mentions "baptism," actually "baptize," in connection with "εὐαγγελίζομαι" is 1 Cor 1:17 (NAG).

Paul's statement to the Galatians—"Before faith came . . . " can be found in Gal 3:23 (NIV).

The references in the Law to not committing adultery and telling the truth in a court of law can be found, for example, in the Ten Commandments. The relevant commandments can be located in Exod 20:14, 16; Deut 5:18, 20 (NIV).

There is mention of certain gleanings being left for the poor in Lev 23:22 (NIV).

The statement by Jesus that he came to fulfill the Law (and the prophets) and his teaching that his disciples should be trustworthy in their dealings with one another and that they should not commit adultery in their minds can be found in Matt 5:17, 33–37 and 27–30 (NIV) respectively. The direction that Jesus, at a Pharisee's house, gave about whom to invite when having a special dinner, found in Luke 14:1 (NIV), and his advice to the rich young ruler about what to give to the poor, located in Luke 18:22 (NIV), are examples of Jesus indicating how his disciples should care for the poor.

The reference by GB to God desiring mercy and not sacrifice can be found in Hos 6:6 (NIV).

Quotes by Jesus of that Hosea passage can be found in Matt 9:13, 12:7 (NIV). The statement by Samuel somewhat along the lines of that in Hosea is located in 1 Sam 15:22 (NIV) and similar statements to that in Hosea can be found in Ps 40:6, 51:16–17; Prov 21:3; Mic 6:6–8 (NIV).

Day 34

Implications for the Proclamation of the Gospel

Over the months GB and TS have developed a warm affection for one another. That affection finds some expression in what they say to each other. This time, TS meets with GB—their last meeting—with four matters on his mind and pushes ahead with them as forthrightly as ever. GB, however, has the last word.

TS: Thanks for the meal. As usual, great! . . . This might be the last occasion that we spend together. Over many days we've dealt with what I think we can call, for simplicity's sake, "The Gospel, Freedom and the Sacraments."

GB: A pity. I mean, if this is our last occasion together. As I've indicated from time to time, I've really valued our chats and I hope that we might meet up with each other again, perhaps to discuss other subjects, or even just to have a meal. I'll be a little sad if this is the last time we get to talk to each other. I know it's really been more my listening to you rather than my contributing much by way of discussion, but it couldn't have been otherwise. And the whole thing has been very helpful—enlightening—and very stimulating. I came to you asking for help and I got it. Many, many thanks.

TS: Maybe some time in the future we could get together again perhaps to talk over something quite different. But today we're winding things up on the subject of baptism and the Lord's Supper. They are two very entrenched Christian customs. If there's any truth to what I've been arguing for then there are certain implications for Christian living and Christian outreach in particular.

GB: Just before we go there— those who believe that Jesus really did command, in some way or another, that we must participate in two or even more ceremonies or rites—what grounds do *you* think they have for believing this?

Implications for the Proclamation of the Gospel

TS: Well, they can appeal to the existence of the many regulations of the Old Testament. They can refer to the beliefs of the Early Fathers, no matter how much some of those beliefs seem to be foreign to the New Testament. They can point to what the reformers said or didn't say in spite of the differences that existed between them. We've touched on these matters. But I don't think they can build a case by appealing to the Scriptures as a whole or any text of the New Testament in particular. There is however one other avenue they could take but many so-called Christian people would be very reluctant to go down that track.

GB: And what's that?

TS: They could deny the trustworthiness of the Scriptures or claim, appealing to who knows what, that in the course of time God has revealed to us things that go beyond what the Scriptures say, even ideas that contradict the Scriptures. In the extreme, they could deny for example that Jesus rose again from the dead and that though he might have been an outstanding teacher and a person of high moral ideals he was only a man after all. They could claim that there are many things written in the Scriptures about him that are probably false—that much of what is written there was invented by some early Christians and their communities. They could even say that it didn't matter what *was* true, that even if the New Testament *didn't* say that Jesus issued these commands, simply claiming that he *did*, is good for the religious life, for the soul or something like that.

GB: But that would be ridiculous—essentially making up your religion to be what you wanted it to be.

TS: Yes. But as I said I don't think that many so-called Christians would want to do that.... Now, I was talking about implications. Let's return to firmer and saner ground. I said that if there is any truth to what I've been arguing for, then there are certain implications for how we live as Christians and in particular, Christian outreach.

GB: And what of the implications for denominational thinking, confessional statements, articles of belief? I'd have thought the implications for such are huge.

TS: To tell you the truth, I cannot envisage any changes at that level. Can you imagine, for example, any denomination that speaks of the administration of the sacraments as approaching or equal to or even surpassing the importance of directly preaching the word of the gospel, changing its mind? In fact, none of us easily give up any of our cherished beliefs and practices, whatever they might be, even if we have doubts as to their good standing before Scripture. And, in general, I think it's even more difficult if we're in a position of some authority within our denomination or group. And somewhat strangely, some of us don't even seem to be sensitive to the fact that amongst Christians, beliefs and practices associated with baptism and the Lord's Supper differ so enormously. You might have thought that awareness of those differences would've made us adhere less tightly to our own beliefs and practices concerning those ceremonies. Perhaps we've simply become very tolerant, being prepared to put up with the beliefs of others no matter what they might be. Perhaps many of us, tolerant or not, stubbornly envisage that we alone possess the truth, while still being very aware of these differences. I don't think there is any point in my discussing any further what I regard as the almost impossible. The various denominations are just not going to change their views, forget about "overnight"—"over centuries"!

GB: Is it hopeless then?

TS: Perhaps not entirely hopeless. What I'd like to happen, what I pray will happen, is that at least some *individuals*, perhaps people of no great importance within their denomination, will begin to question some of their beliefs about these customs. Maybe they could think again about what they do and why, when participating in these ceremonies. If they could see what the flow-on effect might be if these ceremonies, as valuable as they could be, were not understood as obligatory, even that might help.

GB: I remember on the first day when we started chatting that you quoted to me something in a letter of Paul's, a letter apparently written mainly with Gentiles in mind, Gentiles who only a short while earlier had become believers. You mentioned how he said that they had turned from idols to serve the living and true God. To give up their religious heritage—beliefs about the gods and behaviors dictated by those beliefs—to turn from what was the underpinning of their lives, must have been extraordinarily difficult. Yet they did so. The gospel that Paul preached and the way he preached it must have been very persuasive. They just didn't give up on the gods, they turned from those gods to serve the one and only true God. Why is it that we find it so difficult to change some of *our* understandings, some of *our* beliefs and we have the gospel to start with? I know we've raised and discussed this question before and more than once. I'm still somewhat puzzled about what I now think is our obstinacy.

TS: It's our humanity. I think we're obstinate in so many ways. We're all guilty. It's our sinful humanity. And we tend to be obstinate partly because we tend to be arrogant and partly because we wish to save face. It's arrogant to believe that we couldn't be wrong. We save face by not admitting to others or to ourselves that we were wrong. We all need to be willing to learn, to be willing to admit to error where appropriate and to change our views and behavior if necessary. Easy to say! Difficult to do! I think I must have said it earlier but I partly work, in particular thinking of myself, on the principle—"No one gets it all right!"

GB: I think you did say something along those lines, so many days ago. . . . You've been very gentle with me concerning the decisions I've made and why I've made them. You've been very supportive. And I've tried to be respectful of you. I've not asked you whether you've been baptized and to what extent or in what way you participate in a "Lord's Supper" type of ceremony if indeed you do. And I am not asking you for that sort of information now. But I do want to say that I'm grateful to you and for a

Implications for the Proclamation of the Gospel

number of reasons, chiefly, however, because you've tried to be biblical in the way you've argued. Others might not think so, but *I* think so. And to repeat your mantra, you've made it abundantly clear that whatever the custom or the ceremony people have in mind, they should make sure that it's helpful, not misleading, that a claim for Biblical precedence is not being made where that's difficult to justify and finally, that it's not seen as obligatory. Thank you for that advice.

TS: I don't quite know how to respond. As I've just said, no one gets it all right! But that doesn't mean we shouldn't try to get things right. That's all I've been attempting to do. And it's been a wonderful pleasure to work with you and to learn about you. I know I've mainly been, as it were, in the chair, but I couldn't help it. You were so willing to reflect and to raise questions. You have been so open-minded. I could never have asked for more. And, of course, I wanted to help and I thought I could. But back to the matter of the implications that flow from the conclusions that I've been pressing upon you—what would follow if these ceremonies were not obligatory and if we didn't treat them as obligatory?

GB: As usual, go for it!

TS: I've only a few things to say. Firstly, what the gospel is all about would be clearer. That's the main thing I want to point out. The gospel is all about God and his son, all that God has planned, all that God has done and all that he will do concerning himself and his Son. Of course it has to do with us—it has been announced to us and we are the sinners who need to repent and believe—but the proclamation of the gospel should in no way be muddied by reference to the importance of ceremonies, customs or rites. Unfortunately, that's what the outsider sometimes or even often, sees as fundamental to Christianity—what Christians do. Not he, the Lord Jesus, in whom Christians believe! When we make customs or ceremonies obligatory, we detract from the gospel. We actually operate in contradiction to the gospel. The gospel itself suffers. It does so because we build into the gospel, making part of the gospel, what is not there. And this has got to be bad news. Not good news. Let the gospel shine in all its glory, with no darkening or diminishing of its grandeur—the grandeur of the Son. Let there be no confusion about, with no detraction from, the reality of the character of God and all that he's accomplished, all that he is accomplishing and all that he will accomplish. As was obvious when we discussed things last Friday, the gospel words "εὐαγγελιον" and "εὐαγγελιζομαι," in the New Testament, have nothing to say about these ceremonies, except for one instance where the association is of a negative nature! The gospel in gospel proclamation could only be enhanced and not in any way diminished, if the idea that these customs were obligatory was completely off the table, forever.

GB: I'm not arguing against you but it comes to mind that on the day of Pentecost, Peter in proclaiming Christ, did say to the crowd listening to him "Repent and be baptized every one of you." I raised this with you some time ago now.

TS: I thought you might think of that text! But as I said before, I think the evidence is such that being baptized had become, as it were, "the badge of repentance" for those following John the Immerser and then for those following Jesus. When John began to baptize the idea that a person should immerse another was a novel one. However, by the Day of Pentecost, when Peter preached, the custom had become so-welled established and was so pointedly symbolic of the need to undergo radical change, that for him to say "be baptized" was not in any way unexpected.

GB: Yes I understand that. I think I just wanted to hear you say those things again.

TS: And now to the second thing I'd like to say. If we recognize that these customs, these precious ceremonies are not obligatory, we are less likely to be misguided about the essentials of *living* under the gospel. The emphasis, untrammeled with the idea of having to conform to certain regulatory procedures, would be on holy, righteous living—loving God with everything we have—upholding his name, pursuing his honor, seeking his glory—and loving our neighbors as we love ourselves—being generous with our money and our time, caring for the poor, befriending the lonely, supporting the widows, coming to the aid of the oppressed, nurturing the orphaned, encouraging the down-hearted, visiting the sick, comforting the sorrowing—all while rejoicing in the sure and certain hope of eternal life and enjoying the comfort, the peace and the freedom God has given and gives to us his children. We are so tempted to want to look to the observance of certain rituals as marks of our conformity to the will of God. Look to the Gospels, the Acts of the Apostles and the letters of the New Testament! See where the emphasis lies! We don't have to look closely. It's obvious!

GB: You don't have to convince *me*. Well, not now! As I've said before, I know what it's like to live under regulations and how deluding that can be. That sort of life characterizes my past through and through. I was trapped. I was blind. I was lost. I was stupid! How amazingly wonderful it is to be free, to live out a life by the grace of God in the power of his Holy Spirit, serving my Maker and my Savior!

TS: Yes, no need to convince you. Now to the third thing I'd like to say. It has to do with making decisions about customs and ceremonies in the light of the gospel that knows no obligatory customs or ceremonies. Customs and the like vary from society to society. Some are helpful. Some are not. And when we proclaim the gospel in a society we cannot ignore these customs. The gospel does not ignore them. Under the influence of the gospel, in the life of the believers, some of those customs will change, but not necessarily all. However, the believers will see even those customs that do not change or do not radically change, in a different light. They will now be recognized as indications of God's kindness towards them—customs that enable them to live in stable, enjoyable relationships with one another and in a healthy relationship with their Father's creation. Other customs, new ones, under the good hand of God, might be introduced into the special world of the believers—in God's church in that society.

Implications for the Proclamation of the Gospel

GB: Even baptism and something like the Lord's Supper!

TS: Yes, of course. If however, we recognize that the customs of being baptized and participating in the Lord's Supper, customs that we cherish, are not obligatory, then we have the freedom to be flexible as to how, when and if these customs could or should be introduced to any new group of Christians. Whatever we do, we would not say to any new believer "You must now adopt this custom" without any thought being given to the world in which they live. Whatever customs or ceremonies we would like to have introduced, I'll say these words again, they should be helpful and not misleading and claims about precedence that cannot be justified should not be made and they should not be seen as obligatory. Look, to give what I know is a very peculiar example—I don't know much about desert communities—consider the oddity of insisting that when members of such a community become Christians they must be baptized by full immersion, when in their world copious amounts of water are never available or if so, only very occasionally. In those circumstances what would such insistence say about the gospel? It would hugely distort it.

GB: Can I throw in another example, maybe also a peculiar one but not an impossible one? What if in a particular society, inviting someone to a so-called meal where only a piece of bread and a sip of wine was served, was regarded as one of the worst of insults to that person and that the custom most worthy of praise was to have, once a year, a splendid and huge feast but only with people with whom you were very close? One can imagine the new believers never having Holy Communion as we might, but instead having a great banquet once a year with each other, all of whom would now be in a close relationship with each other, all because of the relationship they had with the Lord. They might also go to one or other of the other feasts with their old friends, as well! Some members of that society might be a little startled by a new notion of "closeness" but they would see nothing insulting about people being invited to the believers' banquet itself.

TS: Our examples really relate to cutting-edge missionary endeavors but the principles are still the same no matter what the circumstances. Customs are simply customs and there is flexibility under the gospel to depart from, to modify, or to introduce, customs, but only in so far as they are in conformity with the gospel or not opposed to the gospel. But now to my final point! It really relates very much to the first—what the gospel is all about. It has to do with the nature of its uniqueness. See what it means to be able to say, "There are no obligatory ceremonies, customs, rites or mantras in the gospel." The gospel is God's word and action for human beings that he's created, human beings living in a world that he's created. It holds out a sure hope to an immoral and blind humanity that can do nothing to save itself. It speaks of the saving sacrificial death and the almighty powerful resurrection of the Son, whom God has made ruler over all things. It tells and warns of the certain judgement to come. It points to the work of the Holy Spirit in power bringing life and immortality to human beings—dying and dead in their sins. It makes clear that no ceremony, custom, rite or mantra will accomplish what God by his Holy Spirit achieves in those who come to bow the knee before him in submission, utter dependency and loving adoration. And to say, "No custom, no ceremony, no rite, no mantra is at all involved in *the* gospel" is to say what cannot be said for any other so-called gospel, whatever its origin, antiquity, number of adherents, so-called spirituality, its imagined depth of meaning, or the sincerity or zeal of its devotees.

GB: Wow. We need to make that uniqueness more obvious don't we? People must begin to see how extraordinarily different *the* gospel is from all other gospels! It should make them sit up and take notice!

TS: You know by now that I'm not at all opposed to people being baptized or people taking part in the Lord's Supper. To be baptized, particularly as an adult, must be a wonderful experience, making that public declaration that one has given away one's old life, and turned to a new life under the banner of the Lord Jesus. It must also be a very encouraging thing for those who have prayed for and tried to help the person being baptized. The ceremony can be a blessing in so many ways. And to take part with others in a meal, simple or otherwise, that has as its focus a remembrance of the death of Jesus can only be another blessing to all those who sincerely believe in him. It's just that they are ceremonies—they are customs. They are not obligatory rites.

GB: When it comes to baptism I don't think what you've argued for will affect ordinary believers, lay people, all that much, at least not if they've been baptized as infants. Their baptism is behind them and they weren't voluntary participants. But I've come across a few, mainly some older men and women whom I could imagine would think that what you've been saying about the Lord's Supper would take from them some of the preciousness with which they view that wonderful ceremony.

TS: I understand what you're saying. And let's not ignore an adult choosing to be baptized as an adult. If such a person views the ceremony as a sign of an absolutely radical reorientation of his or her life with a new but sharp and intense focus directed towards Christ Jesus in whom he or she places unswerving faith, claiming him as Lord, and has then soberly, freely and conscientiously, undergone the ceremony of baptism, what greater preciousness can there be? And if with respect to the Lord's Supper, believers center their attention on the extraordinary death of Jesus, the great cost involved and the unmerited grace displayed and not on their feelings when they participate, if they embrace the reality that that death unites all those who are in him, fellow believers, all equally sinners saved by that grace, and if they come to the ceremony freely, willingly and genuinely in devotion to him and not out of any sense of compunction, again, what greater preciousness can there be? Such preciousness relates to what the ceremonies point to not on some notion that they are obligatory.

GB: I wholeheartedly agree.

Implications for the Proclamation of the Gospel

TS: Anyway, no matter what we want out of a ceremony, I'm sure I've said it before, there's no satisfactory substitute for the truth. And for all the worth of our customs, we need to remember that it's far easier to take part in a religious ceremony than it is to love God with all of one's being and to love one's neighbor as oneself. Such love requires considerable rethinking of, and making considerable changes to, how we customarily live. All of us have customs and we believers need to reflect upon the customs that *we* have—I'm not now referring to baptism and the Lord's Supper—and recognize that we might need to change some of those customs and the perspectives associated with them. For example, there's the value we place on other believers and their gifts, our views of leadership, our understanding of what it means to teach and how we best learn and our ideas on how best to preach the gospel in our culture, in our society and to members of our society, having different backgrounds and coming from different perspectives. We mustn't let any of our customs dictate what we do, allow or don't allow, if those customs with their associated perspectives are or become unhelpful.

GB: You're giving me ideas for some future get-togethers! But here and now I want you to know I really do appreciate the significance of those four things you've just said—about the gospel itself, living under the gospel, making decisions about customs in the light of the gospel and the uniqueness of the gospel. I suppose one could collect them together under the heading of "Proclaiming the Gospel." It is the true gospel that must be proclaimed and what is proclaimed must truthfully indicate how believers are to live and the various ceremonies and customs they could adopt. And the gospel must be so proclaimed as to make it abundantly clear that it is the absolutely unique, great and awesome gospel of the Lord Jesus Christ.

TS: Amen! I think that with that injunction of yours, you have the final word!

Final Comment

I wish that TS and GB had been real people, that I had recorded their dialogue and that what is written in this book was a genuine reflection of what they had said. Alas, they are completely fictitious as is their dialogue. Yet they could have been real and their dialogue could have been much along the lines as reported because the arguments generated by TS and reacted to by GB are "real." What you think of the arguments however, is up to you, the reader. As TS said to GB "You have the final word." Well, while this world lasts and beyond this world, no word is really final, except for that which is uttered or approved of by God.

Bibliography

The Acts of John. See Ferguson, Everett. *Baptism in the Early Church.* Grand Rapids: Eerdmans, 2009.

The Acts of Paul and Thecla. See Ferguson, Everett. *Baptism in the Early Church.* Grand Rapids: Eerdmans, 2009. See also http://www.newadvent.org/fathers/0816.htm.

The Acts of Peter. See Ferguson, Everett. *Baptism in the Early Church.* Grand Rapids: Eerdmans, 2009. See also http://www.earlychristianwritings.com/text/actspeter.html.

Agassi, Joseph. *The Continuing Revolution: A History of Physics from the Greeks to Einstein.* New York: McGraw Hill, 1968.

The Apocalypse of Peter. See Ferguson, Everett. *Baptism in the Early Church.* Grand Rapids: Eerdmans, 2009. See also http://www.earlychristianwritings.com/text/apocalypsepeter-roberts.html.

The Apostolic Tradition. See http://www.bombaxo.com/hippolytus.html.

Appian. *Appian's Roman History IV. The Civil Wars Books 3.27–5.* Translated by Horace White. Cambridge: Harvard University Press, 1913.

Arnold, Jack L. *Reformation Men and Theology.* Lesson 10. See thirdmill.org/newfiles/jac_arnold/CH.Arnold.RMT.10.html.

Astrampsychus Oracula. See *Thesaurus Linguae Graecae.*

Athas, George. Sydney. Personal Communication.

Athenaeus. *II Athenaeus. The Learned Banqueters. Books III, 106e–V.* Edited and translated by S. Douglas Olson. Cambridge: Harvard University Press, 2006.

———. *IV Athenaeus. The Learned Banqueters. Books 8–10.420e.* Edited and translated by S. Douglas Olson. Cambridge: Harvard University Press, 2008.

———. *V Athenaeus. The Learned Banqueters. Books 10.420e–11.* Edited and translated by S. Douglas Olson. Cambridge: Harvard University Press, 2009.

———. *VII Athenaeus. The Learned Banqueters. Books 13.594b–14.* Edited and translated by S. Douglas Olson. Cambridge: Harvard University Press, 2011.

———. *VIII Athenaeus. The Learned Banqueters. Book 15. Indexes.* Edited and translated by S. Douglas Olson. Cambridge: Harvard University Press, 2012.

Augustine. *Confessions.* In *St Augustine Confessions.* Translated by William Watts. Cambridge: Harvard University Press, 1912. See also http://www.newadvent.org/fathers/110106.htm.

———. *Epistulae.* In *St Augustine Select Letters.* Translated by James H. Baxter. Cambridge: Harvard University Press, 1953. See also http://www.newadvent.org/fathers/1102022.htm.

———. *Exposition on Psalm 34.* See http://www.newadventure.org/fathers/1801034.htm.

———. *On Christian Doctrine.* See http://www.newadvent.org/fathers/12023.htm.

Bibliography

———. *Sermon 272.* See http://www.earlychurchtexts.com/public/augustine_sermon_272_eucharist.htm.
Barrett, C. K. *The First Epistle to the Corinthians.* Peabody: Hendrickson, 1968.
———. *Church, Ministry and Sacraments in the New Testament.* Exeter: Paternoster, 1985.
Bauckham, Richard J. *Jude, 2 Peter.* Word Biblical Commentary. 50 Waco: Word Books, 1983.
Blomberg, Craig L. *Contagious Holiness: Jesus' meals with sinners.* New Studies in Biblical Theology 19 Downers Grove: Intervarsity, 2005.
Bokser, B. M. *The Origins of the Seder: The Passover rite and Early Rabbinic Judaism.* Oakland: University of California, 1984.
Bolt, Peter. Sydney. Personal Communication.
Brenton, Lancelot, C. L. *The Septuagint with Apocrypha: Greek and English.* London: Samuel Bagster & Sons, 1851.
Bruce, F. F. *The Book of the Acts* (revised). Grand Rapids: Eerdmans, 1988.
Burkert, Walter. *Greek Religion.* Cambridge: Harvard University Press, 1985.
Carson, D. A. *Matthew.* Grand Rapids: Zondervan, 1984.
———. *The Gospel According to John.* Grand Rapids: Eerdmans, 1991.
Casey, Maurice. Nottingham. Personal Communication via Stephanie Fisher. Nottingham, and George Athas. Sydney.
Cheung, Alex T. *Idol Food in Corinth: Jewish background and Pauline legacy.* Sheffield: Sheffield, 1999.
Chrysostom, John. *epistulum i ad Corinthos.* See *Thesaurus Linguae Graecae.*
Chung-Kim, Esther. *Inventing Authority: The Use of the Church Fathers in Reformation Debates over the Eucharist.* Waco: Baylor University Press, 2011.
Clement of Alexandria. *Miscellanies.* In *Alexandrian Christianity.* Library of Christian Classics. II Edited by J. E. L. Oulton and Henry Chadwick. London: SCM, 1954.
———. *Paedagogus.* See http://www.newadvent.org/fathers/0209.htm.
Clement of Rome. *2 Clement.* See Ferguson, Everett. *Baptism in the Early Church.* Grand Rapids: Eerdmans, 2009.
———. *The First Epistle to the Corinthians.* In *Early Christian Fathers.* Library of Christian Classics. I Edited by Cyril C. Richardson. London: SCM, 1953. See also http://www.newadvent.org/fathers/1010.htm.
Conant, T. J. *The Meaning and Use of Baptizein.* Grand Rapids: Kregel, 1977.
Corley, K. E. *Private Women Public Meals: Social Conflict in the Synoptic Tradition.* Peabody: Hendrickson, 1993.
Council of Gangra. See http://www.newadvent.org/fathers/3804.htm.
Cyprian. *Epistle 1. To Donatius.* See http://www.newadvent.org/fathers/050601.htm.
———. *Epistle 62. To Caecilius.* See http://www.newadvent.org/fathers/050662.htm.
Demosthenes. *Demosthenes Orations II.* 18–19. *De Corona, De Falsa Legatione.* Translated by C. A. Vince and J. H. Vince. Cambridge: Harvard University Press, 1926.
The Didache. See http://www.newadvent.org/fathers/0714.htm.
Diodorus Siculus. *Diodorus Siculus. Library of History I. Books I-II 34.* Translated by C. H. Oldfather. Cambridge: Harvard University Press, 1933.
———. *Diodorus Siculus. Library of History II. Books II 35-IV 58.* Translated by C. H. Oldfather. Cambridge: Harvard University Press, 1935.
———. *Diodorus Siculus. Library of History III. Books IV 59-VIII.* Translated by C. H. Oldfather. Cambridge: Harvard University Press, 1939.

Bibliography

———. *Diodorus Siculus. Library of History VIII. Books XVI 66–XVII.* Translated by C. B. Welles. Cambridge: Harvard University Press, 1963.

Diogeneis Sinopensis Epistulae. See *Thesaurus Linguae Graecae.*

Duck, Ruth C. *Gender and the Name of God.* New York: The Pilgrim Press, 1991.

Dunn, James D. G. "Baptism." In *The Theology of Paul the Apostle*, 443–59. Grand Rapids: Eerdmans, 1998.

———. "The Birth of a Metaphor–Baptized in Spirit (Part I)." *Expository Times* LXXXIX 5 February (1978) 134–38.

———. "The Birth of a Metaphor–Baptized in Spirit (Part II)." *Expository Times* LXXXIX 6 March (1978) 173–75.

The Epistle of the Apostles. See http://www.earlychristianwritings.com/text/apostolorum.html.

The Epistle of Barnabas. See Ferguson, Everett. *Baptism in the Early Church.* Grand Rapids: Eerdmans, 2009.

Eusebius, *Ecclesiastical History.* In *A New Eusebius.* Edited by J. Stevenson. London: SPCK, 1965. See also http://www.newadvent.org/fathers/250105.htm.

Ferguson, Everett. *Baptism in the Early Church.* Grand Rapids: Eerdmans, 2009.

Fotopoulos, J. *Food Offered to Idols in Roman Corinth.* Wissenschaftlichte Untersuchungen zum Neuen Testament 2 Reihe Tübingen: Mohr Siebeck, 2003.

Garland, David E. *1 Corinthians.* Grand Rapids: Baker 2003.

The Gospel of Nicodemus. See Ferguson, Everett. *Baptism in the Early Church.* Grand Rapids: Eerdmans, 2009.

Grimm, Harold J. *The Reformation Era.* New York: Macmillan, 1954.

Grosheide, F. W. *Commentary on the First Epistle to the Corinthians.* Grand Rapids: Eerdmans, 1953.

Hero. *Pneumatica.* See *Thesaurus Linguae Graecae.* See also *The Pneumatics of Hero of Alexandria.* Translated by J. G. Greenwood and edited by Bennet Woodcroft. London: Macdonald, 1971.

Ignatius. *To the Ephesians.* In *Ignatius of Antioch: A commentary on the letters of Ignatius of Antioch.* Hermeneia: a critical and historical commentary on the Bible. Edited by William R. Schoedel. Philadelphia: Fortress, 1985. 33–100. See also www.newadvent.org/fathers/0104.htm.

———. *To the Magnesians.* In *Ignatius of Antioch: A commentary on the letters of Ignatius of Antioch.* Hermeneia: a critical and historical commentary on the Bible. Edited by William R. Schoedel. Philadelphia: Fortress, 1985. 101–33. See also http://www.newadvent.org/fathers/0105.htm.

———. *To the Philadelphians.* In *Ignatius of Antioch: A commentary on the letters of Ignatius of Antioch.* Hermeneia: a critical and historical commentary on the Bible. Edited by William R. Schoedel. Philadelphia: Fortress, 1985. 193–215. See also http://www.newadvent.org/fathers/0108.htm.

———. *To the Romans.* In *Ignatius of Antioch: A commentary on the letters of Ignatius of Antioch.* Hermeneia: a critical and historical commentary on the Bible. Edited by William R. Schoedel. Philadelphia: Fortress, 1985. 163–91. See http://www.newadvent.org/fathers/0107.htm.

———. *To the Smyrnaeans.* In *Ignatius of Antioch: A commentary on the letters of Ignatius of Antioch.* Hermeneia: a critical and historical commentary on the Bible. Edited by William

R. Schoedel. Philadelphia: Fortress, 1985. 217–53. See also http://www.newadvent.org/fathers/0109.htm.

Irenaeus. *Against Heresies*. See http://www.newadvent.org/fathers/0103.htm.

———. *The Demonstration of the Apostolic Preaching*. See Ferguson, Everett. *Baptism in the Early Church*. Grand Rapids: Eerdmans, 2009.

———. *Fragment 34*. See Ferguson, Everett. *Baptism in the Early Church*. Grand Rapids: Eerdmans, 2009. See also http://www.newadvent.org/fathers/0134.htm.

———. *Fragmenta deperditorum, Fragment 36*. See *Thesaurus Linguae Graecae*. See also http://www.newadvent.org/fathers/0134.htm.

Jeremias, Joachim. *The Eucharistic Words of Jesus*. Study edition. London: SCM, 1966.

The Jerusalem Bible. London: Darton, Longman, and Todd, 1966.

Joseph and Aseneth. See http://archive.org/stream/josephasenathcon00broo/josephasenathcon00broo_djvu.txt.

Josephus. *Josephus II. The Jewish War. Books I–III*. Translated by H. St. J. Thackeray. Cambridge: Harvard University Press, 1927.

———. *Josephus III. The Jewish War. Books IV–VII*. Translated by H. St. J. Thackeray. Cambridge: Harvard University Press, 1928.

———. *Josephus V Jewish Antiquities. Books V–VIII*. Translated by H. St. J. Thackeray and Ralph Marcus. Cambridge: Harvard University Press, 1934.

———. *Josephus VI. Jewish Antiquities. Books IX–XI*. Translated by Ralph Marcus. Cambridge: Harvard University Press, 1937.

———. *Josephus IX. Jewish Antiquities. Books XVIII–XX. Index*. Translated by Louis H. Feldman. Cambridge: Harvard University Press, 1965.

Judge, E. A. *The First Christians in the Roman World*. Augustan and New Testament Essays. Edited by James R. Harrison. Tubingen: Mohr Siebeck, 2008.

———. *The Social Pattern of Christian Groups in the First Century*. London: Tyndale, 1960.

———. Sydney. Personal Communication.

Justin. *Apology 1*. See http://www.newadvent.org/fathers/0126.htm.

Kew, C. *Closer Communion: The Sacraments in Scripture and History*. London: Salvationist, 1980.

Knox, David Broughton. *D. Broughton Knox Selected Works: Church and Ministry*. 2 Edited by Kirsten Renee Birkett. Kingsford Sydney: Matthias Media, 2003.

Knox, Ronald. *The Knox Translation of the Bible*. Second edition. Cambridge: Cambridge University Press, 1956.

Layton, P. *The Sacraments and the Bible: Measuring the Salvationist viewpoint alongside Scripture*. London: Shield, 2007.

Liber Jubilaearum. Fragment. See *Thesaurus Linguae Graecae*.

Liddell, H. G. and Scott, R. eds. *An Intermediate Greek-English Lexicon*. London: Oxford University Press, 1889, founded upon the seventh edition of *Liddell and Scott's Greek-English Lexicon*.

LXX. In Brenton, Lancelot, C. L. *The Septuagint with Apocrypha: Greek and English*. Originally—London: Bagster & Sons, 1851. Peabody: Hendrickson, 1986.

MacCulloch, Diarmaid. *Reformation: Europe's House Divided 1490–1700*. London: Penguin, 2003.

McGrath, Alister E. *Reformation Thought: An Introduction*. Third edition, Oxford: Blackwell, 1999.

Bibliography

Mandelkern, Solomon. *Veteris Testamenti Concordantiae Hebraicae Atque Chaldicae.* Edited by F. Margolini and M. Gottsteinii, Tel Aviv: Schocken, 1971.

Marcus Martialis. *Martial Epigrams. I.* Edited and translated by D. R. Shackleton Bailey. Cambridge: Harvard University Press, 1993.

May, George. "The Lord's Supper: Ritual or Relationship? Making a Meal of it in Corinth Part 1: Meals in the Gospels and Acts." *Reformed Theological Review* 60 3 December (2001) 138–50.

———. "The Lord's Supper: Ritual or Relationship? Making a Meal of it in Corinth Part 2: Meals at Corinth." *Reformed Theological Review* 61 1 April (2002) 1–18.

———. Sydney. Personal Communication.

Menander. *Menander III. Samia, Sykyonioi, Synaristosai, Phasma, Unidentified Fragments.* Edited and translated by W. G. Arnott. Cambridge: Harvard University Press, 2000.

Minucius Felix. *Octavius.* See http://www.newadvent.org/fathers/0410.htm.

M'Neile, Hugh. *Baptism doth save: a letter to the Right Rev the Lord Bishop of Exeter.* 1851. See https://archive.org/stream/a622218600mcneuoft/a622218600mcneuoft_djvu.txt.

Moore, Richard. *The Complete Notes of the Doway Bible and Rhemish Testament.* Dublin: Tims 1837.

Moulton, F. W. and A. S. Geden. *A Concordance to the Greek Testament.* Fourth edition Edinburgh: T. & T. Clark, 1963.

Moulton, J. H. and G. Milligan. *The Vocabulary of the Greek New Testament.* London: Hodder and Stoughton, 1930.

Murphy-O'Connor, Jerome. "Baptized for the Dead" (1 Cor. xv, 29) A Corinthian Slogan." *Revue Biblique* 88 (1981) 532–43.

———. *St Paul's Corinth: Texts and Archaeology.* Good News Studies 6 Wilmington: Glazier, 1983.

Nestle-Aland. *Greek-English New Testament.* Ninth revised edition. Stuttgart: Deutsche Bibelgesellschaft, 2001.

The New Jerusalem Bible. London: Darton, Longman and Todd, 1985.

Origen. *Against Celsus.* See http://www.newadvent.org/fathers/0416.htm.

———. *Homilae in Jeremiam.* See *Thesaurus Linguae Graecae.*

Peterson, David G. *The Acts of the Apostles.* Grand Rapids: Eerdmans, 2009.

Philo Judaeus. *De Vita Contemplativa.* See Blomberg, Craig L., *Contagious Holiness: Jesus' meals with sinners.* New Studies in Biblical Theology 19 Downers Grove: Intervarsity, 2005. See also http://humweb.ucsc.edu/gweltaz/courses/history/hist_5B/Lectures/therapeutae.pdf.

———. *Philo I.* Translated by F. H. Colson and G. H. Whitaker. Cambridge: Harvard University Press, 1929.

———. *Philo VI.* Translated by F. H. Colson. Cambridge: Harvard University Press, 1935.

———. *Philo VIII.* Translated by F. H. Colson. Cambridge: Harvard University Press, 1939.

———. *Philo X.* Translated by F. H. Colson. Cambridge: Harvard University Press, 1962.

Phua, R. L. -S. *Idolatry and Authority, A study of 1 Corinthians 8.1—11.1 in the Light of the Jewish Diaspora.* Library of New Testament Studies 299. Edited by M. Goodacre. London: T. & T. Clark, 2005.

Pindar. *Pindar, Olympians Odes, Pythinian Odes.* Translated by William H. Race. Cambridge: Harvard University Press, 1997.

Plato. *Plato II. Laches. Protagoras. Meno. Euthydemus.* Translated by W. R. M. Lamb. Cambridge: Harvard University Press, 1924.

Bibliography

———. *Plato III Lysis. Symposium. Gorgias.* Translated by W. R. M. Lamb. Cambridge: Harvard University Press, 1925.

———. *Plato IV Cratylus, Parmenides, Greater Hippias, Lesser Hippias.* Translated by Harold N. Fowler. Cambridge: Harvard University Press, 1926.

———. *Plato The Republic.* Translated by H. D. P. Lee. Harmondsworth: Penguin, 1955.

Pliny. *Epistolae.* In *A New Eusebius.* Edited by J. Stevenson. London: SPCK, 1965. See also http://ancienthistory.about.com/library/bl/bl_text_plinyltrstrajan.htm.

Plutarch. *Plutarch Lives I. Theseus and Romulus, Lycurgus and Numa, Solon and Publicola.* Translated by Bernadotte Perrin. Cambridge: Harvard University Press, 1914.

———. *Plutarch's Lives V. Agesilaus and Pompey. Pelopidas and Marcellus.* Translated by Bernadotte Perrin. Cambridge: Harvard University Press, 1917.

———. *Plutarch's Lives VII. Demosthenes and Cicero. Alexander and Caesar.* Translated by Bernadotte Perrin. Cambridge: Harvard University Press, 1919.

———. *Plutarch's Lives IX. Demetrius and Antony Pyrrhus and Gaius Marius.* Translated by Bernadotte Perrin. Cambridge: Harvard University, 1920.

———. *Plutarch's Moralia II.* Translated by Frank Cole Babbitt. Cambridge: Harvard University Press, 1961.

———. *Plutarch's Moralia III.* Translated by Frank Cole Babbitt. Cambridge: Harvard University Press, 1931.

———. *Plutarch's Moralia IV.* Translated by Frank Cole Babbitt. Cambridge: Harvard University Press, 1936.

———. *Plutarch's Moralia VIII.* Translated by P. A. Clement and H. B. Hoffleit. Cambridge: Harvard University Press, 1969.

———. *Plutarch's Moralia IX.* Translated by Edwin L. Minar, Jr., F. H. Sandbach, and W. C. Helmbold. Cambridge: Harvard University Press, 1969.

———. *Plutarch's Moralia XII.* Translated by Harold Cherniss and William C. Helmbold. Cambridge: Harvard University Press, 1968.

Polanyi, Michael. "The Growth of Science in Society." *Minerva* 5 4 (1967) 533–45.

———. "The Republic of Science." *Minerva* 1 1 (1962) 54–73.

Polybius. *Polybius I. The Histories, Book I–II.* Translated by W. R. Paton. Cambridge: Harvard University Press, 2010.

———. *Polybius VI. The Histories, Books 28–39. Fragments.* Translated by W. R. Paton and revised by F. W. Walbank and Christian Habicht. Fragments edited and translated by S. Douglas Olson. Cambridge: Harvard University Press, 2012.

Richardson, Cyril, C., ed. *Early Christian Fathers.* Library of Christian Classics. I London: SCM, 1953.

Robinson, D. W. B. "The Doctrine of Baptism." *The Churchman* LXXVI 2 (1962) 83–89.

———. "Towards a definition of baptism." *The Reformed Theological Review* xxxiv 1 January–April (1975) 1–15.

———. Sydney. Unpublished Paper.

The Rule of the Congregation. See Blomberg, Craig L. *Contagious Holiness: Jesus' meals with sinners.* New Studies in Biblical Theology 19 Downers Grove: Intervarsity, 2005. See also https://www.bc.edu/dam/files/research_sites/cjl/sites/partners/cbaa_seminar/qumran.htm.

The Shepherd of Hermas. See Ferguson, Everett. *Baptism in the Early Church.* Grand Rapids: Eerdmans, 2009. See also http://www.newadvent.org/fathers/02011.htm.

Bibliography

Sirach. *Book of Wisdom*. See Blomberg, Craig L. *Contagious Holiness: Jesus' meals with sinners*. New Studies in Biblical Theology 19 Downers Grove: Intervarsity, 2005. See also http://st-takla.org/pub_Deuterocanon/Deuterocanon-Apocrypha_El-Asfar_El-Kanoneya_El-Tanya__5-Wisdon-of-Joshua-Son-of-Sirach.html.

Smith, D. E. *From Symposium to Eucharist: The Banquet in the Early Christian World*. Minneapolis: Fortress, 2003.

Soranus. *Gynaeciorum*. See *Thesaurus Linguae Graecae*. See also *Soranus' Gynecology*. Translated by Owsei Temkin. Baltimore: John Hopkins University, 1991.

Stephenson, J., ed. *A New Eusebius*. London: SPCK, 1965.

Strabo. *The Geography of Strabo III Books VI and VII*. Translated by Horace L. Jones. Cambridge: Harvard University Press, 1924.

———. *The Geography of Strabo V Books X–XII*. Translated by Horace L. Jones. Cambridge: Harvard University Press, 1928.

———. *The Geography of Strabo VI Books XIII and XIV*. Translated by Horace L. Jones. Cambridge: Harvard University Press, 1929.

Strack, H. L. and P. Billerbeck. *Kommentar zum Neuen Testament aus Talmud und Midrasch IV* Munich 1928.

Synod of Antioch. See http://www.newadvent.org/fathers/3805.htm.

Synod of Hippo. See http://www.cristoraul.com/readinghall/Western-Civilization-Jewels/HEFELE/Book-8/109.html.

Tertullian. *Apologeticus*. In *Tertullian: Apology de Spectaculis. Minucius Felix: Octavius*. Translated by T. R. Glover, and Gerald H. Rendall. Cambridge: Harvard University Press, 1931. See also http://www.newadvent.org/fathers/0301.htm.

———. *De Oratione*. In Evans, Ernest, ed. *Tertullian's Tract on the Prayer*. London: SPCK, 1953. See also http://www.newadvent.org/fathers/0322.htm.

———. *De Resurrectione Mortuorum*. In Evans, Ernest, ed. *Tertullian's Treatise on the Resurrection*. London: SPCK, 1960. See also http://www.newadvent.org/fathers/0316.htm.

———. *On Baptism*. In Ferguson, Everett. *Baptism in the Early Church*. Grand Rapids: Eerdmans, 2009. See also http://www.newadvent.org/fathers/0321.htm.

———. *On the soldier's crown*. In *A New Eusebius*. Edited by J. Stevenson. London: SPCK, 1965. See also http://www.newadvent.org/fathers/0304.htm.

Theophrastus. *Fragment* 122. See *Thesaurus Linguae Graecae*. See also *Athenaeus. V Athenaeus. The Learned Banqueters. Books 10.420e–11*. Edited and translated by S. Douglas Olson. Cambridge: Harvard University Press, 2009.

Thesaurus Linguae Graecae. Irvine: University of California, 2007.

Tobit. *The Book of Tobit*. See Blomberg, Craig L., *Contagious Holiness: Jesus' meals with sinners*. New Studies in Biblical Theology 19 Downers Grove: Intervarsity, 2005. See also http://st-takla.org/pub_Deuterocanon/Deuterocanon-Apocrypha_El-Asfar_El-Kanoneya_El-Tanya__1-Tobit.html.

Tomson, P. J. *Paul and the Jewish Law: Halakha in the Letters of the Apostle to the Gentiles*. Compendia Rerum Iudaicarum ad Novum Testamentum. Section III Jewish Traditions in Early Christian Literature 1 Van Gorum Assen/Maastricht. Minneapolis: Fortress, 1990.

Trullian Council. See http://www.ccel.org/ccel/schaff/npnf214.xiv.iii.lxxv.html.

Tyndale. 1 Corinthians. See http://wesley.nnu.edu/biblical_studies/tyndale/1co.txt.

Bibliography

Unknown Author. *The War Cry* 28 February (1987). See http://www.waterbeachsalvationarmy.org.uk/what-to-know-more/why-does-the-salvation-army-not-baptise-or-hold-communion/.

Whitaker, E. C. "The History of the Baptismal Formula." *Journal of Ecclesiastical History* 16 April (1965) 1–12.

White, J. R. "Baptized on Account of the Dead: The Meaning of 1 Corinthians 15:29 in Its Context." *Journal of Biblical Literature* 116 (1997) 487–99.

Woodbridge, John D. and Frank A. James III. *Church History 2: From Pre-Reformation to the Present Day*. Grand Rapids: Zondervan, 2013.

Woodhouse, J. W. "What is this meal?" *Briefing* 123 October (1993) 2–6.

———. "The Body of the Lord." *Briefing* 124 November (1993) 2–5.

Wright, N. T. *Paul and the Faithfulness of God*. Minneapolis: Fortress Press, 2013.

Wycliffe, J. 1 Corinthians. *The Wycliffe Bible*. See http://wesley.nnu.edu/biblical_studies/wycliffe/1co.txt.

———. "On the Eucharist." In *Advocates of Reform: From Wyclif to Erasmus*. Library of Christian Classics. XIV Edited by M. Spinka. London: SCM, 1953.

Vitae Aesopi. *Vita Pl vel Accursiana*. See *Thesaurus Linguae Graecae*.

Xenophon. *Xenophon VI Cyropaedia II*. Translated by Walter Miller. Cambridge: Harvard University Press, 1914.

www.ingramcontent.com/pod-product-compliance
Lightning Source LLC
Chambersburg PA
CBHW080724300426
44114CB00019B/2485